Hands-On Kubernetes on Windows

Effectively orchestrate Windows container workloads using
Kubernetes

Piotr Tylenda

BIRMINGHAM - MUMBAI

Hands-On Kubernetes on Windows

Copyright © 2020 Packt Publishing

Commissioning Editor: Vijin Boricha
Acquisition Editor: Shrilekha Inani
Content Development Editor: Ronn Kurien
Senior Editor: Richard Brookes-Bland
Technical Editor: Dinesh Pawar
Copy Editor: Safis Editing
Project Coordinator: Neil Dmello
Proofreader: Safis Editing
Indexer: Manju Arasan
Production Designer: Deepika Naik

First published: March 2020

Production reference: 1300320

Published by Packt Publishing Ltd.
Livery Place
35 Livery Street
Birmingham
B3 2PB, UK.

ISBN 978-1-83882-156-2

www.packt.com

Packt.com

Subscribe to our online digital library for full access to over 7,000 books and videos, as well as industry leading tools to help you plan your personal development and advance your career. For more information, please visit our website.

Why subscribe?

- Spend less time learning and more time coding with practical eBooks and Videos from over 4,000 industry professionals

- Improve your learning with Skill Plans built especially for you

- Get a free eBook or video every month

- Fully searchable for easy access to vital information

- Copy and paste, print, and bookmark content

Did you know that Packt offers eBook versions of every book published, with PDF and ePub files available? You can upgrade to the eBook version at www.packt.com and as a print book customer, you are entitled to a discount on the eBook copy. Get in touch with us at customercare@packtpub.com for more details.

At www.packt.com, you can also read a collection of free technical articles, sign up for a range of free newsletters, and receive exclusive discounts and offers on Packt books and eBooks.

Contributors

About the author

Piotr Tylenda is an experienced DevOps and software engineer with a passion for Kubernetes and Azure technologies. In his projects, he has focused on the adoption of microservices architecture for monolithic applications, developing big data pipelines for e-commerce, and architecting solutions for scalable log and telemetry analytics for hardware. His most notable contribution to Kubernetes' open source ecosystem is the development of Ansible automation for provisioning and deploying hybrid Windows/Linux Kubernetes clusters. Currently, he works at Microsoft Development Center Copenhagen in Denmark in a team developing a Microsoft Dynamics 365 Business Central SaaS offering.

I would like to thank my wonderful wife, Agnieszka, who supported and motivated me during the process of writing this book. If it weren't for you, this book would have never become a reality!

About the reviewer

Amit Malik is an IT enthusiast and technology evangelist focused on cloud and emerging technologies. He is currently employed by Spektra Systems as the director of technology, where he helps Microsoft partners grow their cloud businesses by using effective tools and strategies. He specializes in the cloud, DevOps, software-defined infrastructure, application modernization, data platforms, and emerging technologies around AI. Amit holds various industry-admired certifications from all major OEMs in the cloud and data space, including Azure Solutions Architect Expert. He is also a **Microsoft Certified Trainer** (**MCT**). Amit is also an active community member for various technology groups and is a regular speaker at industry conferences and events.

Packt is searching for authors like you

If you're interested in becoming an author for Packt, please visit `authors.packtpub.com` and apply today. We have worked with thousands of developers and tech professionals, just like you, to help them share their insight with the global tech community. You can make a general application, apply for a specific hot topic that we are recruiting an author for, or submit your own idea.

Table of Contents

Preface

Starting with version 1.14, Kubernetes has brought the most anticipated feature of the year 2019: production-level support for Windows Server container workloads. This is a huge milestone that enables migration to cloud-native technologies for all enterprises that rely heavily on Windows technologies at their core. Developers and system operators can now leverage the same tools and pipelines to deploy both Windows and Linux workloads, scale them in a similar way, and undertake efficient monitoring. From a business perspective, container adoption for Windows means lower operational costs and better hardware utilization than plain VMs.

You are holding in your hands a book that will guide you in terms of how to use Kubernetes and Docker containers in the Microsoft Windows ecosystem – it covers both hybrid Windows/Linux Kubernetes cluster deployment and handles cluster operations using a Windows client machine. Since support for Windows in Kubernetes is a fairly new concept, you can expect the official documentation and guides to still be scarce. In this book, we aim to systematize your knowledge regarding Kubernetes scenarios that involve Windows. Our aim was to create the ultimate guide for Kubernetes on Windows.

Who this book is for

The primary audience for this book is Kubernetes DevOps architects and engineers who need to integrate Windows container workloads into their Kubernetes clusters. If you are a Windows application (especially .NET Framework) developer and you haven't used Kubernetes yet, this book is also for you! In addition to the strategies regarding the deployment of hybrid Windows/Linux Kubernetes clusters, we cover the fundamental concepts behind Kubernetes and how they map to the Windows environment. And if you are interested in migrating existing .NET Framework applications to Windows Server containers running on Kubernetes, you will definitely find guidance in terms of how to approach this problem.

What this book covers

Chapter 1, *Creating Containers*, describes different container types that are currently used, in particular, across the Linux and Windows operating systems. The main objective of this chapter is demonstrating how to build a sample Windows container, run it, and perform basic operations.

Chapter 2, *Managing State in Containers*, discusses the possible approaches for managing and persisting state in containerized applications and explains how to mount local and cloud storage volumes (Azure Files SMB share) on containers in order to run clustered database engines such as MongoDB using Windows containers.

Chapter 3, *Working with Container Images*, focuses on container images, which are the standard way of distributing containerized applications. The objective of this chapter is to demonstrate how to use Docker Hub and Azure Container Registry and how to deliver container images safely in deployment pipelines.

Chapter 4, *Kubernetes Concepts and Windows Support*, familiarizes you with core Kubernetes services such as kubelet, kube-proxy, and kube-apiserver, as well as the most commonly used Kubernetes objects, such as Pod, Service, Deployment, and DaemonSet. You will learn why Windows support in Kubernetes is important and what the current limitations are as regards Windows containers and Windows nodes. We will also focus on creating simple development Kubernetes clusters for different use cases.

Chapter 5, *Kubernetes Networking*, describes the networking model of Kubernetes and available Pod network solutions. You will learn how to choose the most suitable networking mode for Kubernetes clusters with Windows nodes.

Chapter 6, *Interacting with Kubernetes Clusters*, shows how to interact and access Kubernetes clusters from a Windows machine using kubectl. As an example, we will show how to work with local development clusters and what the most common and useful kubectl commands are.

Chapter 7, *Deploying Hybrid On-Premises Kubernetes Clusters*, demonstrates how to approach the provisioning of VMs and the deployment of hybrid Windows/Linux Kubernetes clusters with Linux master/nodes and Windows nodes. On-premises deployment is the most universal type of deployment as it can be performed using any cloud service provider or in a private data center.

Chapter 8, *Deploying Hybrid Azure Kubernetes Service Engine Clusters*, provides an overview of how to approach the deployment of a hybrid Windows/Linux Kubernetes cluster using AKS Engine and demonstrates an example deployment of a sample Microsoft IIS application.

Chapter 9, *Deploying Your First Application*, demonstrates how to deploy a simple web application to Kubernetes imperatively and declaratively and discusses the recommended way to manage applications running in Kubernetes. We will also cover scheduling Pods on Windows nodes exclusively and how to scale Windows applications running on Kubernetes.

Chapter 10, *Deploying a Microsoft SQL Server 2019 and ASP.NET MVC Application,* describes how to deploy a sample voting application implemented in ASP.NET MVC (running in Windows containers) to an AKS Engine cluster, together with Microsoft SQL Server 2019 (running in Linux containers). You will also learn how you can debug .NET applications running in Kubernetes using Visual Studio Remote Debugger.

Chapter 11, *Configuring Applications to Use Kubernetes Features,* describes how to implement and configure more advanced features of Kubernetes, including namespaces, ConfigMaps and Secrets, persistent storage, health and readiness checking, autoscaling, and rolling deployments. This chapter also shows how role-based access control (RBAC) works in Kubernetes.

Chapter 12, *Development Workflow with Kubernetes,* shows how to use Kubernetes as a platform for microservices development. You will learn how to package applications using Helm and how to improve your development experience using Azure Dev Spaces. Additionally, the chapter describes how to use Azure Application Insights and Snapshot Debugger for your containerized application running in Kubernetes.

Chapter 13, *Securing Kubernetes Clusters and Applications,* covers the security of Kubernetes clusters and containerized applications. We will discuss the general recommended security practices for Kubernetes and Windows-specific considerations.

Chapter 14, *Monitoring Kubernetes Applications Using Prometheus,* focuses on how to approach the monitoring of Kubernetes clusters, especially Windows nodes and .NET applications running on Windows nodes. You will learn how to deploy a full monitoring solution using a Prometheus Helm chart and how to configure it to monitor your applications.

Chapter 15, *Disaster Recovery,* discusses backing up a Kubernetes cluster and disaster recovery strategies. The main focus is to show what components require backups in order to restore the cluster safely and how to automate this process.

Chapter 16, *Production Considerations for Running Kubernetes,* is a set of general recommendations for running Kubernetes in production environments.

To get the most out of this book

Having some general knowledge of Docker and Kubernetes is advised but not required. We are going to cover the fundamental concepts of containerization on Windows and Kubernetes itself in dedicated chapters. For those chapters that focus on the deployment of Windows applications to Kubernetes, it is recommended that you have basic experience with .NET Framework, C#, and ASP.NET MVC. Please note that for each guide and example in this book, there is a counterpart available in the official GitHub repository: `https://github.com/PacktPublishing/Hands-On-Kubernetes-on-Windows`

Throughout the book, you will require your own Azure subscription. You can read more about how to obtain a limited free account for personal use here: `https://azure.microsoft.com/en-us/free/`.

Software/Hardware covered in the book	OS Requirements
Visual Studio Code, Docker Desktop, Kubectl, Azure CLI with 16 GB RAM	Windows 10 Pro, Enterprise, or Education (version 1903 or later; 64-bit), Windows Server 2019, Ubuntu Server 18.04

If you are using the digital version of this book, we advise you to type the code yourself or access the code via the GitHub repository (link available in the next section). Doing so will help you avoid any potential errors related to the copying and pasting of code.

Download the example code files

You can download the example code files for this book from your account at `www.packt.com`. If you purchased this book elsewhere, you can visit `www.packtpub.com/support` and register to have the files emailed directly to you.

You can download the code files by following these steps:

1. Log in or register at `www.packt.com`.
2. Select the **Support** tab.
3. Click on **Code Downloads**.
4. Enter the name of the book in the **Search** box and follow the onscreen instructions.

Once the file is downloaded, please make sure that you unzip or extract the folder using the latest version of:

- WinRAR/7-Zip for Windows
- Zipeg/iZip/UnRarX for Mac
- 7-Zip/PeaZip for Linux

The code bundle for the book is also hosted on GitHub at `https://github.com/ PacktPublishing/Hands-On-Kubernetes-on-Windows`. In case there's an update to the code, it will be updated on the existing GitHub repository.

We also have other code bundles from our rich catalog of books and videos available at `https://github.com/PacktPublishing/`. Check them out!

Download the color images

We also provide a PDF file that has color images of the screenshots/diagrams used in this book. You can download it here: `http://www.packtpub.com/sites/default/files/ downloads/9781838821562_ColorImages.pdf`.

Conventions used

There are a number of text conventions used throughout this book.

`CodeInText`: Indicates code words in text, database table names, folder names, filenames, file extensions, pathnames, dummy URLs, user input, and Twitter handles. Here is an example: "Mount the downloaded `WebStorm-10*.dmg` disk image file as another disk in your system."

A block of code is set as follows:

```
html, body, #map {
 height: 100%;
 margin: 0;
 padding: 0
 }
```

When we wish to draw your attention to a particular part of a code block, the relevant lines or items are set in bold:

```
[default]
exten => s,1,Dial(Zap/1|30)
exten => s,2,Voicemail(u100)
exten => s,102,Voicemail(b100)
exten => i,1,Voicemail(s0)
```

Any command-line input or output is written as follows:

```
$ mkdir css
$ cd css
```

Bold: Indicates a new term, an important word, or words that you see on screen. For example, words in menus or dialog boxes appear in the text like this. Here is an example: "Select **System info** from the **Administration** panel."

Warnings or important notes appear like this.

Tips and tricks appear like this.

Get in touch

Feedback from our readers is always welcome.

General feedback: If you have questions about any aspect of this book, mention the book title in the subject of your message and email us at customercare@packtpub.com.

Errata: Although we have taken every care to ensure the accuracy of our content, mistakes do happen. If you have found a mistake in this book, we would be grateful if you would report this to us. Please visit www.packtpub.com/support/errata, selecting your book, clicking on the Errata Submission Form link, and entering the details.

Piracy: If you come across any illegal copies of our works in any form on the internet, we would be grateful if you would provide us with the location address or website name. Please contact us at copyright@packt.com with a link to the material.

If you are interested in becoming an author: If there is a topic that you have expertise in, and you are interested in either writing or contributing to a book, please visit authors.packtpub.com.

Reviews

Please leave a review. Once you have read and used this book, why not leave a review on the site that you purchased it from? Potential readers can then see and use your unbiased opinion to make purchase decisions, we at Packt can understand what you think about our products, and our authors can see your feedback on their book. Thank you!

For more information about Packt, please visit packt.com.

Section 1: Creating and Working with Containers

The objective of this section is to present different containerization technologies and the benefits of choosing one variant over another. You will see how to containerize an application on Windows and understand the key steps involved in creating and maintaining the images.

This section contains the following chapters:

- Chapter 1, *Creating Containers*
- Chapter 2, *Managing State in Containers*
- Chapter 3, *Working with Container Images*

Creating Containers

1

The concepts of *containers* and *OS-level virtualization* have their roots in the `chroot` system call in Unix V7 operating systems (OSes), which date back to the late 1970s. Starting with a simple concept of process isolation and *chroot jails*, where the process is running in an apparently isolated root directory, containerization has undergone rapid evolution and became a mainstream technology in the 2010s with the advent of **Linux Containers** (**LXC**) and Docker. In 2014, Microsoft announced support for Docker Engine in the incoming release of Windows Server 2016. This is where the story of Windows containers and Kubernetes on Windows begins.

In this chapter, we will provide you with a better understanding of containers for the Windows OS by highlighting important differences between containerization on Linux and Windows and container runtime types on Windows, namely Windows Server Containers (or process isolation) and Hyper-V isolation. We will also learn how to install Docker Desktop for Windows 10 for development scenarios and create our first example container running on your machine.

This chapter will cover the following topics:

- Linux versus Windows containers
- Understanding Windows container variants
- Installing Docker Desktop for Windows tooling
- Building your first container

Technical requirements

The requirements for this chapter are as follows:

- **Intel Virtualization Technology (Intel VT)** or **AMD Virtualization (AMD-V)** technology features enabled in the BIOS
- A minimum of 4 GB of RAM
- Windows 10 Pro, Enterprise, or Education (version 1903 or later, 64-bit) installed
- Visual Studio Code

For more information regarding the hardware requirements for running Docker and containers on Windows, please refer to `https://docs.microsoft.com/en-us/virtualization/windowscontainers/deploy-containers/system-requirements`.

Windows 10 versions starting with Anniversary Update (version 1607, build 14393) are supported, but version 1903 is recommended for the best experience since it comes with all the necessary features. For more details regarding Windows 10 versions and container runtimes compatibility, please refer to `https://docs.microsoft.com/en-us/virtualization/windowscontainers/deploy-containers/version-compatibility`.

Visual Studio Code can be downloaded for free from the official web page at: `https://code.visualstudio.com/`.

You can download the latest code samples for this chapter from this book's official GitHub repository at: `https://github.com/PacktPublishing/Hands-On-Kubernetes-on-Windows/tree/master/Chapter01`.

Linux versus Windows containers

Containerization on both Linux and Windows aims to achieve the same goal – creating predictable and lightweight environments that are isolated from other applications. For Linux, a classic example of container usage can be running a Python RESTful API written in Flask, without worrying about conflicts between Python modules that are required by other applications. Similarly, for Windows, the containers can be used to host an **Internet Information Services** (**IIS**) web server that's entirely isolated from other workloads running on the same machine.

Compared to traditional hardware virtualization, containerization comes at the cost of being tightly coupled with the host OS since it uses the same kernel to provide multiple isolated user spaces. This means that running Windows containers on the Linux OS or running Linux containers on the Windows OS is not possible natively without the additional help of traditional hardware virtualization techniques.

In this book, we will focus on the Docker container platform, which is required for running containers on Windows. Now, let's summarize the current state of containerization support on Linux and Windows that's provided by Docker Engine and what the possible solutions are when it comes to development and production scenarios.

Docker containerization on Linux

Originally, Docker Engine was developed primarily for the Linux OS, which provides the following kernel features for the Docker runtime:

- **Kernel namespaces**: This is the core concept for containers and makes it possible to create isolated process workspaces. Namespaces partition kernel resources (such as network stacks, mount points, and so on) so that each process workspace can access its own set of resources and ensures they can't be accessed by processes from other workspaces. This is what ensures the isolation of containers.
- **Control groups**: Resource usage limits and isolation is a secondary core concept in containerization. On Linux, this feature is provided by *cgroups*, which enables resource limiting (CPU usage, RAM usage, and so on) and priority access to resources for one process or a group of processes.
- **Layer filesystem capabilities**: On Linux, *UnionFS* is one of the many implementations of *union mount* – a file system service that allows files and directories coming from separate filesystems to be unified into one transparent, coherent filesystem. This feature is crucial for Docker container images that consist of immutable layers. During the container runtime, the read-only layers are transparently overlaid together with a writable container layer.

Docker Engine is responsible for providing a basic runtime for containers, abstracting container management, and exposing functionalities using the REST API to the client layer, such as the Docker CLI. The architecture of Docker on Linux can be summarized with the following diagram:

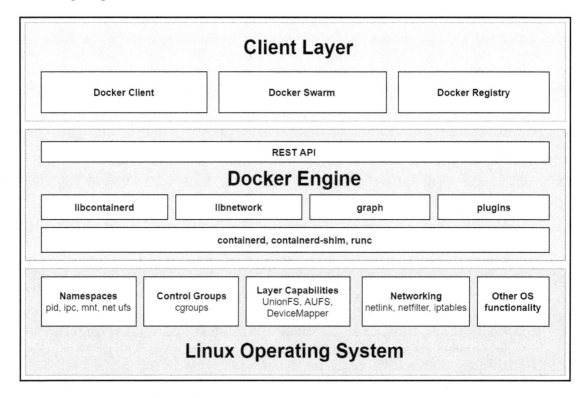

From a Linux OS perspective, the container runtime architecture is presented in the following diagram. This architecture applies to container engines on Linux in general, not only Docker:

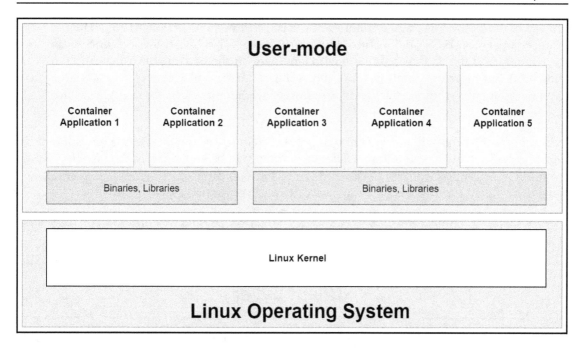

Next, we will look at Docker containerization on Windows.

Docker containerization on Windows

In 2014, when Microsoft announced support for Docker Engine in the incoming release of Windows Server 2016, the Docker container engine had already matured on Linux and was proven to be an industry standard for container management. This fact has driven design decisions for Docker and containerization support for Windows, which eventually received a similar architecture for running process-isolated Windows Server containers. The Windows kernel features that are used by Docker Engine roughly map to the following:

- **Kernel namespaces**: This functionality is provided by, among others, Object Namespaces and the Process Table in the Windows kernel.
- **Control groups**: Windows has its own concept of *Job Objects*, which allows a group of processes to be managed as a single unit. Essentially, this feature provides similar functionality to *cgroups* on Linux.
- **Layer filesystem capabilities**: The *Windows Container Isolation File System* is a filesystem driver that provides a virtual filesystem view for processes that are executed in Windows containers. This is analogous to *UnionFS* or other implementations of *union mount* for the Linux OS.

On top of these low-level functionalities, the services layer, which consists of a **Host Compute Service** (**HCS**) and a **Host Network Service** (**HNS**), abstracts a public interface for running and managing containers with language bindings available for C# and Go (hcsshim). For more information about the current container platform tools, please refer to the official documentation at: `https://docs.microsoft.com/en-us/virtualization/ windowscontainers/deploy-containers/containerd#hcs`.

It is important to know that there are two types of Windows containers: process-isolated and Hyper-V-isolated. The difference between them will be explained in the next section – isolation is a runtime property of the containers and you can expect them to, in general, behave similarly and differ only from a security and compatibility perspective.

The following diagram summarizes the containerization architecture and Docker support for Windows:

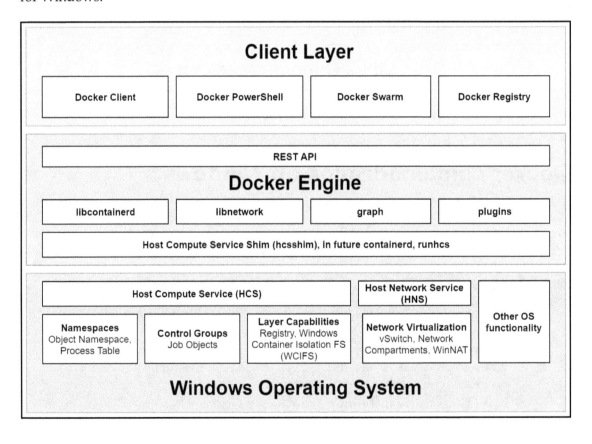

For comparison with the high-level architecture of containerization on Linux, the following diagram presents the multi-container runtime architecture for Windows. At this point, we are only considering *process-isolated Windows Server containers*, which closely resemble containers on Linux, but in the next section, we will also cover the architecture of *Hyper-V isolation* for containers on Windows:

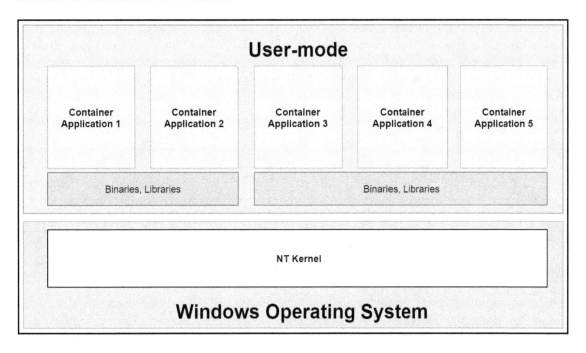

Next, let's look at the some differences between containers on Linux and Windows.

Key differences between containers on Linux and Windows

Docker containers on Linux and Windows aim to solve the same problems in principle and currently, the container management experience is starting to converge on these platforms. Nevertheless, if you come from the Linux ecosystem and have used Docker extensively there, you may be surprised by some differences that you can find. Let's briefly summarize them.

The largest and the most apparent limitation is the Windows host OS and Windows container OS compatibility requirements. In the case of Linux, you can safely assume that if the host OS kernel is running the minimum required version of 3.10, any Linux container will run without any problems, no matter which distribution it is based on. For Windows, it is possible to run containers with base OS versions that are exactly the same as the host OS version that's supported without any limitations. Running a newer container OS version on an old host OS is not supported, and what's more, running older container OS versions on a newer host OS comes with the requirement of using *Hyper-V isolation*. For example, a host running Windows Server version 1803 build 17134 can use containers with base image version Windows Server version 1803 build 17134 natively, but running containers with Windows Server version 1709 build 16299 will require Hyper-V isolation, and starting a container with Windows Server 2019 build 17763 is not possible at all. The following table visualizes this principle:

Host OS version	Container base image OS version	Compatibility
Windows Server, version 1803 build 17134	Windows Server, version 1803 build 17134	*Process* or *Hyper-V* isolation
Windows Server, version 1803 build 17134	Windows Server, version 1709 build 16299	*Hyper-V* isolation
Windows Server, version 1803 build 17134	Windows Server 2019 build 17763	Not supported
Windows Server 2019 build 17763	Windows Server 2019 build 17763	*Process* or *Hyper-V* isolation

For a more detailed compatibility matrix, please refer to the official Microsoft documentation at: https://docs.microsoft.com/en-us/virtualization/ windowscontainers/deploy-containers/version-compatibility#choose-which-container-OS-version-to-use.

It is worth mentioning that the requirements for Hyper-V isolation may be a significant limitation in cloud environments or when running Docker on **virtual machines** (**VMs**). In such cases, Hyper-V isolation requires the nested virtualization feature to be enabled by the hypervisor. We will cover Hyper-V isolation in detail in the next section.

Another important aspect you may notice is the difference in sizes between the base images for Linux and Windows containers. Currently, the minimal Windows Server image, mcr.microsoft.com/windows/nanoserver:1809, is 98 MB in size, whereas, for example, the minimalistic image for Alpine Linux, alpine:3.7, is only 5 MB in size. The full Windows Server image, mcr.microsoft.com/windows/servercore:ltsc2019, is over 1.5 GB, while the base image for Windows, mcr.microsoft.com/windows:1809, is 3.5 GB. But it is worth mentioning that since the first release of Windows Server 2016 Core image, when the image size was 6 GB, these numbers constantly go down.

These differences can be seen more as the limitations of Docker containers on Windows. However, there is one aspect where Windows provides more flexibility than Linux – support for running Linux containers on Windows. Docker Desktop for Windows 10 supports such a scenario out of the box. Although this feature is still in development, it is possible to host Linux containers alongside Windows containers on Windows 10 with the help of Hyper-V isolation. We will cover this feature in more detail in the next section. The opposite scenario with Windows containers running on Linux has no native solution and requires manually hosting additional Windows VM on a Linux host.

Windows Server also supports running Linux containers, providing that the **Linux Containers on Windows** (**LCOW**) experimental feature is enabled.

In the next section, we will focus on the differences between different Windows container runtime variants.

Understanding Windows container variants

Windows containers come in two distinct levels of isolation: process and Hyper-V. Process isolation is also known as **Windows Server Containers** (**WSC**). Initially, process isolation was available on the Windows Server OS only, whereas on desktop versions of the Windows OS, you could run containers using Hyper-V isolation. Starting with Windows 10, version 1809 (October 2018 Update) and Docker Engine 18.09.1, process isolation is also available on Windows 10.

In the official documentation, you may find the terms Windows container *types* and *runtimes*. They also refer to the isolation levels, and these terms are used interchangeably.

Now, let's take a look at how these isolation levels differ, what the use cases for them are, and how to create containers by specifying the desired isolation type.

Process isolation

Process-isolated containers, also known as **WSC**, is the default isolation mode provided for containers on Windows Server. The architecture of process isolation is similar to what you have when running containers on the Linux OS:

- Containers use the same shared kernel.
- Isolation is provided at the kernel level using features such as process tables, object namespaces, and job objects. More information can be found in the *Docker containerization on Windows* section.

This is summarized in the following diagram:

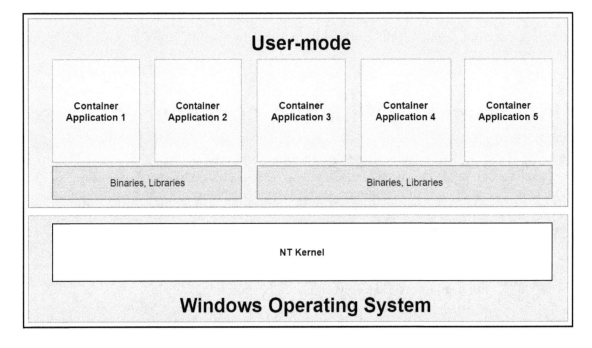

Process isolation provides a lightweight runtime for containers (compared to Hyper-V isolation) and offers a greater density of deployment, better performance, and lower spin-up time. However, there are a few points you should consider when using this type of isolation:

- The Docker container base image has to match the version of the container host OS. For example, if you are running Windows 10, version 1903, you can only run containers that have used base image version 1903 of Windows 10 or Windows Server. This means you have to rebuild the image for each version of Windows that is being released (only major *feature updates*).
- This should be only for the execution of trusted code. In order to execute untrusted code, Hyper-V isolation is advised.

With Windows 10, version 1809 and later, it is possible to use process isolation for the container runtime, provided that you are running Docker Desktop for Windows 2.0.1.0 (*Edge* release channel) or later and Docker Engine 18.09.1+. For Windows 10, the default isolation level for containers is Hyper-V and in order to use process isolation, it has to be specified explicitly while creating a container using the `--isolation=process` argument:

```
docker run -d --isolation=process mcr.microsoft.com/windows/nanoserver:1903
cmd /c ping localhost -n 100
```

This option can be also specified as a parameter to the Docker daemon using the `--exec-opt` parameter. For more details, please see the official Docker documentation at the: https://docs.docker.com/engine/reference/commandline/run/#specify-isolation-technology-for-container---isolation.

> Using process-isolated containers on the Windows 10 OS is only recommended for development purposes. For production deployments, you should still consider using Windows Server for process-isolated containers.

Hyper-V isolation

Hyper-V isolation is the second type of isolation available for Windows containers. In this type of isolation, each container is running inside a dedicated, minimal Hyper-V virtual machine and can be briefly summarized as follows:

- Containers do not share the kernel with host OS. Each container has its own Windows kernel.
- Isolation is provided at the virtual machine hypervisor level (requires Hyper-V role to be installed).
- There are no compatibility limitations between the host OS version and container base OS version.
- This is recommended for the execution of untrusted code and multi-tenant deployments as it provides better security and isolation.

The details of the Hyper-V isolation architecture can be seen in the following diagram:

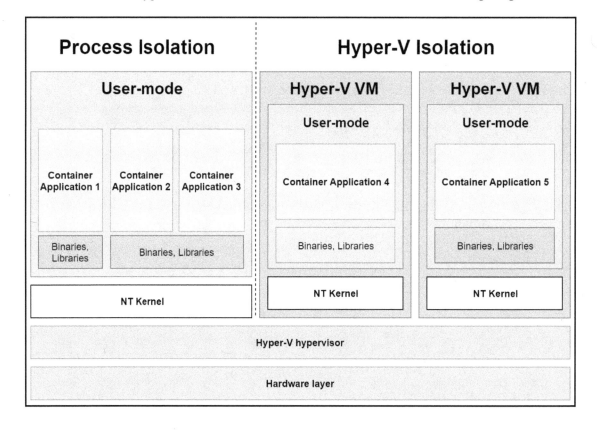

This type of isolation comes at a cost that you have to take into account when choosing the isolation level:

- Hyper-V isolation involves virtualization overhead, higher memory, and CPU usage footprint compared to process isolation, but still provides much better performance than running a full VM with Windows Nano Server. You can check the memory requirements for running containers with different isolation levels in the following table.
- Container spin-up time is slower compared to process isolation.
- Requires nested virtualization when used for containers running on a VM. This may be a limitation for some hypervisors and cloud deployments. The following table shows the memory requirements for Windows Server 1709 containers:

Container base image	Process isolation (WSC)	Hyper-V isolation
Nano Server	30 MB	110 MB + 1 GB pagefile
Server Core	45 MB	360 MB + 1 GB pagefile

The container images remain unchanged compared to process isolation; you only need to specify a different isolation level when creating the actual container. You can do this using the `--isolation=hyperv` parameter:

```
docker run -d --isolation=hyperv mcr.microsoft.com/windows/nanoserver:1809
cmd /c ping localhost -n 100
```

Note that in this case, even if you are running Windows 10, version 1903, you can use the container base image version 1809 without any limitations.

Hyper-V isolation is the default level of isolation when running containers on Windows 10, so the `--isolation=hyperv` parameter is not required. The opposite is also true; process isolation is the default level for Windows Server and if you want to use Hyper-V isolation, you have to specify it explicitly. The default isolation level can be changed in the `daemon.json` configuration file by specifying the `isolation` parameter in `exec-opts`. For more information, please refer to `https://docs.docker.com/engine/reference/commandline/dockerd/#daemon-configuration-file` and `https://docs.docker.com/engine/reference/commandline/dockerd/#docker-runtime-execution-options`.

Linux containers on Windows

In April 2017, Docker announced LinuxKit, a solution for running Linux containers on platforms that are not shipped with the Linux kernel, namely Windows and macOS. LinuxKit is a toolkit for building portable and lightweight Linux subsystems that contain only the bare minimum for running Linux containers on a given platform. Although Docker, since the first release in 2016, was able to run Linux containers on Windows to some limited extent, the announcement of LinuxKit was the milestone that started the story of **Linux Containers on Windows (LCOW)** as we know them today.

Running Linux containers on Windows is not recommended for production deployments yet. Using LinuxKit and MobyLinuxVM is intended only for Desktop for Windows and development purposes. At the same time, the LCOW feature is still experimental and is not suitable for production.

LinuxKit and MobyLinuxVM

Docker for Windows (which was the initial name of Docker Desktop for Windows at that time) eventually came with a dedicated Hyper-V virtual machine based on LinuxKit named MobyLinuxVM. The purpose of this virtual machine is to provide a minimal runtime for Linux containers that can technically be run side by side with Windows containers.

By default, Docker Desktop for Windows runs in Linux containers mode, which utilizes MobyLinuxVM. In order to switch to Windows containers mode, you have to navigate to the Docker Desktop tray icon and select **Switch to Windows containers...**. Docker will restart and switch to native Windows containers.

In this solution, MobyLinuxVM runs its own Docker daemon and technically acts as a separate container host enclosed inside a virtual machine. Similarly, Windows has its own Docker Daemon that's responsible for Windows containers and also provides the Docker Client (CLI), which communicates with both Docker Daemons. This architecture can be seen in the following diagram:

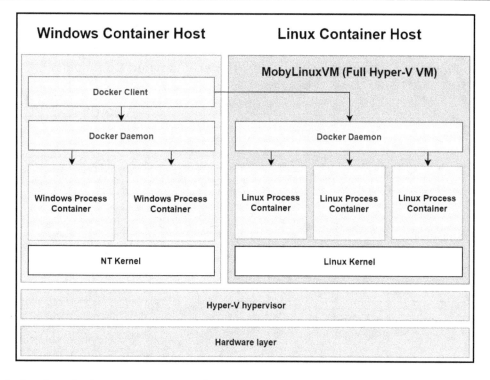

Now, let's take a look at a more up-to-date approach for running Linux containers on Windows: LinuxKit LCOW.

LinuxKit LCOW and Hyper-V isolation

Contrary to the MobyLinuxVM approach, **Linux Containers on Windows (LCOW)** uses Hyper-V isolated containers to achieve similar results. LCOW is available for Windows 10, which comes with Docker for Windows 17.10, and for Windows Server, version 1709, which comes with a preview release of Docker Enterprise Edition.

The main difference compared to MobyLinuxVM is the possibility to natively run Linux and Windows containers side by side using *the same* Docker Daemon. This solution is the current strategy for supporting Linux containers running on Windows but as the long-term solution, in June 2019, Docker and Microsoft started a collaboration to integrate the Windows Subsystem for Linux version 2 as the primary Linux container runtime on Windows. Eventually, both LinuxKit LCOW and MobyLinuxVM with Docker Desktop for Windows will be retired.

The following diagram shows LCOW:

Windows Container Host		Hyper-V Isolated Containers		
Docker Client		LCOW	LCOW	LCOW
Docker Daemon		gRPC	gRPC	gRPC
Windows Process Container	Windows Process Container	Linux Process Container	Linux Process Container	Linux Process Container
NT Kernel		Linux Kernel	Linux Kernel	Linux Kernel
Hyper-V hypervisor				
Hardware layer				

In order to enable LCOW support in Docker Desktop (version 18.02 or later), you have to enable the **Experimental features** option in Docker Settings > Daemon. Creating an LCOW container requires specifying the `--platform linux` parameter (if platform selection is unambiguous, that is, the image only exists in Linux, then it can be omitted in newer versions of Docker Desktop):

```
docker run -it --platform linux busybox /bin/sh
```

The preceding command will create a busybox Linux container and enter the interactive Bourne shell (sh).

 As of Docker Desktop for Windows 2.0.4.0, it is not possible to run the development Kubernetes cluster provided by Docker *("batteries included")* with the LCOW feature enabled.

In this section, you learned how containers are currently supported on the Windows platform and the key differences between the provided runtimes. Now, we can start installing **Docker Desktop for Windows**.

Installing Docker Desktop for Windows tooling

Creating applications for Kubernetes on Windows requires an environment for developing and testing Docker containers. In this section, you will learn how to install Docker Desktop for Windows, which is the recommended tooling environment for development, building, shipping, and running Linux and Windows containers on Windows 10. First, let's recap on the prerequisites and Docker's minimum requirements before continuing with the installation process:

- A minimum of 4 GB of RAM.
- The **Intel Virtualization Technology (Intel VT)** or **AMD Virtualization (AMD-V)** technology features enabled in the BIOS. Note that if you are using a VM as your development machine, Docker Desktop for Windows does not guarantee support for nested virtualization. If you want to find out more about this scenario, please refer to `https://docs.docker.com/docker-for-windows/troubleshoot/#running-docker-desktop-for-windows-in-nested-virtualization-scenarios`.
- Windows 10 Pro, Enterprise, or Education (version 1903 or later, 64-bit) installed. The current Docker Desktop supports version 1703 or later, but for the best experience when going through the examples in this book, it is recommended that you upgrade it to version 1903 or later. You can check your version of Windows by opening the **Start** menu, selecting the **Settings** icon, and navigating to **System > About**. You will find the necessary details under **Windows Specifications**.

Docker Desktop for Windows is also known as Docker for Windows and Docker **Community Edition** (**CE**) for Windows. This is especially important if you are following older installation guides.

If you are interested in the installation of Docker Enterprise for Windows Server, please refer to `Chapter 7`, *Deploying a Hybrid On-Premises Kubernetes Cluster*.

Stable and Edge channels

Depending on your requirements, you can choose from two release channels for Docker Desktop for Windows: **Stable** and **Edge**. You should consider using a Stable channel if you are OK with the following:

- You want the recommended and reliable platform to work with containers. Releases in a Stable channel follow the release cycle of Docker platform stable releases. You can expect releases in the Stable channel to be performed once per quarter.
- You want to have a choice of whether to send usage statistics.

You should consider using an Edge channel if you are OK with the following:

- You want to get the experimental features as soon as possible. This may come at a cost of some instability and bugs. You can expect releases in the Edge channel to be performed once per month.
- You are OK with usage statistics being collected.

Now, let's proceed with the installation itself.

Installation

The installation process described in this section follows the recommendations from the official Docker documentation. Let's begin:

 If you are using chocolatey to manage application packages on your Windows system, it is also possible to use the official trusted package for Docker Desktop, available from: `https://chocolatey.org/packages/docker-desktop`.

1. In order to download Docker Desktop for Windows, navigate to `https://hub.docker.com/editions/community/docker-ce-desktop-windows`. Downloading it requires registering for the service. You can also choose direct links for downloading the Stable channel release (`https://download.docker.com/win/stable/Docker%20for%20Windows%20Installer.exe`) or the Edge channel release (`https://download.docker.com/win/edge/Docker%20Desktop%20Installer.exe`).

Docker Desktop for Windows will automatically enable the Hyper-V role if needed and restart the machine. If you are a VirtualBox user or Docker Toolbox user, you will no longer be able to run VirtualBox VMs as Type-1 and Type-2 hypervisors cannot run side by side. You will be still able to access your existing VM images but will not be able to start the VMs.

2. Navigate to the directory where the installer has been downloaded to and double-click on it.

3. Enable Windows container support by default by selecting the **Use Windows containers instead of Linux containers** option:

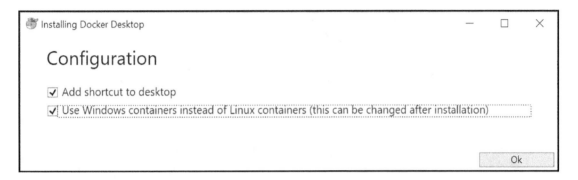

4. Proceed with the installation:

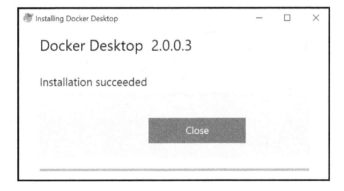

5. You may be prompted to restart your machine if the Hyper-V role was enabled by the installer.

6. Launch the **Docker Desktop** application.
7. Wait until Docker is fully initialized. You will see the following prompt:

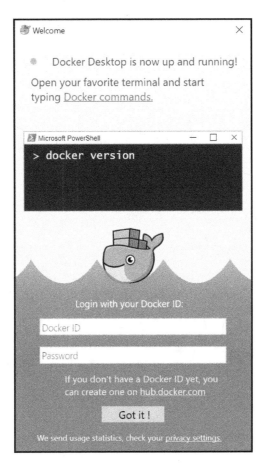

After installation, we need to verify whether Docker has been installed properly and can run a simple *hello world* container image.

Verifying the installation

Now, let's verify whether the installation was successful:

1. Confirm that the Docker Client is working properly by opening Powershell and executing the following command:

```
docker version
```

2. You should see an output similar to the following:

```
Client: Docker Engine - Community
 Version: 18.09.2
 API version: 1.39
 Go version: go1.10.8
 Git commit: 6247962
 Built: Sun Feb 10 04:12:31 2019
 OS/Arch: windows/amd64
 Experimental: false

Server: Docker Engine - Community
 Engine:
  Version: 18.09.2
  API version: 1.39 (minimum version 1.12)
  Go version: go1.10.6
  Git commit: 6247962
  Built: Sun Feb 10 04:13:06 2019
  OS/Arch: linux/amd64
  Experimental: false
```

3. Run a simple container based on the official Powershell image:

```
docker run -it --rm mcr.microsoft.com/powershell pwsh -c 'Write-Host
"Hello, World!"'
```

4. During the first run of this command, the missing container image layers will be downloaded. After some time, you will see **Hello, World!** written to the console output by Powershell:

5. Congratulations! You have successfully installed Docker Desktop for Windows and run your first container.

In the next subsection, you will learn how to enable process isolation for containers.

Running process-isolated containers

On Windows 10, in order to run process-isolated containers, you have to explicitly specify the `--isolation=process` parameter while creating the container. As we mentioned previously, it is also necessary to specify the container image version that matches your OS. Let's get started:

1. Assuming you are running Windows 10, version **1903**, let's execute the following command, which attempts to create a process-isolated container in detached (background) mode. Run a ping command stating the number of echo requests to be sent to your localhost machine, that is, `100`:

```
docker run -d --rm --isolation=process
mcr.microsoft.com/windows/nanoserver:1809 cmd /c ping localhost -n
100
```

The selected version of the **mcr.microsoft.com/windows/nanoserver** image is 1809, which does not match your OS version. Therefore, it will fail with an error informing you that the container's base image OS version does not match the host OS:

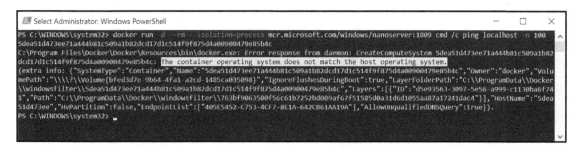

2. Now, let's execute a similar command but now specify the proper, matching version (1903) of the container base image:

    ```
    docker run -d --rm --isolation=process
    mcr.microsoft.com/windows/nanoserver:1903 cmd /c ping localhost -n
    100
    ```

    In this case, the container has started successfully, which can be verified by using the docker ps command:

3. Now, let's check how process isolation differs in practice from Hyper-V isolation. We will compare the visibility of the container processes in the host OS between these two isolation types.

4. First, get the container ID of your newly created process-isolated container. This container should run for a few minutes as it performs 100 echo requests to localhost before it terminates and is removed automatically. In our example, the container ID is
a627beadb1297f492ec1f73a3b74c95dbebef2cfaf8f9d6a03e326a1997ec2c

1. Using the `docker top <containerId>` command, it is possible to list all the processes running inside the container, including their **process IDs (PID)**:

```
docker top
a627beadb1297f492ec1f73a3b74c95dbebef2cfaf8f9d6a03e326a1997ec2c1
```

The following screenshot shows the output of the preceding command:

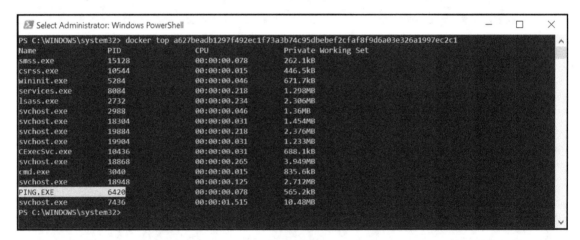

In the preceding screenshot, the PID of the `ping.exe` process inside the container is `6420`. In order to list `ping.exe` processes running in the context of the host OS, use the `Get-Process` cmdlet in Powershell:

```
Get-Process -Name ping
```

The following screenshot shows the output of the preceding command:

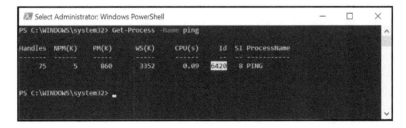

The preceding output reveals that the `ping.exe` process running inside the container is also visible from the host and has exactly the same PID: `6420`.

For comparison, we will create a similar container, but this time specify the `--isolation=hyperv` parameter in order to enforce Hyper-V isolation. On Windows 10, when running a default Docker configuration, you can omit the `--isolation` parameter altogether since the default isolation level is Hyper-V. We can create the container (with a different base image OS version than the host) using the following command:

```
docker run -d --rm --isolation=hyperv
mcr.microsoft.com/windows/nanoserver:1809 cmd /c ping localhost -n 100
```

The following screenshot shows the output of the preceding command:

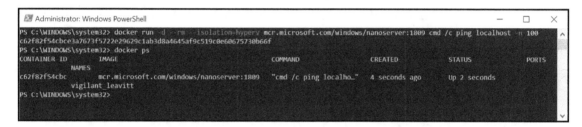

The container has started successfully. In this case, the container ID is **c62f82f54cbce3a7673f5722e29629c1ab3d8a4645af9c519c0e60675730b66f**. Inspecting the processes running inside the container reveals that `ping.exe` has a PID of `1268`:

When inspecting the processes running on the host, you will see that there is no `ping.exe` process with a PID of `1268` (and nor is there a `cmd.exe` process with a PID of `1216`, which is the main process in the container):

```
Administrator: Windows PowerShell                                              —   □   ×
PS C:\WINDOWS\system32> Get-Process -Name ping
Get-Process : Cannot find a process with the name "ping". Verify the process name and call the cmdlet again.
At line:1 char:1
+ Get-Process -Name ping
+ ~~~~~~~~~~~~~~~~~~~~~~~
    + CategoryInfo          : ObjectNotFound: (ping:String) [Get-Process], ProcessCommandException
    + FullyQualifiedErrorId : NoProcessFoundForGivenName,Microsoft.PowerShell.Commands.GetProcessCommand

PS C:\WINDOWS\system32>
```

The reason for this is that the processes running in the Hyper-V container are not sharing the kernel with host as they are executed in separate, lightweight Hyper-V VM with their own kernel matching the container base image OS version.

Now, it's time to run your first Linux container on Windows using LCOW!

Running LCOW containers

By default, Docker Desktop for Windows hosts Linux containers using MobyLinuxVM, which provides a minimal, fully-functional environment for hosting Linux containers. This approach is meant only for development and testing purposes as it is not available on Windows Server. Windows Server currently has experimental support for LCOW and it is also possible to enable this feature in Docker Desktop.

To enable LCOW support in Docker Desktop, you have to enable experimental features in the Docker Daemon. Let's take a look:

1. Open the Docker Desktop tray icon and select **Settings**.
2. Navigate to the **Daemon** tab.

3. Enable the **Experimental features** checkbox:

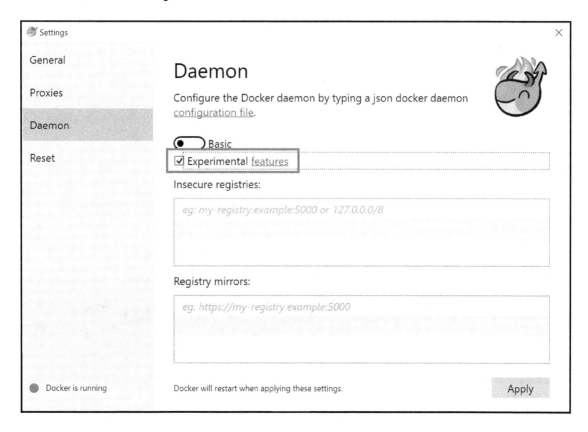

4. **Apply** the changes. Docker Desktop will restart.

Open PowerShell and create a container that uses Linux as the base image by providing the `--platform=linux` parameter to `docker run`. In this example, we're creating a **busybox** container in interactive mode and starting a Bourne shell:

```
docker run --rm -it --platform=linux busybox /bin/sh
```

 If the image exists in a version for one platform, it is not necessary to provide the `--platform` parameter. After downloading the image, it is also no longer necessary to specify the `--platform` parameter to run the container.

After the container is started, the Bourne shell prompt will appear (`/ #`). Now, you can verify that you are indeed running inside a Linux container by using the `uname` command, which prints Linux kernel information:

```
uname -a
```

The following screenshot shows the output of the preceding command:

```
Administrator: Windows PowerShell                                    —    □    ×
PS C:\WINDOWS\system32> docker run --rm -it --platform=linux busybox /bin/sh
/ # uname -a
Linux 9998acd00f52 4.14.35-linuxkit #1 SMP Mon Apr 23 11:11:13 UTC 2018 x86_64 GNU/Linux
/ #
```

In a separate Powershell window, without closing the Bourne shell in the container, execute the `docker inspect <containerId>` command in order to verify that the container is indeed running using LCOW using Hyper-V isolation:

In this section, you learned how to install Docker Desktop for Windows tooling and how to verify its functionality, including running Linux containers on Windows. In the next section, you will learn how to approach building your first Windows container image with the help of Visual Studio Code.

Building your first container

In the previous section, you have learned how to install Docker Desktop for Windows and how to run simple Windows and Linux containers. This section will demonstrate how to build a custom Docker image using `Dockerfile` and how to perform the most common actions on running containers, such as accessing logs and perform `exec` into a container.

A Dockerfile is a text file that contains all the commands that the user would execute in order to assemble a container image. As this book does not focus on Docker only, this section will be a short recap of common Docker operations. If you are interested in Dockerfiles themselves and building containers, please refer to the official documentation at: `https://docs.docker.com/engine/reference/builder/`.

As an example, we will prepare a Dockerfile that creates a Windows container image of Microsoft IIS hosting a demonstration HTML web page. The image definition won't be complicated in order to demonstrate operation principles.

Preparing a Visual Studio Code workspace

The first step is preparing the Visual Studio Code workspace. Visual Studio Code requires you to install an additional extension for managing Docker. Let's get started:

1. In order to do that, open the **Extensions** view by pressing *Ctrl + Shift + X*.
2. In **Extensions: Marketplace**, search for `docker` and install the official Docker extension from Microsoft:

All of the operations demonstrated in this section can be performed without Visual Studio Code, in any code/text editor and using the command line. Visual Studio Code is a useful, multi-platform IDE for developing and testing applications running in Docker containers.

After the installation is complete, Docker Explorer will become available:

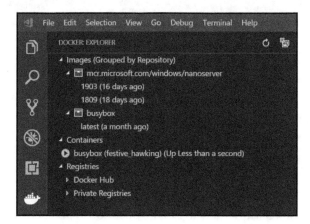

3. You can also leverage new Docker-oriented commands from the **Command Palette** after pressing *Ctrl + Shift* + P and typing docker into the search bar:

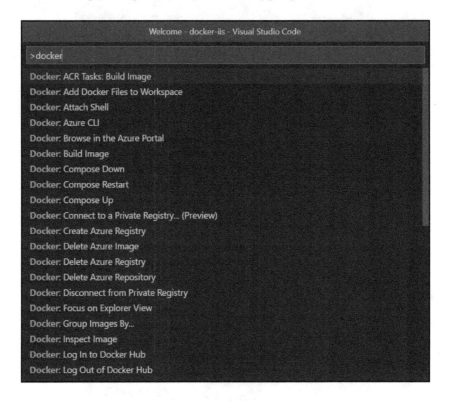

4. Now, initialize the workspace by opening the desired folder using the *Ctrl + K, Ctrl + O* shortcut or navigating to **File | Open Folder...**.

In the next subsection, we will create a demonstration HTML web page that will be hosted inside the Windows container.

Creating a sample HTML web page

We will start creating our Docker image by creating a minimalistic HTML "Hello World!" web page. This step mimics implementing an application without any containerization and is a common scenario in application development: you are running a non-containerized application and then you move it to a Docker container.

> You can also use the files from this book's GitHub repository to do this, available from: `https://github.com/PacktPublishing/Hands-On-Kubernetes-on-Windows/tree/master/Chapter01/01_docker-helloworld-iis`.

Add a new file in Visual Studio Code in your workspace using the *Ctrl + N* shortcut or by navigating to **File > New File**. Use the following sample HTML code in the new file:

```
<!DOCTYPE html>
<html>
    <head>
        <title>Hello World!</title>
    </head>
    <body>
        <h1>Hello World from Windows container!</h1>
    </body>
</html>
```

Save the file (using *Ctrl + S*) as `index.html` in your workspace.

Let's proceed with creating the Dockerfile itself.

Creating a Dockerfile

As we will be hosting the web page in the container using IIS, we need to create a **Dockerfile** that uses the `mcr.microsoft.com/windows/servercore/iis` official image as the base image for the build. We will use a Docker image with the `windowsservercore-1903` tag to ensure that we are running a version that matches the host OS and make it possible to use process isolation.

Create a new file in your workspace named `Dockerfile`, containing the following:

```
FROM mcr.microsoft.com/windows/servercore/iis:windowsservercore-1903

RUN powershell -NoProfile -Command Remove-Item -Recurse
C:\inetpub\wwwroot\*
WORKDIR /inetpub/wwwroot
COPY index.html .
```

Visual Studio Code gives you a lot of snippets while writing the Dockerfile, providing that you have named the file following the expected convention. You can also bring up the list of snippets by pressing *Ctrl +* SPACE while editing.

In the next subsection, you will learn how to manually build a Docker image based on the Dockerfile you have just created.

Building a Docker image

Building a Docker image is performed using the `docker build` command. You have two options when it comes to performing this step:

- Use Visual Studio Code's **Command Palette**.
- Use the Powershell command line.

In Visual Studio Code, do the following:

1. Use the *Ctrl + Shift + P* shortcut in order to open the **Command Palette**.
2. Search for **Docker: Build Image** and execute it by providing the image name and tag in the following format (or use the default suggested name based on the directory name):

   ```
   <image name>:<tag>
   ```

3. If you are logged into a custom registry or using Docker Hub, you can also specify the following:

   ```
   <registry or username>/<image name>:<tag>
   ```

 The concepts of Docker Registry and the public Docker Hub will be covered in `Chapter 3`, *Working with Container Images*.

We will use the following image name and tag in this example: `docker-helloworld-iis:latest`.

The Visual Studio Code command is equivalent to performing the following actions in Powershell:

1. Change the working directory to the folder that contains the `Dockerfile`; for example:

   cd c:\src\Hands-On-Kubernetes-on-Windows\Chapter01\docker-helloworld-iis

2. Execute the `docker build` command while specifying the `-t` argument in order to provide the image name and tag and use the current directory, `.`, as the build context:

   docker build -t docker-helloworld-iis:latest .

The following screenshot shows the output of the preceding command:

```
Administrator: Windows PowerShell                                          —    □    ×

PS C:\src\Hands-On-Kubernetes-on-Windows\Chapter01\docker-helloworld-iis> docker build -t docker-helloworld-iis:latest .
Sending build context to Docker daemon  3.072kB
Step 1/4 : FROM mcr.microsoft.com/windows/servercore/iis:windowsservercore-1903
windowsservercore-1903: Pulling from windows/servercore/iis
5b663e3b9104: Pull complete
0887519c3911: Pull complete
5f5ccf5b51ed: Pull complete
344c67f74218: Pull complete
e5c24911f88d: Pull complete
Digest: sha256:ae9a7767fa62ac8fd11139fe8a5616858925e344ea615497466dbfb57dc6de5b
Status: Downloaded newer image for mcr.microsoft.com/windows/servercore/iis:windowsservercore-1903
 ---> 7e02fd27f6a7
Step 2/4 : RUN powershell -NoProfile -Command Remove-Item -Recurse C:\inetpub\wwwroot\*
 ---> Running in 355f1d2f868a
Removing intermediate container 355f1d2f868a
 ---> 58856b244b32
Step 3/4 : WORKDIR /inetpub/wwwroot
 ---> Running in 6a28c10d249b
Removing intermediate container 6a28c10d249b
 ---> c5c48a90708f
Step 4/4 : COPY index.html .
 ---> c162de57646a
Successfully built c162de57646a
Successfully tagged docker-helloworld-iis:latest
PS C:\src\Hands-On-Kubernetes-on-Windows\Chapter01\docker-helloworld-iis>
```

After a successful build, you can use the `docker-helloworld-iis` local image to create new containers. We will cover this in the next subsection.

Running Windows containers

Now, let's create a process-isolated Windows container with our example web page. In Visual Studio Code, navigate to the **Command Palette** (*Ctrl + Shift + P*) and find the **Docker: Run** command. As the image, choose `docker-helloworld-iis`. A terminal with the appropriate command will open.

This is the equivalent to performing the `docker run` command in Powershell, as follows (if port *tcp/80* on your host machine is already in use, use any other port that's available):

```
docker run -d --rm --isolation=process -p 80:80 docker-helloworld-iis
```

After successfully starting the container, navigate to `http://localhost:80/` in a web browser. You should see the following output:

Next, we will be inspecting container logs, which are one of the most useful tools for debugging container issues.

Inspecting container logs

Accessing the main process' standard output and standard error logs in the container is crucial for debugging issues with containerized applications. This is also a common scenario when using Kubernetes, where you can perform similar operations using Kubernetes CLI tools.

The current architecture of the official Microsoft IIS Docker image does not provide any logs to the `stdout` of `ServiceMonitor.exe` (the main process in the container), so we will demonstrate this on the simple `ping.exe` example that we used previously. Run the following container in order to create the container:

```
docker run -d --rm --isolation=process
mcr.microsoft.com/windows/nanoserver:1903 cmd /c ping localhost -n 100
```

Now, in Visual Studio Code, you can inspect the logs by opening the **Command Palette** (*Ctrl* + *Shift* + *P*) and executing the `Docker: Show Logs` command. After selecting the container name, the logs will be shown in the terminal. Alternatively, you can use the **Docker Explorer** tab, expand the **Containers** list, right-click the container you want to inspect, and select **Show Logs**:

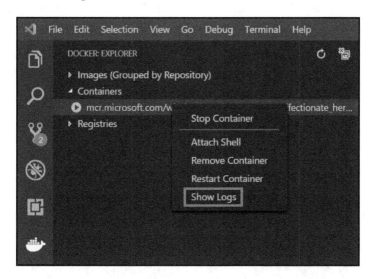

This will open a terminal in Visual Studio Code so that you can start streaming logs from the container's `stdout` and `stderr` instances.

For the PowerShell command line, you have to use the `docker logs` command:

```
docker logs <containerId>
```

It is also worth noting that in debugging scenarios, you may find the `-f` and `--tail` parameters useful:

```
docker logs -f --tail=<number of lines> <containerId>
```

The `-f` parameter instructs the log output to be followed in real-time, whereas the `--tail` parameter makes it possible to show only a specified number of last lines from the output.

Apart from inspecting container logs, you will often need to `exec` into a running container. This will be covered in the next subsection.

Exec into a running container

In debugging and testing scenarios, it is often required to execute another process inside a running container in an ad hoc manner. This is especially useful for creating a shell instance (for Windows, with cmd.exe or powershell.exe, and for Linux, with bash or sh) in the container and interactively debugging the container. Such an operation is called performing exec into a running container.

Visual Studio Code enables this through **Docker Explorer**. In the **Docker Explorer** tab, find the container you would like to exec into, right-click it, and choose **Attach Shell**:

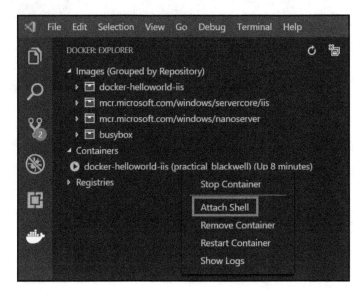

By default, for Windows containers, this command will exec using the powershell.exe command. If you are running images based on Windows Nano Server, you will not be able to use powershell.exe and you'll have to use cmd.exe instead. To customize which command is used during **Attach Shell**, open **Settings** (*Ctrl + ,*), search for **docker**, and customize the **docker.attachShellCommand.windowsContainer** setting.

In the Powershell command line, the equivalent docker exec command is as follows:

```
docker exec -it <containerId> powershell.exe
```

The preceding command creates a new `powershell.exe` process inside the running container in interactive mode with the attached terminal (the `-it` parameter). As you can see, a new interactive instance of the Powershell terminal opens:

```
Administrator: C:\Windows\System32\WindowsPowerShell\v1.0\powershell.exe        —    □    ×
Windows PowerShell
Copyright (C) Microsoft Corporation. All rights reserved.

Try the new cross-platform PowerShell https://aka.ms/pscore6

PS C:\inetpub\wwwroot>
```

 You can only exec into containers that have the main process running. If the container is exited, terminated, or placed in a paused state, it will **not** be possible to use the `exec` command.

Let's try inspecting the contents of `index.html` inside the container's working directory:

```
cat .\index.html
```

The following screenshot shows the output of the preceding command:

```
Administrator: C:\Windows\System32\WindowsPowerShell\v1.0\powershell.exe        —    □    ×
PS C:\inetpub\wwwroot> cat .\index.html
<!DOCTYPE html>
<html>
    <head>
        <title>Hello World!</title>
    </head>
    <body>
        <h1>Hello World from Windows container!</h1>
    </body>
</html>
PS C:\inetpub\wwwroot>
```

This reveals the expected contents of the `index.html` file that we created and added to the image earlier.

We can also inspect the IIS worker process (`w3wp.exe`) for the application pool hosting `index.html`. This is a common scenario during debugging when not all the logs are available directly via container output logs:

```
cat ..\logs\LogFiles\W3SVC1\u_ex<current date>.log
```

The following screenshot shows the output of the preceding command:

```
Administrator: C:\Windows\System32\WindowsPowerShell\v1.0\powershell.exe                    —    □    ×
PS C:\inetpub\wwwroot> cat ..\logs\LogFiles\W3SVC1\u_ex190607.log
#Software: Microsoft Internet Information Services 10.0
#Version: 1.0
#Date: 2019-06-07 21:55:24
#Fields: date time s-ip cs-method cs-uri-stem cs-uri-query s-port cs-username c-ip cs(User-Agent) cs(Referer) sc-status sc
-substatus sc-win32-status time-taken
2019-06-07 21:55:24 172.22.172.206 GET / - 80 - 10.0.75.1 Mozilla/5.0+(Windows+NT+10.0;+Win64;+x64)+AppleWebKit/537.36+(KH
TML,+like+Gecko)+Chrome/70.0.3538.102+Safari/537.36+Edge/18.18362 - 200 0 0 113
#Software: Microsoft Internet Information Services 10.0
#Version: 1.0
#Date: 2019-06-07 22:20:28
#Fields: date time s-ip cs-method cs-uri-stem cs-uri-query s-port cs-username c-ip cs(User-Agent) cs(Referer) sc-status sc
-substatus sc-win32-status time-taken
2019-06-07 22:20:28 172.22.172.206 GET / - 80 - 10.0.75.1 Mozilla/5.0+(Windows+NT+10.0;+Win64;+x64)+AppleWebKit/537.36+(KH
TML,+like+Gecko)+Chrome/70.0.3538.102+Safari/537.36+Edge/18.18362 - 304 0 0 57
2019-06-07 22:20:28 172.22.172.206 GET /favicon.ico - 80 - 10.0.75.1 Mozilla/5.0+(Windows+NT+10.0;+Win64;+x64)+AppleWebKit
/537.36+(KHTML,+like+Gecko)+Chrome/70.0.3538.102+Safari/537.36+Edge/18.18362 - 404 0 2 9
2019-06-07 22:20:29 172.22.172.206 GET / - 80 - 10.0.75.1 Mozilla/5.0+(Windows+NT+10.0;+Win64;+x64)+AppleWebKit/537.36+(KH
TML,+like+Gecko)+Chrome/70.0.3538.102+Safari/537.36+Edge/18.18362 - 304 0 0 0
2019-06-07 22:20:29 172.22.172.206 GET /favicon.ico - 80 - 10.0.75.1 Mozilla/5.0+(Windows+NT+10.0;+Win64;+x64)+AppleWebKit
/537.36+(KHTML,+like+Gecko)+Chrome/70.0.3538.102+Safari/537.36+Edge/18.18362 - 404 0 2 0
2019-06-07 22:20:42 172.22.172.206 GET / - 80 - 10.0.75.1 Mozilla/5.0+(Windows+NT+10.0;+Win64;+x64)+AppleWebKit/537.36+(KH
TML,+like+Gecko)+Chrome/70.0.3538.102+Safari/537.36+Edge/18.18362 - 200 0 0 0
PS C:\inetpub\wwwroot>
```

Using `docker exec` is one of the most powerful commands that you have in your container toolbox. If you learn how to use it, you'll be able to debug your applications almost as if they were hosted in a non-containerized environment.

Summary

In this chapter, you learned about the key aspects of the Windows containers architecture and the differences between the isolation modes provided by the Windows container runtime. We also covered how to install Docker Desktop for Windows and demonstrated how to perform the most important operations using the Docker CLI on the Windows platform.

This and the next two chapters will be the foundations of what you are going to learn about regarding Kubernetes on Windows in the rest of this book. In the next chapter, we will focus on managing state in Windows containers, that is, how to persist data when running containers.

Questions

1. What are the kernel features that Windows exposes in order to enable containerization?
2. What are the key differences between containerization on Linux and on Windows?
3. What is the difference between Hyper-V isolation and process isolation? When should you use Hyper-V isolation?
4. How can we enable LCOW on Windows 10?
5. What command can we use to access logs for the main process in a Docker container?
6. How can we start a new Powershell process inside a running container?

You can find the answers to these questions in the *Assessments* section of this book.

Further reading

This chapter has provided a recap of Docker containers on Windows. For more information concerning Windows containers, please refer to two excellent Packt books:

- *Docker on Windows: From 101 to production with Docker on Windows, at* `https://www.packtpub.com/virtualization-and-cloud/docker-windows-second-edition`.
- *Learning Windows Server Containers, at* `https://www.packtpub.com/virtualization-and-cloud/learning-windows-server-containers`.
- You can also check out the official Microsoft documentation on Windows containers, at `https://docs.microsoft.com/en-us/virtualization/windowscontainers/about/`.

Managing State in Containers 2

Managing the state of an application is one of the key aspects when architecting any software solution, regardless of whether it is a monolith desktop application or a complex, distributed system hosted in a cloud environment. Even if most of your services in the system are stateless, some part of your system will be stateful, for example, a cloud-hosted NoSQL database or a dedicated service you have implemented yourself. And if you are aiming at good scalability for your design, you have to ensure that the storage for your stateful services scales appropriately. In these terms, services or applications hosted in Docker containers are no different – you need to manage the state, especially if you want the data to be persisted on container restarts or failures.

In this chapter, we will provide you with a better understanding of how state can be persisted in Docker containers running on Windows and how these concepts relate to data persistence in Kubernetes applications. You will learn about the concepts of *volumes* and *bind mounts* and how they can be used in order to share state between containers and the container host.

This chapter covers the following topics:

- Mounting local volumes for stateful applications
- Using remote/cloud storage for container storage
- Running clustered solutions inside containers

Technical requirements

For this chapter, you will need the following:

- Windows 10 Pro, Enterprise, or Education (version 1903 or later, 64-bit) installed.
- Docker Desktop for Windows 2.0.0.3 or later installed

The installation of Docker Desktop for Windows and its detailed requirements were covered in Chapter 1, *Creating Containers*.

You will also need your own Azure account. You can read more about how to obtain a limited free account for personal use here: https://azure.microsoft.com/en-us/free/.

You can download the latest code samples for this chapter from this book's official GitHub repository: https://github.com/PacktPublishing/Hands-On-Kubernetes-on-Windows/tree/master/Chapter02.

Mounting local volumes for stateful applications

To understand native Docker storage options for stateful applications, we have to take a look at how the layer filesystem is organized. The main role of this filesystem service is to provide a single virtual logical filesystem for each container based on Docker images.

Docker images consist of a series of read-only layers, where each layer corresponds to one instruction in a Dockerfile. Let's take a look at the following Dockerfile from the previous chapter:

```
FROM mcr.microsoft.com/windows/servercore/iis:windowsservercore-1903

RUN powershell -NoProfile -Command Remove-Item -Recurse
C:\inetpub\wwwroot\*
WORKDIR /inetpub/wwwroot
COPY index.html .
```

When building a Docker image, (*almost*) each instruction creates a new layer that contains only a set of differences in the filesystem that a given command has introduced. In this case, we have the following:

- FROM
  mcr.microsoft.com/windows/servercore/iis:windowsservercore-1903
  : This instruction defines the base layer (or a set of layers) from the base image.

- `RUN powershell -NoProfile -Command Remove-Item -Recurse C:\inetpub\wwwroot\*`: The layer that's created by this instruction will reflect the deletion of contents in the `C:\inetpub\wwwroot\` directory from the original base image.
- `WORKDIR /inetpub/wwwroot`: Even though this instruction is not causing any filesystem changes, it will still create **no operation** (**nop**) layer to persist this information.
- `COPY index.html .`: This final instruction creates a layer that consists of `index.html` in the `C:\inetpub\wwwroot\` directory.

If you have an existing Docker image, you can inspect the layers yourself using the `docker history` command:

```
docker history <imageName>
```

For example, for the image resulting from the preceding Dockerfile, you can expect the following output:

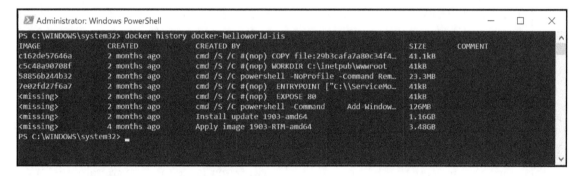

The bottom five layers come from the `mcr.microsoft.com/windows/servercore/iis:windowsservercore-1903` base image, whereas the top three layers are a result of the instructions we described previously.

When a new container is created, the filesystem for it is created, which consists of read-only image layers and a writeable top layer, also called a container layer. For the container, the layers are transparent and processes "see" it as a regular filesystem – on the Windows system, this is guaranteed by the *Windows Container Isolation File System* service. Any changes that are made to the container filesystem by the processes inside it are persisted in the writeable layer. This concept can be seen in the following diagram:

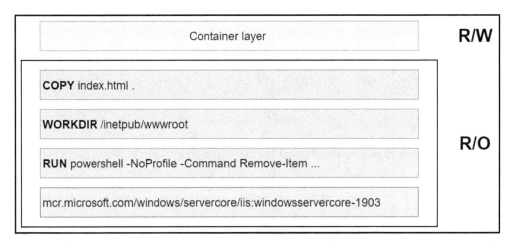

Now that we know the principles of the layer filesystem in Docker, we can focus on *volumes* and *bind mounts*.

Volumes and bind mount

At this point, it may seem that having a writeable container layer for each container is enough to provide state persistence for your application. Data is persisted, even if you stop and restart the same container afterward. Unfortunately, you would easily discover that containers and their writeable layers are tightly coupled and that you cannot easily share data between different containers or even new instances of the same image. A simple scenario where this becomes apparent is as follows:

1. Build a container image based on your current Dockerfile.
2. Start a new container based on this build.

3. Introduce some modifications to the writeable container layer; for example, a process inside the container modifies a file that stores data for the application.

4. Now, you would like to create a new version of your image by modifying the Dockerfile with additional instructions. At the same time, you want to recreate the container and reuse the data in the file that has already been modified in the container's writable layer.

You will realize that after recreating the container with the new image version, all of the changes that you made to the file using the application state will be gone. Apart from this, using the container layer to store data has more disadvantages:

- The writeable layer is coupled with the container host, which means it isn't possible to easily move the data to a different host.
- Layer filesystems provide worse performance than direct access to the host filesystem.
- You cannot share the writeable layer between different containers.

A general rule of thumb is to avoid storing data in a writeable container layer, especially for I/O-intensive applications.

Docker provides two solutions for persistent storage that can be mounted into a container: volume and bind mounts. In both cases, the data is exposed as a directory in the container filesystem and will be persisted, even if the container is stopped and deleted. In terms of performance, both volumes and bind mounts access the host's filesystem directly, which means there is no layer filesystem overhead. It is also possible to share data between multiple containers using these Docker features.

Bind mounts provide a simple functionality of mounting any *file* or *directory* from the container host to a given container. This means that a bind mount will act as a shared file or directory between the host and a container. In general, it is not recommended to use bind mounts as they are harder to manage than volumes, but there are certain use cases when bind mounts are useful, especially on the Windows platform, where volume support is limited.

Bind mounts allow you to share any files from the container host. This means that if you mount sensitive directories such as `C:\Windows\` to an untrusted container, you risk a security breach.

Volumes provide similar functionality to bind mounts but they are fully managed by Docker, which means you don't have to worry about physical paths in the container's host filesystem. You can create *anonymous* or *named* volumes and then mount them into containers. Any data in the volume will not be deleted unless you explicitly delete the volume using Docker. A very common use case for volumes is providing persistent storage for containers that are running a database instance – when the container is recreated, it will use the same volume that contains the data that was written by the previous container instance.

The basic functionality of volumes is that they provide storage in the container host filesystem. It is also possible to use *volume drivers (plugins)*, which use volume abstraction to access remote cloud storage or network shares. Note that, currently, on the Windows platform, there is limited support for volume plugins and most of them can only be used on the Linux OS. More on the available plugins can be found at `https://docs.docker.com/engine/extend/legacy_plugins/#volume-plugins`.

Now, let's take a look at how to perform basic operations on Docker volumes.

Creating and mounting volumes

Creating a new volume can be performed explicitly using the `docker volume create` command. It is also possible to create named and anonymous volumes automatically when the container starts. To manually create a Docker named volume, follow these steps:

1. Execute the following command:

   ```
   docker volume create <volumeName>
   ```

2. After creation, you can inspect the details of the volume using the `docker volume inspect` command:

```
Administrator: Windows PowerShell                                    —    □    ×
PS C:\WINDOWS\system32> docker volume inspect test-named-volume
[
    {
        "CreatedAt": "2019-08-08T08:48:08+02:00",
        "Driver": "local",
        "Labels": {},
        "Mountpoint": "C:\\ProgramData\\Docker\\volumes\\test-named-volume\\_data",
        "Name": "test-named-volume",
        "Options": {},
        "Scope": "local"
    }
]
PS C:\WINDOWS\system32>
```

As you can see, the volume data is stored as a regular directory in the host filesystem when using the default *local* driver.

To mount a volume to a container, you have to use the `--mount` or `--volume` (short parameter: `-v`) parameters for the `docker run` command. Originally, `--volume` was used for stand-alone containers, whereas `--mount` was used for swarm containers, but starting with Docker 17.06, `--mount` can also be used for standalone containers and is the recommended practice as it provides more robust options. More about these flags can be found in the official documentation: `https://docs.docker.com/storage/volumes/#choose-the--v-or---mount-flag`.

Follow these steps to learn how to mount a volume:

1. Assuming that you would like to mount `test-named-volume` from the previous example in a new PowerShell container under the `C:\Data` directory, you have to specify the `--mount` parameter, as follows:

```
docker run -it --rm `
            --isolation=process `
            --mount source=test-named-volume,target=C:\Data `
            mcr.microsoft.com/powershell:windowsservercore-1903
```

Omitting the `source=<volumeName>` parameter will cause the creation of an *anonymous* volume that can be accessed using the volume ID later. Bear in mind that if you run a container with the `--rm` option, anonymous volumes will be automatically deleted when the container is exited.

2. After the container has started and the terminal has been attached, try creating a simple file in the directory where a volume has been mounted:

```
echo "Hello, Volume!" > C:\Data\test.txt
```

3. Now, exit the container (which will cause it to stop and be automatically removed due to the --rm flag) and inspect the volume directory on the host:

```
PS C:\WINDOWS\system32> cat C:\ProgramData\Docker\volumes\test-
named-volume\_data\test.txt
Hello, Volume!
```

4. To demonstrate that the named volume can be easily mounted in another container, let's create a new container based on the mcr.microsoft.com/windows/servercore:1903 image and with a volume mount target that's different from the one in the previous example:

```
docker run -it --rm `
            --isolation=process `
            --mount source=test-named-volume,target=C:\ServerData `
            mcr.microsoft.com/windows/servercore:1903
```

5. If you inspect the volume directory in the container, you will notice that the test.txt file is present and contains the expected content:

```
C:\>more C:\ServerData\test.txt
Hello, Volume!
```

It is also possible to use the VOLUME command in a Dockerfile in order to force the automatic creation of a volume on container start, even if the --mount parameter was not provided for the docker run command. This is useful if you would like to explicitly inform others of where state data is stored by your application and also when you need to ensure that the layer filesystem is not introducing additional overhead. You can find an example of the VOLUME command's usage in the following Dockerfile in the repository for this book: https://github.com/PacktPublishing/Hands-On-Kubernetes-on-Windows/blob/master/Chapter02/03_MongoDB_1903/Dockerfile#L44.

In the next subsection, we'll take a quick look at how to remove volumes using the Docker CLI.

Removing volumes

To remove existing named or anonymous volumes using the `docker volume rm` command, they cannot be used in any container (even stopped ones). The standard procedure would be as follows:

```
docker stop <containerId>
docker rm <containerId>
docker volume rm <volumeId>
```

For anonymous volumes, if you use the `--rm` flag for the `docker run` command, the container will be removed on exit, along with its anonymous volumes. This flag should be used depending on the scenario – in most cases, it is useful for testing and development purposes to make cleanup easier.

During development, you may occasionally need to perform a full cleanup of all of the volumes on your Docker host, for example, if you need to free disk space. The Docker CLI provides a dedicated command that will remove any volumes that are not used in any container:

```
docker volume prune
```

Next, we will take a look at bind mounts and how they differ from volumes.

Mounting a local container host directory using bind mounts

Bind mounts are the simplest form of persistent storage that is shared between the container and the host machine. In this way, you can mount any existing directory from the host filesystem in the container. It is also possible to "overwrite" an existing directory in the container with host directory contents, which may be useful in some scenarios. In general, volumes are the recommended storage solution, but there are a few cases where bind mounts can be useful:

- Sharing configuration between the host and the container. A common use case may be DNS configuration or the `hosts` file.

- In development scenarios, sharing build artifacts that were created on the host so that they can be consumed inside the container.
- On Windows, mounting SMB file shares as directories in the container.

 Volumes can be seen as an *evolution* of bind mounts. They are fully managed by Docker, without tight coupling to the container host filesystem being visible to the user.

Creating a bind mount for a container requires the `docker run` command to be specified with an additional parameter, `type=bind`, for the `--mount` flag. In this example, we will mount the host's `C:\Users` directory as `C:\HostUsers` in the container:

```
docker run -it --rm `
        --isolation=process `
        --mount type=bind,source=C:\Users,target=C:\HostUsers `
        mcr.microsoft.com/powershell:windowsservercore-1903
```

You can verify that any changes performed to `C:\HostUsers` will also be visible on the host machine in `C:\Users`.

 Windows-specific features and the limitations of bind mounts can be found in the official documentation from Microsoft: `https://docs.microsoft.com/en-us/virtualization/windowscontainers/manage-containers/container-storage#bind-mounts`.

In the next section, we are going to learn how to leverage bind mounts in order to use remote or cloud storage in Windows containers.

Using remote/cloud storage for container storage

Storing data locally in a container host filesystem is not suitable for use cases that require high-availability, failover, and ease of data backup. In order to provide storage abstraction, Docker provides volume drivers (plugins), which can be used to manage volumes that are hosted on remote machines or in cloud services. Unfortunately, at the time of writing this book, Windows containers running on-premises do not support the volume plugins that are currently available on Linux OS. This leaves us with three choices when it comes to using cloud storage in Windows containers:

- Use Docker for Azure and the Cloudstor volume plugin, which is a partially managed solution for running Docker in *swarm* mode on Azure VMs. In this book, we will not cover Docker for Azure as this solution is separate from Kubernetes, including Azure offerings for managed Kubernetes. If you are interested in more details about this service, please refer to `https://docs.docker.com/docker-for-azure/persistent-data-volumes/`.
- Use cloud storage directly in application code using cloud service provider SDKs. This is the most obvious solution, but it requires embedding storage management into your application code.
- Use bind mounts and **Server Message Block** (**SMB**) global mappings in order to mount Azure Files, which is a fully managed cloud file share that can be accessed via the SMB protocol.

Soon, we will demonstrate how to leverage the last option: SMB global mappings for Azure Files. But first, we have to install the Azure CLI in order to manage Azure resources.

Installing the Azure CLI and Azure PowerShell module

In order to manage Azure resources efficiently from the command line, it is recommended to use the official Azure CLI. The official installation notes can be found at `https://docs.microsoft.com/en-us/cli/azure/install-azure-cli-windows?view=azure-cli-latest`. Let's get started:

1. Installing the Azure CLI from PowerShell requires running the following commands as an Administrator:

   ```
   Invoke-WebRequest -Uri https://aka.ms/installazurecliwindows -
   OutFile .\AzureCLI.msi
   Start-Process msiexec.exe -Wait -ArgumentList '/I AzureCLI.msi
   /quiet'
   Remove-Item .\AzureCLI.msi
   ```

2. After installing the Azure CLI, you need to restart your PowerShell window. Next, log in to your Azure account:

   ```
   az login
   ```

The preceding command will open your default browser and instruct you to log in to your Azure account.

3. Now, run the following command to verify that you have been logged in properly:

```
az account show
```

You should be able to see your subscription details, similar to this:

```
Administrator: Windows PowerShell                         —    □    ×

PS C:\src> az account show
{
  "environmentName": "AzureCloud",
  "id": "                             ",
  "isDefault": true,
  "name": "Pay-As-You-Go",
  "state": "Enabled",
  "tenantId": "                             ",
  "user": {
    "name": "                             ",
    "type": "user"
  }
}
PS C:\src>
```

On top of that, we need to install the Azure PowerShell module since some operations are not available in the Azure CLI.

4. Installation for the currently logged-in user can be performed using the following command:

```
Install-Module -Name Az -AllowClobber -Scope CurrentUser
```

The official installation steps can be found here: https://docs.microsoft.com/ en-us/powershell/azure/install-az-ps?view=azps-2.5.0#install-the- azure-powershell-module-1.

5. If you run into problems while importing the newly installed module, you'll also need to set a PowerShell execution policy to RemoteSigned as an Administrator:

```
Set-ExecutionPolicy RemoteSigned
```

6. Logging in to Azure using the PowerShell module has to be done separately from the Azure CLI and can be performed using the following command:

```
Connect-AzAccount
```

At this point, you should be able to manage your resources using the Azure CLI and the Azure PowerShell module, without opening the Azure Portal website! Let's take a look at how to create an Azure Files SMB share.

Creating Azure Files SMB share

Assuming that you are following along with these examples on a fresh Azure subscription, let's create an Azure Resource Group and Azure Storage Account first:

1. In a PowerShell window, execute the following code:

```
az group create `
    --name docker-storage-resource-group `
    --location westeurope
```

You can choose a location that is the most suitable for you (in order to show a list of available locations, run `az account list-locations`). In this example, we are using the `westeurope` Azure location.

You can also use the PowerShell script in this book's GitHub repository to do this: `https://github.com/PacktPublishing/Hands-On-Kubernetes-on-Windows/blob/master/Chapter02/01_CreateAzureFilesSMBShare.ps1`. Remember to run this script as an Administrator since global mappings for SMB share must be added from a privileged account.

2. After the successful creation of an Azure Resource Group, continue by creating an Azure Storage Account:

```
az storage account create `
    --name dockerstorageaccount `
    --resource-group docker-storage-resource-group `
    --location westeurope `
    --sku Standard_RAGRS `
    --kind StorageV2
```

The preceding command will create a `general-purpose v2` storage account with `read-access geo-redundant` storage called `dockerstorageaccount` in `docker-storage-resource-group`. This operation can take up to a few minutes to complete.

3. Next, you have to create the actual Azure Files SMB share. First, create a connection string for your Azure Storage Account and store it as a variable in PowerShell:

```
$azureStorageAccountConnString = az storage account show-
connection-string `
    --name dockerstorageaccount `
    --resource-group docker-storage-resource-group `
    --query "connectionString" `
    --output tsv

if (!$azureStorageAccountConnString) {
    Write-Error "Couldn't retrieve the connection string."
}
```

Remember to keep the connection string safe as it can be used to manage your storage account!

4. Using the connection string stored in the `$azureStorageAccountConnString` variable, create the share:

```
az storage share create `
    --name docker-bind-mount-share `
    --quota 2 `
    --connection-string $azureStorageAccountConnString
```

This will create a share called `docker-bind-mount-share` with a quota limit of 2 GB, which we will now use in our Docker container.

Mounting Azure Files SMB share in a container

In order to mount the new Azure Files SMB share as a bind mount in a container, we will leverage the *SMB Global Mapping* feature that was introduced in Window Server 1709. Global mappings have been introduced specifically for this purpose, that is, mounting SMB shares on the host so that they're visible to containers. Let's get started:

1. First, ensure that you are logged in so that you can execute Azure PowerShell (using the `Connect-AzAccount` command).
2. Next, let's define a few variables that will be used in the commands we'll execute

soon:

```
$resourceGroupName = "docker-storage-resource-group"
$storageAccountName = "dockerstorageaccount"
$fileShareName = "docker-bind-mount-share"
```

The names being used here are exactly the same as the ones we used in the previous subsection while creating the Azure Files SMB share.

3. The next step is to define the `$storageAccount` and `$storageAccountKeys` variables:

```
$storageAccount = Get-AzStorageAccount `
 -ResourceGroupName $resourceGroupName `
 -Name $storageAccountName
$storageAccountKeys = Get-AzStorageAccountKey `
   -ResourceGroupName $resourceGroupName `
     -Name $storageAccountName
```

These variables will be used for the retrieval of file share details and credentials for access, both of which are needed for SMB Global Mapping.

4. Now, *optionally*, you can persist your share credentials in Windows Credential Manager using the `cmdkey` command:

```
Invoke-Expression -Command `
    ("cmdkey
/add:$([System.Uri]::new($storageAccount.Context.FileEndPoint).Host
) " + `
    "/user:AZURE\$($storageAccount.StorageAccountName)
/pass:$($storageAccountKeys[0].Value)")
```

5. We will also need details regarding Azure Files SMB share, so let's define a new variable called `$fileShare`:

```
$fileShare = Get-AzStorageShare -Context $storageAccount.Context |
Where-Object {
    $_.Name -eq $fileShareName -and $_.IsSnapshot -eq $false
}
```

6. At this point, you can also check if the file share details have been retrieved successfully. By doing this, you will be able to detect if, for example, $fileShareName contains the wrong share name:

```
if ($fileShare -eq $null) {
    Write-Error "Azure File share not found"
}
```

7. The last step, before creating an SMB Global Mapping, is to define a credentials object, which will be used for mapping creation:

```
$password = ConvertTo-SecureString `
    -String $storageAccountKeys[0].Value `
    -AsPlainText `
    -Force
$credential = New-Object System.Management.Automation.PSCredential `-ArgumentList "AZURE\$($storageAccount.StorageAccountName)",
$password
```

8. Finally, we can use the New-SmbGlobalMapping command in order to create the mapping for Azure Files SMB share:

```
New-SmbGlobalMapping `
    -RemotePath
"\\$($fileShare.StorageUri.PrimaryUri.Host)\$($fileShare.Name)" `
    -Credential $credential `
    -Persistent $true `
    -LocalPath G:
```

If you need to remove SMB Global Mapping, you can do so using the Remove-SmbGlobalMapping command.

The preceding command will mount your Azure Files SMB share persistently as the G: drive. You can use this path later for bind mounts for Docker containers. Now, you can test if your mapping works correctly by moving some test files to the G: drive using Windows Explorer.

The principle of using bind mount for a globally mapped SMB share can be used for any SMB-compatible server, such as the following:

- A traditional file server hosted in your local network
- A third-party implementation of the SMB protocol, such as NAS appliances
- A traditional SAN or **Scale-out File Server (SoFS)** on top of **Storage Spaces Direct (S2D)**

Globally mapped SMB shares, when used as bind mounts, are transparently visible for the containers as regular directories in the local filesystem. All of the "heavy lifting" is performed by the container host, which is responsible for managing the SMB share connection.

Let's demonstrate this feature by creating a simple PowerShell process-isolated container:

1. First, create a directory called `G:\ContainerData` in the SMB share for our demonstration container:

   ```
   New-Item -ItemType Directory -Force -Path G:\ContainerData
   ```

2. Now, we can run the container by providing the new directory in the Azure Files SMB share as a bind mount with `C:\Data` as the target:

   ```
   docker run -it --rm `
               --isolation=process `
               --mount type=bind,source=G:\ContainerData,target=C:\Data
   `mcr.microsoft.com/powershell:windowsservercore-1903
   ```

   With this, we can easily prove that our solution works and that the container state files are indeed stored in Azure Cloud!

3. In the running container, create a file that contains data. For example, get a list of the currently running processes and store it as a `processes.txt` file:

   ```
   Get-Process > C:\Data\processes.txt
   ```

4. Now, log in to Azure Portal (`https://portal.azure.com/`) and do the following:
    1. Navigate to **Storage accounts** from the main menu.
    2. Open the **dockerstorageaccount** account.
    3. In the storage account menu, open **Files** under the **File service** group.
    4. Open the **docker-bind-mount-share** file share from the list.

You will see a familiar directory structure. Navigate into the **ContainerData** directory to see that the `processes.txt` file is indeed there and contains the data that was stored in the container:

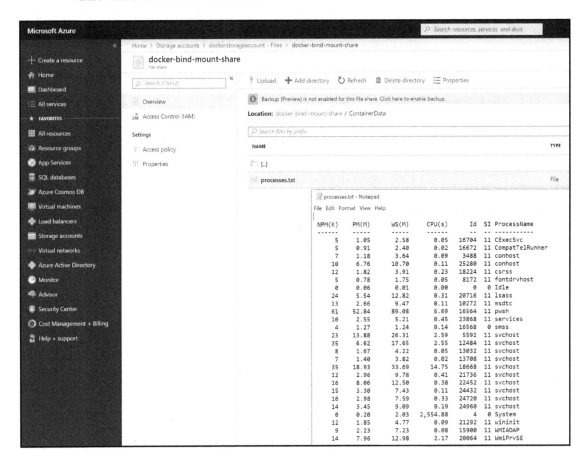

In Kubernetes, a similar procedure can be performed in a managed way using *volumes* (not to be confused with Docker volumes). We will focus on this in Chapter 11, *Configuring Applications to Use Kubernetes Features*. You can also refer to the official documentation: https://kubernetes.io/docs/concepts/storage/.

Please note that this scenario can also be achieved with a regular SMB File Server hosted in your local network, which may be a suitable solution if you use them in your infrastructure already.

Congratulations! You have successfully created a Windows container that uses Azure Cloud storage to persist container state. In the next section, we will learn how to run MongoDB inside Windows containers as an example of a multi-container solution.

Running clustered solutions inside containers

MongoDB is a free and open source cross-platform, document-oriented database program that can run in cluster mode (using shards and ReplicaSets). In this example, we will run a three-node MongoDB ReplicaSet as that is much easier to configure than a full sharded cluster and is sufficient to demonstrate the principle of storing container state data persistently.

If you would like to learn more about MongoDB and advanced sharded cluster components, please refer to the official documentation: https://docs.mongodb.com/manual/core/sharded-cluster-components/.

Our MongoDB ReplicaSet architecture will look as follows:

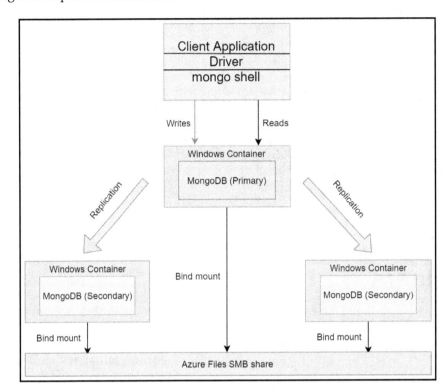

The primary node is responsible for managing all write operations, and there can only be one primary in a ReplicaSet. The secondary nodes are only replicating the primary's *oplog* and apply the data operations so that their datasets reflect the dataset of the primary. The main benefits of such a MongoDB deployment are as follows:

- **Automatic failover**: If the primary becomes unavailable, the rest of the secondary nodes will perform new leader election and resume cluster functionality.
- **Possibility to use secondaries to read data**: You can specify read preference so that clients offload the primary for read operations. However, you have to take note of the fact that asynchronous replication may result in secondaries being slightly off-sync with the primary node.

Now, let's create our MongoDB ReplicaSet!

Creating a MongoDB ReplicaSet

Follow these steps to create the ReplicaSet:

1. First, let's create a Docker network called `mongo-cluster` for the new cluster using the `docker network create` command:

   docker network create --driver nat mongo-cluster

    If you would like to learn more about Docker networks, please refer to the official documentation: `https://docs.docker.com/network/`. For Windows-specific documentation, please go to `https://docs.microsoft.com/en-us/virtualization/windowscontainers/container-networking/network-drivers-topologies`.

   We will use Azure Files SMB share (globally mapped to the `G:` drive), which we created in the previous section, in order to store MongoDB's state using bind mounts.

2. We need to create new directories in our SMB share, two for each MongoDB node:

   ```
   New-Item -ItemType Directory -Force -Path G:\MongoData1\db
   New-Item -ItemType Directory -Force -Path G:\MongoData1\configdb
   New-Item -ItemType Directory -Force -Path G:\MongoData2\db
   New-Item -ItemType Directory -Force -Path G:\MongoData2\configdb
   New-Item -ItemType Directory -Force -Path G:\MongoData3\db
   New-Item -ItemType Directory -Force -Path G:\MongoData3\configdb
   ```

Currently, the official MongoDB image for Windows only exists in Windows Server Core 1803, which means we would have to use Hyper-V isolation to run such containers on Windows 1903. This means that we can't leverage SMB Global Mappings, so we need to create our own MongoDB image based on Windows Server Core 1903. This will make it possible for us to use process isolation. The image we are going to build is based on the official MongoDB image for the 4.2.0 RC8 version, which can be found here: `https://github.com/docker-library/mongo/blob/a3a213fd2b4b2c26c71408761534fc7eaafe517f/4.2-rc/windows/windowsservercore-1803/Dockerfile`. To perform the build, follow these steps:

1. Download the Dockerfile from this book's GitHub repository: `https://github.com/PacktPublishing/Hands-On-Kubernetes-on-Windows/blob/master/Chapter02/03_MongoDB_1903/Dockerfile`.

2. In PowerShell, navigate to the location where you downloaded the Dockerfile (using a new, separate directory is recommended).
3. Execute the `docker build` command in order to create a custom MongoDB image named `mongo-1903` in your local image registry:

```
docker build -t mongo-1903:latest .
```

The build process will take a few minutes as MongoDB has to be downloaded and installed in the build container.

This image also exposes the MongoDB data as volumes under `C:\data\db` and `C:\data\configdb` inside the container (https://github.com/PacktPublishing/Hands-On-Kubernetes-on-Windows/blob/master/Chapter02/03_MongoDB_1903/Dockerfile#L44). Taking all of these into account, let's create our first MongoDB process-isolated container named `mongo-node1`, which will be running in the background (using the -d option):

```
docker run -d `
            --isolation=process `
            --volume G:\MongoData1\db:C:\data\db `
            --volume G:\MongoData1\configdb:C:\data\configdb `
            --name mongo-node1 `
            --net mongo-cluster `
            mongo-1903:latest `
            mongod --bind_ip_all --replSet replSet0
```

When running this container, we are providing a custom command to run the container process, that is, `mongod --bind_ip_all --replSet replSet0`. The `--bind_ip_all` argument instructs MongoDB to bind to all the network interfaces that are available in the container. For our use case, the `--replSet replSet0` argument ensures that the daemon runs in ReplicaSet mode, expecting to be in a ReplicaSet named `replSet0`.

After the successful creation of the first node, repeat this process for the next two nodes, changing their name and volume mount points appropriately:

```
docker run -d `
            --isolation=process `
            --volume G:\MongoData2\db:C:\data\db `
            --volume G:\MongoData2\configdb:C:\data\configdb `
            --name mongo-node2 `
            --net mongo-cluster `
            mongo-1903:latest `
            mongod --bind_ip_all --replSet replSet0

docker run -d `
            --isolation=process `
```

```
--volume G:\MongoData3\db:C:\data\db `
--volume G:\MongoData3\configdb:C:\data\configdb `
--name mongo-node3 `
--net mongo-cluster `
mongo-1903:latest `
mongod --bind_ip_all --replSet replSet0
```

After the creation process has finished, you can verify that the containers are running properly using the `docker ps` command:

The preceding steps have also been provided as a PowerShell script in this book's GitHub repository: `https://github.com/PacktPublishing/Hands-On-Kubernetes-on-Windows/blob/master/Chapter02/02_InitializeMongoDBReplicaSet.ps1`.

The next stage is to configure the ReplicaSet. We will do this using the mongo shell. Follow these steps:

1. Create an instance of the mongo shell. If you're already running a MongoDB container (for example, mongo-node1), the easiest way to do this is to `exec` into an existing container and run the mongo process:

   docker exec -it mongo-node1 mongo

2. After a few seconds, you should see the mongo shell console prompt, >. You can initialize the ReplicaSet using the `rs.initiate()` method:

```
rs.initiate(
  {
    "_id" : "replSet0",
    "members" : [
      { "_id" : 0, "host" : "mongo-node1:27017" },
      { "_id" : 1, "host" : "mongo-node2:27017" },
      { "_id" : 2, "host" : "mongo-node3:27017" }
    ]
  }
)
```

The preceding command creates a ReplicaSet called `replSet0` using our three nodes. These can be identified by their DNS names in the `mongo-cluster` Docker network.

For more details regarding the initialization of ReplicaSets, please refer to the official documentation: `https://docs.mongodb.com/manual/reference/method/rs.initiate/`.

3. You can also verify the state of initialization using the `rs.status()` command in the mongo shell. After a short time, when the ReplicaSet is fully initialized, in the command JSON output, you should be able to see the ReplicaSet in one node with `"stateStr": "PRIMARY"` and two other nodes with `"stateStr": "SECONDARY"` in the command's output.

In the next subsection, we will quickly verify our ReplicaSet by generating test data and reading it in another container.

Writing and reading test data

Follow these steps to write and read test data:

1. First, in the mongo shell for the ReplicaSet primary node (as a prompt, you will see `replSet0:PRIMARY>`), let's add 1,000 sample documents in the `demo` collection:

```
for (var i = 1; i <= 1000; i++) {
  db.demo.insert( { exampleValue : i } )
}
```

2. You can quickly verify the inserted documents by using the `find()` method on the `demo` collection:

```
db.demo.find()
```

3. Now, we will create a minimalistic .NET Core 3.0 console application running in a Docker container. This will connect to the ReplicaSet running in our Docker container, query our `demo` collection, and write a value of `exampleValue` for each document to standard output.

You can find the source code and Dockerfile for this in this book's GitHub repository: `https://github.com/PacktPublishing/Hands-On-Kubernetes-on-Windows/tree/master/Chapter02/04_MongoDB_dotnet`.

If, during the execution of this scenario, you experience any instability issues with MongoDB, consider upgrading the `mongo-1903` Dockerfile to the latest MongoDB version.

To read our test data, we need to build the application Docker image and create a container that's running in the `mongo-cluster` network. Perform the following steps to do so:

1. Clone the repository and navigate to the `Chapter02/04_MongoDB_dotnet` directory in PowerShell.
2. Execute `docker build` in the current directory in order to create the `mongo-dotnet-sample` Docker image:

```
docker build -t mongo-dotnet-sample:latest .
```

3. Run the sample container. This needs to be connected to the `mongo-cluster` network:

```
docker run --isolation=process `
  --rm `
  --net mongo-cluster `
  mongo-dotnet-sample:latest
```

In the output, you should see an increasing sequence of numbers, which is the values of `exampleValue` in our test documents:

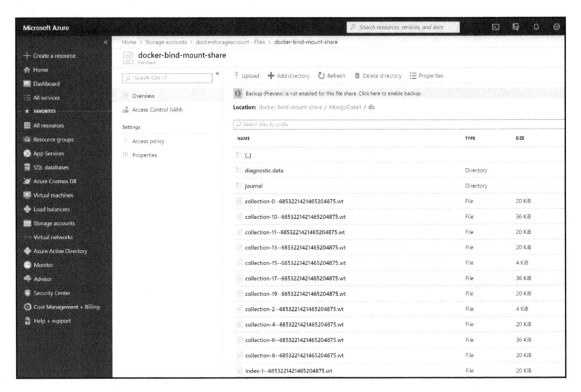

If you are curious, you can check what the SMB share contains on Azure Portal (`https://portal.azure.com/`):

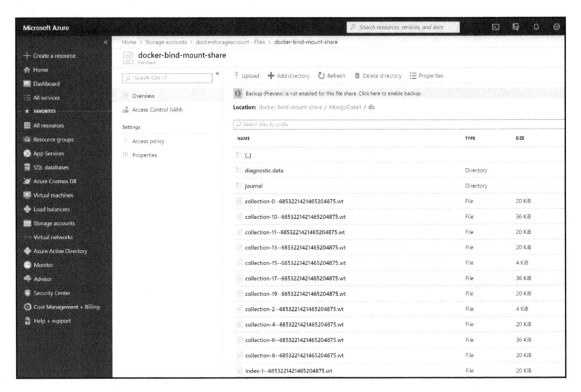

Congratulations! You have successfully created and tested a MongoDB ReplicaSet running in a Windows container with Azure Files SMB share being used as a bind mount for storing data. Let's quickly summarize what we have learned in this chapter.

Summary

In this chapter, you learned the key aspects of Docker storage on Windows: using volumes and bind mounts. With the help of Azure, you successfully set up your Azure Files SMB share, which can be used to store container state data using SMB global mappings. Last but not least, you wrapped all this up by setting up your own three-node MongoDB ReplicaSet backed by Azure Cloud storage and verified your setup!

The next chapter will be the last one to focus purely on Docker on the Windows platform. You can expect to learn about the fundamentals of how to work with Docker images and how to use them in your application development life cycle. After that, we will be ready to begin our journey with Kubernetes.

Questions

1. What is the container layer in the Docker storage architecture?
2. What is the difference between volumes and bind mounts?
3. Why is storing container state data in the container layer not recommended?
4. How can you mount Azure Files SMB share transparently in a container?
5. Can you use bind mounts in containers that run in Hyper-V isolation?
6. What command removes all unused volumes on the container host?
7. What are volume drivers (plugins)?

You can find the answers to these questions in the *Assessments* section of this book.

Further reading

- For more information concerning managing state and volumes in Docker (not only on Windows), please refer to the following Packt book:
- *Learn Docker – Fundamentals of Docker 18.x* (`https://www.packtpub.com/networking-and-servers/learn-docker-fundamentals-docker-18x`).
- You can also refer to the official Docker documentation, which gives a good overview of possible storage options for Docker itself: `https://docs.docker.com/storage/`.

Working with Container Images

3

Container-based software development lifecycle requires easy image packaging and reliable ways to distribute containerized applications - these are key aspects that the Docker ecosystem has solved. We used Dockerfiles and Docker images in the previous chapters. Simply put, a Dockerfile defines build instructions for creating a Docker image, an immutable, layered snapshot of container data that can be used for instantiating containers. These two concepts allow us to create easy and standardized packaging for container applications. In order to provide reliable and scalable distribution for Docker images, we can use image registries.

In this chapter, we will focus on the usage of Docker registries, mainly the publicly accessible Docker Hub and private Azure Container Registry, and we will also introduce Docker Content Trust – a concept for publishing and managing signed collections of content. With this introduction to container image management, you will be ready to fully enter the world of Kubernetes on Windows!

This chapter will cover the following topics:

- Storing and sharing container images
- Using cloud container builders
- Image tagging and versioning
- Ensuring the integrity of the image supply chain

Technical requirements

For this chapter, you will need the following:

- Windows 10 Pro, Enterprise, or Education (version 1903 or later, 64-bit) installed.
- Docker Desktop for Windows 2.0.0.3 or later installed.
- The Azure CLI installed. You can find detailed installation instructions in Chapter 2, *Managing State in Containers*.

The installation of Docker Desktop for Windows and its detailed requirements were covered in Chapter 1, *Creating Containers*.

To be able to use cloud-hosted registries, you will need your own Azure account. If you haven't created an account for the previous chapters, you can find out how to obtain a limited free account for personal use here: https://azure.microsoft.com/en-us/free/.

You can download the latest code samples for this chapter from this book's official GitHub repository: https://github.com/PacktPublishing/Hands-On-Kubernetes-on-Windows/tree/master/Chapter03.

Storing and sharing container images

So far, you have already pulled your first hello-world container with the docker pull hello-world command and even used the docker run hello-world command. Under the hood, a few things happen during an image pull:

1. Docker Engine connects to the so-called Docker image registry. The registry can be specified explicitly, but by default, this is the official public registry, called Docker Hub (https://hub.docker.com/).
2. Docker Engine authenticates to the registry, if needed. This can be the case if you are running a private registry or paid plan for Docker Hub.
3. The selected hello-world image is downloaded as a set of layers identified by SHA256 digests. Each layer is unpacked after being downloaded.
4. The image is stored locally.

A similar procedure happens if you execute the docker run command and the image is not present in the local store. The first time, it will be pulled, and later, the locally cached image will be used.

 If you are familiar with GitHub or other source repository managed hosting, you will find many concepts in image management and image registries similar.

So, intuitively, the image registry is an organized, hierarchical system for storing Docker images. The hierarchy of images consists of the following levels:

- **Registry**: This is the top level of the hierarchy.
- **Repository**: Registries host multiple repositories, which are storage units for images.

- **Tag**: A versioning label for a single image. Repositories group multiple images identified by the same image name and different tags.

Each image in the registry is identified by an image name and tag, and the hierarchy above is reflected in the final image name. The following scheme is used: `<registryAddress>/<userName>/<repositoryName>:<tag>`, for example, `localregistry:5000/ptylenda/test-application:1.0.0`. When using Docker commands, some of these parts are optional and if you do not provide a value, the default will be used:

- `<registryAddress>` is the DNS name or IP address (together with the port) of the registry that is used for storing the image. If you omit this part, the default Docker Hub registry (`docker.io`) will be used. Currently, there is no way of changing the default value of the registry address, so if you would like to use a custom registry, you have to always provide this part.
- `<userName>` identifies the user or organization that owns the image. In the case of Docker Hub, this is a so-called Docker ID. Whether this part is required depends on the registry – for Docker Hub, if you do not provide a Docker ID, it will assume official images, which are a curated set of Docker repositories that are maintained and reviewed by Docker.
- `<repositoryName>` is a unique name within your account. The image name is formed as `<registryAddress>/<userName>/<repositoryName>`.
- `<tag>` is a unique label within a given image repository that is used for organizing images, in most cases using a versioning scheme, for example, `1.0.0`. If this value is not provided, the default, `latest`, will be used. We will focus on tagging and versioning images later in this chapter.

 With multi-architecture Docker image variants, it is possible to have different images under the same image name and tag for different architectures. The version of the image will be automatically chosen based on the architecture of the machine running the Docker client. Identifying such images can be performed explicitly using an additional `@sha256:<shaTag>` part after the image tag, for example, `docker.io/adamparco/demo:latest@sha256:2b77acdfea5 dc5baa489ffab2a0b4a387666d1d526490e31845eb64e3e73ed20`. For more details, please go to `https://engineering.docker.com/2019/04/ multi-arch-images/`.

Now that you know how Docker images are identified, let's take a look at how to push an image to the Docker registry.

Pushing an image to the Docker registry

Sharing container images using the registry is performed via an image push. This process uploads the required image layers to the selected repository in a registry and makes it available for pull by other users that have access to a given repository. In the case of Docker Hub, which we will use for this demonstration, your repositories will be public, unless you have a paid plan.

Pushing images to Docker Hub requires authentication. If you haven't already registered at Docker Hub, please navigate to `https://hub.docker.com/` and follow the instructions there. After registration, you will need your Docker ID and password in order to log in to the services using the `docker login` command:

```
PS C:\WINDOWS\system32> docker login
Login with your Docker ID to push and pull images from Docker Hub. If you
don't have a Docker ID, head over to https://hub.docker.com to create one.
Username: packtpubkubernetesonwindows
Password:
Login Succeeded
```

Throughout this book, we will be using the `packtpubkubernetesonwindows` Docker ID in order to demonstrate our examples. It is recommended that you create your own account to be able to fully follow the examples in this book. Follow these steps:

1. The first step is to create an image that can actually be pushed to the registry. We will use the following Dockerfile to create the image:

    ```
    FROM
    mcr.microsoft.com/windows/servercore/iis:windowsservercore-1903

    WORKDIR /inetpub/wwwroot
    RUN powershell -NoProfile -Command ; \
        Remove-Item -Recurse .\* ; \
        New-Item -Path .\index.html -ItemType File ; \
        Add-Content -Path .\index.html -Value \"This is an IIS
    demonstration!\"
    ```

    This Dockerfile creates an IIS web host image, which serves a minimalistic web page that displays **This is an IIS demonstration!**.

2. Save the Dockerfile in your current directory. To build it, issue the following `docker build` command:

    ```
    docker build -t <dockerId>/iis-demo .
    ```

Bear in mind that you have to supply your Docker ID as part of the repository name in order to be able to push the image to Docker Hub.

3. After a successful build, you are ready to perform an image push to the registry. This can be performed with the `docker push` command:

```
docker push <dockerId>/iis-demo
```

The following screenshot shows the output of the preceding command:

```
Administrator: Windows PowerShell                                                        —  □  ×
PS C:\src\Hands-On-Kubernetes-on-Windows\Chapter03\01_iis-demo> docker push packtpubkubernetesonwindows/iis-demo
The push refers to repository [docker.io/packtpubkubernetesonwindows/iis-demo]
a739ac2b5de1: Pushed
0ac556df41fa: Pushed
22654ee65998: Pushed
f1627a8358bf: Pushed
118f3762d074: Pushed
4b775a679e59: Skipped foreign layer
734d75c7186c: Skipped foreign layer
latest: digest: sha256:fac1e2272d408bad97c27ddf518fc57cf7cba3aed4203401f905780142f1a601 size: 1993
PS C:\src\Hands-On-Kubernetes-on-Windows\Chapter03\01_iis-demo>
```

Docker pushes the image as a set of layers, which also optimizes the push process if already known layers are being used. Also, note that in the case of Windows-based images, you will see a **Skipped foreign layer** message. The reason for this is that any layers that come from a registry other than Docker Hub, such as **Microsoft Container Registry** (**MCR**), will not be pushed to Docker Hub.

Now, you can also navigate to the Docker Hub web page and check your image details – for the example image, you can check it here: `https://cloud.docker.com/repository/docker/packtpubkubernetesonwindows/iis-demo/`. Any user that has access to your repository can now use the `docker pull <dockerId>/iis-demo` command in order to use your image.

You have successfully pushed your first image to Docker Hub! Now, let's take a look at pushing images to custom image registries.

Using a custom local registry

When it comes to choosing storage for your images, you are not limited to using the default Docker Hub. In fact, in most cases, when you are running production code, you may want to use a locally hosted Docker Registry, which is an open source, highly scalable application for storing and distributing Docker images. You should consider this solution in the following situations:

- You want to distribute Docker images in an isolated network
- You need strict control where the images are stored and distributed
- You would like to compliment your CI/CD workflow to enable faster and more scalable delivery of images

Detailed information about the deployment of Docker Registry can be found in the official documentation: https://docs.docker.com/registry/deploying/.

For Kubernetes deployments, it is a common practice to host your own Docker Registry alongside or even inside the Kubernetes cluster. There are numerous automations available for this use case, for example, the official Helm chart for the deployment of registries on Kubernetes: https://github.com/helm/charts/tree/master/stable/docker-registry.

In order to use a custom image registry, all you need to do is specify the registry address (and port, if needed) in the image name when using pull or push commands, for example, localregistry:5000/ptylenda/test-application:1.0.0, where localregistry:5000 is the domain name and port of a locally hosted Docker registry. In fact, you have already used a custom Docker image registry when you pulled images for your demonstration Windows IIS application: mcr.microsoft.com/windows/servercore/iis:windowsservercore-1903. The mcr.microsoft.com registry is the MCR, which is the official registry for Microsoft Published images. The main difference between other public registries and MCR is that it is tightly integrated with Docker Hub and leverages its UI for providing a browsable catalog of images. Docker Engine is capable of using any system that exposes the Docker Registry HTTP API (https://docs.docker.com/registry/spec/api/) as a container image registry.

Currently, it is not possible to change the default container image registry for Docker Engine. Unless you specify the registry address in the image name, the target registry will always be assumed to be docker.io.

Apart from hosting your own local image registry, there are a couple of cloud-based alternatives that provide private image registries:

- **Azure Container Registry (ACR)** https://azure.microsoft.com/en-in/ services/container-registry/). We will cover this registry in the next section as part of a demonstration of how to use cloud hosting for container builds.
- Docker Enterprise and its Docker Trusted Registry (https://www.docker.com/ products/image-registry).
- IBM Cloud Container Registry (https://www.ibm.com/cloud/container-registry).
- Google Cloud Container Registry (https://cloud.google.com/container-registry/).
- RedHat Quay.io and Quay Enterprise (https://quay.io). Quay is an interesting solution if you would like to host not only the registry but also the build automation and web catalog on-premises, similar to Docker Hub.

In the next section, you will learn how to use Docker Hub to automate Docker image builds and how to host your own registry using ACR.

Using cloud container builders

One of the features that Docker Hub offers is **automated builds (autobuilds)**. This is especially useful in Continuous Integration and Continuous Deployment scenarios where you would like to ensure that each push to your code repository results in a build, a publish, and potentially a deployment.

 Currently, Docker Hub does not support Windows images, but this is likely to change in the near future. We will demonstrate this usage on a Linux image, but all the principles remain the same. For Windows container cloud builds, check out the next section about Azure Container Registry.

To set up automated builds, complete the following steps:

1. Create a GitHub repository where your application code resides, together with a Dockerfile that defines the Docker image for the application.
2. Create a Docker Hub repository and add an autobuild trigger. This trigger can also be added after creating the repository.

3. Customize the build rules.

4. Optionally, enable autotests. This is a validation feature provided by Docker Hub where you can define your test suite in order to test each new image push.

Let's begin by creating a GitHub repository!

Creating a GitHub repository

If you don't have a GitHub account, you can create one for free at `https://github.com/join`. In this example, we will create a dedicated public repository called `nginx-demo-index` in the `hands-on-kubernetes-on-windows` organization. Let's get started:

1. Navigate to `https://github.com/` and use the + sign to create a new repository:

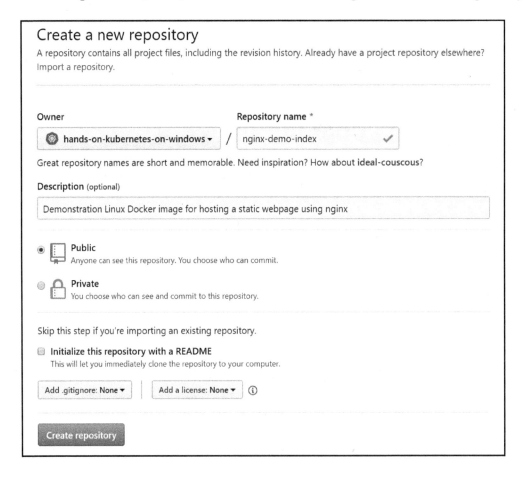

Hosting an organization is not required; you can just use your own personal namespace. The repository is intended to only contain the application source code (in our case, just a static `index.html` web page) and the Dockerfile that's required to build the image, which aligns with the suggested best practices for Docker development.

2. After you have created the repository, we can push some source code for the image. You can find the source code for our minimalistic Docker image for hosting a static web page using nginx in this book's GitHub repository: `https://github.com/PacktPublishing/Hands-On-Kubernetes-on-Windows/tree/master/Chapter03/02_nginx-demo-index`.

3. In order to clone the newly created repository, in PowerShell, navigate to the directory where you would like to have the repository and use the `git clone` command:

   ```
   git clone https://github.com/<userName>/<repositoryName>.git
   ```

4. Copy all the required source files to the repository and perform a push using the `git push` command:

   ```
   git add -A
   git commit -am "Docker image source code"
   git push -u origin master
   ```

5. At this point, you should be able to see the files in the repository when you navigate to GitHub web page, for example, `https://github.com/hands-on-kubernetes-on-windows/nginx-demo-index`:

The next step is to create the actual Docker Hub repository and configure autobuild. Let's proceed!

Creating a Docker Hub repository with autobuild

Integrating a Docker Hub repository with autobuild requires connecting your GitHub account to your Docker Hub account and creating the repository itself. Let's get started:

1. Open `https://hub.docker.com/` and navigate to **Account Settings**. In the **Linked Accounts** section, click **Connect** for **GitHub** provider:

2. Authorize Docker Hub Builder to access your repositories. At this point, if you need to, you can also grant access to any organization.
3. After the accounts have been connected, open `https://hub.docker.com/` again and click the **Create Repository** section's + button:

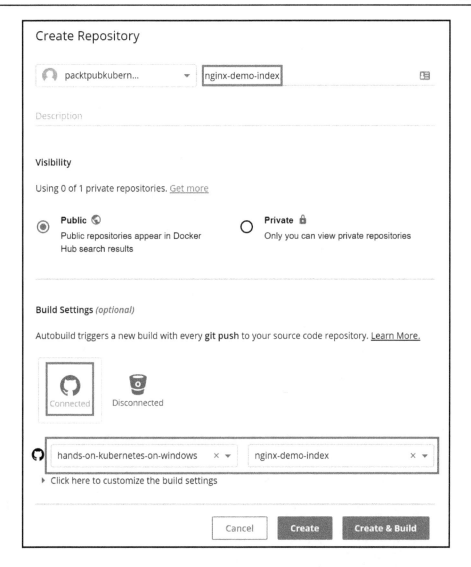

4. Fill in all the required details. In our case, the name of our repository will be `packtpubkubernetesonwindows/nginx-demo-index`.

5. In **Build Settings**, choose the GitHub icon and select the GitHub repository that you have just created, as shown in the preceding screenshot.

6. Inspect the build settings by clicking **Click here to customize the build settings** in order to understand what the default configuration is:

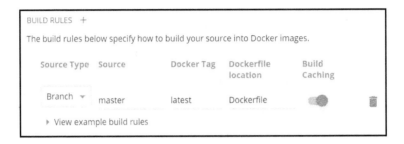

7. The default settings are suitable for our image as we would like to trigger the build whenever new code is pushed to the **master** branch. A Dockerfile with the name **Dockerfile** in the root of your GitHub repository should be used for building images.
8. Click **Create & Build** to save and immediately start a build based on the current code in the repository.
9. In **Recent Builds**, you should see a **Pending** build of your image:

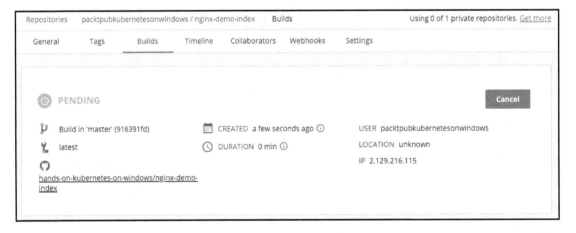

10. After a few minutes, the build should finish and the `packtpubkubernetesonwindows/nginx-demo-index:latest` image should be available. You can verify this by pulling the image using the `docker pull packtpubkubernetesonwindows/nginx-demo-index:latest` command.

Now, let's take a look at how to easily trigger Docker image builds with a new code commit.

Triggering the Docker Hub autobuild

With the autobuild setup created in the previous section, triggering a new Docker image build is as simple as committing new code to your GitHub repository. In order to do that, you have to do the following:

1. Introduce a change to the source code for the image on GitHub; for example, modify the `index.html` file:

```
<!DOCTYPE html>
<html>
    <head>
        <title>Hello World!</title>
    </head>
    <body>
        <h1>Hello World from nginx container! This is a new version
of image for autobuild.</h1>
    </body>
</html>
```

2. Commit and push the code change:

```
git commit -am "Updated index.html"
git push -u origin master
```

3. In the **Builds** tab for this image repository on Docker Hub, you should almost immediately see that a new image build has been triggered (source commit: `https://github.com/hands-on-kubernetes-on-windows/nginx-demo-index/tree/5ee600041912cdba3c82da5331542f48701f0f28`):

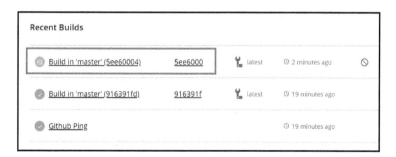

> If your build fails, you can always inspect the Docker build logs in the build details and **Build logs** tab.

4. After the build succeeds, verify your image by running a new container on your Windows machine:

```
docker run -it --rm `
        -p 8080:80 `
        packtpubkubernetesonwindows/nginx-demo-index:latest
```

5. The image will be automatically pulled from the Docker Hub repository. Navigate to `http://localhost:8080` in your web browser. You should see the following output:

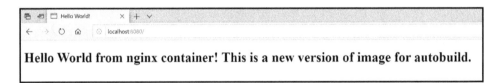

Congratulations – you have successfully created and triggered a Docker image autobuild on Docker Hub! In the next section, you will learn how to create a similar setup for Windows-based images using Azure Container Registry.

Creating Azure Container Registry

Azure Container Registry (**ACR**) is a fully managed private Docker registry provided by Azure Cloud. In this section, we will create a new instance of ACR using the Azure CLI. You will learn how to achieve similar build automation as provided by Docker Hub but with the possibility of building Windows images and using a private registry.

> You can find detailed installation instructions for the Azure CLI in Chapter 2, *Managing State in Containers*.

To create an Azure Container Registry instance, follow these steps:

1. Ensure that you are logged in to the Azure CLI by using the `az login` command in PowerShell. Proceed by creating a dedicated resource group for your ACR instance. In this example, we will use the `acr-resource-group` resource group and `westeurope` as the Azure location:

```
az group create `
    --name acr-resource-group `
    --location westeurope
```

 You can also use the PowerShell script available in this book's GitHub repository: `https://github.com/PacktPublishing/Hands-On-Kubernetes-on-Windows/blob/master/Chapter03/03_CreateAzureContainerRegistry.ps1`. Remember to provide a globally unique ACR name in order to be able to create the instance.

2. Next, create a basic-tier ACR instance with a globally unique name (for demonstration purposes, we have provided `handsonkubernetesonwinregistry`, but you have to provide your own unique name as it will be a part of the registry's DNS name):

```
az acr create `
  --resource-group acr-resource-group `
  --name handsonkubernetesonwinregistry `
  --sku Basic
```

 If you are interested in other service tiers of Azure Container Registry, please refer to the official documentation: `https://docs.microsoft.com/en-us/azure/container-registry/container-registry-skus`.

You will be provided with detailed information regarding your newly created registry:

```
{
  "adminUserEnabled": false,
  "creationDate": "2019-08-18T21:20:53.081364+00:00",
  "id": "/subscriptions/cc9a8166-829e-401e-
a004-76d1e3733b8e/resourceGroups/acr-resource-
group/providers/Microsoft.ContainerRegistry/registries/handsonkuber
netesonwinregistry",
  "location": "westeurope",
  "loginServer": "handsonkubernetesonwinregistry.azurecr.io",
  "name": "handsonkubernetesonwinregistry",
  "networkRuleSet": null,
```

```
      "provisioningState": "Succeeded",
      "resourceGroup": "acr-resource-group",
      "sku": {
        "name": "Basic",
        "tier": "Basic"
      },
      "status": null,
      "storageAccount": null,
      "tags": {},
      "type": "Microsoft.ContainerRegistry/registries"
    }
```

The most important information is `"loginServer":` `"handsonkubernetesonwinregistry.azurecr.io"`, which will be used for pushing and pulling Docker images.

3. Finally, the last step is to log in to the registry so that you can use the registry in the Docker CLI:

```
az acr login `
  --name handsonkubernetesonwinregistry
```

With ACR set up, we are ready to build a Docker image using ACR in the cloud environment.

Building a Docker image using Azure Container Registry

For demonstration purposes, we will use a simple Windows IIS image that hosts a static HTML web page. You can find the Docker image source in this book's GitHub repository: `https://github.com/PacktPublishing/Hands-On-Kubernetes-on-Windows/tree/master/Chapter03/04_iis-demo-index`. To build the image in ACR, follow these steps:

1. Clone the repository with the image source code and navigate to the `Chapter03/04_iis-demo-index` directory in PowerShell.

2. Execute the `az acr build` command in order to begin the Docker image build in the cloud environment (remember to provide the Docker build context directory, which in this example is denoted by the *dot* for the current directory):

```
az acr build `
     --registry handsonkubernetesonwinregistry `
     --platform windows `
     --image iis-demo-index:latest .
```

3. The `az acr build` command starts an ACR quick task. This uploads the Docker build context to the cloud and runs the build process remotely. After a few minutes, the build process should finish. You can expect output similar to the local `docker build` command.

4. Now, you can verify the image by running a container on your local machine and pulling the image from ACR. You need to use the full DNS name for the registry (in this example, this is `handsonkubernetesonwinregistry.azurecr.io`):

```
docker run -it --rm `
          -p 8080:80 `
          handsonkubernetesonwinregistry.azurecr.io/iis-demo-
index:latest
```

5. Navigate to `http://localhost:8080` in a web browser and verify that the container is running as expected:

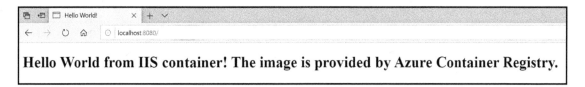

You have successfully executed your ACR build quick task! Now, we can start automating the ACR build trigger for a GitHub repository code push in a similar fashion to how we would using Docker Hub.

Automatic builds for Azure Container Registry

Azure Container Registry offers similar functionality to Docker Hub for the automation of Docker image builds on code push. The pipeline is highly customizable and can support building multiple container images at once, but in this example, we will focus on automating a single image build on the GitHub repository code push.

> For more advanced multi-step and multi-container scenarios, check out the official documentation: `https://docs.microsoft.com/en-us/azure/container-registry/container-registry-tutorial-multistep-task`.

Integrating ACR and GitHub can be performed as follows:

1. Create a new GitHub repository and push the Docker image source code. In this example, we will use source code from `https://github.com/PacktPublishing/Hands-On-Kubernetes-on-Windows/tree/master/Chapter03/04_iis-demo-index`, which will be pushed to a new GitHub repository, that is, `https://github.com/hands-on-kubernetes-on-windows/iis-demo-index`.

2. Generate a GitHub **Personal Access Token** (**PAT**) in order to access the repository in ACR. Navigate to `https://github.com/settings/tokens/new`.

3. Enter a PAT description and choose the **repo:status** and **public_repo** scopes (for private repositories, you need to use a full **repo** scope):

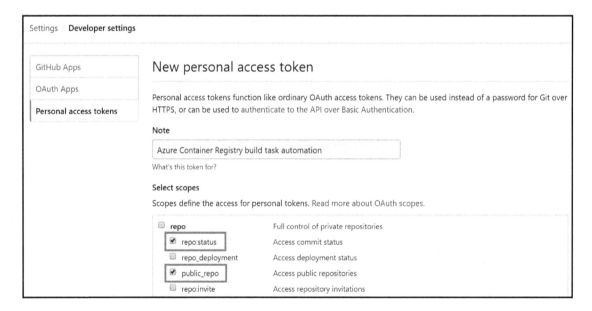

4. Click the **Generate token** button.

5. You will be provided with a PAT value. Copy the token to a secure location as you will need it to set up integration.

6. Now, let's create an ACR task called `iis-demo-index-task`. This will be triggered automatically when code is pushed to `https://github.com/hands-on-kubernetes-on-windows/iis-demo-index`. The required parameters are similar to the build configuration for Docker Hub:

```
az acr task create `
    --registry handsonkubernetesonwinregistry `
    --name iis-demo-index-task `
    --platform windows `
    --image "iis-demo-index:{{.Run.ID}}" `
    --context
https://github.com/hands-on-kubernetes-on-windows/iis-demo-index `
    --branch master `
    --file Dockerfile `
    --git-access-token <gitHubPersonalAccessTokenValue>
```

> If you run into an `az acr task create: 'utputformat' is not a valid value for '--output'. See 'az acr task create --help'.` error being returned by the Azure CLI, ensure that you are escaping/quoting curly brackets for PowerShell properly.

7. Test your ACR task definition using the `az acr task run` command:

```
az acr task run `
    --registry handsonkubernetesonwinregistry `
    --name iis-demo-index-task
```

8. In the source code for your Docker image, introduce a change and commit and push it to the GitHub repository. For example, modify the static text so that it reads as follows:

```
Hello World from IIS container! The image is provided by Azure
Container Registry and automatically built by Azure Container
Registry task.
```

9. Retrieve the ACR task logs to verify that the task was indeed triggered:

```
az acr task logs --registry handsonkubernetesonwinregistry
```

You should see an output similar to the following, which indicates that a new task instance was triggered by the push:

```
Administrator: Windows PowerShell                                                    —    □    ×
PS C:\src\Hands-On-Kubernetes-on-Windows\Chapter03\04_iis-demo-index> az acr task logs --registry handsonkubernetesonwin
registry
Showing logs of the last created run.
Run ID: cb5
2019/08/18 22:55:29 Downloading source code...
2019/08/18 22:55:40 Finished downloading source code
2019/08/18 22:55:42 Using acb_vol_7f760829-2575-48fe-8e6a-6872b10c280a as the home volume
2019/08/18 22:55:42 Setting up Docker configuration...
2019/08/18 22:55:55 Successfully set up Docker configuration
2019/08/18 22:55:55 Logging in to registry: handsonkubernetesonwinregistry.azurecr.io
2019/08/18 22:56:01 Successfully logged into handsonkubernetesonwinregistry.azurecr.io
2019/08/18 22:56:01 Executing step ID: build. Timeout(sec): 28800, Working directory: '', Network: ''
```

10. When the task is finished, pull the image tagged with **Run ID** (in this case, this is **cb5**). You can also use the `latest` tag, but this requires removing a locally cached image using the `docker rmi` command:

    docker pull handsonkubernetesonwinregistry.azurecr.io/iis-demo-index:cb5

11. Create a new container using the handsonkubernetesonwinregistry.azurecr.io/iis-demo-index:cb5 image:

    ```
    docker run -it --rm `
                -p 8080:80 `
                handsonkubernetesonwinregistry.azurecr.io/iis-demo-
    index:cb5
    ```

12. Navigate to http://localhost:8080 in a web browser and verify that the container is running as expected. Also, verify that the static HTML page contains changes that were introduced in the code push:

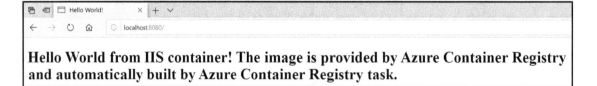

Hello World from IIS container! The image is provided by Azure Container Registry and automatically built by Azure Container Registry task.

Other cloud service providers have similar offerings for setting up Docker image registries and build pipelines. If you are interested in Google Cloud Platform services, please check out GCP Cloud Build: `https://cloud.` `google.com/cloud-build/docs/quickstart-docker`.

You have successfully set up your Docker image build pipeline using GitHub and Azure Container Registry – congratulations! Now, we will take a quick look at best practices for image tagging and versioning.

Image tagging and versioning

Docker images use tags in order to provide different versions of the same image in the repository – each image tag corresponds to a given Docker image ID. Specifying tags for Docker images is often performed during an image build, but you can also add tags explicitly using the `docker tag` command:

```
docker pull mcr.microsoft.com/dotnet/core/sdk
docker tag mcr.microsoft.com/dotnet/core/sdk:latest mydotnetsdk:v1
docker tag mcr.microsoft.com/dotnet/core/sdk:latest mydotnetsdk:v2
```

In this example, we pulled the `latest` image tag (as it was not specified explicitly) of the .NET Core SDK and then tagged the image with the `mydotnetsdk:v1` and `mydotnetsdk:v2` tags in the local image cache. Now, it is possible to use these tags while performing operations on your local machine, like so:

```
docker run -it --rm mydotnetsdk:v1
```

Let's take a look at the `latest` tag, which is often used when working with Docker.

Using the latest tag

By default, the Docker CLI assumes a special tag called `latest`. This means that if you perform the `docker pull applicationimage` command or the `docker run -it` `applicationimage` command, or use `FROM applicationimage` in your Dockerfile, the `applicationimage:latest` tag will be used. Similarly, when you execute `docker` `build -t applicationimage .`, the resulting Docker image will be tagged with the `latest` tag and each subsequent build will produce a new version of `applicationimage:latest`.

It is important to understand that `latest` behaves just like any other Docker image tag. It can be seen as a default value that is always used by Docker whenever no tag has been provided by user. This has some consequences that may cause confusion, as follows:

- During an image build, if you specify your tag for the image, the latest tag will not be added. This means that if you push `applicationimage:v1` to the registry, it doesn't mean that `applicationimage:latest` will be updated. You have to perform it explicitly.
- When the image owner pushes a new Docker image version to the repository and it is tagged again with the `latest` tag, this doesn't mean that your locally cached image will be updated and used during `docker build`. You have to tell the Docker CLI to attempt to pull a newer version of the image by using the `--pull` argument for `docker build`.
- Using the `latest` tag for the Dockerfile's `FROM` instruction can lead to different images being built in different points in time, which is generally not desirable. For example, you may be building your image using the `mcr.microsoft.com/dotnet/core/sdk` image at a point in time when `latest` points to version 2.2 of the SDK, but after a few months, building the same Dockerfile will result in version 3.0 being used as the base.

The general best practice (this is also the same for Kubernetes) is to avoid deploying production containers using the `latest` tag and use the `latest` tag just for development scenarios and ease of use for your local environment. Similarly, to ensure that your Docker images are predictable and self-descriptive, you should avoid using base images with the `latest` tag in a Dockerfile – use a specific tag instead.

Semantic versioning

In order to efficiently manage the versioning and tagging of Docker images, you can use **Semantic Versioning (Semver)** as a general strategy. This versioning scheme is widely adopted among image distributors and helps consumers understand how your image evolves.

Generally, Semver suggests the scheme of using three numbers – major, minor, and patch – separated with dots, `<major>.<minor>.<patch>`, where each number is incremented as needed. As an example, 2.1.5 means that the major version of the image is 2, the minor version is 1, and the patch version is currently 5. The meaning of these release numbers and incrementation rules are similar to what you would expect for versioning non-containerized applications:

- **Major**: Increment if you are introducing features that break compatibility or introduce other breaking changes.
- **Minor**: Increment if you are introducing features that are fully compatible with previous releases. Consumers do not need to upgrade usages of your application.
- **Patch**: Increment if you are publishing bug fixes or patches.

 More details regarding Semver as a general concept can be found here: `https://semver.org/`.

The best practices for using Semver when building/pushing Docker images can be summarized as follows:

- When building a new version of your image, always create a new patch tag (for example, **2.1.5**).
- Always overwrite existing major and minor tags (for example, **2** and **2.1**).
- Never overwrite patch tags. This ensures that image consumers who would like to use a specific version of your application can be sure that it does not change over time.
- Always overwrite the existing `latest` tag.

The following set of commands shows an example of building and tagging a new version of the `applicationimage` Docker image:

```
# New build a new version of image and push latest tag
docker build -t applicationimage:latest .
docker push applicationimage:latest

# New major tag
docker tag applicationimage:latest applicationimage:2
docker push applicationimage:2

# New minor tag
docker tag applicationimage:latest registry:2.1
docker push applicationimage:2.1

# New patch tag
docker tag applicationimage:latest applicationimage:2.1.5
docker push applicationimage:2.1.5
```

You may also introduce additional tags that add correlation to your build system IDs or git commit SHA-1 hash, which was used for the image build.

Ensuring the integrity of the image supply chain

Providing content trust of the image supply chain is one of the most important, but often neglected, topics in managing Docker images. In any distributed system that communicates and transfers data over an untrusted medium (such as the internet), it is crucial to provide a means of content trust – a way of verifying both the source (publisher) and the integrity of data entering the system. For Docker, this is especially true for pushing and pulling images (data), which is performed by Docker Engine.

The Docker ecosystem describes the concept of **Docker Content Trust** (**DCT**), which provides a means of verifying the digital signatures of data being transferred between the Docker Engine and the Docker Registry. This verification allows the publishers to sign their images and the consumer (Docker Engine) to verify the signatures to ensure the integrity and source of the images.

In the Docker CLI, it is possible to sign an image using the `docker trust` command, which is built on top of Docker Notary. This is a tool that's used for publishing and managing trusted collections of content. Signing images requires a Docker Registry with an associated Notary server, for example, Docker Hub.

 To learn more about content trust for a private Azure Container Registry, please refer to `https://docs.microsoft.com/en-us/azure/container-registry/container-registry-content-trust`.

Signing an image

As an example, we will sign one of the Docker images we have built and pushed to Docker Hub in this chapter, that is, `packtpubkubernetesonwindows/iis-demo-index`. To follow along, you will need to perform the operations on your own image repository, `<dockerId>/iis-demo-index`. Signing can be performed with the following steps:

1. Generate a delegation key pair. Locally, this can be done using the following command:

   ```
   docker trust key generate <pairName>
   ```

2. You will be asked for a passphrase for the private key. Choose a safe password and continue. The private delegation key will be stored in `~/.docker/trust/private` by default (also on Windows) and the public delegation key will be saved in the current working directory.

3. Add the delegation public key to the Notary server (for Docker Hub, it is `notary.docker.io`). Loading the key is performed for a particular image repository, which in Notary is identified by a **Globally Unique Name (GUN)**. For Docker Hub, they have the form of `docker.io/<dockerId>/<repository>`. Execute the following command:

```
docker trust signer add --key <pairName>.pub <signerName>
docker.io/<dockerId>/<repository>

# For example
docker trust signer add --key packtpubkubernetesonwindows-key.pub
packtpubkubernetesonwindows
docker.io/packtpubkubernetesonwindows/iis-demo-index
```

4. If you are performing the delegation for your repository for the first time, you will be automatically asked for initiation using the local Notary canonical root key.

5. Tag the image so that it has a specific tag that can be signed, like so:

```
docker tag packtpubkubernetesonwindows/iis-demo:latest
packtpubkubernetesonwindows/iis-demo:1.0.1
```

6. Use the private delegation key to sign the new tag and push it to Docker Hub, like so:

```
docker trust sign packtpubkubernetesonwindows/iis-demo:1.0.1
```

7. Alternatively, this can be performed by `docker push`, providing that you have set the `DOCKER_CONTENT_TRUST` environment variable in PowerShell before pushing:

```
$env:DOCKER_CONTENT_TRUST=1
docker tag packtpubkubernetesonwindows/iis-demo:latest
packtpubkubernetesonwindows/iis-demo:1.0.2
docker push packtpubkubernetesonwindows/iis-demo:1.0.2
```

8. Now, you can inspect the remote trust data for the repository:

```
docker trust inspect --pretty
docker.io/packtpubkubernetesonwindows/iis-demo:1.0.1
```

Next, let's try running a container with DCT enabled on the client side.

Enabling DCT for the client

In order to enforce DCT when using the Docker CLI for `push`, `build`, `create`, `pull`, and `run`, you have to set the `DOCKER_CONTENT_TRUST` environment variable to 1. By default, DCT is disabled for Docker client. Follow these steps:

1. Set the `DOCKER_CONTENT_TRUST` environment variable in the current PowerShell session:

```
$env:DOCKER_CONTENT_TRUST=1
```

2. Run a new container using the signed image that we just created:

```
docker run -d --rm docker.io/packtpubkubernetesonwindows/iis-demo:1.0.1
```

3. You will notice that the container starts without any problem. Now, try creating a new container using the `latest` tag, which was not signed:

```
PS C:\src> docker run -d --rm
docker.io/packtpubkubernetesonwindows/iis-demo:latest
C:\Program Files\Docker\Docker\Resources\bin\docker.exe: No valid
trust data for latest.
See 'C:\Program Files\Docker\Docker\Resources\bin\docker.exe run --
help'.
```

This short scenario shows how DCT can be used to ensure the integrity and source of the image that's used for container creation.

Summary

In this chapter, you learned how the Docker ecosystem provides an infrastructure for storing and sharing container images using Docker Registry. The concepts of the image registry and automated cloud builds have been demonstrated using a public Docker Hub and a private Azure Container Registry, which you set up from scratch using the Azure CLI. You also learned about the best practices for tagging and versioning images using the semantic versioning scheme. Finally, you were introduced to ensuring image integrity using **Docker Content Trust** (**DCT**).

In the next chapter, we are going to perform our first deep dive into the Kubernetes ecosystem in order to understand some key concepts and how they currently fit Windows containers support.

Questions

1. What is Docker Registry and how does it relate to Docker Hub?
2. What is an image tag?
3. What is the standard image repository naming scheme for Docker Hub?
4. What is Azure Container Registry and how does it differ from Docker Hub?
5. What is the `latest` tag and when is it recommended to use it?
6. How can we version (tag) images using semantic versioning?
7. Why would you use Docker Content Trust?

You can find the answers to these questions in the *Assessments* section of this book.

Further reading

- For more information concerning managing Docker container images and image registries, please refer to the following Packt books:
    - *Docker on Windows: From 101 to production with Docker on Windows* (`https://www.packtpub.com/virtualization-and-cloud/docker-windows-second-edition`)
    - *Learn Docker – Fundamentals of Docker 18.x* (`https://www.packtpub.com/networking-and-servers/learn-docker-fundamentals-docker-18x`)

- If you would like to know more about Azure Container Registry and how it fits into the Azure ecosystem, take a look at the following Packt book:
  - *Azure for Architects – Second Edition* (`https://www.packtpub.com/virtualization-and-cloud/azure-architects-second-edition`)
- You can also refer to the official Docker documentation, which gives a good overview of Docker Hub (`https://docs.docker.com/docker-hub/`) and the open source Docker Registry (`https://docs.docker.com/registry/`).

2
Section 2: Understanding Kubernetes Fundamentals

Understanding Kubernetes fundamentals is crucial to developing and deploying container applications. Here, you will understand how Kubernetes relates to container management and what the key components of this platform are.

This section contains the following chapters:

- Chapter 4, *Kubernetes Concepts and Windows Support*
- Chapter 5, *Kubernetes Networking*
- Chapter 6, *Interacting with Kubernetes Clusters*

4
Kubernetes Concepts and Windows Support

In the previous chapters, we focused on containerization and Docker support on the Windows platform. These concepts were mainly limited to single-machine scenarios, where the application requires only one container host. For production-grade distributed container systems, you have to consider different aspects, such as scalability, high availability, and load balancing, and this always requires orchestrating containers running on multiple hosts.

Container orchestration is a way of managing the container life cycle in large, dynamic environments – it ranges from provisioning and deploying containers to managing networks, providing redundancy and high-availability of containers, automatically scaling up and down container instances, automated health checks, and telemetry gathering. Solving the problem of container orchestration is non-trivial – this is why **Kubernetes** (k8s for short, where 8 denotes the number of omitted characters) was born.

The story of Kubernetes dates back to the early 2000s and the Borg system, which was developed internally by Google for managing and scheduling jobs at a large scale. Subsequently, in the early 2010s, the Omega cluster management system was developed at Google as a clean-slate rewrite of Borg. While Omega was still used internally by Google only, in 2014, Kubernetes was announced as an open source container orchestration solution that takes its roots from both Borg and Omega. In July 2015, when the 1.0 version of Kubernetes was released, Google partnered with the Linux Foundation to form the **Cloud Native Computing Foundation** (**CNCF**). This foundation aims at empowering organizations so that they can build and run scalable applications in modern, dynamic environments such as public, private, and hybrid clouds. Four years later, in April 2019, Kubernetes 1.14 was released, which delivered production-level support for Windows nodes and Windows containers. This chapter is all about the current state of Kubernetes with regard to Windows!

Cloud-native application is a commonly used term in container orchestration for applications that leverage containerization, cloud computing frameworks, and the loose coupling of components (microservices). But it doesn't necessarily mean that cloud-native applications must run in a cloud – they adhere to a set of principles that make them easy to be hosted on-premises or in the public/private cloud. If you are interested in learning more about CNCF, please refer to the official web page: `https://www.cncf.io/`.

In this chapter, we will cover the following topics:

- Kubernetes high-level architecture
- Kubernetes objects
- Windows and Kubernetes ecosystem
- Kubernetes limitations on Windows
- Creating your own development cluster from scratch
- Production cluster deployment strategies
- Managed Kubernetes providers

Technical requirements

For this chapter, you will need the following:

- Windows 10 Pro, Enterprise, or Education (version 1903 or later, 64-bit) installed
- Docker Desktop for Windows 2.0.0.3 or later installed
- The Chocolatey package manager for Windows installed (`https://chocolatey.org/`)
- Azure CLI installed

How to install Docker Desktop for Windows and its system requirements was covered in `Chapter 1`, *Creating Containers*.

Using the Chocolatey package manager is not mandatory, but it makes installation and application version management much easier. The installation process is documented here: `https://chocolatey.org/install`.

For Azure CLI, you can find detailed installation instructions in `Chapter 2`, *Managing State in Containers*.

To learn about managed Kubernetes providers, you will need your own Azure account in order to create an AKS instance with Windows nodes. If you haven't already created an account for the previous chapters in this book, you can read more about how to obtain a limited free account for personal use here: `https://azure.microsoft.com/en-us/free/`.

You can download the latest code samples for this chapter from this book's official GitHub repository: `https://github.com/PacktPublishing/Hands-On-Kubernetes-on-Windows/tree/master/Chapter04`.

Kubernetes high-level architecture

In this and the next section, we will focus on the Kubernetes high-level architecture and its core components. If you are already familiar with Kubernetes in general but you would like to know more regarding Kubernetes support for Windows, you can skip to the *Windows and Kubernetes ecosystem* section.

What is Kubernetes?

In general, Kubernetes can be seen as the following:

- A container (microservices) orchestration system
- A cluster management system for running distributed applications

As a container orchestrator, Kubernetes solves common challenges that arise when deploying containerized, cloud-native applications at scale. This includes the following:

- Provisioning and deploying containers on multiple container hosts (nodes)
- Service discovery and load balancing network traffic
- Automatically scaling container instances up and down
- Automated rollouts and rollbacks of new container image versions
- Automatic, optimal bin-packing of containers with regard to resources such as CPU or memory
- Application monitoring, telemetry gathering, and health checks
- Orchestrating and abstracting storage (local, on-premises, or the cloud)

At the same time, Kubernetes can also be described as a cluster management system – the master (or multiple masters, in highly available deployments) is responsible for effectively coordinating multiple worker nodes that handle the actual container workloads. These workloads are not limited to Docker containers only – Kubernetes uses the **Container Runtime Interface** (**CRI**) on worker nodes to abstract container runtimes. Eventually, cluster clients (for example, DevOps engineers) can manage the cluster using the RESTful API that's been exposed by the master. Cluster management is performed using a declarative model, which makes Kubernetes very powerful – you describe the desired state and Kubernetes does all the heavy lifting in order to transform the current state of the cluster into the desired state.

Imperative cluster management by using ad hoc commands is also possible but it is generally discouraged for production environments. The operations are performed directly on a live cluster and there is no history of previous configurations. In this book, we will use the declarative object configuration technique whenever possible. For a more detailed discussion regarding Kubernetes cluster management techniques, please refer to the official documentation: https://kubernetes.io/docs/concepts/overview/working-with-objects/object-management/.

The high-level architecture for Kubernetes can be seen in the following diagram. We'll go through each component in the next few paragraphs:

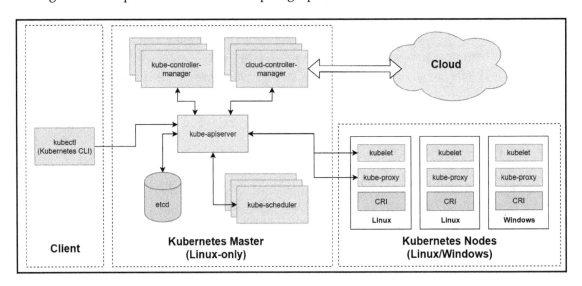

Let's begin by focusing on the role of Kubernetes master, also known as the control plane.

Kubernetes master – control plane

In the Kubernetes cluster, the master (control plane) consists of a set of components that are responsible for global decisions regarding the cluster, such as scheduling and deploying application instances to worker nodes, as well as managing cluster events. Additionally, the master exposes an API for communication for both worker nodes and managing clients.

Master components are not restricted to running on a dedicated host; it is also possible to have them running on worker nodes. The master node can act as a worker node, just like any node in a Kubernetes cluster. However, in general, these are not recommended due to reliability reasons – what's more, for production environments, you should consider running a highly available Kubernetes setup, which requires multiple master nodes running components redundantly.

One of the most significant limitations of running Kubernetes master services is that they have to be hosted on a Linux machine. It is not possible to have a Windows machine with master components, which means that even if you are planning to run Windows containers only, you still need Linux machine(s) as a master. Currently, there are no plans for the implementation of Windows-only Kubernetes clusters, although this may change as the development of the Windows Subsystem for Linux 2 progresses.

We will briefly go through the components that compose the master. Let's begin by taking a look at the Kubernetes API Server (or `kube-apiserver`, which is the binary name of this component).

kube-apiserver

The **Kubernetes API Server** (**kube-apiserver**) is the central component in the Kubernetes control plane and acts as a gateway for all interactions between clients and cluster components. Its main responsibilities are as follows:

- Exposing cluster APIs that have been implemented as a set of RESTful endpoints over HTTPS. The API is used by clients managing the cluster as well as by internal Kubernetes components. All the resources in the Kubernetes cluster are abstracted as Kubernetes API objects.
- Persisting cluster state in the `etcd` cluster – each action performed by a client or state update reported by a cluster component has to go through the API Server and be persisted in the cluster store.
- Authentication and authorization of users and service accounts.

- Validation of requests.
- Providing the *watch* API to inform subscribers (for example, other cluster components) about changes in the cluster state using incremental notification feeds. The watch API is the key concept that makes Kubernetes highly extensible and distributed in nature.

In highly available Kubernetes deployments, `kube-apiserver` is hosted on multiple master nodes, behind a dedicated load balancer.

etcd cluster

To persist the cluster state, Kubernetes uses `etcd` – a distributed, reliable key-value store that utilizes the Raft distributed consensus algorithm in order to provide sequential consistency. The `etcd` cluster is the most important part of the control plane – this is the source of truth for the whole cluster, both for the current state and the desired state of the cluster.

Generally, single-node `etcd` clusters are only recommended for testing purposes. For production scenarios, you should always consider running at least a five-member cluster (with an odd number of members) in order to provide sufficient fault tolerance.

 When choosing an `etcd` cluster deployment topology, you can consider either a stacked etcd topology or an external etcd topology. A stacked etcd topology consists of one etcd member per Kubernetes master instance, whereas an external etcd topology utilizes an etcd cluster deployed separately from Kubernetes and is available via a load balancer. You can find out more about these topologies in the official documentation: https://kubernetes.io/docs/setup/production-environment/tools/kubeadm/ha-topology/.

The *watch* protocol that's exposed by `etcd` is also a core functionality for the watch API in Kubernetes, which is provided by `kube-apiserver` for other components.

kube-scheduler

The main responsibility of the **Kubernetes Scheduler** (**kube-scheduler**) component is scheduling container workloads (Kubernetes Pods) and assigning them to healthy worker nodes that fulfill the criteria required for running a particular workload.

A **Pod** is a group of one or more containers with a shared network and storage and is the smallest Deployment unit in the Kubernetes system. We will cover this Kubernetes object in the next section.

Scheduling is performed in two phases:

- Filtering
- Scoring

In the filtering phase, `kube-scheduler` determines the set of nodes that are capable of running a given Pod. This includes checking the actual state of nodes and verifying any resource requirements specified by the Pod definition. At this point, if there are no nodes that can run a given Pod, the Pod cannot be scheduled and remains pending. Next, in the scoring step, the scheduler assigns scores for each node based on a set of policies. Then, the Pod is assigned by the scheduler to the node with the highest score.

You can read more about available policies in the official documentation: `https://kubernetes.io/docs/concepts/scheduling/kube-scheduler/#kube-scheduler-implementation`.

 Kubernetes design offers a great deal of extensibility and possibility to replace components. Kube-scheduler is one of the components that's used to demonstrate this principle. Even if its internal business logic is complex (all efficient scheduling heuristics are rather complex...), the scheduler only needs to watch for *unassigned* Pods, determine the best node for them, and inform the API Server about the assignment. You can check out an example implementation of a custom scheduler here: `https://banzaicloud.com/blog/k8s-custom-scheduler/`.

Now, let's take a look at `kube-controller-manager`.

kube-controller-manager

The **Kubernetes Controller Manager (kube-controller-manager)** is a component that is responsible for running core reconciliation and control loops in the cluster. The Controller Manager consists of a set of separate, specialized controllers that act independently. The main aim of controllers is to observe the *current* and the *desired* cluster state that's exposed by API Server and command changes that attempt to transform the *current* state to the *desired* one.

The most important controllers that are shipped in `kube-controller-manager` binary are as follows:

- **Node Controller (formally named nodelifecycle)**: This observes the status of the node and reacts when it is unavailable.
- **ReplicaSet Controller (replicaset)**: This is responsible for ensuring that the correct number of Pods for each ReplicaSet API object is running.
- **Deployment Controller (deployment)**: This is responsible for managing associated ReplicaSet API objects and performing rollouts and rollbacks.
- **Endpoints Controller (endpoint)**: This manages Endpoint API objects.
- **Service Account Controller (serviceaccount) and Token Controller (serviceaccount-token)**: This is responsible for creating default accounts and access tokens for new namespaces.

You can think of kube-controller-manager as a Kubernetes brain that ensures that the *current* state of the cluster moves toward the *desired* cluster state.

cloud-controller-manager

Originally a part of `kube-controller-manager`, the **Kubernetes Cloud Controller Manager (cloud-controller-manager)** provides cloud-specific control loops. The reason for the separation of Cloud Controller Manager is to allow for the easier evolution of cloud-specific connectors (providers) code, which in most cases, is released at different cadences than the core Kubernetes code.

 As of Kubernetes 1.17, cloud-controller-manager is still in its beta stage. You can check the current status of the feature in the official documentation: `https://kubernetes.io/docs/tasks/administer-cluster/running-cloud-controller`.

When enabling cloud-controller-manager, the cloud-specific control loops in kube-controller-manager must be disabled. Then, the following controllers will depend on the cloud provider's implementation:

- **Node Controller**: The provider is used for determining a node's status and detecting if the node was deleted.
- **Route Controller**: Requires the provider for setting up network routing.
- **Service Controller**: Manages load balancers via the provider.
- **Volume Controller**: Manages storage volumes using the provider.

The list of external cloud providers offered as a part of Kubernetes constantly evolves and can be checked in the official documentation (`https://kubernetes.io/docs/concepts/cluster-administration/cloud-providers/`) and on Kubernetes' organization GitHub page (`https://github.com/kubernetes?q=cloud-provider-type=language=`).

Kubernetes nodes – data plane

In the Kubernetes cluster, the data plane consists of nodes (formerly known as *minions*) that are responsible for running container workloads scheduled by the master. Nodes can be physical bare-metal machines or virtual machines, which gives flexibility when designing a cluster.

The following diagram summarizes the architecture and components that compose Kubernetes nodes:

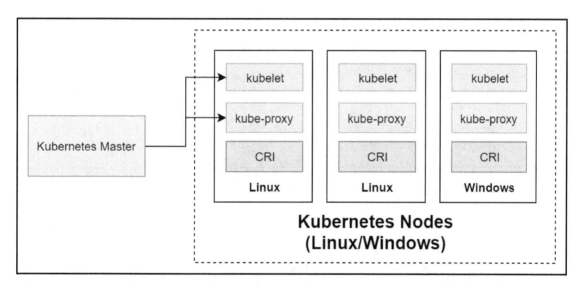

In terms of Windows support, all node components can run both on Windows and Linux machines. This means that Windows Kubernetes nodes are visible to the master in the same way as Linux nodes and from this perspective, they only differ by the type of containers that they can support.

The main components of Kubernetes nodes are as follows:

- **kubelet**: The main Kubernetes agent, which ensures that container workloads (Pods) are executed on the node.
- **Container runtime**: The software that's responsible for managing containers. It's abstracted by the **Container Runtime Interface (CRI)**.
- **kube-proxy**: The network proxy that's responsible for managing the local node network.

Let's take a look at `kubelet` first.

kubelet

Running on every node in the cluster, `kubelet` is a service that's responsible for ensuring that container workloads (Pods) that have been assigned by the control plane are executed. Additionally, it is also responsible for the following:

- Reporting node and Pods statuses to the API Server
- Reporting resource utilization
- Performing the node registration process (when joining a new node to the cluster)
- Executing liveness and readiness Probes (health checks) and reporting their status to the API Server

To perform actual container-related operations, kubelet uses a container runtime.

Container runtime

Kubelet is not directly coupled with Docker – in fact, as we mentioned in the introduction to this section, Docker is not the only **container runtime** that Kubernetes supports. To perform container-related tasks, for example, pulling an image or creating a new container, kubelet utilizes the **Container Runtime Interface (CRI)**, which is a plugin interface that abstracts all common container operations for different runtimes.

The actual definition of the Container Runtime Interface is a protobuf API specification, which can be found in the official repository: `https://github.com/kubernetes/cri-api/`. Any container runtime that implements this specification can be used to execute container workloads in Kubernetes.

Currently, there are numerous container runtimes that can be used with Kubernetes on Linux. The most popular are as follows:

- **Docker**: The *traditional* Docker runtime, abstracted by `dockershim`, which is the CRI implementation for `kubelet`.
- **CRI-containerd**: In short, `containerd` is a component of Docker that is responsible for the management of containers. Currently, CRI-containerd is the recommended runtime for Kubernetes on Linux. For more information, please visit `https://containerd.io/`.
- **CRI-O**: The container runtime implementation dedicated to CRI that follows the **Open Containers Initiative** (**OCI**) specification. For more information, please visit `https://cri-o.io/`.
- **gVisor**: The OCI-compatible sandbox runtime for containers that's integrated with Docker and containerd. For more information, please visit `https://gvisor.dev/`.

The difference between dockershim and CRI-containerd can be seen in the following diagram:

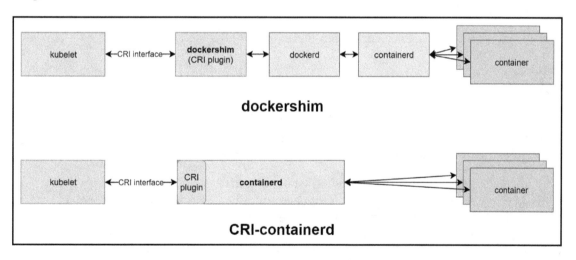

The CRI-containerd runtime offers a much simpler architecture with less communication between daemons and processes, thereby eliminating the traditional Docker Engine. This solution aims at providing a *stripped down* Docker runtime that exposes the crucial components for Kubernetes.

If you are interested in getting a more historical context regarding Docker and containerd separation, you can read the following article: `http://alexander.holbreich.org/docker-components-explained/`.

For Windows, the list is much shorter, and currently includes Docker (Enterprise Edition 18.09+, also abstracted by dockershim) and incoming support for CRI-containerd. This is expected to be available when a stable version of containerd, 1.3, is released and *runhcs shim* is fully supported. This will also come with new support for Hyper-V isolation for containers, which is currently (as of Kubernetes 1.17) implemented without CRI-containerd as a limited experimental feature.

kube-proxy

In the Kubernetes cluster, networking rules and routes on nodes are managed by kube-proxy, which runs on every node. These rules allow communication between Pods and external clients to Pods and are a vital part of the Service API Object. On the Linux platform, kube-proxy configures rules using iptables (most commonly), whereas on the Windows platform, the **Host Networking Service** (**HNS**) is used.

We will cover Kubernetes networking in more detail in the next chapter.

DNS

An internal DNS server is optional and can be installed as an add-on, but it is highly recommended in standard deployments as it simplifies service discovery and networking. Currently, the default DNS server used by Kubernetes is CoreDNS (`https://coredns.io/`).

Kubernetes automatically adds an internal static IP address of the DNS server to the domain name resolution configuration for each container. This means that processes running in Pods can communicate with Services and Pods running in the cluster just by knowing their domain name, which will be resolved to the actual internal IP address. The concept of Kubernetes Service objects will be covered in the next section.

Now, let's take a look at the most commonly used Kubernetes objects.

Kubernetes objects

Setting up a Kubernetes cluster with Windows nodes is complex and will be covered later in this book, and the principles will be demonstrated on Linux examples. From a Kubernetes API Server perspective, Windows and Linux nodes operate in almost the same way.

In the Kubernetes cluster, the cluster state is managed by the kube-apiserver component and is persisted in the etcd cluster. The state is abstracted and modeled as a set of Kubernetes objects – these entities describe what containerized applications should be run, how they should be scheduled, and are the policies concerning restarting or scaling them. If there is anything you would like to achieve in your Kubernetes cluster, then you have to create or update Kubernetes objects. This type of model is called a **declarative model** – you declare your intent and Kubernetes is responsible for changing the current state of the cluster to the desired (intended) one. The declarative model and the idea of maintaining the desired state is what makes Kubernetes so powerful and easy to use.

In this book, we will follow the convention from the official documentation, where objects are capitalized; for example, Pod or Service.

The anatomy of each Kubernetes Object is exactly the same; it has two fields:

- **Spec**: This defines the *desired state* of the Object. This is where you define your requirements when creating or updating an Object.
- **Status**: This is provided by Kubernetes and describes the *current state* of the Object.

Working with Kubernetes objects always requires using the Kubernetes API. Most commonly, you will manage Kubernetes objects using the **command-line interface** (**CLI**) for Kubernetes, which comes as a kubectl binary. It is also possible to interact with the Kubernetes API directly using client libraries.

The installation of `kubectl` and examples of its usage will be covered in `Chapter 6`, *Interacting with Kubernetes Clusters*.

Now, let's take a quick look at how an example Kubernetes Object is structured. When interacting directly with the Kubernetes API, objects must be specified in JSON format. However, `kubectl` allows us to use YAML manifest files, which are translated into JSON when you perform operations. Using YAML manifest files is generally recommended and you can expect most of the examples that you find in the documentation to follow this convention. As an example, we will use a definition of a Pod that consists of a single nginx web server Linux container, stored in a file called `nginx.yaml`:

```
apiVersion: v1
kind: Pod
metadata:
  name: nginx-pod-example
  labels:
    app: nginx-host
spec:
  containers:
  - name: nginx
    image: nginx:1.17
    ports:
    - containerPort: 80
```

The required parts in the manifest file are as follows:

- `apiVersion`: The version of the Kubernetes API being used for this Object.
- `kind`: The type of Kubernetes Object. In this case, this is `Pod`.
- `metadata`: Additional metadata for the Object.
- `spec`: The Object Spec. In the example specification, the nginx container uses the `nginx:1.17` Docker image and exposes port `80`. The Spec is different for every Kubernetes Object and has to follow the API documentation. For example, for Pod, you can find the API reference here: `https://kubernetes.io/docs/reference/generated/kubernetes-api/v1.17/#podspec-v1-core`.

Creating the Pod is now as simple as running the following `kubectl apply` command:

```
kubectl apply -f nginx.yaml
```

If you would like to try out this command without a local Kubernetes cluster, we recommend using one for Kubernetes playground; for example, https://www.katacoda. com/courses/kubernetes/playground:

1. In the **master** window, run the following `kubectl` command, which will apply a manifest file hosted on GitHub:

   ```
   kubectl apply -f
   https://raw.githubusercontent.com/PacktPublishing/Hands-On-Kubernet
   es-on-Windows/master/Chapter04/01_pod-example/nginx.yaml
   ```

2. After a few seconds, the Pod will be created and its STATUS should be Running:

   ```
   master $ kubectl get pod -o wide
   NAME                     READY   STATUS     RESTARTS   AGE   IP
   NODE         NOMINATED NODE   READINESS GATES
   nginx-pod-example   1/1     Running    0          15s   10.40.0.1
   node01    <none>           <none>
   ```

3. Use the `curl` command in the **master** window to get the Pod's IP (in this case, `10.40.0.1`) to verify that the container is indeed running. You should see the raw contents of the default nginx web page:

   ```
   curl http://10.40.0.1:80
   ```

> `kubectl` currently offers two declarative approaches for managing Kubernetes objects: manifest files and kustomization files. Using the kustomize approach is much more powerful as it organizes manifest files and configuration generation in a predictable structure. You can learn more about kustomize here: https://github.com/kubernetes-sigs/ kustomize/tree/master/docs.

Now, let's take a closer look at the Pod API Object.

Pods

Kubernetes uses Pods as its basic, atomic unit for Deployment and scaling, and represents processes running in the cluster – an analogy from Microsoft Hyper-V would be a single virtual machine that you deploy as an atomic unit in your Hyper-V cluster. A Kubernetes Pod consists of one or more containers that share kernel namespaces, IPC, network stack (you address them by the same cluster IP and they can communicate via localhost), and storage. To understand Pods, it is good to know the origin of the name: in the English language, a pod is a group of whales, and Docker uses a whale for its logo – think of a whale as a Docker container!

In their simplest form, you can create single-container Pods – this is what we did in the introduction to this section when demonstrating nginx Pod creation. For some scenarios, you may need multiple-container Pods, where the main container is accompanied by additional containers that serve multiple purposes. Let's take a look at a few of these:

- **Sidecar containers**, which can perform various *helper* operations, such as log collection, data synchronization for the main container, and so on.
- **Adapter containers**, which can normalize output or monitor the data of the main container so that it can be used by other services.
- **Ambassador containers**, which proxy the communication of the main container with the outside world.
- **Init containers**, which are specialized containers that run before application containers in the Pod. For example, they may set up the environment, which isn't performed in the main container image.

 Technically, even single-container Pods contain an extra infra container, which is often a pause image. It acts as a *parent* container for all containers in the pod and enables kernel namespaces sharing. If you are interested in more details regarding infra containers, please refer to this article: `https:/`
`/www.ianlewis.org/en/almighty-pause-container`.

The concept of a Pod can be seen in the following diagram:

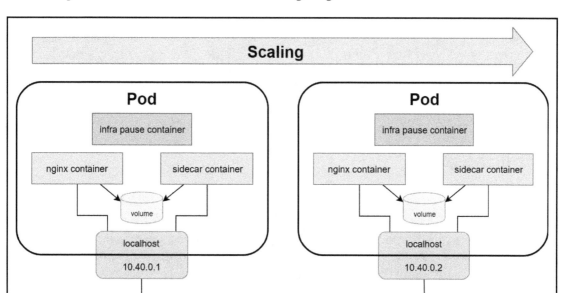

There are a couple of considerations that you should keep in mind when using Pods:

- Pod's containers always run on one node and once a Pod is created, it is always bound to one node.
- You scale your application by adding more Pods, not by adding more containers inside the same Pod.
- A Pod is considered *ready* and able to serve requests when *all* its containers are ready. The status of a container is determined by Probes, for example, liveness and readiness Probes, which can be defined in the Spec.
- Pods are ephemeral. They are created, they die, and new ones are recreated in their place (if needed).
- When a Pod is recreated, it receives a new cluster IP. This means that your application design should never rely on static IP assignments and assume that the Pod may even be recreated on a different node.

You will rarely create bare Pods independently, as we did in the introduction to the section. In most cases, they are managed through Deployments.

Pods have a finite life cycle and if the containers inside crash or exit, they may not be automatically recreated, depending on the restart policy. To maintain a desired number of Pods with a certain Spec and metadata in the cluster, you need `ReplicaSet` objects.

ReplicaSets

Kubernetes builds many powerful concepts on top of Pods, which makes container management easy and predictable. The simplest one is the `ReplicaSet` API Object (the successor of ReplicationController), which aims at maintaining a fixed number of healthy Pods (replicas) to fulfill certain conditions. In other words, if you say *I want three nginx Pods running in my cluster*, ReplicaSet does that for you. If a Pod is destroyed, `ReplicaSet` will automatically create a new Pod replica to restore the desired state.

Let's look at an example ReplicaSet manifest `nginx-replicaset.yaml` file that creates three replicas of the nginx Pod:

```
apiVersion: apps/v1
kind: ReplicaSet
metadata:
  name: nginx-replicaset-example
spec:
  replicas: 3
  selector:
    matchLabels:
      environment: test
  template:
    metadata:
      labels:
        environment: test
    spec:
      containers:
      - name: nginx
        image: nginx:1.17
        ports:
        - containerPort: 80
```

There are three main components of the `ReplicaSet` Spec:

- `replicas`: Defines the number of Pod replicas that should run using the given `template` and matching `selector`. Pods may be created or deleted in order to maintain the required number.
- `selector`: A label selector, which defines how to identify Pods that the ReplicaSet will acquire. Note that this may have a consequence of acquiring existing bare Pods by `ReplicaSet`!
- `template`: Defines the template for Pod creation. Labels used in metadata must positively match the `selector`.

You can apply the `ReplicaSet` manifest in a similar manner to how we applied a Pod in the Katacoda playground:

```
kubectl apply -f
https://raw.githubusercontent.com/PacktPublishing/Hands-On-Kubernetes-on-Wi
ndows/master/Chapter04/02_replicaset-example/nginx-replicaset.yaml
```

You can observe how three Pod replicas are created using the following command:

```
kubectl get pod -o wide -w
```

ReplicaSets mark the newly created or acquired Pods by assigning themselves to the `.metadata.ownerReferences` property of the Pod (if you are curious, you can check by using the `kubectl get pod <podId> -o yaml` command). This means that if you create exactly the same ReplicaSet, with exactly the same selectors but with a different name, for example, `nginx-replicaset-example2`, they will not *steal* Pods from each other. However, if you have already created bare Pods with matching labels, such as `environment: test`, the ReplicaSet will acquire them and may even delete the Pods if the number of replicas is too high!

If you really need to create a single Pod in Kubernetes cluster, it is a much better idea to use a `ReplicaSet` with the `replicas` field set to 1, which will act as a container *supervisor*. In this manner, you will prevent the creation of bare Pods without owners that are tied to the original node only.

This can be seen in the following diagram:

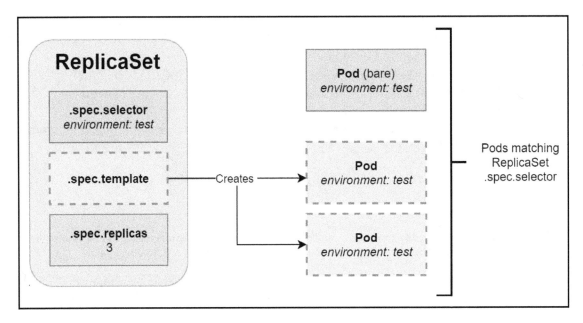

Usually, you don't create ReplicaSets on your own as they are not capable of performing rolling updates or rolling back to earlier versions easily. To facilitate such scenarios, Kubernetes provides objects built on top of ReplicaSets: Deployment and StatefulSet. Let's take a look at Deployment first.

Deployments

At this point, you already know the purpose of Pods and ReplicaSets. Deployments are Kubernetes objects that provide declarative updates for Pods and ReplicaSets. You can declaratively perform operations such as the following by using them:

- Perform a *rollout* of a new ReplicaSet.
- Change the Pod template and perform a controlled rollout. The old ReplicaSet will be gradually scaled down, whereas the new ReplicaSet will scale up at the same rate.
- Perform a *rollback* to an earlier version of the Deployment.
- Scale the ReplicaSet up or down.

The relationship of Deployment to ReplicaSets and Pods can be seen in the following diagram:

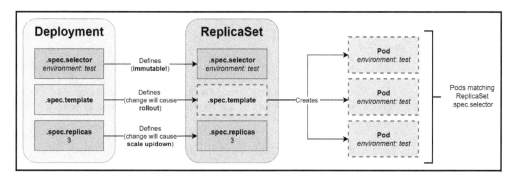

You should **avoid** managing ReplicaSets created by a Deployment on your own. If you need to make any changes to the ReplicaSet, perform the changes on the owning Deployment Object.

Note that the issue of the *accidental* acquisition of Pods by ReplicaSets managed by Deployments does not exist. The reason for this is that Pods and ReplicaSets use a special, automatically generated label called `pod-template-hash` that guarantees the uniqueness of the selection.

Let's take a look at an example Deployment manifest in the `nginx-deployment.yaml` file:

```yaml
apiVersion: apps/v1
kind: Deployment
metadata:
  name: nginx-deployment-example
spec:
  replicas: 3
  selector:
    matchLabels:
      environment: test
  template:
    metadata:
      labels:
        environment: test
    spec:
      containers:
      - name: nginx
        image: nginx:1.17
        ports:
        - containerPort: 80
```

As you can see, the basic structure is almost identical to ReplicaSet, but there are significant differences in how Deployment behaves when you perform a declarative update. Let's quickly demonstrate this in the playground:

1. Create manually the Deployment manifest file or download it using the wget command:

    ```
    wget
    https://raw.githubusercontent.com/PacktPublishing/Hands-On-Kubernet
    es-on-Windows/master/Chapter04/03_deployment-example/nginx-
    deployment.yaml
    ```

2. Apply the Deployment manifest file using the following command:

    ```
    kubectl apply -f nginx-deployment.yaml --record
    ```

    The --record flag adds a metadata annotation of kubernetes.io/change-cause to API objects that were created or modified by the preceding command. This feature allows you to easily track changes in your cluster.

3. Wait for the Deployment to fully roll out (you can observe the number of ready Pods in your deployment using kubectl get deployment -w).

4. Now, change the Pod Spec in the template in the YAML manifest; for example, change .spec.template.spec.containers[0].image to nginx:1.16 and apply the Deployment manifest again.

5. Immediately after that, observe how the rollout progresses using the following command:

    ```
    master $ kubectl rollout status deployment nginx-deployment-example
    Waiting for deployment "nginx-deployment-example" rollout to
    finish: 1 out of 3 new replicas have been updated...
    Waiting for deployment "nginx-deployment-example" rollout to
    finish: 2 out of 3 new replicas have been updated...
    Waiting for deployment "nginx-deployment-example" rollout to
    finish: 1 old replicas are pending termination...
    deployment "nginx-deployment-example" successfully rolled out
    ```

The Spec of Deployment is much richer than ReplicaSet. You can check the official documentation for more details: `https://kubernetes.io/docs/concepts/workloads/controllers/deployment/#writing-a-deployment-spec`. The official documentation contains multiple use cases of Deployments, all of which are described in detail: `https://kubernetes.io/docs/concepts/workloads/controllers/deployment/#use-case`.

As you can see, the declarative update to the Deployment template definition caused a smooth rollout of new Pod replicas. The old ReplicaSet was scaled down and, simultaneously, a new ReplicaSet, with a new Pod template, was created and gradually scaled up. You can now try performing the same operation with an `image` update for an existing bare ReplicaSet and you will see that... actually, nothing happens. This is because ReplicaSet only uses a Pod template to create new Pods. Existing Pods will not be updated or removed by such a change.

A rollout is only triggered when the `.spec.template` for Deployment is changed. Other changes to the Deployment manifest will not trigger a rollout.

Next, let's take a look at a concept similar to Deployments: StatefulSets.

StatefulSets

Deployments are usually used to deploy stateless components of your application. For stateful components, Kubernetes provides another API Object named `StatefulSet`. The principle of this operation is very similar to Deployment – it manages ReplicaSets and Pods in a declarative way and provides smooth rollouts and rollbacks. However, there are some key differences:

- StatefulSets ensure a deterministic (sticky) ID of Pods, which consists of `<statefulSetName>-<ordinal>`. For Deployments, you would have a random ID consisting of `<deploymentName>-<randomHash>`.
- For StatefulSets, the Pods are started and terminated in a specific, predictable order while scaling the ReplicaSet.

- In terms of storage, Kubernetes creates PersistentVolumeClaims based on `volumeClaimTemplates` of the StatefulSet Object for each Pod in the StatefulSet and always attaches this to the Pod with the same ID. For Deployments, if you choose to use `volumeClaimTemplates`, Kubernetes will create a single PersistentVolumeClaim and attach the same to all the Pods in the Deployment.
- You need to create a headless Service Object that is responsible for managing the deterministic network identity (DNS names) for Pods. The Headless Service allows us to return all Pod IPs behind the Service as DNS A records instead of a single DNS A record with a Service Cluster IP.

StatefulSets use a similar Spec to Deployments – you can find out more regarding StatefulSets by looking at the official documentation: `https://kubernetes.io/docs/concepts/workloads/controllers/statefulset/`.

DaemonSets

A DaemonSet is another controller-backed Object that is similar to a ReplicaSet but aims at running *exactly one* templated Pod replica per node in the cluster (optionally matching selectors). The most common use cases for running a DaemonSet are as follows:

- Managing monitoring telemetry for a given cluster node, for example, running Prometheus Node Exporter
- Running a log collection daemon on each node, for example, `fluentd` or `logstash`
- Running troubleshooting Pods, for example, node-problem-detector (`https://github.com/kubernetes/node-problem-detector`)

One of the DaemonSets that may run on your cluster out of the box is `kube-proxy`. In a standard cluster deployment performed by kubeadm, `kube-proxy` is distributed to nodes as a DaemonSet. You can also verify this on your Katacoda playground:

```
master $ kubectl get daemonset --all-namespaces
NAMESPACE       NAME            DESIRED   CURRENT   READY    UP-TO-DATE
AVAILABLE    NODE SELECTOR     AGE
kube-system     kube-proxy      2         2         2        2
<none>          12m
kube-system     weave-net       2         2         2        2
<none>          12m
```

If you would like to find out more about DaemonSets, please refer to the official documentation: `https://kubernetes.io/docs/concepts/workloads/controllers/daemonset/`.

Services

Pods that are created by ReplicaSets or Deployments have a finite life cycle. At some point, you can expect them to be terminated and new Pod replicas with new IP addresses will be created in their place. So, what if you have a Deployment running web server Pods that need to communicate with Pods that have been created as a part of another Deployment, for example, backend Pods? Web server Pods cannot assume anything about IP addresses or the DNS names of backend Pods, as they may change over time. This issue is resolved with Service API objects, which provide reliable networking for a set of Pods.

In general, Services target a set of Pods, and this is determined by label selectors. The most common scenario is exposing a Service for an existing Deployment by using exactly the same label selector. The Service is responsible for providing a reliable DNS name and IP address, as well as for monitoring selector results and updating the associated Endpoint Object with the current IP addresses of matching Pods.

For internal clients (Pods in the cluster), the communication to Pods behind a service is transparent – they use the Cluster IP or DNS name of the Service and the traffic is routed to one of the destination Pods. Routing capabilities are provided by kube-proxy, but it is important to know that the traffic is not routed through any master components – kube-proxy implements routing at the operating system kernel level and directly routes this to an appropriate Pod's IP address. In its simplest form, the destination Pod will be chosen randomly, but with **IP Virtual Server** (**IPVS**) proxy mode, you can have more complex strategies, such as least connection or shortest expected delay.

 Services can also expose Pods to external traffic.

The principle of how Service works can be seen in the following diagram:

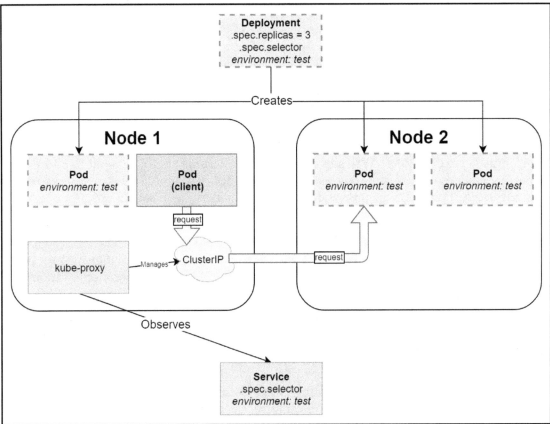

Let's expose an example service for our nginx Deployment:

1. If you don't have a running Deployment on the Katacoda playground, you can create one using the following command:

    ```
    kubectl apply -f
    https://raw.githubusercontent.com/PacktPublishing/Hands-On-Kubernet
    es-on-Windows/master/Chapter04/03_deployment-example/nginx-
    deployment.yaml --record
    ```

2. Expose the Service for a deployment using the following `kubectl expose` command:

```
kubectl expose deployment nginx-deployment-example
```

3. This command is *imperative* and should be avoided in favor of the *declarative* manifest. This command is equivalent to applying the following Service manifest:

```
apiVersion: v1
kind: Service
metadata:
  name: nginx-deployment-example
spec:
  selector:
    environment: test
  type: ClusterIP
  ports:
  - port: 80
    protocol: TCP
    targetPort: 80
```

4. Now, after the Service has been exposed, create an interactive `busybox` Pod and start the Bourne shell process:

```
kubectl run --generator=run-pod/v1 -i --tty busybox --image=busybox
--rm --restart=Never -- sh
```

5. When the container shell prompt appears, download the default web page served by nginx Pods while using the `nginx-deployment-example` Service name as the DNS name:

```
wget http://nginx-deployment-example && cat index.html
```

You can also use a **Fully Qualified Domain Name (FQDN)**, which is in the following form: `<serviceName>.<namespaceName>.svc.<clusterDomain>`. In this case, it is `nginx-deployment-example.default.svc.cluster.local`.

Next, let's take a quick look at objects that provide storage in Kubernetes.

Storage-related objects

In this book, we will cover Kubernetes storage only when needed as it is a broad and complex topic – in fact, storage and managing the stateful components of any cluster is often the hardest challenge to solve. If you are interested in details regarding storage in Kubernetes, please refer to the official documentation: `https://kubernetes.io/docs/concepts/storage/`.

In Docker, we use volumes to provide persistence either on local disk or remote/cloud storage using volume plugins. Docker volumes have a life cycle that's independent of the containers that consume them. In Kubernetes, there is a similar concept of a Volume, which is tightly coupled with a Pod and has the same life cycle as the Pod. The most important aspect of Volumes in Kubernetes is that they support multiple backing storage providers (types) — this is abstracted by Volume Plugins and, more recently, the **Container Storage Interface** (**CSI**), which is an interface for out-of-tree Volume Plugins that are developed independently from Kubernetes core. You can, for example, mount an Amazon Web Services EBS volume or Microsoft Azure Files SMB Share as a Volume for your Pod – the full list of Volume types is available here: `https://kubernetes.io/docs/concepts/storage/volumes/#types-of-volumes`.

One of the Volume types is **PersistentVolumeClaim** (**PVC**), which aims at decoupling Pods from the actual storage. PersistentVolumeClaim is an API Object that models a request for the storage of a specific type, class, or size – think of saying *I would like 10 GB of read/write-once SSD storage*. To fulfill such a request, a **PersistentVolume** (**PV**) API Object is required, which is a piece of storage that has been provisioned by the cluster's automation process. PersistentVolume types are also implemented as plugins, in a similar manner to Volumes.

Now, the whole process of provisioning PersistentVolumes can be dynamic – it requires creating a **StorageClass** (**SC**) API Object and using it when defining PVCs. When creating a new StorageClass, you provide a **provisioner** (or plugin) with specific parameters, and each PVC using the given SC will automatically create a PV using the selected provisioner.

These dependencies can be seen in the following diagram:

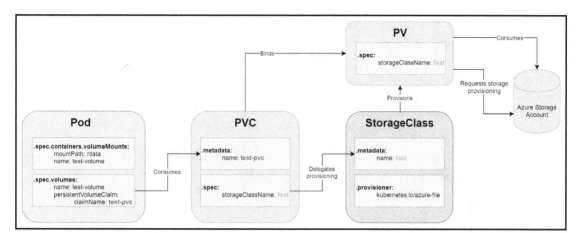

When you would like to deploy a Pod with a PersistentVolume mounted, the sequence of events would be as follows:

1. Create a StorageClass with a desired provisioner.
2. Create a PersistentVolumeClaim that uses the SC.
3. PersistentVolume is dynamically provisioned.
4. When creating a Pod, mount the PVC as a Volume.

> The idea of dynamically provisioned PersistentVolumes is complemented by the concept of StatefulSets. StatefulSets define volumeClaimTemplates, which can be used for the dynamic creation of the PersistentVolumeClaims of a given StorageClass. By doing this, the whole process of storage provisioning is fully dynamic – you just create a StatefulSet and the underlying storage objects are managed by the StatefulSet controller. You can find more details and examples here: `https://kubernetes.io/docs/concepts/workloads/controllers/statefulset/#stable-storage`.

Such storage architecture in Kubernetes ensures the portability of workloads, which means that you can easily move your Deployments and PersistentVolumeClaims to a different cluster. All you need to do is provide a StorageClass that fulfills the requirements of PVC. No modifications need to be made to the StatefulSet or PVC.

The Windows and Kubernetes ecosystem

Initially, Kubernetes was a Linux-centric solution – this was a result of the fact that mainstream containerization also originates from the Linux platform. In 2014, Microsoft and Windows were soon to join the containerization world – Microsoft announced support for Docker Engine in the upcoming release of Windows Server 2016. Kubernetes **Special Interest Group (SIG)** Windows was started in March 2016 and in January 2018, Kubernetes 1.9 provided beta support for Windows Server Containers. This support eventually matured to production level in April 2019 when Kubernetes 1.14 was released.

Why is Windows support for Kubernetes so important? Windows dominates in enterprise workloads and with Kubernetes being the de facto standard in container orchestration, support for Windows brings the possibility of migrating the vast majority of enterprise software to containers. Developers and system operators can now leverage the same tools and pipelines to deploy both Windows and Linux workloads, scale them in a similar way, and monitor them efficiently. From a business perspective, container adoption for Windows means better operational costs and better hardware utilization than plain VMs.

Windows containers support in Kubernetes is constantly evolving and more and more limitations are being replaced by new features. There are two key points that you need to remember in general:

- Currently, Windows machines can only join the cluster as nodes. There is no possibility and no plans for running master components on Windows. Clusters that run both Linux and Windows nodes are known as being hybrid or heterogeneous.
- You will need the latest stable version of Kubernetes and the latest (or almost latest) version of the Windows Server operating system to enjoy the full support that's on offer. For example, for Kubernetes 1.17, you need Windows Server 1809 (Semi-Annual Channel release) or Windows Server 2019 (the same release but coming from the Long-Term Servicing Channel), although the latest Windows Server, 1903, is also supported.

Currently, the amount of documentation regarding Windows support for Kubernetes is limited but growing. The best resources out there are as follows:

- Official Kubernetes documentation: `https://kubernetes.io/docs/setup/ production-environment/windows/intro-windows-in-kubernetes/`.
- Official Windows containerization and Kubernetes support documentation: `https://docs.microsoft.com/en-us/virtualization/ windowscontainers/kubernetes/getting-started-kubernetes-windows`.

- Azure Kubernetes Engine How-Tos for Windows: `https://docs.microsoft.com/en-us/azure/aks/windows-container-cli`.
- SIG-Windows meeting notes and recordings: `https://github.com/kubernetes/community/tree/master/sig-windows`.
- Kubernetes release notes and changelogs (look for SIG-Windows or Windows-related points): `https://github.com/kubernetes/kubernetes/releases`.
- Kubernetes Community Forums for Windows discussion: `https://discuss.kubernetes.io/c/general-discussions/windows`.
- Slack channel for SIG-Windows (you can really find a lot of help here if you run into problems!): `https://kubernetes.slack.com/messages/sig-windows`.

Let's take a look at the current state of Windows support for Kubernetes and the limitations as of version 1.17.

Kubernetes limitations on Windows

Windows Server containers support comes with a set of limitations that constantly change as each new version of Kubernetes is released and new releases of Windows Server arrive. Generally, from a Kubernetes API Server and kubelet perspective, in heterogeneous (hybrid) Linux/Windows Kubernetes clusters, the containers on Windows behave almost the same as Linux containers. However, there are some key differences in the details. First, let's take a look at some high-level, major limitations:

- Windows machines can only join the cluster as worker nodes. There is no possibility and no plans for running master components on Windows.
- Windows Server 1809 or 2019 is the minimal requirement for the OS on worker nodes. You cannot use Windows 10 machines as nodes.
- Docker Enterprise Edition (Basic) 18.09 or later is required as the container runtime. Enterprise Edition is available at no extra cost for the Windows Server operating system.
- The Windows Server operating system is subject to licensing (`https://www.microsoft.com/en-us/cloud-platform/windows-server-pricing`). Windows Container images are subject to the Microsoft Software Supplemental License (`https://docs.microsoft.com/en-us/virtualization/windowscontainers/images-eula`). For development and evaluation purposes, you can also use the Evaluations Center: `https://www.microsoft.com/en-us/evalcenter/evaluate-windows-server-2019`.

- Hyper-V isolation for Windows Server containers running on Kubernetes is in its experimental phase (alpha) and the current design will be deprecated in favor of the containerd implementation of the runtime. Until that time comes, the compatibility rules for process-isolated containers apply – you have to run containers with a base OS image that matches the host OS version. You can find more details in Chapter 1, *Creating Containers*.
- **Linux Containers on Windows** (**LCOW**) is not supported.
- Probably the most relevant to you is as follows: setting up a local Kubernetes development environment for hybrid Linux/Windows clusters is complex and currently, no standard solutions, such as Minikube or Docker Desktop for Windows, support such a configuration. This means you either need an on-premises, multi-node cluster or managed cloud offering to develop and evaluate your scenarios.
- The Windows nodes join process is not automated as much as it is for Linux nodes. Kubeadm will soon support the process of joining Windows nodes, but until then, you have to do this manually (with some help from Powershell scripting).

For container workload/compute, some of the limitations are as follows:

- Privileged containers are not supported on Windows nodes. This may pose some other limitations, such as running CSI plugins that must run in privileged mode.
- Windows does not have an out of memory process killer and currently, the Pods cannot be limited in terms of memory that's used. This is true for process-isolated containers but once containerd Hyper-V isolation is available on Kubernetes, a limit can be enforced.
- You need to specify proper node selectors to prevent, for example, Linux DaemonSets from trying to run on Windows nodes. This is technically not a limitation, but you should be aware that you need to control these selectors for your deployments.

For networking, some of the limitations are as follows:

- Network management for Windows nodes is more complex and Windows container networking is similar to VM networking.
- Fewer network plugins (CNI) are supported on Windows. You need to choose a solution that works for both Linux and Windows nodes in your cluster, for example, Flannel with a host-gw backend.

- L2bridge, l2tunnel, or overlay networks do not support IPv6 stack.
- Kube-proxy for Windows does not support IPVS and advanced load balancing policies.
- Accessing the NodePort Service from the node running the Pod fails.
- Ingress Controllers can run on Windows, but only if they support Windows containers; for example, *ingress-nginx*.
- Pinging external network hosts from inside the cluster with ICMP packets is not supported. In other words, don't be surprised when you are testing connectivity from Pods to the outside world with ping. You can use `curl` or Powershell `Invoke-WebRequest` instead.

For storage, some of the limitations are as follows:

- Expanding mounted volumes is not possible.
- Secrets that are mounted to Pods are written in clear-text using node storage. This may pose security risks and you will need to take additional actions to secure the cluster.
- Windows nodes only support the following volume types:
  - FlexVolume (SMB, iSCSI)
  - azureDisk
  - azureFile
  - gcePersistentDisk
  - awsElasticBlockStore (since 1.16)
  - vsphereVolume (since 1.16)

> The following limitations concern Kubernetes 1.17. Since the list of supported functionalities and current limitations changes, we advise that you check the official documentation for more up to date details: `https://kubernetes.io/docs/setup/production-environment/windows/intro-windows-in-kubernetes/#supported-functionality-and-limitations`.

Even if there is no support for local development clusters with Windows nodes, we'll still take a look at them; it is very likely that support for Windows workloads will be available in the near future.

Creating your own development cluster from scratch

In this section, you will learn how to set up a local Kubernetes cluster for development and learning on the Windows operating system. We will be using minikube, which is the official, recommended toolset, and Docker Desktop for Windows Kubernetes clusters. Please note that the current tooling for local clusters *does not* support Windows containers as it requires a multi-node setup with Linux master and Windows Server nodes. So, in other words, these tools allow you to develop Kubernetes applications running in Linux containers on your Windows machine. Basically, they provide an optimized Linux VM that hosts a one-node Kubernetes cluster.

> If you wish to experiment, you can use Katacoda Kubernetes playground (`https://www.katacoda.com/courses/kubernetes/playground`), which was used to demonstrate Kubernetes objects in this chapter, or Play with Kubernetes (`https://labs.play-with-k8s.com/`), which is provided by Docker, Inc.

minikube

Minikube is available on Windows, Linux, and macOS and aims at providing a stable environment for local development with Kubernetes. The key requirement on Windows is that a VM hypervisor needs to be installed. For Docker Desktop for Windows and Windows containers, we already use Hyper-V, so this will be our choice here. If you haven't enabled Hyper-V yet, please either follow the instructions for installing Docker Desktop for Windows in `Chapter 1`, *Creating Containers*, or follow the official documentation: `https://docs.microsoft.com/en-us/virtualization/hyper-v-on-windows/quick-start/enable-hyper-v`.

To install minikube, you need to perform the following steps:

1. If you don't have a Hyper-V virtual external network switch, create one by opening **Hyper-V Manager** from the **Start** menu and clicking **Virtual Switch Manager...** from the **Actions** tab.
2. Select **External** and click **Create Virtual Switch**.
3. Use **External Switch** as the name of the virtual switch and choose the network adapter that you will use to connect to the internet; for example, your Wi-Fi adapter:

4. Click **OK** to accept the changes.
5. Install kubectl (Kubernetes CLI) using the *Chocolatey* package manager. Execute the following command as an Administrator in a Powershell window:

```
choco install kubernetes-cli
```

6. Install minikube using Chocolatey, also as an Administrator:

```
choco install minikube
```

7. Set Hyper-V as the default virtualization driver for minikube:

```
minikube config set vm-driver hyperv
```

8. Set your virtual external switch to minikube by default:

```
minikube config set hyperv-virtual-switch "External Switch"
```

9. Start minikube. This may take a few minutes as the VM has to be set up and the Kubernetes node needs to be initialized:

```
minikube start
```

If you need to debug issues on the actual minikube VM (for example, connection problems), you can use the `minikube ssh` command or connect to the terminal directly from Hyper-V manager. The login username is `docker` and the password is `tcuser`.

10. Verify that the installation was successful by running the `kubectl` command, which will be configured to connect to the minikube cluster. You should see a variety of Pods running in the `kube-system` namespace:

    ```
    kubectl get pods --all-namespaces
    ```

11. You can use any of the example Kubernetes objects that we used in this chapter or just create your own:

    ```
    kubectl apply -f
    https://raw.githubusercontent.com/PacktPublishing/Hands-On-Kubernet
    es-on-Windows/master/Chapter04/03_deployment-example/nginx-
    deployment.yaml --record
    ```

12. Eventually, you can try using the Kubernetes Dashboard in your web browser. To initialize and open the dashboard, run the following command:

    ```
    minikube dashboard
    ```

Now, we will take a look at another approach to local development that uses Docker Desktop for Windows.

Docker Desktop for Windows

For Windows users, using Docker Desktop for Windows and its built-in local Kubernetes cluster is the easiest approach. It is also recommended if you are working in environments that require a proxy to connect to the internet as the setup is seamless and easier compared to minikube.

If you haven't installed Docker Desktop for Windows yet, you should follow the instructions in `Chapter 1`, *Creating Containers*. To enable the local Kubernetes cluster, you need to follow these steps:

1. Ensure that you are running in Linux containers mode. **DockerDesktopVM** will be responsible for hosting the Kubernetes cluster. To do that, open the tray icon for Docker Desktop for Windows and click **Switch to Linux containers...**.

2. When the operation is finished, open **Settings** from the tray icon.
3. Open the **Kubernetes** section.
4. Check the **Enable Kubernetes** checkbox and click **Apply**.
5. The setup process will take a few minutes to complete .
6. If you have set up minikube, you need to **switch context** to kubectl. From the command line, run the following command:

```
kubectl config use-context docker-desktop
```

7. Alternatively, you can also switch the context from Docker Desktop from the Windows tray:

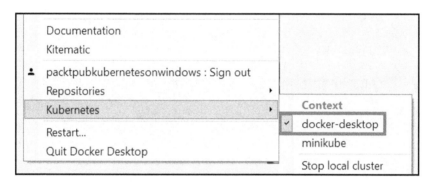

You will learn more about the kubectl configuration and its contexts in Chapter 6, *Interacting with Kubernetes Clusters*.

8. Now, you can start hacking with your local Kubernetes cluster. Let's deploy the Kubernetes Dashboard:

```
kubectl apply -f
https://raw.githubusercontent.com/kubernetes/dashboard/v1.10.1/src/
deploy/recommended/kubernetes-dashboard.yaml
```

9. Wait until all the Pods are **Running**:

```
kubectl get pods --all-namespaces --watch
```

10. Get the default service account token. Copy the `token:` value from the command's output:

    ```
    kubectl describe secret -n kube-system default
    ```

11. Enable the kubectl proxy for the cluster. This process should be running while you are accessing the dashboard:

    ```
    kubectl proxy
    ```

12. Navigate to `http://localhost:8001/api/v1/namespaces/kube-system/services/https:kubernetes-dashboard:/proxy/#!/overview?namespace=kube-system`.

13. Select **Token**, paste your default token, and **Sign In**.

Alternative strategies for setting up a local development Kubernetes cluster with Windows containers support involve the automated setup of VMs on your local machine using, for example, vagrant. You can explore some of the small projects on GitHub that use this approach, but you should expect them to be outdated and no longer supported.

In the next section, we will provide a short overview of the production cluster deployment strategies that we can perform for Kubernetes clusters, especially with Windows nodes.

Production cluster deployment strategies

The deployment of production-level clusters and even the development of clusters with Windows nodes requires a very different approach. There are three important questions that determine your options for the deployment of Kubernetes clusters:

- Are you deploying the cluster in the cloud or using on-premises bare metal or virtual machines?
- Do you need **high availability** (**HA**) set up?
- Do you need Windows containers support?

Let's summarize the most popular deployment tools currently available.

kubeadm

The first one is **kubeadm** (`https://github.com/kubernetes/kubeadm`), which is a command-line tool focused on getting a minimum viable, secure cluster up and running in a user-friendly way. One of the aspects of kubeadm is that it is a tool that is scoped only to a given machine and Kubernetes API communication, so, in general, it is intended to be a building block for other automation tools that manage the cluster as a whole. Its principle is simple: use the `kubeadm init` command on master node(s) and `kubeadm join` on worker nodes. The features of kubeadm can be summarized as follows:

- You can deploy clusters in on-premises environments and cloud environments.
- Highly available clusters are supported but as of version 1.17, this feature is still in its beta stage.
- Official Windows support is currently planned for version 1.18. The current version of kubeadm is a good base for starting a hybrid Kubernetes cluster. First, you bootstrap master node(s) and (optionally) Linux worker nodes and continue with the scripts currently provided by Microsoft for joining Windows nodes (`https://github.com/microsoft/SDN`) or previewing versions of scripts in the sig-windows-tools GitHub repository (`https://github.com/kubernetes-sigs/sig-windows-tools`). We will be using this approach in Chapter 7, *Deploying Hybrid On-Premises Kubernetes Cluster*.

If you are planning to automate how your Kubernetes cluster is provisioned, for example, using Ansible, kubeadm is a good starting point as it provides a good degree of flexibility and easy configuration.

kops

The next option is using **Kubernetes Operations** (**kops**, `https://github.com/kubernetes/kops`), which uses kubeadm internally. Kops aims to manage whole Kubernetes clusters in cloud environments – you can think of it as *kubectl for clusters*. Its main features are as follows:

- Deployment of clusters on Amazon Web Services (officially supported), Google Compute Engine, and OpenStack (both in their beta stages). On-premises deployments are not supported unless you are running your own deployment of OpenStack. VMware vSphere support is in its alpha stage.
- Production-level support for HA clusters.
- Windows nodes are not supported.

In this book, we will not focus on kops due to its lack of support for Windows.

kubespray

Kubespray (https://github.com/kubernetes-sigs/kubespray) is a composition of configurable Ansible playbooks that run kubeadm in order to bootstrap fully-functional, production-ready Kubernetes clusters. The main difference between kubespray and kops is that kops is more tightly integrated with cloud providers, whereas kubespray is aimed at multiple platforms, including bare-metal deployments. Its features can be summarized as follows:

- Support for installing Kubernetes clusters for multiple cloud providers and bare-metal machines.
- Production-level support for HA clusters.
- Windows nodes are currently not supported, but with incoming kubeadm support for Windows nodes, kubespray is the best candidate to extend its support.

As kubespray does not support Windows nodes at this point, we will not focus on it in this book.

AKS Engine

AKS Engine (https://github.com/Azure/aks-engine) is an official, open source tool for provisioning self-managed Kubernetes clusters on Azure. It aims at generating **Azure Resource Manager** (**ARM**) templates that bootstrap Azure VMs and set up the cluster.

AKS Engine should not be confused with **Azure Kubernetes Service** (**AKS**), which is a fully-managed Kubernetes cluster offering by Azure. AKS Engine is used by AKS internally, though.

Its features can be summarized as follows:

- Available only for Azure; other platforms are not supported.
- High availability is implemented through Azure VMSS (https://kubernetes.io/blog/2018/10/08/support-for-azure-vmss-cluster-autoscaler-and-user-assigned-identity/).

- Good Windows support – the official test suites are validated on AKS Engine configuration. We'll use this approach in `Chapter 8`, *Deploying a Hybrid Azure Kubernetes Engine Service Cluster*.

However, please note that AKS Engine offers experimental features that are not available as managed AKS offerings yet. This means that this approach may not always be suitable for running production workloads, depending on which AKS Engine features you use.

Managed Kubernetes providers

As the popularity of Kubernetes constantly grows, there are multiple, **fully-managed** Kubernetes offerings being provided by different cloud providers and companies specializing in Kubernetes. You can find a long, but not complete, list of Kubernetes providers (not only managed) at `https://kubernetes.io/docs/setup/#production-environment`. In this section, we will summarize the managed offerings of the tier-1 cloud service providers and what they offer in terms of Windows support, namely the following:

- Microsoft Azure: **Azure Kubernetes Service** (**AKS**)
- Google Cloud Platform: **Google Kubernetes Engine** (**GKE**)
- Amazon Web Services: **Elastic Kubernetes Service** (**EKS**)

For **managed** Kubernetes providers, the key principle is that you are not responsible for managing the control plane, the data plane, and the underlying cluster infrastructure. From your perspective, you get a ready cluster of a given size (that may scale on demand) with high availability and the appropriate SLAs in place. You just need to deploy your workload! An alternative, less managed approach is the **turnkey cloud solution**, where you manage the control plane, data plane, and upgrades yourself, but the infrastructure is managed by the cloud provider. A good example of such a solution is the **AKS Engine** running on top of Azure VMs.

All of these cloud providers have Windows containers support in their managed Kubernetes offerings and for all them, this feature is currently in preview. You can expect limited support for the feature and limited backward compatibility.

Azure Kubernetes Service introduced Windows nodes support in May 2019 and is the most mature offering for Windows Containers, with good support in its documentation (`https:/ /docs.microsoft.com/en-us/azure/aks/windows-container-cli`). This offering is built on top of the AKS Engine internally, so you can expect similar features to be available there. You can monitor the official roadmap for incoming Windows support features by going to `https://github.com/Azure/AKS/projects/1`.

Google Kubernetes Engine announced support for Windows Containers in their Rapid release channel in May 2019. Currently, there is limited information available about this alpha feature – for Google Cloud Platform, the most common and well-validated use case is deploying Kubernetes for Windows directly to Google Compute Engine VMs.

Amazon Elastic Kubernetes Service announced preview support for Windows Containers in March 2019. You can find more details about Windows Containers support in EKS in the official documentation: `https://docs.aws.amazon.com/eks/latest/userguide/windows-support.html`

Creating AKS cluster with Windows nodes

To complete this walkthrough, you need an Azure account and Azure CLI installed on your machine. You can find more details in `Chapter 2`, *Managing State in Containers*.

 The following steps are also available as a Powershell script in the official GitHub repository for this book: `https://github.com/PacktPublishing/ Hands-On-Kubernetes-on-Windows/blob/master/Chapter04/05_ CreateAKSWithWindowsNodes.ps1`.

Let's begin by enabling the preview features for AKS:

1. Install the `aks-preview` extension using the Azure CLI from Powershell:

```
az extension add --name aks-preview
```

2. Update the `aks-preview` extension to its latest available version:

```
az extension update --name aks-preview
```

3. Register the `WindowsPreview` feature flag for your subscription to enable multiple node pools. A separate node pool is required for Windows nodes. Note that this operation should be performed on test or development subscriptions as any cluster that is created after enabling this flag will use this feature:

```
az feature register `
    --name WindowsPreview `
    --namespace Microsoft.ContainerService
```

4. This operation will take a few minutes. You have to wait until the `Status` of the feature is `Registered` to be able to continue. To check the current `Status`, run the following command:

```
az feature list `
    -o json `
    --query "[?contains(name,
'Microsoft.ContainerService/WindowsPreview')].{Name:name,State:prop
erties.state}"
```

5. When the feature is registered, execute the following command to propagate the change:

```
az provider register `
    --namespace Microsoft.ContainerService
```

6. Now, wait until the provider finishes the registration and switches status to `Registered`. You can monitor the status using the following command:

```
az provider show -n Microsoft.ContainerService `
    | ConvertFrom-Json `
    | Select -ExpandProperty registrationState
```

The actual cost of AKS is determined by the number and size of the Azure VMs that host the cluster. You can find the predicted costs of running an AKS cluster here: https://azure.microsoft.com/en-in/pricing/details/kubernetes-service/. It is advised that you delete the cluster if you are not planning to use it after this walkthrough to avoid extra costs.

With the preview feature enabled, you can continue creating the actual AKS cluster with Windows nodes. The available versions of Kubernetes depend on the location where you create the cluster. In this walkthrough, we suggest using the `westeurope` Azure location. Follow these steps to create the cluster:

1. Create a dedicated resource group for your AKS cluster, for example, `aks-windows-resource-group`:

```
az group create `
    --name aks-windows-resource-group `
    --location westeurope
```

2. Get the list of available Kubernetes versions in a given location:

```
az aks get-versions `
    --location westeurope
```

3. Choose the desired one. It is advised that you use the latest one; for example, `1.15.3`.

4. Create an `aks-windows-cluster` AKS instance using the selected version and provide the desired Windows username and password (choose a secure one!). The following command will create a two-node pool of Linux nodes running in VMSS high-availability mode:

```
az aks create `
    --resource-group aks-windows-resource-group `
    --name aks-windows-cluster `
    --node-count 2 `
    --enable-addons monitoring `
    --kubernetes-version 1.15.3 `
    --generate-ssh-keys `
    --windows-admin-username azureuser `
    --windows-admin-password "S3cur3P@ssw0rd" `
    --enable-vmss `
    --network-plugin azure
```

5. After a few minutes, when the AKS cluster is ready, add a Windows **node pool** named `w1pool` to the cluster – this operation will take a few minutes. There is a limit of six characters for the Windows node pool name:

```
az aks nodepool add `
  --resource-group aks-windows-resource-group `
  --cluster-name aks-windows-cluster `
  --os-type Windows `
  --name w1pool `
  --node-count 1 `
  --kubernetes-version 1.15.3
```

6. If you do not have `kubectl` installed already, install it using the Azure CLI:

```
az aks install-cli
```

7. Get the cluster credentials for `kubectl`. The following command will add a new context for `kubectl` and switch to it:

```
az aks get-credentials `
    --resource-group aks-windows-resource-group `
    --name aks-windows-cluster
```

8. Verify that the cluster has been deployed successfully! Run any `kubectl` command:

```
kubectl get nodes
kubectl get pods --all-namespaces
```

9. Now, you can start hacking with your first Kubernetes cluster with Windows nodes! For example, create a sample Deployment that runs three replicas of the official ASP.NET sample in Windows containers, exposed behind a Service of the LoadBalancer type:

```
kubectl apply -f
https://raw.githubusercontent.com/PacktPublishing/Hands-On-Kubernet
es-on-Windows/master/Chapter04/06_windows-example/windows-
example.yaml --record
```

10. The container creation process may take up to 10 minutes as the Windows base image needs to be pulled first. Wait for the external load balancer IP to be available:

```
PS C:\> kubectl get service
NAME                TYPE           CLUSTER-IP      EXTERNAL-IP
PORT(S)             AGE
kubernetes          ClusterIP      10.0.0.1        <none>
443/TCP             32m
windows-example     LoadBalancer   10.0.179.85     13.94.168.209
80:30433/TCP        12m
```

11. Navigate to the address in a web browser to check if your application is running properly:

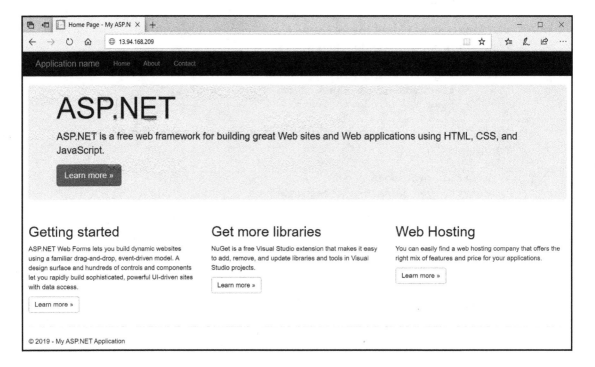

To delete the AKS cluster, use the `az group delete --name aks-windows-resource-group --yes --no-wait` command.

Congratulations! You have successfully created your first, fully-managed Kubernetes cluster with Windows nodes. In the next few chapters, we will look at different approaches for creating Kubernetes clusters with Windows containers support.

Summary

In this chapter, you learned about the key theory behind Kubernetes – its high-level architecture and the most commonly used Kubernetes API objects. On top of that, we summarized how Kubernetes currently fits into the Windows ecosystem and the current limitations in Windows support. Next, you learned how to set up your own Kubernetes development environment for Linux containers using the recommended tools, such as minikube and Docker Desktop for Windows, as well as the possible production cluster deployment strategies available. Finally, we reviewed the managed Kubernetes offerings that support Windows containers and performed a successful deployment of Azure Kubernetes Service cluster with the Windows node pool!

The next chapter will bring you more knowledge regarding Kubernetes architecture – Kubernetes networking in general and in the Windows ecosystem. This will be the last chapter that focuses on the theory of Kubernetes and its working principles.

Questions

1. What is the difference between the control plane and the data plane in Kubernetes?
2. How does the declarative model and the concept of desired state work and what are its benefits?
3. What is the difference between a container and a Pod?
4. What is the purpose of the Deployment API Object?
5. What are the key limitations of Kubernetes support on Windows?
6. What is minikube and when should you use it?
7. What is the difference between AKS and AKS Engine?

You can find answers to these questions in the *Assessments* section of this book.

Further reading

- For more information regarding Kubernetes concepts, please refer to the following PacktPub books:
    - *The Complete Kubernetes Guide* (https://www.packtpub.com/virtualization-and-cloud/complete-kubernetes-guide)
    - *Getting Started with Kubernetes – Third Edition* (https://www.packtpub.com/virtualization-and-cloud/getting-started-kubernetes-third-edition)
    - *Kubernetes for Developers* (https://www.packtpub.com/virtualization-and-cloud/kubernetes-developers)
- You can also refer to the excellent official Kubernetes documentation (https://kubernetes.io/docs/home/), which is always the most up to date source of knowledge about Kubernetes in general. For Windows-specific scenarios, the official Microsoft Virtualization documentation is recommended: https://docs.microsoft.com/en-us/virtualization/windowscontainers/kubernetes/getting-started-kubernetes-windows.

5
Kubernetes Networking

For container orchestration, there are two major challenges to be solved: managing container hosts (nodes) and managing the networking between containers. If you limited your container host cluster to only one node, networking would be fairly simple—for Docker on Linux, you would use the default bridge network driver, which creates a private network (internal to the host), allowing the containers to communicate with each other. External access to the containers requires exposing and mapping container ports as host ports. But now, if you consider a multi-node cluster, this solution does not scale well—you have to use NAT and track which host ports are used, and on top of that, the applications running in containers have to be aware of the networking topology.

Fortunately, Kubernetes provides a solution to this challenge by providing a networking model that has specific, fundamental requirements—any networking solution that complies with the specification can be used as the networking model implementation in Kubernetes. The goal of this model is to provide transparent container-to-container communication and external access to the containers, without containerized applications requiring any knowledge about the underlying networking challenges. Throughout this chapter, we will explain the assumptions of the Kubernetes networking model and how Kubernetes networking issues can be solved in hybrid Linux/Windows clusters.

In this chapter, we will cover the following topics:

- Kubernetes networking principles
- Kubernetes CNI network plugins
- Windows server networking in Kubernetes
- Choosing Kubernetes network modes

Technical requirements

For this chapter, you will need the following:

- Windows 10 Pro, Enterprise, or Education (version 1903 or later, 64-bit) installed
- Docker Desktop for Windows 2.0.0.3 or later installed
- Azure CLI installed if you would like to use the AKS cluster from the previous chapter

Installation of Docker Desktop for Windows and system requirements are covered in Chapter 1, *Creating Containers*.

For Azure CLI, you can find detailed installation instructions in Chapter 2, *Managing State in Containers*.

You can download the latest code samples for this chapter from the official GitHub repository: https://github.com/PacktPublishing/Hands-On-Kubernetes-on-Windows/tree/master/Chapter05

Kubernetes networking principles

As a container orchestrator, Kubernetes provides a networking model that consists of a set of requirements that any given networking solution must fulfill. The most important requirements are as follows:

- Pods running on a node must be able to communicate with all Pods on all nodes (including the Pod's node) without NAT and explicit port mapping.
- All Kubernetes components running on a node, for example kubelet or system daemons/services, must be able to communicate with all Pods on that node.

These requirements enforce a flat, NAT-less network model, which is one of the core Kubernetes concepts that make it so powerful, scalable, and easy to use. From this perspective, Pods are similar to VMs running in a Hyper-V cluster—each Pod has its own IP address assigned (IP-per-Pod model), and containers within a Pod share the same network namespace (like processes on a VM), which means they share the same localhost and need to be aware of port assignments.

In short, networking in Kubernetes has the following challenges to overcome:

- **Intra-Pod communication between containers**: Handled by standard localhost communication.

- **Pod-to-Pod communication**: Handled by underlying network implementation.
- **Pod-to-Service and External-to-Service communication**: Handled by Service API objects, communication is dependent on the underlying network implementation. We will cover this later in this section.
- **Automation of networking setup by kubelet when a new Pod is created**: Handled by **Container Network Interface** (**CNI**) plugins. We will cover this in the next section.

There are numerous implementations of the Kubernetes networking model, ranging from simple L2 networking (for example, Flannel with a host-gw backend) to complex, high-performance **Software-Defined Networking** (**SDN**) solutions (for example, Big Cloud Fabric). You can find a list of different implementations of the networking model in the official documentation: `https://kubernetes.io/docs/concepts/cluster-administration/networking/#how-to-implement-the-kubernetes-networking-model`.

In this book, we will only focus on implementations that are relevant from the Windows perspective:

- L2 network
- Overlay network

Let's begin with the L2 network, which is the simplest network implementation available.

L2 network

Layer 2 (**L2**) refers to the data link layer, which is the second level in the seven-layer OSI reference model for network protocol design. This layer is used to transfer data between nodes in the same local area network (so, think of operating on MAC addresses and switch ports, not IP addresses, which belong to L3). For Kubernetes, an L2 network with routing tables set up on each Kubernetes node is the simplest network type that fulfills the Kubernetes networking model implementation requirements. A good example is Flannel with a host-gw backend. At a high level, Flannel (host-gw) provides networking for Pods in the following way:

1. Each node runs a **flanneld** (or **flanneld.exe** for Windows) agent, which is responsible for allocating a subnet lease from a larger, preconfigured address space called **Pod CIDR** (**Classless Inter-Domain Routing**). In the following diagram, Pod CIDR is `10.244.0.0/16`, whereas Node 1 has leased subnet `10.244.1.0/24` and Node 2 has leased subnet `10.244.2.0/24`.

2. In most cases, the Flannel agent is deployed as a **DaemonSet** during Pod network installation in the cluster. An example DaemonSet definition can be found here: `https://github.com/coreos/flannel/blob/master/Documentation/kube-flannel.yml`.

3. Flannel stores networking information and lease data using the Kubernetes API or **etcd** directly, depending on its configuration.

4. When a new node joins the cluster, Flannel creates a `cbr0` bridge interface for all Pods on a given node. Routing tables in the operating system on nodes are updated, containing one entry for each node in the cluster. For example, for Node 2 in the following diagram, the routing table has two entries, which route communication to `10.244.1.0/24` via the `10.0.0.2` gateway (inter-node communication to Node 1) and communication to `10.244.2.0/24` via the local `cbr0` interface (local communication between Pods on Node 1).

5. When a new Pod is created, a new **veth** device pair is created. An `eth0` device is created in the Pod network namespace and a `vethX` device at the other end of the pair in the host (root) namespace. A virtual Ethernet device is used as a tunnel between network namespaces.

6. In order to trigger the preceding actions, kubelet uses CNI, which is implemented by the Flannel CNI plugin:

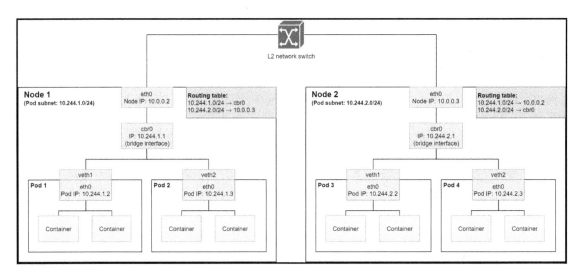

All of the actions performed by Flannel could be performed manually using the command line but, of course, the goal of Flannel is to automate the process of new node registration and new Pod network creation transparently for Kubernetes users.

Let's now quickly analyze what happens when a container in Pod 1, 10.244.1.2 (on Node 1), would like to send a TCP packet to a container in Pod 4, 10.244.2.3 (on Node 2):

1. Pod 1 outbound packet will be sent to the cbr0 bridge interface as it is set as the default gateway for the eth0 Pod interface.
2. The packet is forwarded to the 10.0.0.3 gateway due to the 10.244.2.0/24 → 10.0.0.3 routing table entry at Node 1.
3. The packet goes through the physical L2 network switch and is received by Node 2 at the eth0 interface.
4. Node 2's routing table contains an entry that forwards traffic to the 10.244.2.0/24 CIDR to the local cbr0 bridge interface.
5. The packet is received by Pod 2.

Note that the preceding example uses Linux network interface naming and terminology. The Windows implementation of this model is generally the same but differs on OS-level primitives.

Using an L2 network with routing tables is efficient and simple to set up; however, it has some disadvantages, especially as the cluster grows:

- L2 adjacency of nodes is required. In other words, all nodes must be in the same local area network with no L3 routers in between.
- Synchronizing routing tables between all nodes. When a new node joins, all nodes need to update their routing tables.
- Possible glitches and delays, especially for short-lived containers, due to the way L2 network switches set up new MAC addresses in forwarding tables.

Flannel with a **host-gw** backend has stable support for Windows.

Generally, using Overlay networking is recommended, which allows creating a virtual L2 network over an existing underlay L3 network.

Overlay network

As a general concept, Overlay networking uses encapsulation in order to create a new, tunneled, virtual network on top of an existing L2/L3 network, called an underlay network. This network is created without any changes to the actual physical network infrastructure for the underlay network. Network services in the Overlay network are decoupled from the underlying infrastructure by encapsulation, which is a process of enclosing one type of packet using another type of packet. Packets that are encapsulated when entering a tunnel are then de-encapsulated at the other end of the tunnel.

Overlay networking is a broad concept that has many implementations. In Kubernetes, one of the commonly used implementations is using the **Virtual Extensible LAN (VXLAN)** protocol for tunneling L2 Ethernet frames via UDP packets. Importantly, this type of Overlay network works both for Linux and Windows nodes. If you have a Flannel network with a VXLAN backend, the networking for Pods is provided in the following way:

1. Similarly to the host-gw backend, a flanneld agent is deployed on each node as a DaemonSet.
2. When a new node joins the cluster, Flannel creates a `cbr0` bridge interface for all Pods on a given node and an additional `flannel.<vni>` VXLAN device (a VXLAN tunnel endpoint, or VTEP for short; VNI stands for VXLAN Network Identifier, in this example, 1). This device is responsible for the encapsulation of the traffic. The IP routing table is updated only for the new node. Traffic to Pods running on the same node is forwarded to the `cbr0` interface, whereas all the remaining traffic to Pod CIDR is forwarded to the VTEP device. For example, for Node 2 in the following diagram, the routing table has two entries that route the communication to `10.244.0.0/16` via the `flannel.1` VTEP device (inter-node communication in the Overlay network) and communication to `10.244.2.0/24` is routed via the local `cbr0` interface (local communication between Pods on Node 1 without Overlay).
3. When a new Pod is created, a new veth device pair is created, similar to the case of the host-gw backend:

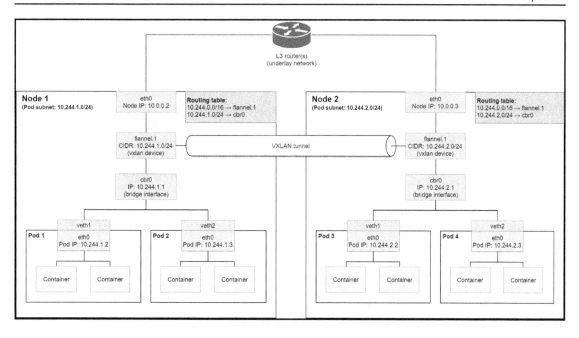

Let's now quickly analyze what happens when a container in Pod 1 10.244.1.2 (on Node 1) would like to send a TCP packet to a container in Pod 4, 10.244.2.3 (on Node 2):

1. Pod 1 outbound packet will be sent to the cbr0 bridge interface as it is set as the default gateway for the eth0 Pod interface.
2. The packet is forwarded to the flannel.1 VTEP device due to the 10.244.0.0/16 → flannel.1 routing table entry at Node 1.
3. flannel.1 uses the MAC address of Pod 4 in the 10.244.0.0/16 Overlay network as the inner packet destination address. This address is populated by the **flanneld** agent in the **forwarding database (FDB)**.
4. flannel.1 determines the IP address of the destination VTEP device at Node 2 using the FDB, and 10.0.0.3 is used as the destination address for the outer encapsulating packet.
5. The packet goes through the physical L2/L3 network and is received by Node 2. The packet is de-encapsulated by the flannel.1 VTEP device.
6. Node 2's routing table contains an entry that forwards traffic to the 10.244.2.0/24 CIDR to the local cbr0 bridge interface.
7. The packet is received by Pod 2.

For Windows, Flannel with an Overlay backend is currently still in the alpha feature stage.

Using a VXLAN backend over a host-gw backend for Flannel has several advantages:

- No need for L2 adjacency of the nodes.
- L2 Overlay networks are not susceptible to spanning tree failures, which can happen in the case of L2 domains spanning multiple logical switches.

The solution described earlier in this section is similar to Docker running in **swarm mode**. You can read more about Overlay networks for swarm mode in the official documentation: `https://docs.docker.com/network/Overlay/`.

The preceding two networking solutions are the most commonly used solutions for hybrid Linux/Windows clusters, especially when running on-premises. For other scenarios, it is also possible to use **Open Virtual Network (OVN)** and **L2 tunneling** for Azure-specific implementations.

Other solutions

In terms of Windows-supported networking solutions for Kubernetes, there are two additional implementations that can be used:

- **Open Virtual Network (OVN)**, for example, as part of a deployment on OpenStack
- **L2 tunneling** for deployments on Azure

OVN is a network virtualization platform for implementing SDN that decouples physical network topology from the logical one. Using OVN, users can define network topologies consisting of logical switches and routers. Kubernetes supports OVN integration using a dedicated CNI plugin **ovn-kubernetes** (`https://github.com/ovn-org/ovn-kubernetes`).

For Azure-specific scenarios, it is possible to leverage Microsoft Cloud Stack features directly using the **Azure-CNI** plugin, which relies on the **L2Tunnel** Docker network driver. In short, Pods are connected to the existing virtual network resources and configurations, and all Pod packets are routed directly to the virtualization host in order to apply Azure SDN policies. Pods get full connectivity in the virtual network provided by Azure, which means that each Pod can be directly reached from outside of the cluster. You can find more details about this solution in the official AKS documentation: `https://docs.microsoft.com/bs-latn-ba/azure/aks/configure-azure-cni`.

Services

In the previous chapter, we covered Services as API objects and explained how they can be used together with Deployments. To briefly recap, Service API objects enable network access to a set of Pods, based on label selectors. In terms of Kubernetes networking, Services are a concept that's built on top of the standard networking model, which aims to do the following:

- Enable reliable communication to a set of Pods using **Virtual IP** (**VIP**). Client Pods do not need to know the current IP addresses of individual Pods, which can change over time. External clients also do not need to know about current IP addresses of Pods.
- Load-balance network traffic (internal as well as external) to a set of Pods.
- Enable service discovery in the cluster. This requires the DNS service add-on to be running in the cluster.

There are four Service types available in Kubernetes, which can be specified in the Service object specification:

- ClusterIP
- NodePort
- LoadBalancer
- ExternalName

We will go through each type separately, but let's first take a look at what a **Service** looks like in the context of Deployments and Pods:

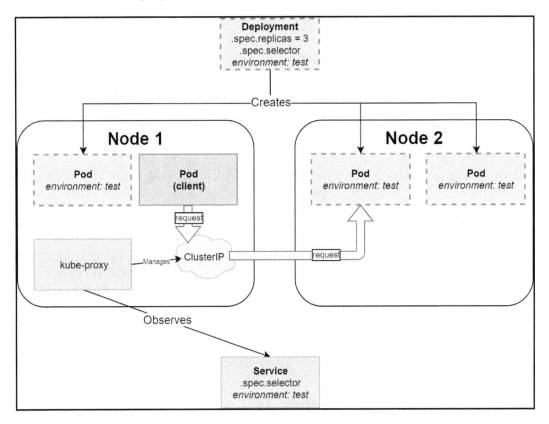

The preceding diagram shows how the simplest internal Service of type ClusterIP exposes an existing Deployment that manages three replicas of Pods labeled with `environment: test`. The ClusterIP Service, with the same label selector, `environment: test`, is responsible for monitoring the result of label selector evaluation and updating **endpoint** API objects with the current set of alive and ready Pod IPs. At the same time, kube-proxy is observing Service and endpoint objects in order to create iptables rules on Linux nodes or HNS policies on Windows nodes, which are used to implement a Virtual IP address with a value of ClusterIP specified in the Service specification. Finally, when a client Pod sends a request to the Virtual IP, it is forwarded using the rules/policies (set up by kube-proxy) to one of the Pods in the Deployment. As you can see, kube-proxy is the central component for implementing Services, and in fact it is used for all Service types, apart from ExternalName.

ClusterIP

The default type of Service in Kubernetes is ClusterIP, which exposes a service using an internal VIP. This means that the Service will only be reachable from within the cluster. Assuming that you are running the following `nginx` Deployment:

```
apiVersion: apps/v1
kind: Deployment
metadata:
  name: nginx-deployment-example
spec:
  replicas: 3
  selector:
    matchLabels:
      environment: test
  template:
    metadata:
      labels:
        environment: test
    spec:
      containers:
      - name: nginx
        image: nginx:1.17
        ports:
        - containerPort: 80
```

 All of the manifest files are available in the official GitHub repository for this book: `https://github.com/PacktPublishing/Hands-On-Kubernetes-on-Windows/tree/master/Chapter05`.

You can deploy a Service of ClusterIP type using the following manifest file:

```
apiVersion: v1
kind: Service
metadata:
  name: nginx-deployment-example-clusterip
spec:
  selector:
    environment: test
  type: ClusterIP
  ports:
  - port: 8080
    protocol: TCP
    targetPort: 80
```

Like for every Service type, the key part is the `selector` specification, which has to match the Pods in the Deployment. You specify `type` as `ClusterIP` and assign `8080` as a port on the Service, which is mapped to `targetPort: 80` on the Pod. This means that client Pod would use the `nginx-deployment-example:8080` TCP endpoint for communicating with nginx Pods. The actual ClusterIP address is assigned dynamically, unless you explicitly specify one in the `spec`. The internal DNS Service in a Kubernetes cluster is responsible for resolving `nginx-deployment-example` to the actual ClusterIP address as a part of service discovery.

 The diagrams in the rest of this section represent how the Services are implemented logically. Under the hood, kube-proxy is responsible for managing all the forwarding rules and exposing ports, as in the previous diagram.

This has been visualized in the following diagram:

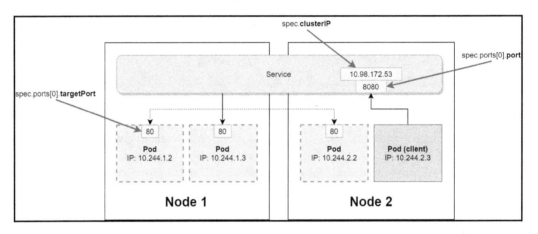

ClusterIP Services are a base for the other types of Service that allow external communication: NodePort and LoadBalancer.

NodePort

The first type of Service allowing external ingress communication to Pods is the NodePort Service. This type of Service is implemented as a ClusterIP Service with the additional capability of being reachable using any cluster node IP address and a specified port. In order to achieve that, kube-proxy exposes the same port on each node in the range 30000-32767 (which is configurable) and sets up forwarding so that any connections to this port will be forwarded to ClusterIP.

You can deploy a NodePort Service using the following manifest file:

```
apiVersion: v1
kind: Service
metadata:
  name: nginx-deployment-example-nodeport
spec:
  selector:
    environment: test
  type: NodePort
  ports:
  - port: 8080
    nodePort: 31001
    protocol: TCP
    targetPort: 80
```

If you do not specify `nodePort` in the Spec, it will be allocated dynamically using the NodePort range. Note that the service still acts as a ClusterIP Service, which means that it is internally reachable at its ClusterIP endpoint.

The following diagram visualizes the concept of a NodePort Service:

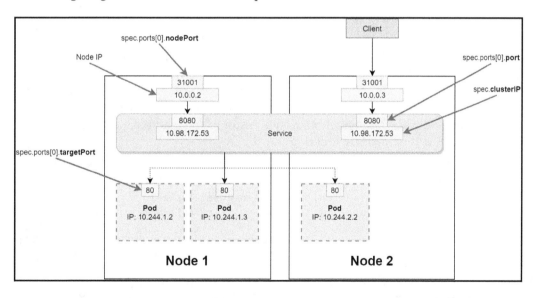

Using a NodePort Service is recommended when you would like to set up your own load-balancing setup in front of the Service. You can also expose the NodePorts directly, but bear in mind that such a solution is harder to secure and may pose security risks.

LoadBalancer

The second type of Service that allows for external ingress communication is LoadBalancer, which is available in Kubernetes clusters that can create external load balancers, for example, managed Kubernetes offerings in the cloud. This type of Service combines the approach of NodePort with an additional external load balancer in front of it, which routes traffic to NodePorts.

You can deploy a LoadBalancer Service using the following manifest file:

```
apiVersion: v1
kind: Service
metadata:
  name: nginx-deployment-example-lb
spec:
  selector:
    environment: test
  type: LoadBalancer
  ports:
  - port: 8080
    protocol: TCP
    targetPort: 80
```

Note that in order to apply this manifest file, you need an environment that supports external load balancers, for example, the AKS cluster that we created in `Chapter 4`, *Kubernetes Concepts and Windows Support*. Katacoda Kubernetes Playground is also capable of creating an "external" load balancer that can be accessed from the Playground terminal. If you attempt to create a LoadBalancer Service in an environment that does not support creating external load balancers, it will result in the load balancer ingress IP address being in the *pending* state indefinitely.

In order to obtain an external load balancer address, execute the following command:

```
PS C:\src> kubectl get svc nginx-deployment-example-lb
NAME                              TYPE            CLUSTER-IP      EXTERNAL-IP
PORT(S)              AGE
nginx-deployment-example-lb       LoadBalancer    10.0.190.215    137.117.227.83
8080:30141/TCP       2m23s
```

The `EXTERNAL-IP` column shows that the load balancer has the IP address `137.117.227.83`, and in order to access your Service you have to communicate with the `137.117.227.83:8080` TCP endpoint. Additionally, you can see that the Service has its own internal ClusterIP , `10.0.190.215`, and NodePort `30141` is exposed. A LoadBalancer Service running on AKS has been visualized in the following diagram:

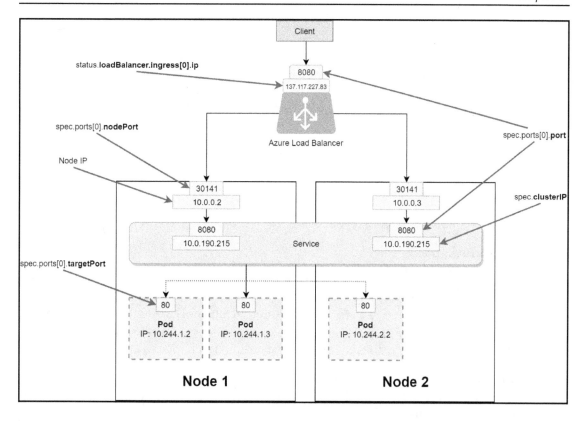

If you are interested in how the Azure Load Balancer in front of the Service is configured, you need to go to `https://portal.azure.com` and navigate to the load balancer resources, where you will find the Kubernetes load balancer instance:

Now, let's take a look at the last type of Service: ExternalName.

ExternalName

In some cases, you need to define a Service that points to an external resource that is not hosted in your Kubernetes cluster. This can include, for example, cloud-hosted database instances. Kubernetes provides a way to abstract communication to such resources and registers them in cluster service discovery by using an ExternalName Service.

ExternalName Services do not use selectors and are just a raw mapping of the Service name to an external DNS name:

```
apiVersion: v1
kind: Service
metadata:
  name: externalname-example-service
spec:
  type: ExternalName
  externalName: cloud.database.example.com
```

During resolution of the Service DNS name (`externalname-example-service.default.svc.cluster.local`), the internal cluster DNS will respond with a CNAME record with a value of `cloud.database.example.com`. There is no actual traffic forwarding using kube-proxy rules involved—the redirection happens at the DNS level.

A good use case for the ExtenalName Service is providing different instances of an external service, for example, a database, depending on the environment type. From the Pods' point of view, this will not require any configuration or connection string changes.

Ingress

LoadBalancer Services only provide L4 load balancing capabilities. This means you cannot use the following:

- HTTPS traffic termination and offloading
- Name-based virtual hosting using the same load balancer for multiple domain names
- Path-based routing to services, for example, as an API gateway

To solve that, Kubernetes provides the Ingress API object (which is not a type of Service), which can be used for L7 load balancing.

Ingress deployment and configuration is a broad topic and is out of scope of this book. You can find more detailed information regarding Ingress and Ingress controllers in the official documentation: `https://kubernetes.io/docs/concepts/services-networking/ingress/`.

Using Ingress requires first the deployment of an Ingress controller in your Kubernetes cluster. An Ingress controller is a Kubernetes controller that is deployed manually to the cluster, most often as a DaemonSet or a deployment that runs dedicated Pods for handling ingress traffic load balancing and smart routing. A commonly used Ingress controller for Kubernetes is **ingress-nginx** (`https://www.nginx.com/products/nginx/kubernetes-ingress-controller`), which is installed in the cluster as a Deployment of an nginx web host with a set of rules for handling Ingress API objects. The Ingress controller is exposed as a Service with a type that depends on the installation. For example, for an AKS cluster that only has Linux nodes, a basic installation of ingress-nginx, exposed as a LoadBalancer Service, can be performed using the following manifests:

```
kubectl apply -f
https://raw.githubusercontent.com/kubernetes/ingress-nginx/master/deploy/st
atic/mandatory.yaml
kubectl apply -f
https://raw.githubusercontent.com/kubernetes/ingress-nginx/master/deploy/st
atic/provider/cloud-generic.yaml
```

In general, the installation of the Ingress controller is dependent on the Kubernetes cluster environment and configuration and has to be adjusted according to your needs. For example, for AKS with Windows nodes, you need to ensure that proper node selectors are used in order to schedule Ingress controller Pods properly.

 You can find the customized nginx Ingress controller definition for AKS with Windows nodes, together with example Services and Ingress definitions, in the official GitHub repository for this book: `https://github.com/PacktPublishing/Hands-On-Kubernetes-on-Windows/tree/master/Chapter05/05_ingress-example`.

When an Ingress controller has been installed in the cluster, the Ingress API Objects may be created and will be handled by the controller. For example, assuming that you have deployed two ClusterIP Services `example-service1` and `example-service2`, the Ingress definition could look as follows:

```
apiVersion: networking.k8s.io/v1beta1
kind: Ingress
metadata:
  name: example-ingress
  annotations:
    nginx.ingress.kubernetes.io/rewrite-target: /
spec:
  rules:
  - http:
      paths:
      - path: /service1
        backend:
          serviceName: example-service1
          servicePort: 80
      - path: /service2
        backend:
          serviceName: example-service2
          servicePort: 80
```

Now, when you perform a HTTP request to `https://<ingressServiceLoadBalancerIp>/service1`, the traffic will be routed by nginx to `example-service1`. Note that you are using only one cloud load balancer for this operation and the actual routing to Kubernetes Services is performed by an Ingress controller using path-based routing.

The principle of this design has been shown in the following diagram:

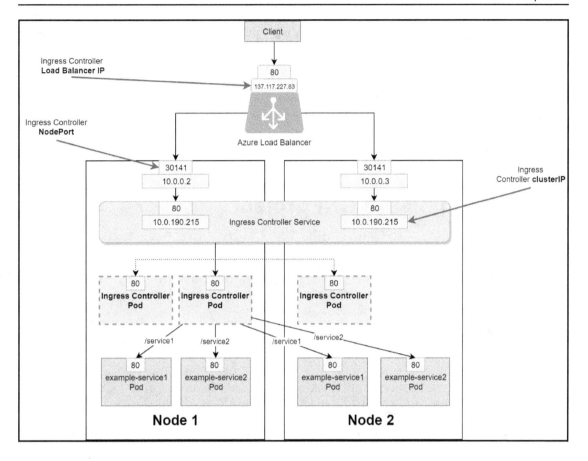

For AKS, you can consider using the HTTP application routing add-on, which automates the management of Ingress controllers and External-DNS controllers for your cluster. More details can be found in the official documentation: `https://docs.microsoft.com/en-us/azure/aks/http-application-routing`.

A general rule of thumb for choosing whether to implement an Ingress or a Service is to use an Ingress for exposing HTTP (and especially HTTPS) endpoints and to use Services for other protocols.

Kubernetes CNI network plugins

In this chapter, we have already mentioned the terms **Container Network Interface** (**CNI**) and **CNI plugins** in the context of Kubernetes networking setup. In fact, CNI is not limited to Kubernetes—this concept originated from the Rkt container runtime and was adopted as a CNCF project aiming to provide a simple and clear interface between any container runtime and network implementation. Container runtimes use CNI plugins in order to connect containers to the network and remove them from the network when needed.

Understanding the CNI project

There are three distinct parts of the CNI project:

- The CNI specification defines the architecture of a generic, plugin-based networking solution for containers and the actual interface that CNI plugins must implement. The specification can be found at `https://github.com/ containernetworking/cni/blob/master/SPEC.md`.
- Libraries for integrating CNI into applications, which is provided in the same repository as the specification: `https://github.com/containernetworking/cni/ tree/master/libcni`.
- CNI plugins reference implementation, which is in a dedicated repository: `https://github.com/containernetworking/plugins`.

The specification of CNI is fairly straightforward, and can be summarized as follows:

- CNI plugins are implemented as stand-alone executables.
- The container runtime is responsible for preparing a new network namespace (or network compartment in the case of Windows) for the container, before interacting with CNI plugins.
- The CNI plugin is responsible for connecting the container to the network, as specified by the network configuration.
- Network configuration is supplied to CNI plugins by the container runtime in JSON format, using standard input.

- Arguments are provided to the CNI plugin using environment variables. For example, the `CNI_COMMAND` variable specifies the operation type that the plugin should perform. The set of commands is limited and consists of `ADD`, `DEL`, `CHECK`, and `VERSION`; the most significant are `ADD` and `DEL`, which add a container to the network and delete it from the network respectively.

For CNI plugins, there are three general types of plugin, which have different responsibilities during network configuration:

- Interface-creating plugins
- **IP Address Management** (**IPAM**) plugins, which are responsible for IP address allocation for containers
- Meta plugins, which may act as adapters for other CNI plugins or provide additional configuration for other CNI plugins or transform their outputs

Currently, on Windows you can only use the following reference implementations: the host-local IPAM plugin, the win-bridge and win-Overlay interface-creating plugins, and the flannel meta plugin. Third-party plugins can be also used; for example, Microsoft provides the Azure-CNI plugin for integrating containers with Azure SDN (`https://github.com/Azure/azure-container-networking/blob/master/docs/cni.md`).

In Kubernetes, CNI plugins are used by kubelet when managing a Pod's life cycle to ensure the connectivity and reachability of the Pod. The most basic operation performed by Kubelet is executing the `ADD` CNI command when a Pod is created and the `DELETE` CNI command when a Pod is destroyed. CNI plugins may be also used for adjusting the kube-proxy configuration in some cases.

Choosing the CNI plugin and defining the network configuration for the CNI plugin is performed during the Pod network add-on installation step when deploying a new cluster. Most commonly, the installation is performed by the deployment of a dedicated DaemonSet, which performs the installation of CNI plugins using init containers and runs additional agent containers on each node if needed. A good example of such an installation is the official Kubernetes manifest for Flannel: `https://github.com/coreos/flannel/blob/master/Documentation/kube-flannel.yml`.

CoreOS Flannel

When working with Linux/Windows hybrid Kubernetes clusters, especially on-premises, you will usually install **Flannel** as a Pod network add-on (`https://github.com/coreos/flannel`). Flannel is a minimalistic L2/L3 virtual network provider for multiple nodes, specifically for Kubernetes and containers. There are three main components in Flannel:

- A **flanneld** (or `flanneld.exe` on Windows machines) agent/daemon running on each node in the cluster, usually deployed as a DaemonSet in Kubernetes. It is responsible for allocating an exclusive subnet lease for each node out of a larger Pod's CIDR. For example, in this chapter, we have been heavily using `10.244.0.0/16` as the Pod CIDR in the cluster and `10.244.1.0/24` or `10.244.2.0/24` as subnet leases for individual nodes. Lease information and node network configuration is stored by `flanneld` using the Kubernetes API or directly in `etcd`. The main responsibility of this agent is synchronizing subnet lease information, configuring the Flannel backend, and exposing the configuration (as a file in the container host filesystem) on the node for other components, such as the Flannel CNI plugin.
- The Flannel **backend**, which defines how the network between Pods is created. Examples of backends supported on both Windows and Linux that we have already used in this chapter are Vxlan and host-gw. You can find more about Flannel backends at `https://github.com/coreos/flannel/blob/master/Documentation/backends.md`.
- The Flannel **CNI plugin**, which is executed by kubelet when adding a Pod to a network or removing a Pod from a network. The Flannel CNI plugin is a meta plugin that uses other interface-creating and IPAM plugins to perform the operations. Its responsibility is to read the subnet information provided by `flanneld`, generate JSON configuration for an appropriate CNI plugin, and execute it. The target plugins choice depends on which backend is used by Flannel; for example, for a vxlan backend on Windows nodes, the Flannel CNI plugin will invoke the host-local IPAM plugin and the win-Overlay plugin. You can find more about this meta plugin in the official documentation: `https://github.com/containernetworking/plugins/tree/master/plugins/meta/flannel`.

Let's take a look at what happens step by step on a Windows node with Flannel running on a vxlan backend—from Flannel agent deployment to Pod creation by kubelet (similar steps occur for Linux nodes but with different target CNI plugins being executed):

1. The `flanneld.exe` agent is deployed to the node as a DaemonSet or is started manually (as the current documentation for Windows suggests).

2. The agent reads the supplied `net-conf.json` file, which contains the Pod CIDR and the vxlan backend configuration:

   ```
   {
       "Network": "10.244.0.0/16",
       "Backend": {
           "Type": "vxlan",
           "VNI": 4096,
           "Port": 4789
       }
   }
   ```

3. The agent acquires a new subnet lease, `10.244.1.0/24`, for the node. Lease information is stored using the Kubernetes API. The `vxlan0` network is created, VTEP devices are created, and routing tables and forwarding database are updated.

4. Information about the subnet lease is written to `C:\run\flannel\subnet.env` in the node filesystem. Here's an example:

   ```
   FLANNEL_NETWORK=10.244.0.0/16
   FLANNEL_SUBNET=10.244.1.0/24
   FLANNEL_MTU=1472
   FLANNEL_IPMASQ=true
   ```

5. Whenever a new node joins the cluster, the `flanneld.exe` agent performs any additional reconfiguration to the routing tables and forwarding database.

6. Now, a new Pod is scheduled on this node and kubelet initializes the pod infra container and executes the ADD command on the Flannel meta CNI plugin with the configuration JSON, which delegates interface creation to the `win-overlay` plugin and IPAM management to the `host-local` plugin. The Flannel CNI plugin generates the configuration JSON based on `subnet.env` and input configuration for these plugins.

7. A new IP is leased using the `host-local` IPAM plugin. Flannel is not responsible for managing the IPAM, it just retrieves a new free IP address from a given subnet on the current node.

8. The `win-bridge` plugin configures the **Host Networking Service (HNS)** endpoint for the Pod and effectively connects the Pod to the Overlay network.

To summarize, Flannel automates the process of L2/Overlay network creation for Pods and maintains the network as new Pods are created or new nodes join the cluster. Currently, the L2 network (the host-gw backend) is considered stable on Windows, whereas the Overlay network (the vxlan backend) on Windows is still in alpha—you will find both of these backends useful when working with on-premises Kubernetes clusters. For AKS and AKS-engine scenarios, the most effective way to install Pod networking is to use the default Azure-CNI plugin.

Windows Server networking in Kubernetes

At a high level, Kubernetes networking for Windows nodes is similar to Linux nodes—kubelet is decoupled from networking operations by CNI. The main differences are in the actual implementation of Windows container networking and in the terminology that is used for Windows containers.

Windows container networking is set up similar to Hyper-V virtual machine networking, and in fact it shares many of the internal services, especially **Host Networking Service (HNS)**, which cooperates with **Host Compute Service (HCS)**, which manages the containers' life cycles. When creating a new Docker container, the container receives its own network namespace (compartment) and a **Virtual Network Interface Controller (vNIC** or in the case of Hyper-V, isolated containers or **vmNIC)** located in this namespace. The vNIC is then connected to a **Hyper-V Virtual Switch (vSwitch)**, which is also connected to the host default network namespace using the host vNIC. You can loosely map this construct to the **container bridge interface** (CBR) in the Linux container world. The vSwitch utilizes Windows Firewall and the **Virtual Filtering Platform (VFP)** Hyper-V vSwitch extension in order to provide network security, traffic forwarding, VXLAN encapsulation, and load balancing. This component is crucial for kube-proxy to provide Services' functionalities, and you can think of VFP as *iptables* from the Linux container world. The vSwitch can be internal (not connected to a network adapter on the container host) or external (connected to a network adapter on the container host); it depends on the container network driver. In the case of Kubernetes, you will be always using network drivers (L2Bridge, Overlay, Transparent) that create an external vSwitch.

 VFP utilizes Windows Kernel functionalities to filter and forward network traffic. Until Kubernetes 1.8, VFP was not supported by kube-proxy, and the only way to forward the traffic was to use **userspace** mode, which does all the traffic management in the user space, not the kernel space.

All of the preceding setup is performed by HNS while a container is being created. HNS is in general responsible for the following:

- Creating virtual networks and vSwitches
- Creating network namespaces (compartments)
- Creating vNICs (endpoints) and placing them inside the container network namespace
- Creating vSwitch ports
- Managing VFP network policies (load-balancing, encapsulation)

In the case of Kubernetes, CNI plugins are the only way to set up container networking (for Linux, it is possible not to use them). They perform the actual communication with HNS and HCS in order to set up the selected networking mode. Kubernetes' networking setup has one significant difference when compared to the standard Docker networking setup: the container vNIC is attached to the pod infra container, and the network namespace is shared between all containers in the Pod. This is the same concept as for Linux Pods.

These constructs are visualized in the following diagram:

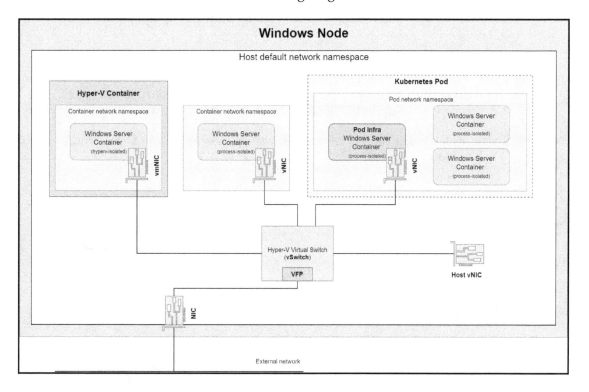

The architecture of Windows container networking for Kubernetes has one more important concept: network drivers (modes). In the next section, we will go through the options and see which of them fit Kubernetes, but first, let's take a quick look at the current limitations of Kubernetes networking on Windows.

Limitations

Windows container networking is constantly evolving, and the implementation of many features is still in progress. Kubernetes has currently a few networking limitations on the Windows platform:

- Host networking mode is not available for Windows Pods.
- Accessing NodePort from the node itself is not supported.
- The IPv6 stack is not supported for L2Bridge, L2Tunnel, and Overlay network drivers.
- ICMP for external networks is not supported. In other words, you will not be able to ping IP addresses outside of your Kubernetes cluster.
- Flannel running on a vxlan backend is restricted to using VNI 4096 and UDP port 4789.
- IPsec encryption for container communication is not supported.
- HTTP proxies are not supported inside containers.
- For Ingress controllers running on Windows nodes, you have to choose a Deployment that supports both Windows and Linux nodes.

You can expect this list to get shorter because new releases of Windows Server and Kubernetes are coming.

Choosing Kubernetes network modes

Network modes (drivers) is a concept from Docker that is a part of the **Container Network Model** (**CNM**). This specification was proposed by Docker to solve container networking setup and management challenges in a modular, pluginable way. Docker's libnetwork is the canonical implementation of the CNM specification.

At this point, you are probably wondering how CNM relates to CNI, which solves a similar problem. Yes, they are competing specifications for container networking! For Linux containers, the implementations of Docker network drivers and CNI can be considerably different. However, for Windows containers, network drivers implemented in libnetwork are a simple shim for HNS that performs all the configuration tasks. CNI plugins, such as win-bridge and win-Overlay, do exactly the same thing: call the HNS API. This means that for Windows, Docker network drivers and CNI plugins are in parity and fully depend on HNS and its native network configurations. If you are interested, you can check out the libnetwork Windows driver implementation and see how it interacts with HNS: `https://github.com/docker/libnetwork/blob/master/drivers/windows/windows.go`.

CNI and CNM have a long history and some significant differences. In the early days of Kubernetes, a decision was made not to use Docker's libnetwork in favor of CNI as an abstraction for container networking management. You can read more about this decision in this Kubernetes blog post: `https://kubernetes.io/blog/2016/01/why-kubernetes-doesnt-use-libnetwork/`. If you are interested in more details about CNI versus CNM, please refer to this article: `https://thenewstack.io/container-networking-landscape-cni-coreos-cnm-docker/`.

In general, for Windows containers, you can use the terms Docker network driver and HNS network driver interchangeably.

There are five HNS network drivers that are currently supported by Windows containers:

- l2bridge
- l2tunnel
- Overlay
- Transparent
- NAT (not used in Kubernetes)

You can create a new Docker network manually using the following command:

```
docker network create -d <networkType> <additionalParameters> <name>
```

Additional parameters are required for some of the network types; you can find more details in the official documentation: `https://docs.microsoft.com/en-us/virtualization/windowscontainers/container-networking/network-drivers-topologies`. The Microsoft SDN repository also provides a simple PowerShell module for interacting with the HNS API, which you can use to analyze your network configuration: `https://github.com/microsoft/SDN/blob/master/Kubernetes/windows/hns.psm1`.

You can find the officially supported networking configurations for Windows containers in the support policy from Microsoft: `https://support.microsoft.com/da-dk/help/4489234/support-policy-for-windows-containers-and-docker-on-premises`.

Let's now go through each type of HNS network to understand how they fit Kubernetes, when to use them, and how they relate to CNI plugins.

L2Bridge

In L2Bridge network mode, containers are connected to a shared external Hyper-V vSwitch, which gives access to the underlay network. Containers also share the same IP subnet as the container host, and the container IP addresses must be statically assigned with the same prefix as the container host IP. MAC addresses are rewritten on ingress and egress to the host's address (this requires MAC spoofing to be enabled; remember this when testing Kubernetes clusters on local Hyper-V VMs).

The following CNI plugins use an L2Bridge network:

- win-bridge
- Azure-CNI
- Flannel with a host-gw backend (as a meta plugin, it invokes win-bridge)

These are the advantages of L2Bridge:

- win-bridge and Flannel (host-gw) are easy to configure
- Stable support in Windows
- Best performance

These are the disadvantages of L2Bridge:

- L2 adjacency between nodes is required

L2Tunnel

L2Tunnel network mode is a special case of L2Bridge in which *all* network traffic from containers is forwarded to the virtualization host in order to apply SDN policies. This network type is intended to be used in Microsoft Cloud Stack only.

The following CNI plugins use L2Tunnel network:

- Azure-CNI

These are the advantages of L2Tunnel:

- Used in AKS and AKS-engine on Azure, and there is stable support.
- You can leverage the features provided by Azure Virtual Network (`https://azure.microsoft.com/en-us/services/virtual-network/`).

These are the disadvantages of L2Tunnel:

- It can only be used on Azure

Overlay

Overlay network mode creates a VXLAN Overlay network using VFP at an external Hyper-V vSwitch. Each Overlay network has its own IP subnet, determined by a customizable IP prefix.

The following CNI plugins use the Overlay network:

- win-Overlay
- Flannel with a vxlan backend (as a meta plugin, it invokes win-Overlay)

These are the advantages of Overlay:

- No limitations in subnet organization.
- No need for L2 adjacency of nodes. You can use this mode in L3 networks.
- Increased security and isolation from the underlay network.

These are the disadvantages of Overlay:

- It's currently in the alpha feature stage on Windows.
- You are restricted to specific VNI (4096) and UDP port (4789).
- Worse performance than L2Bridge.

Transparent

The last HNS network type that is supported in Kubernetes on Windows is Transparent. Containers attached to the Transparent network will be connected to external Hyper-V vSwitch with statically or dynamically assigned IP addresses from the physical network. In Kubernetes, this network type is used for supporting OVN where intra-Pod communication is enabled by logical switches and routers.

The following CNI plugins use the Transparent network:

- ovn-kubernetes

These are the disadvantages of the Transparent network:

- If you would like to use this network type in Kubernetes hosted on-premises, you have to deploy OVN and Open vSwitches, which is a complex task on its own.

Summary

In this chapter, you have learned about the principles of networking in Kubernetes. We have introduced the Kubernetes networking model and the requirements that any model implementation must fulfill. Next, we analyzed the two most important network model implementations from a Windows perspective: the L2 network and Overlay network. In the previous chapter, you were introduced to Service API objects, and in this chapter, you gained a deeper insight into how Services are implemented with regard to the networking model. And eventually, you learned about Kubernetes networking on Windows nodes, CNI plugins, and when to use each plugin type.

The next chapter will focus on interacting with Kubernetes clusters from Windows machines using Kubernetes command-line tools, namely **kubectl**.

Questions

1. What are the requirements for implementing the Kubernetes network model?
2. When can you use Flannel with a host-gw backend in Kubernetes?
3. What is the difference between the ClusterIP and the NodePort Service?
4. What are the benefits of using an Ingress controller over the LoadBalancer Service?

5. What are CNI plugins and how are they used by Kubernetes?
6. What is the difference between internal and external Hyper-V vSwitches?
7. What is the difference between the CNI plugin and a Docker network driver?
8. What is an Overlay network?

You can find answers to these questions in *Assessments* in the back matter of this book.

Further reading

For more information regarding Kubernetes concepts and networking, please refer to the following Packt books and resources:

- The Complete Kubernetes Guide (https://www.packtpub.com/virtualization-and-cloud/complete-kubernetes-guide).
- Getting Started with Kubernetes – Third Edition (https://www.packtpub.com/virtualization-and-cloud/getting-started-kubernetes-third-edition).
- Kubernetes for Developers (https://www.packtpub.com/virtualization-and-cloud/kubernetes-developers).
- Hands-On Kubernetes Networking (video) (https://www.packtpub.com/virtualization-and-cloud/hands-kubernetes-networking-video).
- You can also refer to the excellent official Kubernetes documentation (https://kubernetes.io/docs/concepts/cluster-administration/networking/), which is always the most up-to-date source of knowledge about Kubernetes in general.
- For Windows-specific networking scenarios, the official Microsoft Virtualization documentation is recommended: https://docs.microsoft.com/en-us/virtualization/windowscontainers/kubernetes/network-topologies for Kubernetes and https://docs.microsoft.com/en-us/virtualization/windowscontainers/container-networking/architecture for Windows container networking in general.

6
Interacting with Kubernetes Clusters

As a Kubernetes cluster user or operator, you need to interact with the Kubernetes API to manage Kubernetes Objects or debug applications running in the cluster. Generally, there are two ways to communicate with the Kubernetes API: you can use representational state transfer (RESTful) HTTPS endpoints directly—for example, for programmatic access—or you can use kubectl, which is the Kubernetes command-line tool (or **command-line interface (CLI)**). In general, kubectl wraps RESTful API communication and hides the complexity regarding locating and authenticating to the Kubernetes API server. Operations such as creating or listing Kubernetes Objects and executing into Pod containers are available as neatly organized kubectl sub-commands—you can use these commands when performing ad hoc operations on your cluster or as a part of **continuous integration/continuous deployment (CI/CD)** for your applications.

In this chapter, we will provide you with a better understanding of how to install kubectl on a Windows machine and how to manage multiple Kubernetes clusters using kubectl. You will also learn the most common and useful kubectl commands for managing Kubernetes Objects and debugging containerized applications.

This chapter consists of the following topics:

- Installing Kubernetes command-line tooling
- Accessing Kubernetes clusters
- Working with development clusters
- Looking at common kubectl commands

Technical requirements

For this chapter, you will need the following installed:

- Windows 10 Pro, Enterprise, or Education (version 1903 or later, 64-bit)
- Docker Desktop for Windows 2.0.0.3, or later
- Chocolatey package manager for Windows (`https://chocolatey.org/`)
- The Azure CLI

Installation of Docker Desktop for Windows and system requirements are covered in `Chapter 1`, *Creating Containers*.

Using the Chocolatey package manager is not mandatory, but it makes the installation process and application version management much easier. The installation process is documented here: `https://chocolatey.org/install`.

For the Azure CLI, you can find detailed installation instructions in `Chapter 2`, *Managing State in Containers*.

To follow along using **Azure Kubernetes Service (AKS)**, you will need your own Azure account and AKS instance created. If you haven't already created the account for previous chapters, you can read more about how to obtain a limited free account for personal use here: `https://azure.microsoft.com/en-us/free/`. AKS cluster deployment is covered in `Chapter 4`, *Kubernetes Concepts and Windows Support*. You can also use the PowerShell script provided in that chapter.

You can download the latest code samples for this chapter from the official GitHub repository: `https://github.com/PacktPublishing/Hands-On-Kubernetes-on-Windows/tree/master/Chapter06`.

Installing Kubernetes command-line tooling

Kubectl is available on a variety of operating systems, including Windows. If you have experience with using kubectl on Linux, you can expect that the only difference will be the installation process—the commands and basic principles remain the same. For Windows, you have several options for kubectl installation, as follows:

- Download the kubectl binary directly.

- Use the PowerShell Gallery (`https://www.powershellgallery.com/`).
- Use third-party Windows package managers: Chocolatey (`https://chocolatey.org/`) or Scoop (`https://scoop.sh/`).

> Kubectl can also be installed automatically by Docker Desktop for Windows while creating a local development Kubernetes cluster (executable installed in `C:\Program Files\Docker\Docker\Resources\bin\kubectl.exe`) or using the Azure CLI when creating the AKS cluster instance (using the `az aks install-cli` command, which installs kubectl in `~/.azure-kubectl/kubectl.exe`). This may create conflicts with already installed kubectl instances in different locations—you can always check which kubectl installation is used in PowerShell by using the `(Get-Command kubectl).Path` command. Switching to a different kubectl installation requires the `PATH` environment to be modified and the desired precedence to be ensured.

You can find detailed instructions for all installation types in the official documentation: `https://kubernetes.io/docs/tasks/tools/install-kubectl/`. We will demonstrate how to install kubectl using Chocolatey, as this is the easiest and the most convenient way to install kubectl on Windows. Follow these steps:

1. If you haven't installed the Chocolatey package manager already, you can find the instructions to do so here: `https://chocolatey.org/install`.
2. Open the PowerShell window as Administrator, and install kubectl using the following command:

```
choco install kubernetes-cli
```

3. If you need to upgrade kubectl to the latest version, use the following command:

```
choco upgrade kubernetes-cli
```

4. Verify that kubectl has been installed, using—for example—the following command:

```
kubectl version
```

According to the Kubernetes version skew support policy, you should use a version of kubectl that is within one minor version (older or newer) of kube-apiserver. For example, kubectl 1.15 is guaranteed to work with kube-apiserver 1.14, 1.15, and 1.16. It is advised that you use the latest kubectl version for your cluster whenever possible.

Please note that the version of kubectl installed from Chocolatey may sometimes be older than the latest available stable version. In this case, if you need the latest stable version, follow the instructions for downloading the kubectl binary directly.

In the next section, we are going to demonstrate how you can organize access to multiple Kubernetes clusters.

Accessing Kubernetes clusters

By default, kubectl uses the `kubeconfig` file located in `~\.kube\config` (note that we call it `kubeconfig`, but the filename is `config`), which on Windows machines expands to `C:\Users\<currentUser>\.kube\config`. This YAML configuration file contains all the parameters required for kubectl to connect to the Kubernetes API for your cluster. This configuration file may be also used by different tools than kubectl—for example, *Helm*.

You can use the `KUBECONFIG` environment variable or the `--kubeconfig` flag for individual commands to force kubectl to use a different `kubeconfig`. For the `KUBECONFIG` environment variable, it is possible to specify multiple `kubeconfig` and merge them in runtime. You can read more about this feature in the official documentation: `https://kubernetes.io/docs/concepts/configuration/organize-cluster-access-kubeconfig/#merging-kubeconfig-files`. Please note that, for Windows, you should specify `KUBECONFIG` paths separated by a semicolon, contrary to Linux, where you use a colon.

Coordinating access to multiple Kubernetes clusters is organized in `kubeconfig` using contexts. Each context contains the following information:

- **Cluster**: The address of the Kubernetes API server.
- **User**: The name of the user, which maps to user credentials (specified in `kubeconfig`).
- **Namespace**: Optionally, you can provide the default namespace to use.

If you have been following the previous chapters, where we demonstrated the installation of Minikube and the local Kubernetes cluster in Docker Desktop for Windows, you have already used contexts that have been automatically added during installation of these clusters. When using kubectl, there is always one context marked as current. You can see the current context using the following command:

```
PS C:\src> kubectl config current-context
minikube
```

Listing all of the available contexts in your kubeconfig can be done in the following way:

```
PS C:\src> kubectl config get-contexts
CURRENT   NAME                          CLUSTER               AUTHINFO
NAMESPACE
          aks-windows-cluster   aks-windows-cluster   clusterUser_aks-
windows-resource-group_aks-windows-cluster
          docker-desktop        docker-desktop        docker-desktop
          docker-for-desktop    docker-desktop        docker-desktop
*         minikube              minikube              minikube
```

If you would like to switch to a different context, for example, docker-desktop, execute the following command:

```
PS C:\src> kubectl config use-context docker-desktop
Switched to context "docker-desktop".
```

You can modify the existing contexts or add your own contexts manually from the command line. For example, the following command will add a new context, docker-desktop-kube-system, which will connect to the docker-desktop cluster and use the kube-system namespace by default:

```
kubectl config set-context docker-desktop-kube-system `
        --cluster docker-desktop `
        --user docker-desktop `
        --namespace kube-system
```

When you switch to the new context and run any command, for example, kubectl get pods, it will be executed against the kube-system namespace.

At any given time, you can override the current context settings using --cluster, --user, --namespace, or even --context flags for kubectl commands.

Typically, when working with managed Kubernetes providers or local development tools, the config will be either served as a separate file to download and use via the KUBECONFIG environment variable, or merged directly into the current kubeconfig as a new context (this is what the az aks get-credentials command does, in the case of AKS). If needed, you can perform merging of kubeconfigs manually, using the following PowerShell command:

```
$env:KUBECONFIG="c:\path\to\config;~\.kube\config"
kubectl config view --raw
```

The output of this command can be used as a new default kubeconfig—you should verify if the result is valid before overwriting the default configuration file. You can use the following code snippet to overwrite the default kubeconfig with a merged one:

```
$env:KUBECONFIG="c:\path\to\config;~\.kube\config"
kubectl config view --raw > ~\.kube\config_new
Move-Item -Force ~\.kube\config_new ~\.kube\config
```

Remember about the kubeconfig merging precedence rules: the value in the first file wins if the same key is found in both files.

Now you know how to manage access to Kubernetes clusters using kubeconfig and kubectl contexts, let's focus on strategies for working with development clusters.

Working with development clusters

Developing applications for Kubernetes introduces some unique challenges that are not present for classical development pipelines. The perfect solution would be introducing minimal changes to the pipelines and processes, but, unfortunately, it is not as simple as that. First of all, you need to maintain a development Kubernetes cluster where you deploy, test, and debug your applications. Secondly, you have to containerize your applications and deploy them to the dev cluster, possibly with more flexibility and access than in a secure production cluster.

Informally, for Kubernetes applications development, you have four modes (concepts) that have been illustrated in the following diagram:

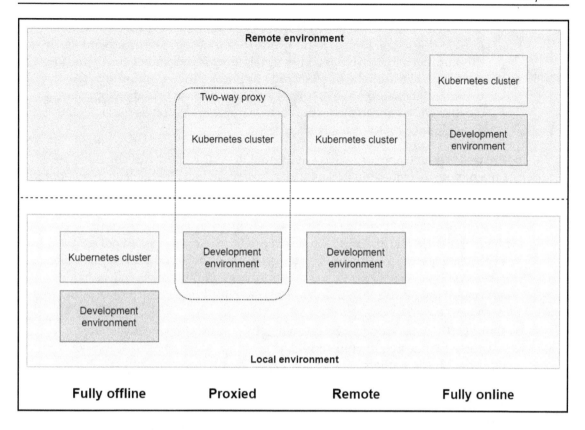

Let's have a look at these four modes:

- **Fully offline**: In a fully offline (local) environment, your development environment and Kubernetes cluster are hosted locally on your machine. A good example of such a configuration is a Minikube or Docker Desktop for Windows local Kubernetes cluster. In both cases, the Kubernetes cluster is hosted in a dedicated local **virtual machine** (**VM**). This development workflow requires the building of Docker images, pushing them to an image registry (local or remote), and using kubectl to deploy the application. You can, of course, leverage the fact that the cluster is running locally, and log in to the cluster nodes and debug the Pod containers. From a Windows containers' perspective, this requires running a full, hybrid Linux/Windows Kubernetes cluster on Hyper-V VMs. This setup requires a local machine that is capable of running at least two VMs: one for the Linux master and one for the Windows worker node. We will be deploying a fully functional hybrid cluster in Chapter 7, *Deploying Hybrid On-Premises Kubernetes Cluster*.

The deployment strategies that are presented in the next chapters can be used for both development and production clusters. The disadvantage of this approach for development is the significant amount of configuration compared to Minikube or other fully offline solutions. Unfortunately, at this point, there are no easy turnkey solutions for hybrid development clusters—if you need a cluster for development as soon as possible, the fully managed AKS is the best option.

- **Proxied**: When using a proxied environment, your Kubernetes cluster is hosted on a remote machine (but it can be also hosted on local VMs!). The development environment is still on your local machine, but you have a two-way network proxy configured so that you can run and debug your applications as if you were "inside" of a Pod in the cluster. In other words, you can simplify your development workflow and skip Docker overhead for development and debugging scenarios. This can be achieved using tools such as Telepresence (`https://www.telepresence.io/`). Unfortunately, Windows is currently supported only through Windows Subsystem for Linux, which means that there is no native Windows support.
- **Remote**: The next mode is remote, whereby you develop locally against a remote cluster, either hosted in your local data center or as a managed Kubernetes offering. This is similar to using a fully offline environment, but you have to beware of extra costs of using managed Kubernetes clusters and limited access to Kubernetes nodes. For Windows, if you are running AKS, you will not be able to log in to the Linux master, but, if you are deploying using AKS engine on bare Azure VMs, you can access both the Linux master and the Windows nodes. The advantage of this environment type is that you can leverage all cloud integrations for Kubernetes, such as LoadBalancer Services or Cloud Volumes. We will be covering AKS engine deployment in `Chapter 8`, *Deploying Hybrid Azure Kubernetes Service Cluster*.
- **Fully Online**: In fully online mode, your development environment, together with the Kubernetes cluster, is hosted remotely. Good examples of such an approach are Eclipse Che (`https://www.eclipse.org/che/docs/`) and Azure Dev Spaces (`https://docs.microsoft.com/en-us/azure/dev-spaces/about`), which fully integrates with Visual Studio Code. Support for Windows nodes is still in development at this point and requires manual configuration (`https://docs.microsoft.com/en-us/azure/dev-spaces/how-to/run-dev-spaces-windows-containers`). In the future, this is the best candidate for offering a seamless Kubernetes development life cycle for Windows containers. We will cover Azure Dev Spaces in `Chapter 12`, *Development Workflow with Kubernetes*.

There are many tools that can boost your Kubernetes application development productivity and reduce the overhead of having "another cluster in the middle of everything". For example, for Windows support, you may want to check out Azure Draft (`https://draft.sh/`), which simplifies the development pipeline using auto-generated Helm charts for your application, or ksync (`https://ksync.github.io/ksync/`), which can be used for syncing your local code/binary changes to Pod containers, without a need for redeployment.

In the next section, we will take a quick look at the most common and useful kubectl commands that you should have in your toolbox.

Looking at common kubectl commands

Kubectl is a powerful tool that provides most of the functionalities you will ever need when interacting with Kubernetes clusters. All of the kubectl commands follow the same syntax, as shown in the following code snippet:

```
kubectl [command] [type] [name] [flags]

# Example:
kubectl get service kube-dns --namespace kube-system
```

`[command]`, `[type]`, `[name]`, and `[flags]` are defined as follows:

- `[command]` specifies the operation—for example `get`, `apply`, `delete`.
- `[type]` is the resource type (a detailed list can be found in the documentation: `https://kubernetes.io/docs/reference/kubectl/overview/#resource-types`), specified in singular, plural, or abbreviated form (case-insensitive)—for example, `service`, `services`, `svc`. You can find more information about each resource by using the `kubectl explain [type]` command.
- `[name]` determines the name of the resource (case-sensitive). If the command allows the name to be omitted, the operation will be applied to all resources of a given type.
- `[flags]` specifies the additional flags, which are either specific for a command or global for kubectl—for example, `--namespace kube-system`.

You can always use `kubectl help` or `kubectl [command] --help` to access comprehensive documentation on how each command works and what the available flags are. The official reference for kubectl can be found here: `https://kubernetes.io/docs/reference/generated/kubectl/kubectl-commands`.

The terms *resource* and *object* are often used in Kubernetes interchangeably, although there are some differences considering Kubernetes internals. Objects are Kubernetes system entities (abstract concepts), whereas resources are the actual RESTful API resources that provide a representation of objects.

Some of the commands, such as `get` or `create`, allow you to specify the output format using the `-o` or `--output` flag. For example, you can use `-o json` to force JSON output format, or `-o jsonpath=<template>` to extract information using JSONPath templates. This is especially useful when implementing automation based on kubectl commands. You can find more information about output types here: `https://kubernetes.io/docs/reference/kubectl/overview/#output-options`.

For *Bash* and *Zsh*, you can increase your kubectl productivity by using autocompletion (`https://kubernetes.io/docs/tasks/tools/install-kubectl/#enabling-shell-autocompletion`). For Windows, there is no autocompletion support for PowerShell yet, but, if you manage your Kubernetes cluster using Windows Subsystem for Linux, you can install Bash autocompletion as well.

Creating resources

In `Chapter 4`, *Kubernetes Concepts and Windows Support*, we have explained the ideas behind *imperative* and *declarative* resource management in Kubernetes. In short, when using imperative management, you rely on commands that create, delete, and replace resources (think of commands in a script). On the other hand, in declarative management, you only describe the desired state of a resource, and Kubernetes performs all the required actions to transform the current state of a resource to the desired one.

Creating a Kubernetes resource in an imperative way can be done using the `kubectl create -f <manifestFile>` command. For the declarative way, you have to use `kubectl apply -f <manifestFile>`. Note that you can apply the `-R` flag and process a directory *recursively* instead of a single file. Let's demonstrate this on an example Deployment manifest file for Linux nginx Pods, which you can download from the GitHub repository for this book: `https://github.com/PacktPublishing/Hands-On-Kubernetes-on-Windows/blob/master/Chapter06/01_deployment-example/nginx-deployment.yaml`.

Assuming that you saved the manifest file as `nginx-deployment.yaml` in the current directory, use PowerShell to execute the following command to create a `nginx-deployment-example` Deployment:

```
kubectl create -f .\nginx-deployment.yaml
```

You can use the URL for manifest files directly in kubectl—for example, `kubectl create -f https://raw.githubusercontent.com/PacktPublishing/Hands-On-Kubernetes-on-Windows/master/Chapter06/01_deployment-example/nginx-deployment.yaml`. Remember to always verify the contents of the manifest file, especially from a security perspective, before deploying them to your cluster.

You can achieve the same using the `kubectl apply` command, as follows:

```
kubectl apply -f .\nginx-deployment.yaml
```

At this point, these commands behave in the same way: they just create the Deployment. But now, if you modify the `nginx-deployment.yaml` file so that the number of replicas is increased to 4, check what happens for the `kubectl create` and `kubectl apply` commands:

```
PS C:\src> kubectl create -f .\nginx-deployment.yaml
Error from server (AlreadyExists): error when creating ".\\nginx-deployment.yaml": deployments.apps "nginx-deployment-example" already exists

PS C:\src> kubectl apply -f .\nginx-deployment.yaml
deployment.apps/nginx-deployment-example configured
```

Creating the Deployment imperatively is not possible because it has been already created—you would have to replace it. In the case of a declarative `apply` command, the change has been accepted, and the existing Deployment has been scaled to 4 replicas.

For declarative management, kubectl offers the `kubectl diff` command, which shows the difference between the current state of resources in the cluster and in the manifest file. Note that you need to have the `diff` tool in your `PATH` environment variable or use any other file-compare tool—for example, Meld (`http://meldmerge.org/`)—and specify it using the `KUBECTL_EXTERNAL_DIFF` environment variable. Increase the number of `replicas` to 5 in `nginx-deployment.yaml`, and check the comparison result, as follows:

```
$env:KUBECTL_EXTERNAL_DIFF="meld"
kubectl diff -f .\nginx-deployment.yaml
```

You can immediately see in the following screenshot which properties will be affected if you execute `kubectl apply`:

A general rule of thumb is that you should stick to declarative resource management whenever possible and leave imperative commands only for development/hacking scenarios. For fully declarative management of your Kubernetes applications, consider kubectl with Kustomize. You can read more about this approach at: https://kubernetes. io/docs/tasks/manage-kubernetes-objects/kustomization/.

Deleting resources

In order to delete resources, you can use the `kubectl delete [type] [name]` command. This is also one of the imperative commands that are still recommended to be used in declarative cluster management, as it is more explicit. Using `kubectl apply` with the `--prune` flag is more dangerous, as you can accidentally delete more resources.

Use the following command to delete the `nginx-deployment-example` Deployment:

```
kubectl delete deployment nginx-deployment-example
```

You can specify the `--all` flag instead of the resource name if you want to delete all resources of a given type.

Describing and listing resources

The next command that you will often use is `kubectl get [type] [name]`, which shows detailed information about resource(s) of a given type. For example, in order to list Pods in the default namespace for the current context, execute the following command:

```
kubectl get pods
```

You can use the `--all-namespaces` or `--namespace=<namespace>` global flags, which allow you to show resources from other namespaces, as illustrated in the following code snippet:

```
kubectl get pods --all-namespaces
```

By default, this command shows limited, predefined columns. You can see more details by using the `-o wide` flag, as follows:

```
kubectl get pods -o wide
```

In some cases, you will find it useful to watch resources. The following command lists all the Pods and periodically refreshes the view with the latest data:

```
kubectl get pods --watch
```

There is also a different command, `kubectl describe`, which can be used for showing resource details, as illustrated in the following code snippet:

```
kubectl describe pod nginx-deployment-example-7f5cfc59d6-2bvvx
```

The difference between the `get` and `describe` commands is that `get` shows a pure representation of a resource from Kubernetes API, whereas `describe` prepares a detailed description, including events, controllers, and other resources.

`kubectl get` supports different outputs than tables—for example, `-o json` or `-o yaml`, which are good for integrations with other tools or dumping a resource state to file, as illustrated in the following code snippet:

```
kubectl get pod nginx-deployment-example-7f5cfc59d6-2bvvx -o yaml
```

If you need more processing of the output, you can use JSONPath (https://github.com/json-path/JsonPath), which is integrated into kubectl. For example, the following expression will list all container images being used in Pods in the cluster:

```
kubectl get pods --all-namespaces -o
jsonpath="{.items[*].spec.containers[*].image}"
```

And lastly, you may find it useful to list all resources from all namespaces with just a single command, as follows:

```
kubectl get all --all-namespaces
```

This should always give you a good overview of what is happening in the cluster!

Editing resources

As mentioned earlier in this section, imperative editing of Kubernetes resources is generally discouraged. `kubectl edit` is a combination of `kubectl get`, opening your favourite text editor, and `kubectl apply` of the modified manifest file, as illustrated in the following code block:

```
kubectl edit deployment nginx-deployment-example
```

On a Windows machine, this command will open `notepad.exe` (or any other editor, if you specify the `EDITOR` or `KUBE_EDITOR` environment variables) with the current state of `nginx-deployment-example`. After editing, save the file, close the editor, and your changes will be applied.

Another approach is using patches, which can be used in declarative management. `kubectl patch` updates a resource by merging the current resource state and a patch that contains only the modified properties. A common use case for patching is when you need to enforce a node selector for an existing DaemonSet in hybrid Linux/Windows clusters. The following JSON patch can be used for ensuring that a DaemonSet such as Flannel or kube-proxy is running only on Linux nodes:

```
{
    "spec": {
        "template": {
            "spec": {
                "nodeSelector": {
                    "beta.kubernetes.io/os": "linux"
                }
            }
        }
    }
}
```

It is possible to use YAML patches as well, but, unfortunately, due to PowerShell escaping rules, we cannot demonstrate this for the `beta.kubernetes.io/os` selector. JSON still requires additional preprocessing in PowerShell.

In order to apply this patch to an `nginx-deployment-example` Deployment, save the patch as a `linux-node-selector.json` file and run the following command:

```
$patch = $(cat .\linux-node-selector.json)
$patch = $patch.replace('"', '\"')
kubectl patch deployment nginx-deployment-example --patch "$patch"
```

You can find more about the patching of resources and merge types in the official documentation: `https://kubernetes.io/docs/tasks/run-application/update-api-object-kubectl-patch/`.

Running an ad hoc Pod

In debugging scenarios, you may find it useful to run an ad hoc Pod and attach to it. You can perform this using the `kubectl run` command—note that this command can generate different resources, but all generators apart from the Pod are deprecated. The following snippet will create a `busybox-debug` Pod with one `busybox` container, and run an interactive Bourne shell session in the container:

```
kubectl run --generator=run-pod/v1 busybox-debug -i --tty --image=busybox --rm --restart=Never -- sh
```

When the shell prompt appears, you can perform actions from inside of the cluster—for example, pinging internal IPs. When you exit the shell, the container will be automatically removed.

You can use a similar approach to create an interactive PowerShell Pod for Windows nodes.

Accessing Pod container logs

Container logs provide crucial information when debugging applications running on Kubernetes. You can access Pod container logs using the `kubectl logs` command, similar to how you would for the Docker CLI, as follows:

```
kubectl logs etcd-docker-desktop -n kube-system
```

This will work if the Pod is running only one container. If the Pod consists of more than one container, you need to use the `--container` or the `--all-containers` flag.

Additionally, you may want to tail n last lines of logs (`--tail=n` flag) and enable live streaming of logs (`--follow` flag), as illustrated in the following code snippet:

```
kubectl logs etcd-docker-desktop -n kube-system --tail=10 --follow
```

Execcing into a Pod container

When debugging applications running on Kubernetes, you can `exec` into containers running in Pods, just as for bare Docker containers. For example, to list all files in the current working directory of the container, use the following `kubectl exec` command:

```
kubectl exec nginx-deployment-example-5997d7d5fb-p9fbn -- ls -al
```

It is possible to attach an interactive Terminal and run a Bash session too, as follows:

```
kubectl exec nginx-deployment-example-5997d7d5fb-p9fbn -it bash
```

For multi-container Pods, you have to use the `--container` flag, or the first container in the Pod will be chosen.

Copying Pod container files

Kubectl gives you the possibility to copy files between your machine and Pod containers (in both ways), analogously to the Docker CLI. For example, to copy the `/var/log/dpkg.log` file from a container running in the `nginx-deployment-example-5997d7d5fb-p9fbn` Pod to your current directory, execute the `kubectl cp` command, as follows:

```
kubectl cp nginx-deployment-example-5997d7d5fb-p9fbn:/var/log/dpkg.log
dpkg.log
```

In general, if you use a Pod container as a source or destination, you need to specify the Pod name and container filesystem path, separated by a colon (`:`). As for other commands, if the Pod is running multiple containers, you need to use the `--container` flag or the first container will be chosen.

Port forwarding and proxying traffic

Kubectl can act as a simple proxy for accessing your Kubernetes cluster. Use port forwarding to Pods if you need to directly communicate from your local machine to a given port on the Pod. This is achieved without manually exposing Service Objects by using the `kubectl port-forward` command. The command can be used for forwarding to an automatically selected Pod based on other Objects selectors—for example, Deployment, as follows:

```
kubectl port-forward deployment/nginx-deployment-example 7000:80
```

This command will forward all traffic from your local machine port 7000 to port 80 for one Pod in an `nginx-deployment-example` Deployment. Navigate to `http://localhost:7000` to verify that the default nginx page is accessible. Terminate the port-forwarding command when you are done.

Additionally, kubectl can provide access to the Kubernetes API server for your local machine. Use the `kubectl proxy` command to expose the API at port 8080, as follows:

```
kubectl proxy --port=8080
```

Now, when you navigate to `http://localhost:8080/api/v1/namespaces/default/pods` in your browser, you will see the Pod Objects that are currently running in the cluster. Congratulations—you have successfully set up kubectl port forwarding!

Summary

In this chapter, you have learned how to install and use the Kubernetes command-line tool, kubectl. We have covered how to organize accessing multiple Kubernetes clusters using kubectl contexts, what are the possible strategies for working with development clusters, and how they fit Windows clusters. On top of that, you now know the basic kubectl commands and a few techniques that can be used for debugging applications running on Kubernetes: running ad hoc Pods, accessing Pod container logs, performing exec into a Pod container, and copying files between your local machine and the Pod container.

The next chapter will focus on the deployment of hybrid Linux/Windows Kubernetes clusters in on-premises scenarios. We will demonstrate how to create a fully functional, multi-node cluster on your local machine using Hyper-V VMs.

Questions

1. What is `kubeconfig`?
2. How would you set up a custom `kubeconfig` location for kubectl?
3. What is the role of context in kubectl?
4. What is the difference between `kubectl create` and `kubectl apply` commands?
5. What is a kubectl resource patch, and when would you use it?
6. What is the command to show live logs from a Pod container?
7. How would you copy a file between your local machine and a Pod container using kubectl?

You can find answers to these questions in *Assessments* of this book.

Further reading

- For more information regarding Kubernetes concepts and the Kubernetes CLI, please refer to the following Packt books:
    - *The Complete Kubernetes Guide* (`https://www.packtpub.com/virtualization-and-cloud/complete-kubernetes-guide`)
    - *Getting Started with Kubernetes – Third Edition* (`https://www.packtpub.com/virtualization-and-cloud/getting-started-kubernetes-third-edition`)
    - *Kubernetes for Developers* (`https://www.packtpub.com/virtualization-and-cloud/kubernetes-developers`)
- You can also refer to the excellent official Kubernetes documentation (`https://kubernetes.io/docs/home/`) and the kubectl reference documentation (`https://kubernetes.io/docs/reference/generated/kubectl/kubectl-commands`).

Section 3: Creating Windows Kubernetes Clusters

3

This section focuses on advanced topics around creating (provisioning and deploying) hybrid Linux/Windows Kubernetes clusters with Linux masters and Windows nodes. The chapters cover deployment in on-premises and cloud (Azure) scenarios.

This section contains the following chapters:

- Chapter 7, *Deploying a Hybrid On-Premises Kubernetes Cluster*
- Chapter 8, *Deploying a Hybrid Azure Kubernetes Service Engine Cluster*

Deploying a Hybrid On-Premises Kubernetes Cluster

In the previous chapters, we have focused on Docker and Kubernetes concepts from a more theoretical standpoint—now, it is time to utilize this knowledge and deploy a Kubernetes cluster from scratch. The goal of this chapter is to have a fully functional, hybrid Windows/Linux Kubernetes cluster in an on-premises environment.

Depending on your needs, you may use this approach to create a minimalistic local development cluster (one Linux **virtual machine** (**VM**)) acting as master and one Windows VM acting as node) or to deploy a production-grade on-premises cluster with Linux and Windows nodes. You are not limited to Hyper-V clusters—this approach can be used for bare-metal machines, VMware clusters, or VMs running in the cloud. Using kubeadm to create Kubernetes clusters gives you the flexibility to deploy the cluster anywhere, as long as the proper networking is set up and the machines are capable of running containerized workloads.

We also recommend using kubeadm as it is a low-level tool that gives a lot of insight into how the cluster is actually created. In the future, you can expect other solutions built on top of kubeadm (such as Kubespray), which supports hybrid clusters. But even then, it is still advised to try a pure kubeadm approach to learn the baseline steps for Kubernetes cluster Deployment.

This chapter covers the following topics:

- Preparing the Hyper-V environment
- Creating a Kubernetes master node using kubeadm
- Installing the Kubernetes network
- Preparing VMs for Windows nodes
- Joining Windows nodes using kubeadm
- Deploying and inspecting your first application

Technical requirements

For this chapter, you will need the following:

- Windows 10 Pro, Enterprise, or Education (version 1903 or later, 64-bit); a Hyper-V host with at least 16 GB RAM (maybe less, if you choose not to install Desktop Experience for Windows Server and Ubuntu Server VMs). You may use any other Windows or Windows Server edition that has Hyper-V available. For Hyper-V, you need the **Intel Virtualization Technology (Intel VT)** or **AMD Virtualization (AMD-V)** technology feature enabled in **Basic Input/Output System (BIOS)**.

> Note: Windows 10 Home cannot be used as a Hyper-V host.

- A minimum of 15 GB disk space for the Linux master VM and 30 GB disk space for each Windows node VM.
- Ubuntu Server 18.04 **Long-Term Support (LTS) International Standards Organization (ISO)** (http://releases.ubuntu.com/18.04.3/ubuntu-18.04.3-live-server-amd64.iso).
- Windows Server 2019 (**Long-Term Servicing Channel (LTSC)**, Desktop Experience available) ISO or Windows Server 1903 (**Semi-Annual Channel (SAC)**, no Desktop Experience) ISO. You should check https://kubernetes.io/docs/setup/production-environment/windows/intro-windows-in-kubernetes/ for the latest recommendations regarding the current Windows Server version. You can obtain evaluation ISOs from the Microsoft Evaluation Center (https://www.microsoft.com/en-us/evalcenter/evaluate-windows-server-2019), or, if you have a Visual Studio subscription (https://my.visualstudio.com/Downloads/Featured), you can download ISOs for development and testing purposes.
- Kubectl installed—the installation process has been covered in Chapter 6, *Interacting with Kubernetes Clusters*.

You can download the latest code samples for this chapter from the official GitHub repository at: https://github.com/PacktPublishing/Hands-On-Kubernetes-on-Windows/tree/master/Chapter07.

Preparing the Hyper-V environment

The first step in a cluster Deployment is preparing the Hyper-V host for Kubernetes master and node VMs.

 If you choose to use a different hypervisor or use bare-metal machines, you may skip this section.

Now, if you have already installed Docker Desktop for Windows on your machine in the previous chapters, then Hyper-V is enabled and configured. All you need is to create an internal **Network Address Translation (NAT)** or an external Hyper-V **Virtual Switch (vSwitch)**, and you are ready to go.

The following diagram shows the design of the cluster that we are going to deploy in this chapter. Bear in mind that the master is *not* configured to be **highly available (HA)**—HA setup is independent of Windows containers' support and you can perform it when preparing Linux master node(s), according to the official documentation (`https://kubernetes.io/docs/setup/production-environment/tools/kubeadm/high-availability/`):

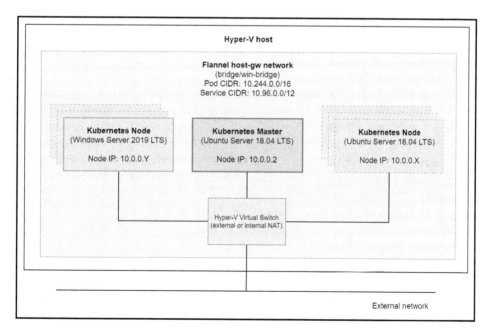

The minimal deployment is an Ubuntu Server 18.04 LTS Kubernetes master (with the possibility to schedule application Pods) with one Windows Server 2019 LTS Kubernetes node. Optionally, you may decide to deploy more Windows and Linux nodes (marked with dotted lines in the diagram), following the same instructions or cloning the VMs.

Enabling Hyper-V

First, let's enable the Hyper-V feature if you haven't enabled it previously, as follows:

1. Open the PowerShell window as Administrator.
2. Execute the following command to enable the Hyper-V feature:

   ```
   Enable-WindowsOptionalFeature -Online -FeatureName Microsoft-Hyper-
   V -All
   ```

3. Reboot the machine.

 If you are using Windows Server as your Hyper-V host, the instructions for enabling the Hyper-V role can be found in the official documentation at: https://docs.microsoft.com/en-us/windows-server/ virtualization/hyper-v/get-started/install-the-hyper-v-role-on- windows-server.

Now, depending on your networking setup, you have to create an appropriate Hyper-V vSwitch. You have two options:

1. **Internal NAT Hyper-V vSwitch**: Use this option if you plan to use the cluster for local development only. Any external inbound communication (apart from your Hyper-V host machine) will require NAT. This option is preferred for a simple Windows 10 development setup, as in most cases you are connected to an external network (Ethernet or Wi-Fi) that does not allow you to manage **Dynamic Host Configuration Protocol** (**DHCP**) and **Domain Name System** (**DNS**) on your own. In other words, if you use an external vSwitch, you will end up with non-predictable IP address assignments for your nodes. Without DNS, you will be not able to ensure proper Kubernetes cluster connectivity.

2. **External Hyper-V vSwitch**: Use this option if your network has a DHCP and DNS server that you (or the network administrator) can manage. This will be the case in most production deployments. You need then to assign appropriate **media access control** (**MAC**) addresses for your VMs in order to receive the desired IP address.

We will follow the convention that the default gateway for the network is `10.0.0.1`, the master node has the IP address `10.0.0.2`, and nodes have subsequent IP addresses `10.0.0.X`.

Creating an internal NAT Hyper-V vSwitch

In order to create the internal NAT vSwitch, perform the following steps:

1. Open the PowerShell window as Administrator.
2. Execute the following command to create an internal vSwitch named `Kubernetes NAT Switch`:

   ```
   New-VMSwitch -SwitchName "Kubernetes NAT Switch" -SwitchType
   Internal
   ```

3. Find the `ifIndex` of the vSwitch you have just created. `ifIndex` will be needed for NAT gateway creation. You can do this by running the following command:

   ```
   Get-NetAdapter
   ```

   The following screenshot shows the output of the preceding command:

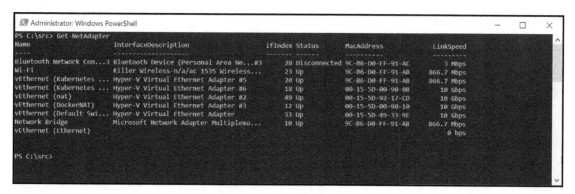

4. Configure the NAT gateway, as follows:

   ```
   New-NetIPAddress -IPAddress 10.0.0.1 -PrefixLength 8 -
   InterfaceIndex <ifIndex>
   ```

5. Create a new NAT network, `Kubernetes NAT Network`, as follows:

   ```
   New-NetNAT -Name "Kubernetes NAT Network" -
   InternalIPInterfaceAddressPrefix 10.0.0.0/8
   ```

If you are using an internal NAT vSwitch, you must provide a static IP address, a gateway IP address, and DNS server information for each VM. The static IP address must be within the range of the NAT internal prefix.

Please note that currently, you can have only one custom internal NAT vSwitch in your system. You can read more in the official documentation at: `https://docs.microsoft.com/en-us/virtualization/hyper-v-on-windows/user-guide/setup-nat-network`.

Creating an external Hyper-V vSwitch

Alternatively, in order to create an external vSwitch, perform the following steps:

1. Use the **Start** menu to launch the Hyper-V Manager.
2. Click **Virtual Switch Manager...** from the **Actions** tab, select **External**, and click **Create Virtual Switch**.
3. Use the name `Kubernetes External Switch` and choose the network adapter that you use for connecting to the internet—for example, your Wi-Fi adapter, as illustrated in the following screenshot:

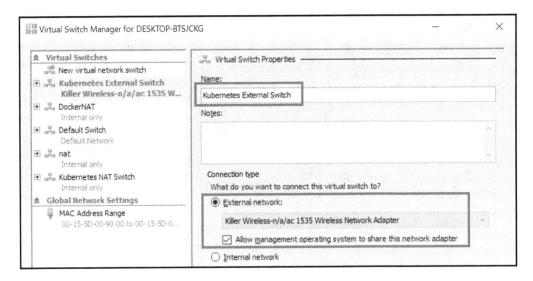

4. Click **OK** to accept the changes.

Now, with the Hyper-V environment ready, you can proceed to the next step—creating the Kubernetes master node running on the Ubuntu Server 18.04 LTS VM.

Creating a Kubernetes master node using kubeadm

For hybrid Windows/Linux Kubernetes clusters, you need to deploy a Linux master—this step remains almost the same as for Linux-only Kubernetes clusters, and you can use any supported operating system for this purpose. We have chosen Ubuntu Server 18.04 LTS as it is widely supported (officially and by the community), has a straightforward installation process, and is easy to manage.

 Instructions in this chapter focus on adding Windows nodes to the Kubernetes cluster. Master preparation steps are minimal. If you are deploying a development cluster on your local machine, using kubeadm to deploy a single control plane in your cluster is sufficient. For production deployments, you should consider deploying an HA master configuration. You can read more about HA and kubeadm at: `https://kubernetes.io/docs/setup/production-environment/tools/kubeadm/high-availability/`.

If you haven't already downloaded the ISO image for Ubuntu Server 18.04 LTS, the official image can be found at: `http://releases.ubuntu.com/18.04.3/ubuntu-18.04.3-live-server-amd64.iso`.

Creating a VM and installing Ubuntu Server

This subsection will guide you through the following steps, which will prepare a new VM with Ubuntu Server:

1. Creating the VM
2. Installing Ubuntu Server
3. Configuring the network
4. Installing additional packages for integration with Hyper-V
5. Setting up a passwordless **Secure Shell (SSH)** login

Creating the VM

First, you need to create a VM that will be used as the master node, running Ubuntu Server 18.04. To do that, open the Hyper-V Manager application and perform the following steps:

1. From the **Actions** menu, choose **New** and click **Virtual Machine**.
2. Click **Next** and choose a **Name** for the master node VM. We will use `Kubernetes Master` for this purpose. Optionally, configure a custom directory for storing VM data to ensure enough disk space for hosting the VM, as illustrated in the following screenshot:

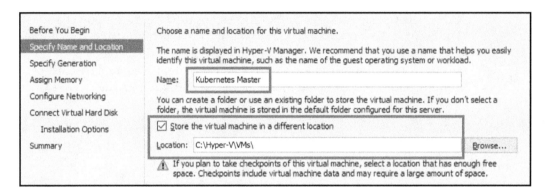

3. In the next dialog, choose **Generation 2** and continue, as illustrated in the following screenshot:

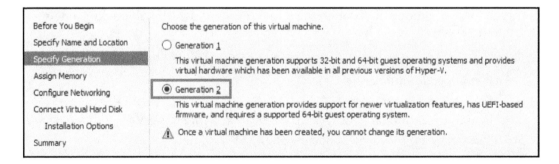

4. Assign at least `2048` MB of RAM for the master node. You may also choose to use the dynamic memory assignment feature. You can find more about hardware minimal requirements in the official documentation, at: `https://kubernetes.io/docs/setup/production-environment/tools/kubeadm/install-kubeadm/#before-you-begin`. For production scenarios, consider using at least `16384` MB of RAM. The following screenshot illustrates the process:

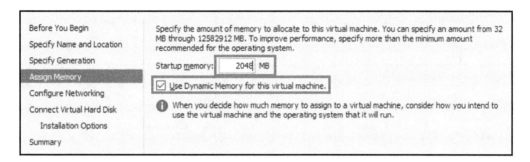

5. Choose an internal NAT or an external switch as the connection for the VM, as shown in the following screenshot:

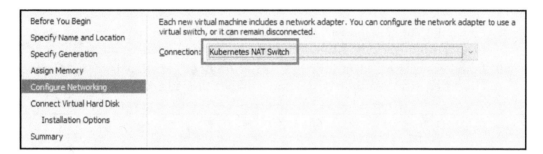

6. Create a new virtual hard disk with 250 GB size. As **virtual hard disks v2 (VHDX)** are dynamically expandable, it is easier to allocate more space from the beginning instead of expanding the disk and partitions later. The following screenshot illustrates the process:

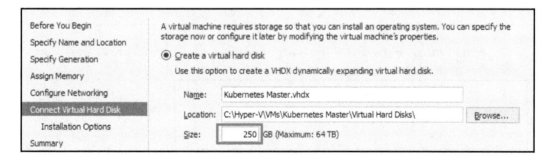

7. Choose to install an operating system from ISO and select your Ubuntu Server 18.04 LTS image file, as shown in the following screenshot:

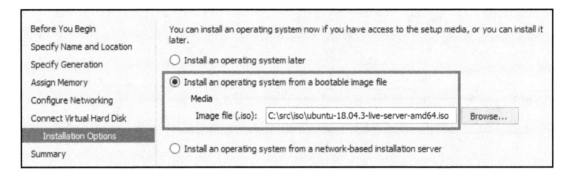

8. Finish the VM creation wizard. Before starting the VM, we need to configure it further. Right-click the **Kubernetes Master** VM and open **Settings**.

9. In the **Security** menu, ensure that the **Secure Boot Template** is set to **Microsoft UEFI Certificate Authority**, as shown in the following screenshot:

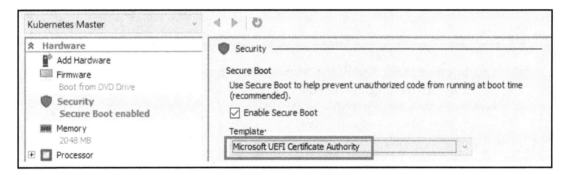

10. In the **Processor** menu, set the **Number of virtual processors** to at least 2, as shown in the following screenshot:

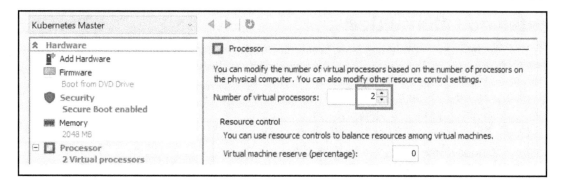

11. In network adapter **Advanced Features** menu, select **Enable MAC address spoofing** for containers. If you are using an external vSwitch and have an external DHCP, you may also want to configure static DHCP assignments. For an internal NAT vSwitch, you can leave the default **Dynamic** setting, as shown in the following screenshot:

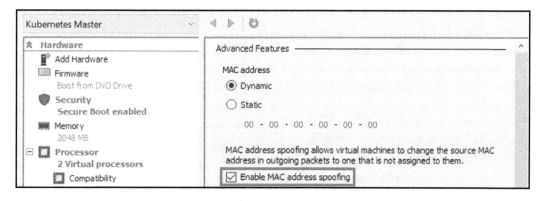

12. Apply all changes and start the VM.

If you think about fully automating this process, you may choose Vagrant (https://www.vagrantup.com/) for development purposes or Packer for production scenarios (https://www.packer.io/). With Vagrant, you can easily create a development VM from scratch and automate the provisioning process using, for example, Ansible. Using Packer, you can produce machine images for VMs or cloud providers in order to use the **Infrastructure-as-Code (IaC)** paradigm.

Installing Ubuntu Server

The VM for the master node has been created, and now we need to install Ubuntu Server 18.04 LTS on the VM. In order to do that, perform the following steps:

1. Connect to the running VM terminal by double-clicking the **Kubernetes Master VM** in Hyper-V manager.
2. Wait for the installer to initialize.
3. Choose **English** as the preferred language.
4. Choose the desired keyboard layout.
5. In **Network connections**, proceed depending on your external network configuration:
   - If you use an internal NAT vSwitch, you have to set up the configuration manually. Open the **eth0** interface and **Edit IPv4**, selecting the **Manual** method. Set **Subnet** 10.0.0.0/8, **Address** 10.0.0.2, **Gateway** 10.0.0.1, **Name servers** 8.8.8.8,8.8.4.4 (or use your provider's DNS server addresses if possible).
   - If you use an external vSwitch, use automatic configuration or manually configure the network according to your requirements.
6. Optionally, configure the **network proxy**. Bear in mind that if you are running behind a network proxy, you will later need to configure Docker to use the proxy.
7. Proceed with the default **Mirror address**.
8. In **Filesystem setup**, configure to **Use An Entire Disk**.
9. Choose the default disk for installation.
10. Proceed with the proposed **Filesystem setup**.
11. In **Profile setup**, you can configure the machine name and the first username. We will use kubernetes-master as the machine name and ubuntu as the username.
12. In the **SSH** menu, choose to **Install OpenSSH Server**.
13. Do not select any additional packages, and continue with the installation.
14. Wait for the installation to finish.
15. Reboot.

Automation of Ubuntu Server installation is possible using Kickstart or preseed configuration files. You can find more information in the official documentation, at: `https://help.ubuntu.com/lts/installation-guide/i386/ch04s06.html`. This approach can be used together with Vagrant or Packer. An example preseed configuration file for Ubuntu Server 18.04 for Packer can be found at: `https://github.com/ptylenda/ironic-packer-template-ubuntu1804-kubernetes-ansible-proxy/blob/master/http/preseed.cfg`.

Let's look at the network configuration.

Configuring the network

If you are using internal NAT vSwitch or an external vSwitch with an external Windows-based DHCP server, there is some additional network configuration required after the machine reboots, as follows:

1. In the VM terminal window, use the username `ubuntu` and your password to log in.

2. Open the following file using `vim` or `nano`:

   sudo vim /etc/netplan/01-netcfg.yaml

   If you are not familiar with the Vim editor, we highly recommend learning the basics. A minimal guide can be found, for example, at: `https://eastmanreference.com/a-quick-start-guide-for-beginners-to-the-vim-text-editor`. Vim is extremely useful for editing files both on Linux and on Windows, without the need for a desktop environment. As an alternative, you can use nano (`https://www.nano-editor.org/`).

3. If you are using an internal NAT vSwitch, enforce the static IP address configuration for the Kubernetes master, as follows:

```
network:
  ethernets:
    eth0:
      dhcp4: no
      addresses: [10.0.0.2/8]
      gateway4: 10.0.0.1
      nameservers:
        addresses: [8.8.8.8,8.8.4.4]
  version: 2
```

4. Alternatively, if you are using an external vSwitch and an external Windows-based DHCP server, set the file contents to the following:

```
network:
  ethernets:
    eth0:
      dhcp4: yes
      dhcp-identifier: mac
  version: 2
```

Setting `dhcp-identifier` to `mac` is crucial for making DHCP leases work properly.

5. Save the file and reboot the machine, using the `sudo reboot` command.

We will now be installing some additional packages.

Installing additional packages for integration with Hyper-V

For any network configuration (both internal NAT and external vSwitch), you should now install additional virtualization tools that enable some dedicated features for integrating with hypervisors, as follows:

1. Log in to the machine again.
2. Update the `apt-get` cache by running the following command:

   ```
   sudo apt-get update
   ```

3. Install additional virtualization tools, as follows:

   ```
   sudo apt-get install -y --install-recommends linux-tools-virtual
   linux-cloud-tools-virtual
   ```

4. Reboot.

Now, let's set up a passwordless SSH login.

Setting up a passwordless SSH login

At this point, it is recommended to switch to using SSH instead of the VM terminal for managing the machine. This will require the following:

1. Installing the SSH client on your Windows machine that you use to connect to the VMs (in most cases, your VM host machine)
2. Generating an SSH key pair in order to disable password authentication for SSH

To install the native SSH client on your Windows machine, perform the following steps:

1. Open the PowerShell window as Administrator
2. Run the following command to get the currently available version of the OpenSSH client:

```
PS C:\WINDOWS\system32> Get-WindowsCapability -Online | ? Name -
like 'OpenSSH*'
Name : OpenSSH.Client~~~~0.0.1.0
State : NotPresent

Name : OpenSSH.Server~~~~0.0.1.0
State : NotPresent
```

3. Install the client, like this:

```
Add-WindowsCapability -Online -Name OpenSSH.Client~~~~0.0.1.0
```

4. To connect to the Kubernetes master node VM, you need to know its IP address. If you are using a static IP address configuration, it is rather straightforward—you use `10.0.0.2`. For a dynamic IP address provided by DHCP, you need to determine it first. Thanks to the virtualization tools installed in the previous steps, you can easily find this in Hyper-V manager in the **Networking** tab, shown at the bottom of the following screenshot:

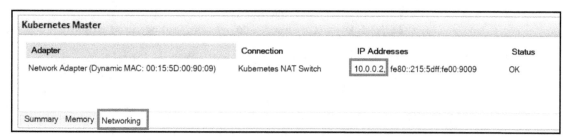

5. In this case, the IP address is `10.0.0.2`, and we can use it to SSH into the VM, as follows:

```
PS C:\WINDOWS\system32> ssh ubuntu@10.0.0.2
The authenticity of host '10.0.0.2 (10.0.0.2)' can't be
established.
ECDSA key fingerprint is
SHA256:X6iv9E7Xix15GFvV+WxiP10Gbkvh1j3xPsBEV/4YcFo.
Are you sure you want to continue connecting (yes/no)? yes
Warning: Permanently added '10.0.0.2' (ECDSA) to the list of known
hosts.
ubuntu@10.0.0.2's password:
Welcome to Ubuntu 18.04.3 LTS (GNU/Linux 4.15.0-65-generic x86_64)
```

If you run into connection problems such as `Connection closed by 10.0.0.2 port 22`, you need to regenerate the SSH host keys. In the VM terminal, run `sudo ssh-keygen -A` and try connecting again. If problems persist, analyze the sshd service logs using `sudo service sshd status`.

The next step is generating an SSH key pair for passwordless login to your Kubernetes master VM. To do this, perform the following steps:

1. Open the PowerShell window.
2. Run the following command to generate the key pair. Do not specify a passphrase:

```
ssh-keygen.exe
```

3. Now, your public key is available in `C:\Users\<user>\.ssh\id_rsa.pub`. Copy it to the Kubernetes Master VM, using the following command. This command ensures that the `authorized_keys` file has proper, secure access permissions:

```
cat ~/.ssh/id_rsa.pub | ssh ubuntu@10.0.0.2 "cat >>
~/.ssh/authorized_keys && chmod 600 ~/.ssh/authorized_keys"
```

4. And the last step is to test passwordless authentication and disable password authentication for the SSH server for the best security, as shown in the following code snippet:

```
ssh ubuntu@192.168.43.105
# You should not be asked for password at this point!
```

5. Edit `/etc/ssh/sshd_config`, as follows:

```
sudo vim /etc/ssh/sshd_config
```

6. Find the `PasswordAuthentication yes` line and comment it out, like this:

```
#PasswordAuthentication yes
```

7. Save the changes and restart the SSH server, like this:

```
sudo service sshd restart
```

8. Reconnect to verify your configuration.

At this point, it is a good idea to export the Hyper-V VM image (or create a checkpoint) for `Kubernetes Master`. This will make it easier to revert to the initial configuration if anything goes wrong during the Kubernetes master configuration.

Installing and configuring Kubernetes prerequisites

Preparing Ubuntu Server 18.04 LTS machines for the Kubernetes master (as well as Kubernetes nodes) requires the following steps:

1. Changing the operating system configuration, such as disabling swap.
2. Installing the Docker container runtime.

All the steps for Ubuntu Server preparation for Kubernetes are also available as a bash script in the official GitHub repository for the book, which can be found at: https://github.com/PacktPublishing/Hands-On-Kubernetes-on-Windows/blob/master/Chapter07/02_ubuntu-prepare-node.sh.

As of Kubernetes 1.17, the list of **validated** Docker versions is as follows: 1.13.1, 17.03, 17.06, 17.09, 18.06, 18.09, 19.03.

In order to configure the operating system for running Kubernetes, perform the following steps:

1. Open the PowerShell window.
2. SSH into the Kubernetes master machine, like this:

   ```
   ssh ubuntu@10.0.0.2
   ```

3. Update `apt-get` and upgrade all packages, as follows:

   ```
   sudo apt-get update
   sudo apt-get dist-upgrade -y
   ```

4. Install the required packages, as follows:

   ```
   sudo apt-get install apt-transport-https ca-certificates curl
   software-properties-common ebtables ethtool -y
   ```

5. Disable the swap partition for the current boot, like this:

   ```
   sudo swapoff -a
   ```

6. Remove the swap partition permanently. Edit `sudo vim /etc/fstab` and remove any lines of type `swap`—for example, the following line:

   ```
   /swap.img       none    swap    sw      0       0
   ```

   Editing `/etc/fstab` should be always performed with a **backup** of the file created. Configuration errors in this file may lead to a non-bootable system!

7. Optionally, reboot the machine to check that the swap partition has not been mounted again. When the machine is rebooted, SSH into the machine and check that `swap` is disabled—the list should be empty, as follows:

   ```
   swapon -s
   ```

8. Ensure that the `br_netfilter` kernel module is loaded during system boot. Use the `sudo vim /etc/modules-load.d/kubernetes.conf` command to create the file and set the following contents:

   ```
   br_netfilter
   ```

9. Configure the `sysctl` variables for Kubernetes (required for the Flannel network). Use the `sudo vim /etc/sysctl.d/99-kubernetes.conf` command to create a new file and ensure that the file has the following contents:

```
net.bridge.bridge-nf-call-ip6tables = 1
net.bridge.bridge-nf-call-iptables = 1
net.bridge.bridge-nf-call-arptables = 1
```

10. Load the `br_netfilter` kernel module for the current boot and reload the `sysctl` variables using the following commands:

```
sudo modprobe br_netfilter
sudo sysctl --system
```

At this point, your Ubuntu Server VM is ready for installing Docker and Kubernetes. In order to install Docker 18.09, which is the latest validated version for usage with Kubernetes 1.16, perform the following steps:

1. Add the official **GNU Privacy Guard** (**GPG**) key for the Docker `apt` package repository, like this:

```
curl -fsSL https://download.docker.com/linux/ubuntu/gpg | sudo apt-key add -
```

 The latest installation instructions for Docker on Ubuntu can be found at: `https://docs.docker.com/install/linux/docker-ce/ubuntu/`. Always cross-check them with the Kubernetes container runtime installation documentation as it contains additional important information, and can be found at: `https://kubernetes.io/docs/setup/production-environment/container-runtimes/#docker`.

2. Add the Docker `apt` package repository, like this:

```
sudo add-apt-repository \
  "deb [arch=amd64] https://download.docker.com/linux/ubuntu \
  $(lsb_release -cs) \
  stable"
```

3. Update the `apt-get` cache to refresh the repository's information, like this:

```
sudo apt-get update
```

4. Install the latest Docker version validated for Kubernetes usage, like this:

```
sudo apt-get install docker-ce=5:18.09.9~3-0~ubuntu-bionic -y
```

5. Disable automatic updates for the `docker-ce` package by running the following command (this will prevent the installation of unvalidated Docker versions):

```
sudo apt-mark hold docker-ce
```

6. Configure the Docker daemon for Kubernetes. Use the `sudo vim /etc/docker/daemon.json` command to create a new file and set the following contents:

```
{
  "exec-opts": ["native.cgroupdriver=systemd"],
  "log-driver": "json-file",
  "log-opts": {
  "max-size": "100m"
  },
  "storage-driver": "overlay2"
}
```

7. Reload `systemctl` and restart the Docker daemon, using the following commands:

```
sudo systemctl daemon-reload
sudo systemctl restart docker
```

8. Verify that Docker is installed properly by running a `hello-world` container, as follows:

```
ubuntu@kubernetes-master:~$ sudo docker run hello-world
Unable to find image 'hello-world:latest' locally
latest: Pulling from library/hello-world
1b930d010525: Pull complete Digest:
sha256:c3b4ada4687bbaa170745b3e4dd8ac3f194ca95b2d0518b417fb47e5879d
9b5f
Status: Downloaded newer image for hello-world:latest

Hello from Docker!
This message shows that your installation appears to be working
correctly.
```

If you are working behind a network proxy, you should ensure you have the following:

- An `/etc/environment` containing the appropriate proxy variables (example guide: `https://kifarunix.com/how-to-set-system-wide-proxy-in-ubuntu-18-04/`).
- A `/etc/systemd/system/docker.service.d` directory containing an additional file with proxy variables (example guide: `https://docs.docker.com/config/daemon/systemd/`).

Your Ubuntu Server VM is now ready to be initialized as the Kubernetes master node. First, let's do the initial planning for the cluster before we install the Kubernetes binaries.

Planning the cluster

Before you begin initialization of the cluster, you need to determine specific subnets and address ranges that will be used by Kubernetes components. This is dependent on your external networking setup (for example, avoiding any IP address conflicts) and the number of Pods and Services you are planning to run in the cluster. In general, it is a good idea to use the defaults, especially for a development cluster running on your local machine behind an internal NAT vSwitch. You need to determine the following values from the table for your cluster:

	Description	Default value
Service subnet	Virtual subnet (non-routable) used by Pods for accessing Services. Routable address translation from virtual IPs is performed by the `kube-proxy` running on nodes.	`10.96.0.0/12`
Cluster (Pod) subnet	Global subnet used by all Pods in the cluster. In general, when using Flannel, each node is assigned a smaller /24 subnet for its Pods. Bear in mind that this subnet must be large enough for all Pods running in the cluster.	`10.244.0.0/16`
Kubernetes DNS service IP	The IP address of the `kube-dns` service used for cluster service discovery and domain name resolution.	`10.96.0.10`

These values will be needed for the next steps when initializing the cluster.

Initializing the cluster

For the initialization of the Kubernetes Ubuntu master and joining Windows nodes, we will be using kubeadm—as of Kubernetes 1.16 (and also 1.17), this is the only well-automated cluster deployment method for hybrid Windows/Linux clusters. The first step is the installation of kubeadm, kubelet, and kubectl on the Ubuntu Server VM. This is also covered in a script available in the GitHub repository, at: `https://github.com/ PacktPublishing/Hands-On-Kubernetes-on-Windows/blob/master/Chapter07/03_ubuntu- install-kubeadm.sh`.

 The official instructions for installing kubeadm and initializing the Kubernetes master can be found at: `https://kubernetes.io/docs/setup/ production-environment/tools/kubeadm/install-kubeadm/` and `https://kubernetes.io/docs/setup/production-environment/ tools/kubeadm/create-cluster-kubeadm/`.

SSH into the Ubuntu Server VM, and perform the following steps:

1. Add the GPG key for the Kubernetes apt package repository, as follows:

```
curl -s https://packages.cloud.google.com/apt/doc/apt-key.gpg |
sudo apt-key add -
```

2. Add the Kubernetes apt package repository. Use the `sudo vim /etc/apt/sources.list.d/kubernetes.list` command to create a new file and set the following contents (note that you currently have to use the `kubernetes-xenial` repository as `bionic` is not available yet):

```
deb https://apt.kubernetes.io/ kubernetes-xenial main
```

3. Update `apt-get` and install the required packages, as follows:

```
sudo apt-get update
sudo apt-get install kubelet kubeadm kubectl -y
```

4. Verify that the latest Kubernetes version has been installed by running the following code:

```
ubuntu@kubernetes-master:~$ kubeadm version
kubeadm version: &version.Info{Major:"1", Minor:"16",
GitVersion:"v1.16.1",
GitCommit:"d647ddbd755faf07169599a625faf302ffc34458",
GitTreeState:"clean", BuildDate:"2019-10-02T16:58:27Z",
GoVersion:"go1.12.10", Compiler:"gc", Platform:"linux/amd64"}
```

5. Disable automatic updates for Kubernetes packages by running the following command (this is especially important as any Kubernetes components' upgrades should be performed consciously and in a controlled manner, taking all compatibility issues into consideration):

```
sudo apt-mark hold kubelet kubeadm kubectl
```

Up to this moment, initializing the Kubernetes master and node is exactly the same. You can follow the same steps when adding more dedicated Ubuntu nodes to the cluster or cloning your VM. If you decide to clone the machine, remember about ensuring that the hostname, MAC address, and product_uuid are unique for each node. Read more about how to ensure this in the official documentation, at: https://kubernetes.io/docs/setup/production-environment/tools/kubeadm/install-kubeadm/#verify-the-mac-address-and-product-uuid-are-unique-for-every-node.

Now, we are ready to initialize the cluster using kubeadm. In order to do this, perform the following steps:

1. Execute the following command, assuming that the Service network is 10.96.0.0/12 and the Pod network is 10.244.0.0/16:

```
sudo kubeadm init --service-cidr "10.96.0.0/12" --pod-network-cidr
"10.244.0.0/16"
```

2. Carefully examine the kubeadm initialization output and note down the kubeadm join information, as follows:

```
Your Kubernetes control-plane has initialized successfully!

To start using your cluster, you need to run the following as a
regular user:

 mkdir -p $HOME/.kube
 sudo cp -i /etc/kubernetes/admin.conf $HOME/.kube/config
 sudo chown $(id -u):$(id -g) $HOME/.kube/config

You should now deploy a pod network to the cluster.
Run "kubectl apply -f [podnetwork].yaml" with one of the options
listed at:
 https://kubernetes.io/docs/concepts/cluster-administration/addons/

Then you can join any number of worker nodes by running the
following on each as root:
```

```
kubeadm join 10.0.0.2:6443 --token c4kkga.50606d1zr7w0s2w8 \
  --discovery-token-ca-cert-hash
sha256:44b2f0f05f79970cc295ab1a7e7ebe299c05fcbbec9d0c08133d4c5ab7fa
db0b
```

3. If your kubeadm token expires (after 24 hours), you can always create a new one using the following command:

```
kubeadm token create --print-join-command
```

4. Copy your **kubectl config** (**kubeconfig**) to the default location, as follows:

```
mkdir -p $HOME/.kube
sudo cp -i /etc/kubernetes/admin.conf $HOME/.kube/config
sudo chown $(id -u):$(id -g) $HOME/.kube/config
```

5. Now, it is recommended to copy the config to your Windows machine in order to be able to manage the cluster without logging into the master node. In the PowerShell window, execute the following commands:

```
scp ubuntu@10.0.0.2:.kube/config config
$env:KUBECONFIG="config;$env:USERPROFILE\.kube\config"
kubectl config view --raw
```

6. Carefully examine the merged config to check that you did not override any existing clusters' configuration. You can read more about merging kubeconfigs in Chapter 6, *Interacting with Kubernetes Clusters*. If the merged configuration is good, you may save it as $env:USERPROFILE\.kube\config and switch context to kubernetes-admin@kubernetes using the following commands:

```
$env:KUBECONFIG="config;$env:USERPROFILE\.kube\config"
kubectl config view --raw > $env:USERPROFILE\.kube\config_new

Move-Item -Force $env:USERPROFILE\.kube\config_new
$env:USERPROFILE\.kube\config

kubectl config use-context "kubernetes-admin@kubernetes"
```

7. Verify that the configuration is working correctly. Retrieve the list of nodes, as follows (note that the NotReady status is caused by no Pod network being installed yet):

```
PS C:\src> kubectl get nodes
NAME                STATUS     ROLES    AGE    VERSION
kubernetes-master   NotReady   master   22m    v1.16.1
```

8. If you do not plan to add any Ubuntu nodes, you may choose to **untaint** the master node in order to allow the scheduling of Linux Pods on the master node. Note that this should be performed for development clusters only. This is achieved by running the following code:

```
kubectl taint nodes --all node-role.kubernetes.io/master-
```

In case you would like to set up the cluster again, you first need to tear down the cluster using kubeadm. Read more about this procedure in the official documentation, at: `https://kubernetes.io/docs/setup/ production-environment/tools/kubeadm/create-cluster-kubeadm/ #tear-down`.

Your Kubernetes master node is almost ready. The last remaining step is the installation of the Pod network. Let's proceed!

Installing the Kubernetes network

After the Kubernetes master has been initialized with kubeadm, the next step is the installation of the Pod network. We have covered Kubernetes networking options in `Chapter 5`, *Kubernetes Networking*, which explains in detail which **Container Network Interface** (**CNI**) plugins are supported for hybrid Windows/Linux clusters. For this on-premises cluster deployment, we will use the Flannel network with a `host-gw` backend (a `win-bridge` CNI plugin on Windows nodes). Remember that you can use this approach only if there is **Layer 2** (**L2**) connectivity (no **Layer 3** (**L3**) routing) between the nodes. In general, a `host-gw` backend is preferable as it is in a stable feature state, whereas an overlay backend is still in an alpha feature state for Windows nodes.

If you are interested in Flannel with overlay backend installation, please refer to the official documentation for detailed steps, at: `https:// kubernetes.io/docs/setup/production-environment/windows/user- guide-windows-nodes/#configuring-flannel-in-vxlan-mode-on-the- linux-control-plane`. Note that you need Windows Server 2019 with the KB4489899 patch installed for overlay networking.

To install Flannel with a `host-gw` backend, perform the following steps (in the PowerShell window or on the Kubernetes master via SSH):

1. Download the latest official manifest file for Flannel for Kubernetes, like this:

```
# Bash
wget
https://raw.githubusercontent.com/coreos/flannel/master/Documentati
on/kube-flannel.yml
```

```
# Powershell
wget
https://raw.githubusercontent.com/coreos/flannel/master/Documentati
on/kube-flannel.yml -OutFile kube-flannel.yml
```

2. Customize the manifest, so that the `net-conf.json` file section has a `host-gw` backend type and proper Pod network defined (default: `10.244.0.0/16`), as follows:

```
net-conf.json: |
  {
    "Network": "10.244.0.0/16",
    "Backend": {
      "Type": "host-gw"
    }
  }
```

3. Apply the modified manifest, like this:

```
kubectl apply -f kube-flannel.yml
```

4. The latest official manifest does not need extra patching for Linux-only scheduling, as it already covers this requirement. If you are following the official guide, you may skip this step.
5. Verify that the Pod network installation has been successful. You should be able to schedule a simple interactive Pod that is running Bourne shell—this will work only if you have an untainted master node for Pod scheduling or have other Linux nodes. This is achieved by running the following code:

```
PS C:\src> kubectl run --generator=run-pod/v1 busybox-debug -i --
tty --image=busybox --rm --restart=Never -- sh
If you don't see a command prompt, try pressing enter.
/ #
```

With the Kubernetes master fully initialized, we can proceed to prepare a VM for the Windows node.

Preparing VMs for Windows nodes

This section follows a similar structure as for the Ubuntu Server VM preparation. For the Windows VM, we will perform the following steps:

1. Creating the VM
2. Installing Windows Server 2019
3. Configuring the network
4. Installing the SSH server
5. Installing and configuring Kubernetes prerequisites

Creating the VM

The steps for creating a Windows Server 2019 VM are almost the same as for Ubuntu Server 18.04. If you are interested in screenshots for the process, please refer to the previous sections.

To create the Windows Server 2019 Kubernetes node VM, open the Hyper-V manager application and perform the following steps:

1. From the **Actions** menu, choose **New** and click **Virtual Machine**.
2. Click **Next**, and choose the **Name** for the Windows node VM. We will use `Kubernetes Windows Node 01` for this purpose. Optionally, configure a custom directory for storing VM data to ensure there is enough disk space to host the VM. You need at least 30 GB of disk space for each node.
3. In the next dialog, choose **Generation 2** and continue.
4. Assign at least `4096` MB of RAM for the Windows node. Using less memory may result in `KubeletHasInsufficientMemory` being reported occasionally and preventing Pods from scheduling. The dynamic memory allocation feature will not work as we are going to enable nested virtualization for this machine. For production scenarios, consider allocating more resources.
5. Choose an internal NAT or an external switch as the connection for the VM. This must be the same switch that you use for the master node.
6. Create a new virtual hard disk with `250` GB size or more. As VHDX are dynamically expandable, it is easier to allocate more space from the beginning instead of expanding the disk and partitions later.
7. Choose to install the operating system from ISO and select your Windows Server 2019 (or 1903) image file.

8. Finish the VM creation wizard. Before starting the VM, we need to configure it further. Right-click the `Kubernetes Windows Node 01` VM and open **Settings**.

9. In the **Processor** menu, set the **Number of virtual processors** to at least 2

10. In the **Network Adapter Advanced Features** menu, select **Enable MAC address spoofing** for containers. If you are using an external vSwitch and have an external DHCP, you may also want to configure static DHCP assignments. For an internal NAT vSwitch, you can leave the default **Dynamic** setting.

11. Apply all changes.

12. Enable nested virtualization with the following command in the PowerShell window, running as Administrator:

```
Set-VMProcessor -VMName "Kubernetes Windows Node 01" -
ExposeVirtualizationExtensions $true
```

The machine is now ready to start the operating system installation.

Installing Windows Server 2019

The installation process for Windows Server 2019 is performed using a graphical interface. If you are considering automating the installation process—for example, for Vagrant or Packer—you should consider using `Autounattend.xml` files provided by virtual floppy drives. You can find an example of such a configuration file on GitHub, at: `https://github.com/ptylenda/kubernetes-for-windows/blob/master/packer/windows/http/Autounattend.xml`.

To perform the installation, perform the following steps:

1. Connect to `Kubernetes Windows Node 01` VM by double-clicking the machine in Hyper-V manager.

2. Start the VM and immediately press any key in order to boot from the installation DVD mounted into the VM.

3. Choose language and locale settings.

4. Click **Install Now**.

5. Provide the product key for your installation.

6. In the next dialog, you can choose whether to install **Desktop Experience** or not. We suggest not installing it as it makes the installation more compact and leaves configuration to command line, which is better for **automation**.

7. Read and accept the license terms.
8. Select the **Custom** installation of Windows Server.
9. Proceed with the default installation target (whole disk, without partitioning).
10. Wait for the installation to finish and for the machine to reboot.
11. During the first login, you have to set the Administrator's password.

Now, you have a Windows Server 2019 VM up and running, but before joining it to the Kubernetes cluster, we need to configure the network and install prerequisites.

Configuring the network

Additional network configuration is needed only if you are running an internal NAT vSwitch—in this case, you need to configure a static IP address, a gateway address, and DNS server information. If you are running an external vSwitch with an external DHCP, the configuration should be performed automatically.

In this guide, we follow the convention that Kubernetes nodes have subsequent IP addresses starting with 10.0.0.3. In order to configure 10.0.0.3 as the static IP address for the first node in the cluster, perform the following steps:

1. Start PowerShell by running the powershell command on the VM.
2. Execute the following command to find the ifIndex of the main Ethernet interface:

    ```
    Get-NetAdapter
    ```

3. Create a new static IP address of 10.0.0.3 for the interface, as follows:

    ```
    New-NetIPAddress -IPAddress 10.0.0.3 -DefaultGateway 10.0.0.1 -
    PrefixLength 8 -InterfaceIndex <ifIndex>
    ```

4. Set DNS server information for the interface, as follows (use appropriate DNS servers if needed):

    ```
    Set-DNSClientServerAddress -InterfaceIndex <ifIndex>
    -ServerAddresses 8.8.8.8,8.8.4.4
    ```

In case you are behind a network proxy, you can define appropriate environment variables at the machine level using the following commands in PowerShell:

```
[Environment]::SetEnvironmentVariable("HTTP_PROXY",
"http://proxy.example.com:80/",
[EnvironmentVariableTarget]::Machine)
[Environment]::SetEnvironmentVariable("HTTPS_PROXY",
"http://proxy.example.com:443/",
[EnvironmentVariableTarget]::Machine)
```

Let's now take a look at how to approach accessing Windows Server VM remotely.

Installing the SSH server

Now, we need a means of connecting to the VM without the Hyper-V terminal—you can still use it if you prefer, but it is more limited than using **Remote Desktop Protocol** (RDP) or SSH. You have the following options:

1. Install the SSH server and use Vim for managing configuration files.
2. Enable the RDP connection (example guide: `https://theitbros.com/how-to-remotely-enable-remote-desktop-using-powershell/`).
3. Use PowerShell Remoting (example guide: `https://docs.microsoft.com/en-us/powershell/module/microsoft.powershell.core/enable-psremoting?view=powershell-6`).

We will demonstrate how to enable the first option, SSH server & Vim, on Windows Server 2019. This option makes access to our Kubernetes cluster uniform, and you can use the same SSH keys for all nodes. Perform the following steps:

1. In the Hyper-V terminal connection for the Windows Server machine, start PowerShell by using the `powershell` command.
2. Verify which is the current version of SSH server that can be installed, by running the following code:

```
Get-WindowsCapability -Online | ? Name -like 'OpenSSH*'

Name : OpenSSH.Client~~~~0.0.1.0
State : NotPresent

Name : OpenSSH.Server~~~~0.0.1.0
State : NotPresent
```

3. Install the `OpenSSH.Server` capability, like this:

```
Add-WindowsCapability -Online -Name OpenSSH.Server~~~~0.0.1.0
```

4. Start the `sshd` service, like this:

```
Start-Service sshd
```

5. Enable automatic startup of the `sshd` service, like this:

```
Set-Service -Name sshd -StartupType 'Automatic'
```

6. Ensure that the appropriate firewall rule is in place (`OpenSSH-Server-In-TCP`), as follows:

```
Get-NetFirewallRule -Name *ssh*
```

7. If it is not present, add it manually, like this:

```
New-NetFirewallRule -Name sshd -DisplayName 'OpenSSH Server (sshd)'
-Enabled True -Direction Inbound -Protocol TCP -Action Allow -
LocalPort 22
```

8. From your development machine, verify that the connection to the VM at `10.0.0.3` is possible via SSH, as follows:

```
PS C:\src> ssh Administrator@10.0.0.3
The authenticity of host '10.0.0.3 (10.0.0.3)' can't be
established.
ECDSA key fingerprint is
SHA256:VYTfjOb1uZmVgHu9BY17q1wpINNEuzb4dsSGtMFQKw4.
Are you sure you want to continue connecting (yes/no)? yes
Warning: Permanently added '10.0.0.3' (ECDSA) to the list of known
hosts.
Administrator@10.0.0.3's password:
Microsoft Windows [Version 10.0.17763.737]
(c) 2018 Microsoft Corporation. All rights reserved.

administrator@WIN-GJD24M0P8DA C:\Users\Administrator>
```

9. By default, the `cmd` shell, which has limited functionality, is started. Start PowerShell in the SSH session by using the `powershell` command.

10. Change the default shell for SSH to be `powershell`, using the following command:

```
New-ItemProperty -Path "HKLM:\SOFTWARE\OpenSSH" -Name DefaultShell
-Value "C:\Windows\System32\WindowsPowerShell\v1.0\powershell.exe"
-PropertyType String -Force
```

9. Install the Chocolatey package manager in order to install the Vim editor, as follows:

```
Set-ExecutionPolicy Bypass -Scope Process -Force; iex ((New-Object
System.Net.WebClient).DownloadString('https://chocolatey.org/instal
l.ps1'))
```

11. Install Vim using Chocolatey, like this:

```
choco install vim -y
```

12. Configure a passwordless SSH login. Add your `~/.ssh/id_rsa.pub` public SSH key to `administrators_authorized_keys` on your Windows Server VM, using the vim `C:\ProgramData\ssh\administrators_authorized_keys` command.

13. Fix permissions for the `administrators_authorized_keys` file, as follows:

```
icacls C:\ProgramData\ssh\administrators_authorized_keys /remove
"NT AUTHORITY\Authenticated Users"
icacls C:\ProgramData\ssh\administrators_authorized_keys
/inheritance:r
```

14. Restart the `sshd` service, like this:

```
Restart-Service -Name sshd -Force
```

All Windows provisioning operations can be performed by a mix of `Autounattend.xml` automated Windows setup (using regular `cmd` and `powershell` scripts) and Ansible, which is supported on Windows hosts. You can check how this approach works with Packer in this minimal example repository, at: `https://github.com/ptylenda/ironic-packer-template-windows2016`.

At this point, your Windows Server VM is connected to the network and is ready for installing Kubernetes prerequisites.

Installing and configuring Kubernetes prerequisites

First, ensure that Windows Server 2019 is up to date. In order to do that, use the Hyper-V terminal connection and perform the following steps:

 If you do not want to use a third-party module for managing updates, you can use the `sconfig` command. Currently, these operations cannot be easily performed via SSH as they require a **graphical user interface** (GUI) interaction.

1. Open a PowerShell session, using the `powershell` command.
2. Install the `PSWindowsUpdate` custom module for managing Windows updates, as follows:

   ```
   Install-Module -Name PSWindowsUpdate
   ```

3. Trigger Windows updates by running the following code (this process may take a bit of time to complete):

   ```
   Get-WUInstall -AcceptAll -Install
   ```

The next step is to install Docker and Kubernetes itself. This can be approached in two ways:

- Manual Docker installation and configuration, as in the official Microsoft documentation, at: `https://docs.microsoft.com/en-us/virtualization/windowscontainers/kubernetes/joining-windows-workers`
- Semi-automated installation using Kubernetes `sig-windows-tools` scripts, as in the official Kubernetes documentation, at: `https://kubernetes.io/docs/setup/production-environment/windows/user-guide-windows-nodes/#join-windows-worker-node`

We will use the second option as it is a more recent approach that aligns with kubeadm support for Windows nodes, available from version 1.16 onward. `sig-windows-tools` scripts perform the following operations:

1. Enable the Windows Server Containers feature.
2. Download the selected container runtime (Docker or **Container Runtime Interface (CRI)**).
3. Pull the required Docker images.
4. Download Kubernetes and Flannel binaries, install them, and add them to the `$env:PATH` variable.
5. Download the selected CNI plugins.

To install all prerequisites for Kubernetes on Windows, perform the following steps:

1. SSH into the Windows Server node VM, like this:

   ```
   ssh Administrator@10.0.0.3
   ```

2. Create and use a new directory where `sig-windows-tools` scripts will be downloaded—for example, `sig-windows-tools-kubeadm`, as follows:

   ```
   mkdir .\sig-windows-tools-kubeadm
   cd .\sig-windows-tools-kubeadm
   ```

3. Download the latest `sig-windows-tools` repository and extract it. Note that the path in the repository may change as it is currently dedicated for `v1.15.0` (you can check the official documentation for the latest version, at: `https://kubernetes.io/docs/setup/production-environment/windows/user-guide-windows-nodes/#preparing-a-windows-node`). Alternatively, you may use the fork in the GitHub repository for the book: `https://github.com/PacktPublishing/Hands-On-Kubernetes-on-Windows/tree/master/Chapter07/07_sig-windows-tools-kubeadm`. The scripts contain a few bug fixes cherry-picked from `sig-windows-tools` that ensure networking works correctly. The code for this step can be seen in the following snippet:

   ```
   Invoke-WebRequest -Uri https://github.com/kubernetes-sigs/sig-windo
   ws-tools/archive/master.zip -OutFile .\master.zip
   tar -xvf .\master.zip --strip-components 3 sig-windows-tools-
   master/kubeadm/v1.15.0/*
   Remove-Item .\master.zip
   ```

4. Now, you need to customize the `Kubeclusterbridge.json` file. This configuration file is used by a helper PowerShell module that installs prerequisites and joins Windows nodes. In the following code block, you can find the configuration for the Windows Server 2019 node. You can also download it from the GitHub repository for the book at: `https://github.com/PacktPublishing/Hands-On-Kubernetes-on-Windows/blob/master/Chapter07/07_sig-windows-tools-kubeadm/Kubeclusterbridge.json`. You need to ensure that `Images` have versions matching your node operating system version and that `Network` has a proper `ServiceCidr` and `ClusterCidr`. Additionally, you need to provide a `KubeadmToken` and `KubeadmCAHash`, which were generated when the Kubernetes master was initialized. You can generate a new token on the Kubernetes master by using the `kubeadm token create --print-join-command` command. The code for this step can be seen in the following snippet:

```
{
    "Cri" : {
        "Name" : "dockerd",
        "Images" : {
            "Pause" : "mcr.microsoft.com/k8s/core/pause:1.2.0",
            "Nanoserver" :
"mcr.microsoft.com/windows/nanoserver:1809",
            "ServerCore" :
"mcr.microsoft.com/windows/servercore:ltsc2019"
        }
    },
    "Cni" : {
        "Name" : "flannel",
        "Source" : [{
            "Name" : "flanneld",
            "Url" :
"https://github.com/coreos/flannel/releases/download/v0.11.0/flanne
ld.exe"
        }
        ],
        "Plugin" : {
            "Name": "bridge"
        },
        "InterfaceName" : "Ethernet"
    },
    "Kubernetes" : {
        "Source" : {
            "Release" : "1.16.1",
            "Url" :
"https://dl.k8s.io/v1.16.1/kubernetes-node-windows-amd64.tar.gz"
        },
        "ControlPlane" : {
```

```
            "IpAddress" : "10.0.0.2",
            "Username" : "ubuntu",
            "KubeadmToken" : "<token>",
            "KubeadmCAHash" : "<discovery-token-ca-cert-hash>"
        },
        "KubeProxy" : {
            "Gates" : "WinDSR=true"
        },
        "Network" : {
            "ServiceCidr" : "10.96.0.0/12",
            "ClusterCidr" : "10.244.0.0/16"
        }
    },
    "Install" : {
        "Destination" : "C:\\ProgramData\\Kubernetes"
    }
}
```

5. At this point, you need to switch to an RDP connection or to a Hyper-V terminal connection. The installation script requires some interaction and elevated privileges that cannot be performed via an SSH PowerShell session.

6. Start the PowerShell session using the `powershell` command, navigate to the `.\sig-windows-tools-kubeadm` directory, and start the installation process, as follows:

```
cd .\sig-windows-tools-kubeadm
.\KubeCluster.ps1 -ConfigFile .\Kubeclusterbridge.json -Install
```

7. The machine will need a reboot during the installation process, and after you log in again, the installation will continue. Verify that the loaded configuration is as expected, by checking the information shown in the following screenshot:

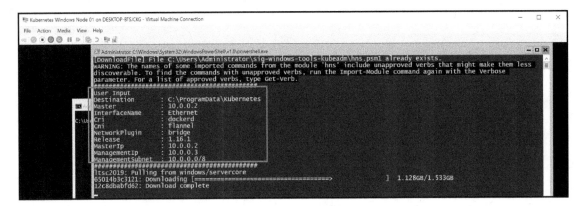

8. You may run into a *race condition* between the fully running Docker daemon and images being pulled. In case of an error, just reboot again or restart the installation process with the same command—remember to close the existing PowerShell session and start a new one before the next attempt. The process of downloading images may take some time, depending on your network connection.

9. After images have been pulled, and the Kubernetes, Flannel, and CNI plugins have been installed, you will be asked to generate a new SSH key pair for accessing the master node from the new Windows node—alternatively, you may do it yourself or reuse an existing key pair. This will make the joining process easier, as cluster configuration has to be retrieved by the joining script using SSH. Execute the command from script output on the `10.0.0.2` master in order to add the public key to `authorized_keys` for the Ubuntu user, as shown in the following screenshot:

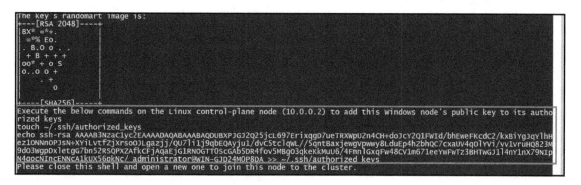

10. When the installation finishes, close the PowerShell window and open a new one, using the `powershell` command.

11. Currently, you need to clean up the `ContainerBootstrap` scheduler task that reruns the script after each boot (this may be fixed in the future releases), as follows:

    Unregister-ScheduledTask -TaskName "ContainerBootstrap"

12. Verify that Docker images have been pulled using the `docker images` command and that Kubernetes binaries have been installed— for example, by running the `kubectl version` command.

Consider exporting the VM image or creating a checkpoint—this will be useful if you choose to add more Windows nodes to the cluster or run into problems during the join process. We can now *finally* proceed to join our first Windows node to the cluster!

Joining Windows nodes using kubeadm

The next task is joining our Windows Server 2019 VM as a node in the Kubernetes cluster. We will use the same `KubeCluster.ps1` script from the Kubernetes `sig-windows-tools` repository, which internally uses **kubeadm** for joining the cluster. The script will perform the following actions:

1. Retrieve the *kubeconfig* file from the `10.0.0.2` master using SSH.
2. Register **kubelet** as a Windows service. This will ensure that the kubelet process is always running on the Windows node.
3. Prepare the CNI plugins' configuration.
4. Create a **Host Networking Service (HNS)** network.
5. Add firewall rules, if needed.
6. Register **flanneld** and **kube-proxy** as Windows services.

 If the join script fails, start a new PowerShell session and rerun the script.

To join the Windows node, proceed with the following steps:

1. In the Hyper-V terminal for the Windows Server VM, start a new PowerShell session using the `powershell` command.
2. Navigate to the directory with the `sig-windows-tools` scripts by running the following command:

   ```
   cd .\sig-windows-tools-kubeadm
   ```

3. Execute the join command, like this:

   ```
   .\KubeCluster.ps1 -ConfigFile .\Kubeclusterbridge.json -Join
   ```

In case of any problems with the `kubeadm join` command (for example, hanging preflight checks), you can edit the `KubeClusterHelper.psm1` file, find the `kubeadm join` command, and add the `--v=3` parameter (or any other verbosity level) to have more detailed info. Additionally, you can examine the services logs in the `C:\ProgramData\Kubernetes\logs` directory. It is also a good idea to verify whether the issue is not already known, at `https://github.com/kubernetes-sigs/sig-windows-tools/issues`—the fix may be already available.

4. Joining a new Windows node is a relatively quick process, and after a few seconds, the operation should finish. Now, verify whether the new node is visible in the cluster and has a `Ready` status, like this:

```
PS C:\src> kubectl get nodes
NAME                STATUS    ROLES     AGE    VERSION
kubernetes-master   Ready     master    26h    v1.16.1
win-gjd24m0p8da     Ready     <none>    11m    v1.16.1
```

5. On the Windows node, verify using the `ipconfig` command that the `cbr0_ep` interface has been created by Flannel, as illustrated in the following screenshot:

```
Administrator: c:\windows\system32\windowspowershell\v1.0\powershell.exe        —     □     ✕

PS C:\Users\Administrator> ipconfig

Windows IP Configuration


Ethernet adapter vEthernet (Ethernet):

   Connection-specific DNS Suffix  . :
   Link-local IPv6 Address . . . . . : fe80::6074:eaec:61ba:4e66%14
   IPv4 Address. . . . . . . . . . . : 10.0.0.3
   Subnet Mask . . . . . . . . . . . : 255.0.0.0
   Default Gateway . . . . . . . . . : 10.0.0.1

Ethernet adapter vEthernet (cbr0_ep):

   Connection-specific DNS Suffix  . :
   Link-local IPv6 Address . . . . . : fe80::71be:b7ae:bbe2:da60%21
   IPv4 Address. . . . . . . . . . . : 10.244.1.2
   Subnet Mask . . . . . . . . . . . : 255.255.255.0
   Default Gateway . . . . . . . . . : 10.244.1.1
```

6. Run a quick smoke test of the new node by creating an ad hoc PowerShell Pod named `powershell-debug`. The Pod spec override must contain `nodeSelector`, which matches Windows nodes, as illustrated in the following code block:

```
kubectl run `
        --generator=run-pod/v1 powershell-debug `
        -i --tty `
        --image=mcr.microsoft.com/powershell:nanoserver-1809 `
        --restart=Never `
        --overrides='{\"apiVersion\": \"v1\", \"spec\":
{\"nodeSelector\": { \"beta.kubernetes.io/os\": \"windows\" }}}'
```

7. The image pull can take a bit of time. You can observe the Pod events by using the following command:

```
kubectl describe pod powershell-debug
```

8. When the Pod starts, verify DNS resolution and connectivity to external addresses—for example, by using the `ping google.com` command, as shown in the following screenshot:

```
Administrator: Windows PowerShell                    —    □    ✕

PowerShell 6.2.3
Copyright (c) Microsoft Corporation. All rights reserved.

https://aka.ms/pscore6-docs
Type 'help' to get help.

PS C:\> ping google.com

Pinging google.com [216.58.215.110] with 32 bytes of data:
Reply from 216.58.215.110: bytes=32 time=102ms TTL=54
Reply from 216.58.215.110: bytes=32 time=43ms TTL=54
Reply from 216.58.215.110: bytes=32 time=45ms TTL=54
Reply from 216.58.215.110: bytes=32 time=34ms TTL=54

Ping statistics for 216.58.215.110:
    Packets: Sent = 4, Received = 4, Lost = 0 (0% loss),
Approximate round trip times in milli-seconds:
    Minimum = 34ms, Maximum = 102ms, Average = 56ms
PS C:\>
```

9. Exit the container and delete the Pod afterward, by running the following command (we did not use the `--rm` flag so that you can easily investigate any problems using the `kubectl describe` command):

```
kubectl delete pod powershell-debug
```

For completeness, in order to remove the Windows node and reset the state of the machine (for example, after a configuration change, in order to install and join again), use the same `KubeCluster.ps1` script and execute the following command:

```
.\KubeCluster.ps1 -ConfigFile .\Kubeclusterbridge.json -Reset
```

Congratulations—now, you have a fully functional, hybrid Windows/Linux Kubernetes cluster running! You may choose to add more Windows or Linux nodes following the same instructions or using VM images (remember about regenerating hostnames, MAC addresses, and `product_uuids`).

Deploying and inspecting your first application

Now, it is time to have some fun with the newly created Kubernetes cluster. We will create a minimal Deployment with the NodePort Service, exposing the application to users. The application itself is the official ASP.NET Core 3.0 sample packaged as a Docker image—feel free to use any other Windows web application container image, or create your own. We have chosen the official sample in order to make the Deployment as fast as possible so that we can focus on Kubernetes operations.

To deploy the sample application, perform the following steps:

1. Create a `windows-example.yaml` manifest file that contains the Deployment and Service definition. You can download it from the GitHub repository (`https://raw.githubusercontent.com/PacktPublishing/Hands-On-Kubernetes-on-Windows/master/Chapter07/09_windows-example/windows-example.yaml`) or directly apply it to the cluster, as follows:

```yaml
apiVersion: apps/v1
kind: Deployment
metadata:
  name: windows-example
  labels:
    app: sample
spec:
```

```
      replicas: 3
      selector:
        matchLabels:
          app: windows-example
      template:
        metadata:
          name: windows-example
          labels:
            app: windows-example
        spec:
          nodeSelector:
            "beta.kubernetes.io/os": windows
          containers:
          - name: windows-example
            image: mcr.microsoft.com/dotnet/core/samples:aspnetapp-
nanoserver-1809
            resources:
              limits:
                cpu: 1
                memory: 800M
              requests:
                cpu: .1
                memory: 300M
            ports:
              - containerPort: 80
---
apiVersion: v1
kind: Service
metadata:
  name: windows-example
spec:
  type: NodePort
  ports:
  - protocol: TCP
    port: 80
    nodePort: 31001
    targetPort: 80
  selector:
    app: windows-example
```

There are three important points in this manifest file, which have been marked in bold:

- **Scheduling for Windows nodes** requires the use of `nodeSelector` with a `"beta.kubernetes.io/os"`: `windows` value. Similarly, if you need to schedule the Pods for Linux nodes, you should use the `"beta.kubernetes.io/os"`: `linux` node selector in hybrid clusters.
- The Pod definition consists of one container based on a `mcr.microsoft.com/dotnet/core/samples:aspnetapp-nanoserver-1809` image. It is important to ensure **compatibility** between the container host operating system version and the container base image version. In this case, Windows Server 2019 LTS is compatible with 1809-based images. If you chose to use Windows Server 1903 nodes, you have to use 1903-based images.
- The **NodePort Service** will be exposed on port **31001** on each node in the cluster. In other words, you can expect that the application will be available at the `10.0.0.2:31001` and `10.0.0.3:31001` endpoints. Note that for LoadBalancer Services, if your infrastructure does not have load balancers, you can consider using **keepalived** (`https://github.com/munnerz/keepalived-cloud-provider`).

2. Open the PowerShell window and apply the manifest file using `kubectl`, like this:

```
kubectl apply -f .\windows-example.yaml
```

3. Wait for the Pods to start—the initial image pull may take a few minutes. You can observe the status of the Pods with the following command:

```
PS C:\src> kubectl get pods --watch
NAME                                READY STATUS    RESTARTS  AGE
windows-example-66cdf8c4bf-4472x    1/1   Running   0         9m17s
windows-example-66cdf8c4bf-647x8    1/1   Running   0         9m17s
windows-example-66cdf8c4bf-zxjdv    1/1   Running   0         9m17s
```

4. Open your internet browser and navigate to `http://10.0.0.2:31001` and `http://10.0.0.3:31001`. You should see the sample application web page that confirms that the deployment was successful, as shown in the following screenshot:

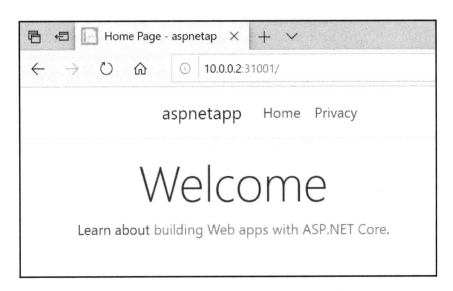

Now, let's perform two common operations that are useful when debugging the application, as follows:

1. Retrieving Pod container logs: To access logs of one of the Pods (`windows-example-66cdf8c4bf-4472x`) in the Deployment, use the following `kubectl logs` command:

```
PS C:\src> kubectl logs windows-example-66cdf8c4bf-4472x
warn:
Microsoft.AspNetCore.DataProtection.Repositories.FileSystemXmlRepos
itory[60]
        Storing keys in a directory
'C:\Users\ContainerUser\AppData\Local\ASP.NET\DataProtection-Keys'
that may not be persisted outside of the container. Protected data
will be unavailable when container is destroyed.
info: Microsoft.Hosting.Lifetime[0]
        Now listening on: http://[::]:80
info: Microsoft.Hosting.Lifetime[0]
        Application started. Press Ctrl+C to shut down.
info: Microsoft.Hosting.Lifetime[0]
        Hosting environment: Production
info: Microsoft.Hosting.Lifetime[0]
```

```
        Content root path: C:\app
warn:
Microsoft.AspNetCore.HttpsPolicy.HttpsRedirectionMiddleware[3]
        Failed to determine the https port for redirect.
```

2. Execute into the Pod container in order to inspect the application configuration. To start a new `cmd` shell (PowerShell is not available in the `nanoserver` image), run the `kubectl exec` command, as follows:

```
PS C:\src> kubectl exec -it windows-example-66cdf8c4bf-4472x cmd
Microsoft Windows [Version 10.0.17763.802]
(c) 2018 Microsoft Corporation. All rights reserved.

C:\app>
```

3. You can now freely access and modify the container, which is useful in debugging and testing scenarios. For example, you can get the contents of the `appsettings.json` file, like this:

```
C:\app>type appsettings.json
{
  "Logging": {
    "LogLevel": {
      "Default": "Information",
      "Microsoft": "Warning",
      "Microsoft.Hosting.Lifetime": "Information"
  }
  },
  "AllowedHosts": "*"
}
```

As you can see, deploying a sample Windows application to a Kubernetes cluster is easy, and all the debugging techniques you know from Linux Kubernetes clusters work exactly the same.

Summary

In this chapter, you have gone through the journey of creating an on-premises Windows/Linux Kubernetes cluster on a Hyper-V host. This approach is useful for creating local development clusters as well as deploying production clusters outside of cloud environments. Let's have a recap of the procedure—we first planned the cluster design and the network for the nodes, Pod, and Service **classless inter-domain routings** (**CIDRs**). Then, we have created the Ubuntu Server 18.04 LTS VM—our Kubernetes master. Creating the master node required an initial configuration of the operating system and the installation of Docker. Initialization was performed using kubeadm. The next important step was the installation of the Kubernetes Pod network, which had to be compatible with both Linux and Windows nodes. In our case, we have chosen Flannel with a `host-gw` backend, which is currently the only stable network solution for hybrid clusters running on-premises. And after that, you have learned how to create the Windows Server 2019 LTS VM and how to join the machine to a Kubernetes cluster using kubeadm and `sig-windows-tools` scripts. Finally, we have deployed a sample ASP.NET Core 3.0 application and performed common operations, such as accessing container logs or executing into a container.

In the next chapter, you will learn how to perform a similar cluster Deployment using AKS Engine. Currently, this is the best and the most stable approach for deploying hybrid Kubernetes clusters in the cloud.

Questions

1. When should you use an internal NAT Hyper-V vSwitch? What are the use cases for an external vSwitch?
2. Which configuration steps are required for preparing a Linux node or master?
3. What are a Service subnet range and a Pod subnet range?
4. How do you generate a new kubeadm token for joining the cluster?
5. How do you allow scheduling of application Pods to the master node?
6. What is the recommended networking solution for on-premises clusters with Linux and Windows nodes?
7. Which steps do you need to perform to join a Windows node to the cluster?
8. What is the command for accessing Pod container logs?

You can find answers to these questions in *Assessments* in back matter of this book.

Further reading

- Currently, most of the resources regarding the Deployment of hybrid Windows/Linux clusters are available online. There are two official guides for creating such clusters:
  - The Kubernetes guide, available at: `https://kubernetes.io/docs/setup/production-environment/windows/intro-windows-in-kubernetes/`.
  - The Microsoft guide, available at: `https://docs.microsoft.com/en-us/virtualization/windowscontainers/kubernetes/getting-started-kubernetes-windows`.

Both guides are often updated, so it is worth checking them as the Deployment procedure may be simplified over time.

- You may also find useful the following **Software-Defined Networking (SDN)** repository from Microsoft, available at: `https://github.com/microsoft/SDN/tree/master/Kubernetes/windows`. It contains many helper scripts that are gradually adopted into the official deployment instructions and kubeadm integration.
- For kubeadm usage and documentation, please refer to `https://kubernetes.io/docs/setup/production-environment/tools/kubeadm/create-cluster-kubeadm/`.
- If you need help with troubleshooting and common problems, you can use the following guides:
  - `https://docs.microsoft.com/en-us/virtualization/windowscontainers/kubernetes/common-problems`.
  - `https://kubernetes.io/docs/setup/production-environment/windows/intro-windows-in-kubernetes/#troubleshooting`.
  - `https://techcommunity.microsoft.com/t5/Networking-Blog/Troubleshooting-Kubernetes-Networking-on-Windows-Part-1/ba-p/508648`—troubleshooting guide, specific to Windows containers networking problems.

8
Deploying a Hybrid Azure Kubernetes Service Engine Cluster

The previous chapter gave an overview of how to create a hybrid Windows/Linux Kubernetes cluster in an on-premises environment. This approach can also be used for Deployments in Infrastructure-as-a-Service cloud environments, but if you are working with Azure, you have an easier solution: **Azure Kubernetes Service (AKS) Engine** (`https://github.com/Azure/aks-engine`). This project aims to provide an Azure-native way of deploying self-managed Kubernetes clusters using **Azure Resource Manager (ARM)** templates, which can leverage all Azure cloud integrations for Kubernetes, for example LoadBalancer services. What's more, with AKS Engine, you have support for the Deployment of a Kubernetes cluster with Windows nodes, requiring minimal configuration and node preparation compared to on-premises environments. In other words, you will be able to provision a production-grade, highly available hybrid cluster in a matter of minutes.

It is important to briefly summarize how AKS Engine relates to other concepts, such as AKS, acs-engine, and the Azure Stack:

- AKS Engine and AKS are not the same Azure offering. AKS is an Azure service that offers you the ability to create a fully managed Kubernetes cluster – we gave an overview of AKS and demonstrated how to deploy a hybrid Windows/Linux cluster using AKS in Chapter 4, *Kubernetes Concepts and Windows Support*. AKS Engine is internally used by AKS but you cannot manage AKS using AK

- acs-engine is a predecessor of AKS Engine, so you may find a lot of documentation mentioning acs-engine instead of AKS Engine. AKS Engine is a backward-compatible continuation of acs-engine.
- Technically, you can also use AKS Engine for on-premises environments if you use the Azure Stack. You can read more here: `https://docs.microsoft.com/en-us/azure-stack/user/azure-stack-kubernetes-aks-engine-overview`.

In this chapter, we will focus on AKS Engine and deploying a hybrid Windows/Linux cluster in the Azure cloud. We will cover the following topics:

- Installing AKS Engine
- Creating an Azure resource group and a service principal
- Using the API model and generating an Azure resource manager template
- Deploying a cluster
- Deploying and inspecting your first application

Technical requirements

For this chapter, you will need the following:

- Windows 10 Pro, Enterprise, or Education (version 1903 or later, 64-bit) installed
- An Azure account
- The Chocolatey package manager for Windows installed (`https://chocolatey.org/`)
- Optionally, Visual Studio Code installed if you would like to visualize the ARM template produced by AKS Engine

Using the Chocolatey package manager is not mandatory but it makes the installation process and application version management much easier. The installation process is documented here: `https://chocolatey.org/install`.

To follow along, you will need your own Azure account in order to create Azure resources for Kubernetes clusters. If you haven't already created an account in the previous chapters, you can read more about how to obtain a limited free account for personal use here: `https://azure.microsoft.com/en-us/free/`.

You can download the latest code samples for this chapter from the official GitHub repository: `https://github.com/PacktPublishing/Hands-On-Kubernetes-on-Windows/tree/master/Chapter08`.

Installing AKS Engine

AKS Engine itself is a command-line tool that can generate an Azure Resource Manager (ARM) template based on a supplied configuration file. To use AKS Engine, you need the following which have installation processes described in previous chapters:

- **The Azure CLI and Azure Cloud Shell**: Instructions are available in Chapter 2, *Managing State in Containers*, in the *Using remote/cloud storage for container storage* storage.
- **kubectl**: Instructions are available in Chapter 6, *Interacting with Kubernetes Clusters*, in the *Installing Kubernetes command-line tooling* section.
- **SSH client for Windows:** Instructions are available in Chapter 7, *Deploying a Hybrid On-Premises Kubernetes Cluster*, in the *Creating a Kubernetes master node using kubeadm* section.

With all the tools installed on your machine, you can proceed to installing AKS Engine itself. The recommended installation approach on Windows is using Chocolatey. Alternatively, you can download AKS Engine binaries (https://github.com/Azure/aks-engine/releases/latest), extract them, and add them to your $env:PATH environment variable. To install AKS Engine using Chocolatey, proceed with the following steps:

1. Open a PowerShell window as an administrator.
2. To install the aks-engine package, execute the following command:

```
choco install aks-engine
```

3. If you want to install a specific version of AKS Engine, for example 0.42.0, use the following command:

```
choco install aks-engine --version=0.42.0
```

4. Verify that your installation was successful:

```
PS C:\src> aks-engine version
Version: v0.42.0
GitCommit: 0959ab812
GitTreeState: clean
```

Now, you are ready to continue to the next step – configuring prerequisites for your Kubernetes cluster. Let's begin by gathering initial cluster information and creating an Azure resource group.

Creating an Azure resource group and a service principal

Before we deploy a Kubernetes cluster using AKS Engine, we need to perform the following initial steps:

1. You need to ensure that you have appropriate permissions within the Azure subscription to create and assign Azure Active Directory service principals. If you created an Azure account just for the walk through, you will have the permissions by default.

2. Determine `SubscriptionId` of the Azure subscription that you are going to use for deploying the cluster. You can do that by opening a PowerShell window and executing the following commands:

   ```
   PS C:\src> az login
   PS C:\src> az account list -o table
   Name            CloudName       SubscriptionId
   State      IsDefault
   --------------  -----------     ------------------------------------  -
   ------     -----------
   Pay-As-You-Go   AzureCloud      cc9a8166-829e-401e-a004-76d1e3733b8e
   Enabled    True
   ```

   We will use `cc9a8166-829e-401e-a004-76d1e3733b8e` as the `SubscriptionId` in the next paragraphs.

3. Determine a globally unique `dnsPrefix` that you would like to use for the hostnames within your cluster. Alternatively, you can rely on an auto generated prefix by AKS Engine. We will use `handson-aks-engine-win` as the prefix in the next paragraphs.

4. Choose which Azure location you would like to use for deploying the cluster. We will use `westeurope` in the examples that follow.

5. Choose a name for your new Azure resource group for your cluster. We will use `aks-engine-windows-resource-group` in the next paragraphs.

6. Choose a username and password for the Windows nodes. We will use `azureuser` and `S3cur3P@ssw0rd` for this purpose – remember to use your own secure password!

7. Generate an SSH key pair that you can use for connecting to Linux nodes. If you choose to have an OpenSSH server on Windows nodes, you can later use the same key pair for accessing the Windows nodes.

The steps described in the next paragraphs for prerequisite creation and AKS Engine Deployment are captured in the PowerShell script available here: https://github.com/PacktPublishing/Hands-On-Kubernetes-on-Windows/blob/master/Chapter08/01_aks-engine/01_CreateAKSEngineClusterWithWindowsNodes.ps1.

Now, please follow the steps for creating an Azure resource group and an Azure Active Directory service principal:

1. Open a PowerShell window and log in using the Azure CLI:

   ```
   az login
   ```

2. Create an Azure resource group for your cluster using the following command:

   ```
   az group create `
     --name aks-engine-windows-resource-group `
     --location westeurope
   ```

3. Create an Azure Active Directory service principal for your cluster. Use an appropriate Subscription ID and Resource Group name:

   ```
   az ad sp create-for-rbac `
     --role="Contributor" `
     --scopes="/subscriptions/cc9a8166-829e-401e-
   a004-76d1e3733b8e/resourceGroups/aks-engine-windows-resource-group"
   ```

Please note that if scope is limited to a given resource group, you will not be able to use the Container Monitoring add-on. We'll cover the configuration of the AAD service principal for this purpose in the next sections.

4. Examine the output of the previous command and take note of appId and password. You cannot retrieve the password later:

   ```
   {
     "appId": "7614823f-aca5-4a31-b2a5-56f30fa8bd8e",
     "displayName": "azure-cli-2019-10-19-12-48-08",
     "name": "http://azure-cli-2019-10-19-12-48-08",
     "password": "8737c1e6-b1b1-4c49-a195-f7ea0fe37613",
     "tenant": "86be0945-a0f3-44c2-8868-9b6aa96b0b62"
   }
   ```

The last step is generating an SSH key pair for accessing Linux nodes in the cluster:

1. Open a PowerShell window.
2. If you have followed the previous chapters, you may already have an SSH key pair generated that you can reuse and skip the next step. To check whether you have an existing SSH key pair, use the following command:

   ```
   ls ~\.ssh\id_rsa.pub
   ```

3. If you need to generate a key pair, execute the following command (using defaults is advised):

   ```
   ssh-keygen
   ```

Now, you have all the information that is required for AKS Engine Deployment. All we need to do is to prepare the AKS Engine apimodel and generate an ARM template for our cluster.

Using apimodel and generating an Azure resource manager template

At its core, AKS Engine uses an **apimodel** (or a cluster definition) JSON file in order to generate Azure resource manager templates that can be used for deploying a Kubernetes cluster directly to Azure. The documentation and schema for apimodel can be found here: `https://github.com/Azure/aks-engine/blob/master/docs/topics/clusterdefinitions.md`. AKS Engine comes with out-of-the-box support for Windows nodes in cluster definitions. You can find examples in the official AKS Engine GitHub repository: `https://github.com/Azure/aks-engine/tree/master/examples/windows`.

Let's now create a custom apimodel based on the minimal Windows cluster example definition (`https://github.com/Azure/aks-engine/blob/master/examples/windows/kubernetes.json`). We will also include two Linux nodes in order to run a hybrid Windows/Linux configuration (one Linux master, two Windows nodes, and two Linux nodes). Follow these steps:

1. Download the following file and save it as `kubernetes-windows.json`: `https://raw.githubusercontent.com/Azure/aks-engine/master/examples/windows/kubernetes.json`.

2. Change `properties.orchestratorProfile.orchestratorRelease` to the desired Kubernetes release, for example, `1.16`.

3. Modify `properties.masterProfile.dnsPrefix` to the selected DNS prefix. In examples, we use `handson-aks-engine-win`, but you need to choose your unique prefix.

4. Add a Linux nodes pool by adding the following JSON object to `properties.agentPoolProfiles`:

```
{
    "name": "linuxpool1",
    "count": 2,
    "vmSize": "Standard_D2_v3",
    "availabilityProfile": "AvailabilitySet"
}
```

5. Modify `properties.windowsProfile.adminUsername` and `properties.windowsProfile.adminPassword` to your selected username and password for Windows nodes.

6. Copy the contents of `~\.ssh\id_rsa.pub` to `properties.linuxProfile.ssh.publicKeys.keyData`.

7. Use the service principal `appId` in `properties.servicePrincipalProfile.clientId` and `password` in `properties.servicePrincipalProfile.secret`.

8. An example customized file has the following contents:

```
{
  "apiVersion": "vlabs",
    "properties": {
        "orchestratorProfile": {
            "orchestratorType": "Kubernetes",
            "orchestratorRelease": "1.16"
        },
        "masterProfile": {
            "count": 1,
            "dnsPrefix": "handson-aks-engine-win",
            "vmSize": "Standard_D2_v3"
        },
        "agentPoolProfiles": [{
                "name": "linuxpool1",
                "count": 2,
                "vmSize": "Standard_D2_v3",
                "availabilityProfile": "AvailabilitySet"
            }, {
                "name": "windowspool2",
```

```json
                    "count": 2,
                    "vmSize": "Standard_D2_v3",
                    "availabilityProfile": "AvailabilitySet",
                    "osType": "Windows",
                    "osDiskSizeGB": 128,
                    "extensions": [{
                            "name": "winrm"
                        }
                    ]
                }
            ],
            "windowsProfile": {
                "adminUsername": "azureuser",
                "adminPassword": "S3cur3P@ssw0rd",
                "sshEnabled": true
            },
            "linuxProfile": {
                "adminUsername": "azureuser",
                "ssh": {
                    "publicKeys": [{
                            "keyData": "<contents of
~\.ssh\id_rsa.pub>"
                        }
                    ]
                }
            },
            "servicePrincipalProfile": {
                "clientId": "8d4d1104-7818-4883-88d2-2146b658e4b2",
                "secret": "9863e38c-896f-4dba-ac56-7a3c1849a87a"
            },
            "extensionProfiles": [{
                    "name": "winrm",
                    "version": "v1"
                }
            ]
        }
    }
```

The apimodel is ready to be used by AKS Engine. Generate the ARM template using the following command:

```
aks-engine generate .\kubernetes-windows.json
```

This will generate the ARM template (with parameters), the full apimodel, and kubeconfigs (for each possible Azure location) in the `_output\<dnsPrefix>` directory. You can inspect these files in order to understand how the cluster is designed – optionally, if you have Visual Studio Code installed, you can use the following excellent extension for visualizing ARM templates – `https://marketplace.visualstudio.com/items?itemName=bencoleman.armview`:

1. In VS Code, after you have installed the extension, open the `_output\<dnsPrefix>\azuredeploy.json` ARM template file.
2. Use the following icon to visualize the ARM template:

3. Load the ARM template parameters `_output\<dnsPrefix>\azuredeploy.parameters.json` using the following icon:

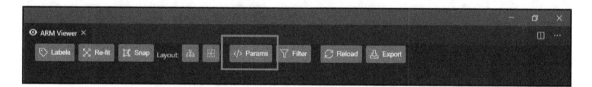

4. You can now inspect the ARM template in a convenient way:

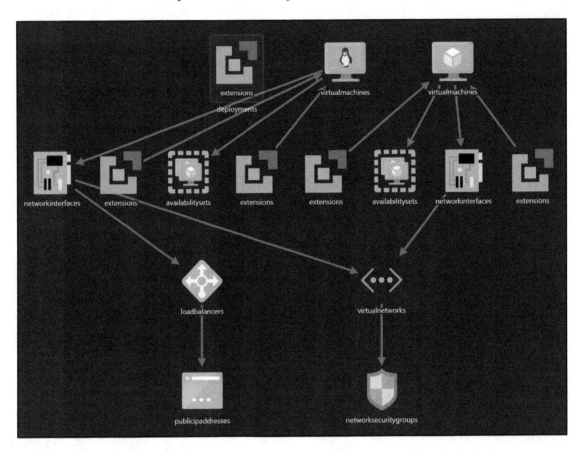

At this point, we are ready to proceed with deploying the cluster using the Azure CLI!

Deploying the cluster

In order to deploy the Kubernetes cluster from the Azure resource manager template, we will use the `az group deployment create` command. This Azure CLI command requires passing the ARM template (`_output\<dnsPrefix>\azuredeploy.json`) and the ARM parameters file (`_output\<dnsPrefix>\azuredeploy.parameters.json`). To deploy the cluster, perform the following steps:

1. Execute the command:

```
az group deployment create `
    --name kubernetes-windows-cluster `
    --resource-group aks-engine-windows-resource-group `
    --template-file ".\_output\<dnsPrefix>\azuredeploy.json" `
    --parameters ".\_output\<dnsPrefix>\azuredeploy.parameters.json"
```

If you run into any problems, you can check the ARM Deployment failure details in the Azure portal by navigating to your resource group and clicking the **Deployment: Failed** link in the upper-right corner. For any `InternalServerErrors`, you may just try choosing another Azure location, such as `westus`.

2. After a few minutes, when the Deployment is finished, the list of created resources and output variables will be returned in JSON format:

```
...
"agentStorageAccountSuffix": {
  "type": "String",
  "value": ""
},
"masterFQDN": {
  "type": "String",
  "value": "<dnsPrefix>.westeurope.cloudapp.azure.com"
},
"primaryAvailabilitySetName": {
  "type": "String",
  "value": "windowspool2-availabilitySet-70017404"
},
...
```

3. Extract the `masterFQDN` property. This is your Kubernetes master DNS name.

Alternatively, you can take the approach of using the `aks-engine` `deploy` command, which combines customizing cluster definition and generating and deploying an ARM template into one command. Note that in order to use container monitoring features you must use the `aks-engine deploy` command at this point.

Now, we need to connect to our new cluster. AKS Engine, along with the ARM template, generates a set of `kubeconfigs` for all possible Azure locations in the form of `.\_output\<dnsPrefix>\kubeconfig\kubeconfig.<azureLocation>.json`. In our case, we used the location `westeurope`, so the kubeconfig is `.\_output\<dnsPrefix>\kubeconfig\kubeconfig.westeurope.json`. To use this kubeconfig for your kubectl, you can use one of the config management techniques provided in `Chapter 6`, *Interacting with Kubernetes Clusters*. For example, to merge this file with your existing, default kubeconfig, perform the following steps:

1. Inspect the contents of `.\_output\<dnsPrefix>\kubeconfig\kubeconfig.westeurope.json` in order to know the cluster name and context name. Both should be the same as your `<dnsPrefix>`.

2. Perform a test merge of the file with the default kubeconfig. Use the following command:

   ```
   $env:KUBECONFIG=".\_output\<dnsPrefix>\kubeconfig\kubeconfig.westeu
   rope.json;$env:USERPROFILE\.kube\config"
   kubectl config view --raw
   ```

3. Carefully inspect the output in order to determine whether the merged config contains all the clusters and contexts you expect.

4. Save the merged file as the default config and switch to using the new `<dnsPrefix>` context:

   ```
   $env:KUBECONFIG=".\_output\<dnsPrefix>\kubeconfig\kubeconfig.westeu
   rope.json;$env:USERPROFILE\.kube\config"
   kubectl config view --raw > $env:USERPROFILE\.kube\config_new

   Move-Item -Force $env:USERPROFILE\.kube\config_new
   $env:USERPROFILE\.kube\config

   kubectl config use-context "<dnsPrefix>"
   ```

5. Test the connection to your new cluster:

```
PS C:\src\temp> kubectl get nodes --all-namespaces
NAME                        STATUS    ROLES     AGE    VERSION
7001k8s000                  Ready     agent     16m    v1.16.1
7001k8s001                  Ready     agent     16m    v1.16.1
k8s-linuxpool1-70017404-0   Ready     agent     13m    v1.16.1
k8s-linuxpool1-70017404-1   Ready     agent     13m    v1.16.1
k8s-master-70017404-0       Ready     master    18m    v1.16.1
PS C:\src\temp> kubectl get pods --all-namespaces
NAMESPACE      NAME                                         READY
STATUS      RESTARTS     AGE
kube-system    azure-cni-networkmonitor-ftnqs               1/1
Running    0            18m
kube-system    azure-ip-masq-agent-vqdhz                    1/1
Running    0            18m
. . .
```

Please note that clusters deployed by AKS Engine are billed depending on the resources that have been used in the ARM templates. You should use the Azure pricing calculator in order to determine the predicted cost. If you do not need the cluster anymore, it is advised to delete it to avoid any unwanted costs. To delete the AKS Engine cluster, use the following command: `az group delete --name aks-engine-windows-resource-group --yes --no-wait`.

Congratulations! You have deployed a fully functional, hybrid Windows/Linux cluster on Azure using AKS Engine! Let's take a look at how to deploy a simple application to the cluster and how to interact with the cluster.

Deploying and inspecting your first application

In this section, we will perform a similar exercise as in the previous chapter – we are going to deploy a sample ASP.NET Core 3.0 application (using a Deployment Object) to our AKS Engine cluster and demonstrate basic kubectl operations. Many aspects of working with an AKS Engine cluster remain the same as in the case of on-premises clusters – the biggest difference is that you can easily utilize Azure features and integrations. To demonstrate this, we will expose the application using a service of type LoadBalancer instead of NodePort. Thanks to the Kubernetes cloud provider for Azure, the LoadBalancer service will be natively integrated with an Azure Load Balancer instance.

Basic operations

To deploy the sample application, follow these steps:

1. Create a `windows-example.yaml` manifest file that contains a Deployment and Service definition. You can download it from the GitHub repository (`https://raw.githubusercontent.com/PacktPublishing/Hands-On-Kubernetes-on-Windows/master/Chapter08/03_windows-example/windows-example.yaml`) or directly apply it to the cluster:

```yaml
apiVersion: apps/v1
kind: Deployment
metadata:
  name: windows-example
  labels:
    app: sample
spec:
  replicas: 3
  selector:
    matchLabels:
      app: windows-example
  template:
    metadata:
      name: windows-example
      labels:
        app: windows-example
    spec:
      nodeSelector:
        "beta.kubernetes.io/os": windows
      containers:
      - name: windows-example
        image: mcr.microsoft.com/dotnet/core/samples:aspnetapp-nanoserver-1809
        resources:
          limits:
            cpu: 1
            memory: 800M
          requests:
            cpu: .1
            memory: 300M
        ports:
          - containerPort: 80
---
apiVersion: v1
kind: Service
metadata:
  name: windows-example
```

```
spec:
  type: LoadBalancer
  ports:
  - protocol: TCP
    port: 80
  selector:
    app: windows-example
```

There are three important points in this manifest file, which have been marked in bold:

- **Scheduling for Windows nodes** requires using `nodeSelector` with the `"beta.kubernetes.io/os"`: `windows` value. Similarly, if you need to schedule the Pods for Linux nodes, you should use the `"beta.kubernetes.io/os"`: `linux` node selector in hybrid clusters. This remains exactly the same as for on-premises clusters.

- The Pod definition consists of one container based on the `mcr.microsoft.com/dotnet/core/samples:aspnetapp-nanoserver-1809` image. It is important to ensure **compatibility** between the container's host operating system version and the container's base image version – this requirement is the same as in an on-premises cluster. You can control what Windows Server version you have in your AKS Engine cluster using the custom `windowsSku` property in `properties.windowsProfile` in the AKS Engine apimodel JSON file. You can read more in the official documentation: `https://github.com/Azure/aks-engine/blob/master/docs/topics/windows-and-kubernetes.md#choosing-the-windows-server-version`. For an existing cluster, you can check the Windows Server version of nodes using the `kubectl get nodes -o wide` command.

- The Service spec has the type set to `LoadBalancer`. This will result in the creation of an externally accessible Azure Load Balancer for the Service. You can read more about this type of Service in `Chapter 5`, *Kubernetes Networking*.

2. Open a PowerShell window and apply the manifest file using `kubectl`. If you haven't merged your `kubeconfigs`, remember to set the proper `$env:KUBECONFIG` variable first and switch to an appropriate kubectl context:

```
kubectl apply -f .\windows-example.yaml
```

3. Wait for the Pods to start – the initial image pull may take a few minutes. You can observe the status of the Pods with the following command:

```
PS C:\src> kubectl get pods --watch
NAME                                READY  STATUS    RESTARTS  AGE
windows-example-66cdf8c4bf-f5bd8    1/1    Running   0
101s
windows-example-66cdf8c4bf-g4v4s    1/1    Running   0
101s
windows-example-66cdf8c4bf-xkbpf    1/1    Running   0
101s
```

4. Wait for external IP creation of the Service. You can observe the status of the Service using the following command:

```
PS C:\src> kubectl get services --watch
NAME              TYPE           CLUSTER-IP     EXTERNAL-IP
PORT(S)           AGE
kubernetes        ClusterIP      10.0.0.1       <none>
443/TCP           24m
windows-example   LoadBalancer   10.0.158.121   52.136.234.203
80:32478/TCP      3m55s
```

5. Open your internet browser and navigate to the Azure Load Balancer address – in the case of this example, it is `http://52.136.234.203/`. You should see the sample application web page, which confirms that the deployment was successful:

Performing common operations, such as accessing Pod container logs or executing ad hoc processes inside of a Pod container is exactly the same as for on-premises clusters – we will briefly revise how to do that:

1. In order to access logs for one of the Pods (`windows-example-66cdf8c4bf-f5bd8`) created as part of the Deployment, use the following `kubectl logs` command:

   kubectl logs windows-example-66cdf8c4bf-f5bd8

2. To **exec** into the same Pod container, for example, start an interactive `cmd` shell and run the `kubectl exec` command:

   kubectl exec -it windows-example-66cdf8c4bf-f5bd8 cmd

3. You can now freely access and modify the container, which is useful in debugging and testing scenarios. For example, you can get the contents of the `appsettings.json` file:

   ```
   C:\app>type appsettings.json
   {
     "Logging": {
       "LogLevel": {
         "Default": "Information",
         "Microsoft": "Warning",
         "Microsoft.Hosting.Lifetime": "Information"
       }
     },
     "AllowedHosts": "*"
   }
   ```

Next, let's see how to connect to the actual virtual machines that are used in the AKS Engine cluster.

Connecting to virtual machines

In order to connect to a Linux master virtual machine, you can use SSH and directly connect to it as it is exposed to the public network:

1. In a PowerShell window, execute the following command (your public SSH key will be used for authentication):

   ssh azureuser@<dnsPrefix>.westeurope.cloudapp.azure.com

2. Now you can perform any maintenance or debugging operations, for example, accessing kubelet service logs:

```
azureuser@k8s-master-70017404-0:~$ sudo journalctl -u kubelet -o
cat
Stopped Kubelet.
Starting Kubelet...
net.ipv4.tcp_retries2 = 8
Bridge table: nat
Bridge chain: PREROUTING, entries: 0, policy: ACCEPT
Bridge chain: OUTPUT, entries: 0, policy: ACCEPT
Bridge chain: POSTROUTING, entries: 0, policy: ACCEPT
Chain PREROUTING (policy ACCEPT)
```

For Windows nodes (or other Linux nodes), the procedure is a bit more complicated as the VMs are in a private IP range. This means you need to use SSH local port forwarding via the Linux master node in order to connect using a remote desktop connection or SSH:

1. First, query for the private IP address of the Windows node that you would like to connect to. You can see all the names of the nodes using the following command:

```
az vm list --resource-group aks-engine-windows-resource-group -o
table
```

2. Use the name to get the private IP address of the node, for example, `7001k8s000`:

```
PS C:\src> az vm show -g aks-engine-windows-resource-group -n
7001k8s000 --show-details --query 'privateIps'
"10.240.0.4,10.240.0.5,10.240.0.6,10.240.0.7,10.240.0.8,10.240.0.9,
10.240.0.10,10.240.0.11,10.240.0.12,10.240.0.13,10.240.0.14,10.240.
0.15,10.240.0.16,10.240.0.17,10.240.0.18,10.240.0.19,10.240.0.20,10
.240.0.21,10.240.0.22,10.240.0.23,10.240.0.24,10.240.0.25,10.240.0.
26,10.240.0.27,10.240.0.28,10.240.0.29,10.240.0.30,10.240.0.31,10.2
40.0.32,10.240.0.33,10.240.0.34"
```

3. Use one of the private IPs in order to create an SSH tunnel from your local `5500` port via the master node to the `3389` port (RDP) on the Windows node:

```
ssh -L 5500:10.240.0.4:3389
azureuser@<dnsPrefix>.westeurope.cloudapp.azure.com
```

4. In a different PowerShell window, start an RDP session via the tunnel:

```
mstsc /v:localhost:5500
```

5. Provide your Windows node credentials (as in apimodel) and connect:

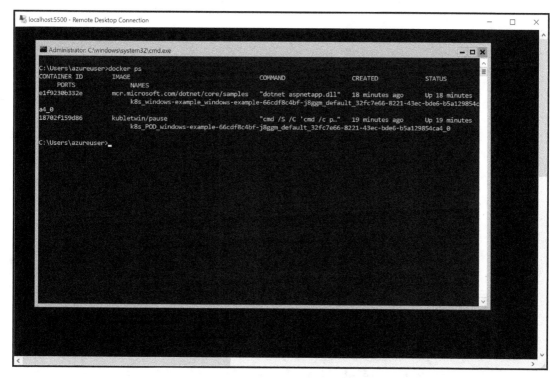

6. Alternatively, you can also use SSH from the master node:

```
ssh 10.240.0.4
```

Now, let's take a look at how to enable Azure Log Analytics and Azure Monitor for containers.

Enabling Azure Log Analytics and Azure Monitor for containers

AKS Engine comes with integration for Azure Log Analytics and Azure Monitor for containers, which is provided by **Operations Management Suite** (**OMS**) agents running on cluster nodes. When deploying your Kubernetes cluster, you can specify an additional `container-monitoring` add-on in the Kubernetes cluster definition – please note that, currently, you have to enable container monitoring when creating a new cluster; you cannot modify an existing cluster definition.

Additionally, this feature comes out of the box only if you use the `aks-engine deploy` command. If you would like to use this feature, perform the following steps:

1. If you have an existing cluster in `aks-engine-windows-resource-group`, delete it first.

2. Modify your cluster definition (apimodel) so that the `properties.orchestratorProfile.kubernetesConfig` property has the following contents. Alternatively, you can use `https://github.com/PacktPublishing/Hands-On-Kubernetes-on-Windows/tree/master/Chapter08/05_windows-apimodel-container-monitoring/kubernetes-windows.json` as the base:

```
{
    "addons": [{
            "name": "container-monitoring",
            "enabled": true
        }
    ]
}
```

3. Ensure that your service principal (in this example `appId: 7614823f-aca5-4a31-b2a5-56f30fa8bd8e`) additionally has the `Log Analytics Contributor` role for your Azure subscription:

```
az role assignment create `
    --assignee 7614823f-aca5-4a31-b2a5-56f30fa8bd8e `
    --role "Log Analytics Contributor" `
    --scope="/subscriptions/cc9a8166-829e-401e-a004-76d1e3733b8e"
```

4. Execute AKS Engine Deployment, using the service principal `appId` as `--client-id` and the `password` as `--client-secret`:

```
aks-engine deploy `
  --subscription-id cc9a8166-829e-401e-a004-76d1e3733b8e `
  --resource-group aks-engine-windows-resource-group `
  --location westeurope `
  --api-model .\kubernetes-windows.json `
  --client-id 7614823f-aca5-4a31-b2a5-56f30fa8bd8e `
  --client-secret 8737c1e6-b1b1-4c49-a195-f7ea0fe37613 `
  --force-overwrite
```

5. After a few minutes, your cluster will be ready and you can merge your default kubeconfig with the AKS Engine kubeconfig.

This `container-monitoring` add-on will make two things possible:

1. Using Azure Log Analytics to query Kubernetes and your application logs using the Kusto query language (`https://docs.microsoft.com/en-us/azure/azure-monitor/log-query/get-started-portal`)

2. Using the Azure Monitor service to monitor containers running in your cluster (`https://docs.microsoft.com/en-us/azure/azure-monitor/insights/container-insights-overview`)

 Note that until the `https://github.com/Azure/aks-engine/issues/2066` issue in AKS Engine is resolved, Kubernetes 1.16 will not integrate with the Log Analytics and Monitor services properly. You can try deploying your cluster again with a different Kubernetes version in apimodel.

These services provide the basic building blocks for monitoring, alerting, and debugging for your containerized applications running on Kubernetes – you can leverage the multiple Azure portal UI features to make analysis and management easier, for example:

1. Use the following URL to access Azure Monitor for containers: `https://aka.ms/azmon-containers`. Azure Monitor deserves a separate, dedicated book to cover all its features – as a quick example, you can explore the default dashboards that are provided for monitoring your Kubernetes cluster:

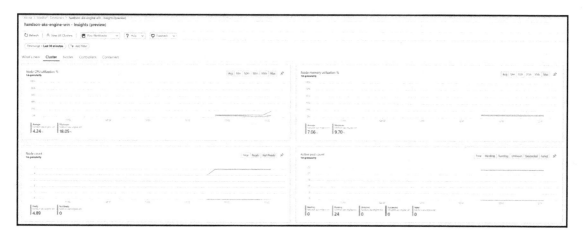

2. Use the following URL to access Azure Log Analytics: `https://portal.azure.com/#blade/Microsoft_Azure_Monitoring/AzureMonitoringBrowseBlade/logs`. Expand the **ContainerInsights** database and select, for example, the **KubeEvents** table. You can now execute a simple Kusto query to check what data is in the table:

```
KubeEvents
| limit 50
```

The following screenshot shows the output of the preceding command:

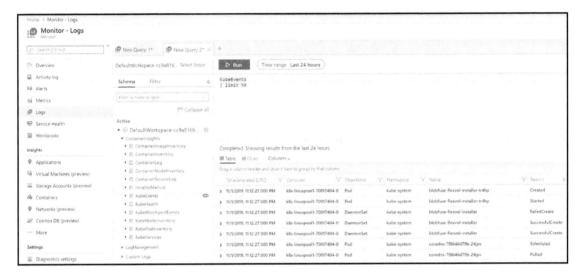

You can learn more about the Log Analytics tables available for container monitoring in the official documentation: `https://docs.microsoft.com/en-us/azure/azure-monitor/insights/containers#monitor-containers`. For the Kusto query language documentation, please refer to `https://docs.microsoft.com/en-us/azure/azure-monitor/log-query/query-language`. Setting up proper monitoring and log analytics solutions is **crucial** for running distributed applications. If you are not using Azure for your clusters, you can consider different solutions, such as Prometheus and Elasticsearch, that provide similar functionalities.

Summary

In this chapter, you have learned how to deploy a hybrid Windows/Linux Kubernetes cluster running on Azure using AKS Engine. Currently, this approach is the most suitable solution for running self-managed, production-grade clusters with Windows nodes. The Deployment procedure is simple – first, install all prerequisites and AKS Engine on your local machine, then create a dedicated Azure resource group and Azure Active Directory service principal. After that, you need to define an apimodel (cluster definition) JSON file for AKS Engine to generate an Azure resource manager template and use the template to deploy the cluster. Additionally, you have learned how to deploy a sample Windows container application and how to perform basic operations using kubectl. On top of that, we have shown how to connect to the virtual machines in the cluster for debugging and monitoring purposes and how to enable Azure Monitor and Azure Log Analytics for your cluster.

The next chapter will focus further on deploying applications to a Kubernetes cluster and how to perform "day-2" operations in your cluster.

Questions

1. What is the difference between AKS and AKS Engine?
2. What is the basic principle of how AKS Engine works?
3. Can you manage AKS clusters using AKS Engine and vice versa?
4. What are the prerequisites for using AKS Engine?
5. What is apimodel in AKS Engine?
6. How do you connect to the Kubernetes Linux master?
7. How do you connect to a Kubernetes Windows node?

You can find the answers to these questions in *Assessments* of this book.

Further reading

- Currently, most of the resources regarding the Deployment of hybrid Windows/Linux clusters using **AKS Engine** are available online. Please check the official documentation on GitHub for more details:
    - https://github.com/Azure/aks-engine/blob/master/docs/topics/windows.md
    - https://github.com/Azure/aks-engine/blob/master/docs/topics/windows-and-kubernetes.md

- In general, many of the topics concerning **AKS** (the managed Kubernetes Azure offering, **not** AKS Engine itself) are useful, as they touch on how to integrate Kubernetes with the Azure ecosystem. You can find more about AKS itself in the following Packt book:
    - *DevOps with Kubernetes – Second Edition* (https://www.packtpub.com/virtualization-and-cloud/devops-kubernetes-second-edition)

- If you need help with troubleshooting and common problems, you can use the following guides:
    - https://github.com/Azure/aks-engine/blob/master/docs/howto/troubleshooting.md
    - https://docs.microsoft.com/en-us/virtualization/windowscontainers/kubernetes/common-problems
    - https://kubernetes.io/docs/setup/production-environment/windows/intro-windows-in-kubernetes/#troubleshooting
    - https://techcommunity.microsoft.com/t5/Networking-Blog/Troubleshooting-Kubernetes-Networking-on-Windows-Part-1/ba-p/508648 – a troubleshooting guide specifically for Windows container networking problems

Section 4: Orchestrating Windows Containers Using Kubernetes

In this section, we will use Kubernetes to create both simple and complex application architectures using containers. We will learn how to deploy, scale, and monitor such applications, utilizing the power of the platform.

This section contains the following chapters:

9
Deploying Your First Application

In the previous chapters, we covered Kubernetes key operation principles and deployment strategies for Windows/Linux hybrid clusters. Now it is time to focus more on deploying and working with Kubernetes applications. To demonstrate the essential operations for Kubernetes applications, we will use the AKS Engine hybrid Kubernetes cluster that we created in Chapter 8, *Deploying Hybrid Azure Kubernetes Service Engine Cluster*. You can use the on-premises hybrid cluster as well, but you should expect limited functionality; for example, services of the LoadBalancer type will not be available.

This chapter covers the following topics:

- Imperatively deploying an application
- Using Kubernetes manifest files
- Scheduling Pods on Windows nodes
- Accessing your application
- Scaling the application

Technical requirements

For this chapter, you will need the following:

- Windows 10 Pro, Enterprise, or Education (version 1903 or later, 64-bit) installed
- An Azure account
- Windows/Linux Kubernetes cluster deployed using AKS Engine

To follow along, you will need your own Azure account to create Azure resources for the Kubernetes cluster. If you haven't already created the account for the previous chapters, you can read more about how to obtain a limited free account for personal use here: `https://azure.microsoft.com/en-us/free/`.

Deploying a Kubernetes cluster using AKS Engine has been covered in `Chapter 8`, *Deploying Hybrid Azure Kubernetes Service Engine Cluster*.

You can download the latest code samples for this chapter from the official GitHub repository: `https://github.com/PacktPublishing/Hands-On-Kubernetes-on-Windows/tree/master/Chapter09`.

Imperatively deploying an application

In the Kubernetes world, you can choose from two approaches when managing your applications: imperative management and declarative management. The imperative approach consists of executing imperative kubectl commands, such as `kubectl run` or `kubectl expose`, and imperative object configuration management, where you use commands such as `kubectl create` or `kubectl replace`. In short, you manage the cluster by executing ad-hoc commands that modify the Kubernetes objects and result in a changed desired state for the cluster—sometimes, you may not even know how the desired state has exactly changed after an imperative command. By contrast, in the declarative approach, you modify object configurations (manifest files) and create or update them in the cluster using the `kubectl apply` command (alternatively, you can use Kustomization files).

Using declarative management is, in general, more close to the spirit of Kubernetes—the whole architecture is focused on persisting the desired cluster state and constantly performing operations that change the current cluster state to the desired state. A general rule of thumb is that in production environments, you should always use declarative management, either using standard manifest files or Kustomization files. You can easily provide source control for your object configurations and integrate this into continuous integration/deployment pipelines. Imperative management is useful for development and proof-of-concept scenarios—the operations are performed directly on a live cluster.

Remember that, for this approach, you will not have an easy way of knowing the history of the previous configurations!

Now, let's first try the imperative approach for deploying a simple web application. We will perform the following operations:

1. Create a single bare Pod or a ReplicationController.
2. Expose it using a Service (LoadBalancer type).

To create imperatively a pod or a ReplicationController, we will use the `kubectl run` command. This command allows you to create different container-management objects using generators. You can find the complete list of generators in the official documentation: `https://kubernetes.io/docs/reference/kubectl/conventions/#generators`—since Kubernetes 1.12, all generators apart from `run-pod/v1` are deprecated. The main reason for this is the relatively high complexity of the `kubectl run` command and the encouragement of a proper, declarative approach for advanced scenarios.

To deploy a sample application based on the `mcr.microsoft.com/dotnet/core/samples:aspnetapp` Docker image, perform the following steps:

1. Open a PowerShell window and ensure that you are using the `kubeconfig` file, which allows you to connect to your AKS Engine hybrid cluster.
2. Determine which version of the Windows Server operating system is available on the nodes in your cluster.For example, for Windows Server 2019 Datacenter nodes, you need to use container images that have base layer version 1809. This means that we have to use the `mcr.microsoft.com/dotnet/core/samples:aspnetapp-nanoserver-1809` Docker image in our example:

   ```
   kubectl get nodes -o wide
   ```

3. Execute the `kubectl run` command with the `run-pod/v1` generator to run a single pod, `windows-example`, for the sample application with `nodeSelector` set to nodes and the OS type,and `windows`:

   ```
   kubectl run `
           --generator=run-pod/v1 `
           --image=mcr.microsoft.com/dotnet/core/samples:aspnetapp-
   nanoserver-1809 `
           --overrides='{\"apiVersion\": \"v1\", \"spec\":
   {\"nodeSelector\": { \"beta.kubernetes.io/os\": \"windows\" }}}' `
           windows-example
   ```

4. The pod will be scheduled on one of the Windows nodes, and you can monitor the progress of pod creation using the following command:

```
PS C:\src> kubectl get pods -w
NAME              READY   STATUS            RESTARTS   AGE
windows-example   0/1     ContainerCreating  0         7s
```

5. When the pod changes its status to `Running`, you can continue with exposing the pod using the LoadBalancer Service:

```
kubectl expose pod windows-example `
        --name windows-example-service `
        --type LoadBalancer `
        --port 8080 `
        --target-port 80
```

6. Wait for `EXTERNAL-IP` of the service to be available:

```
PS C:\src> kubectl get service -w
NAME                      TYPE          CLUSTER-IP       EXTERNAL-IP
PORT(S)           AGE
kubernetes                ClusterIP     10.0.0.1         <none>
443/TCP           24h
windows-example-service   LoadBalancer  10.0.192.180
213.199.135.14   8080:30746/TCP   5m10s
```

7. Now you can use the external IP of the service and port `8080` to access the application running in the pod. For example, in the web browser, navigate to `http://213.199.135.14:8080/`.

Alternatively, the preceding procedure can be performed in only one `kubectl run` command, which will create the pod and expose it immediately using the LoadBalancer Service:

```
kubectl run `
        --generator=run-pod/v1 `
        --image=mcr.microsoft.com/dotnet/core/samples:aspnetapp-
nanoserver-1809 `
        --overrides='{\"apiVersion\": \"v1\", \"spec\":
{\"nodeSelector\": { \"beta.kubernetes.io/os\": \"windows\" }}}' `
        --expose `
        --port 80 `
        --service-overrides='{ \"spec\": { \"type\":
\"LoadBalancer\" }}' `
        windows-example
```

Note that this command exposes the service using port 80, not 8080. Using service port 80 and target port 8080 requires another layer of complexity in the `--service-overrides` flag.

For the sake of completeness, let's run our `mcr.microsoft.com/dotnet/core/samples:aspnetapp-nanoserver-1809` container behind a Kubernetes ReplicationController object. You can learn more about ReplicationControllers, ReplicaSets, and Deployments in `Chapter 4`, *Kubernetes Concepts and Windows Support*—in general, it is not advisable to run bare Pods in your cluster; you should always manage Pods using at least ReplicaSets or, preferably, Deployments. In Kubernetes 1.17, it is still possible to create a ReplicationController using `kubectl run`—the generator is deprecated but not removed yet. Creating a ReplicationController imperatively requires using a different `--generator` flag with the value `run/v1`:

```
kubectl run `
        --generator=run/v1 `
        --image=mcr.microsoft.com/dotnet/core/samples:aspnetapp-
nanoserver-1809 `
        --overrides='{\"apiVersion\": \"v1\", \"spec\": {\"nodeSelector\":
{ \"beta.kubernetes.io/os\": \"windows\" }}}' `
        --expose `
        --port 80 `
        --service-overrides='{ \"spec\": { \"type\": \"LoadBalancer\" }}' `
        windows-example
```

Even if this approach is quick and does not require any configuration files, you can clearly see that using `kubectl run` for anything else than simple operations is getting complex and error-prone. In most cases, you will be using imperative commands for the following operations:

- Quickly creating Pods in your development clusters
- Creating ad hoc interactive Pods for debugging purposes
- Predictably deleting Kubernetes resources—more on this in the next section

Let's now perform similar Deployment by using Kubernetes manifest files and the declarative management approach.

Using Kubernetes manifest files

Declarative management of Kubernetes objects is much closer to the spirit of Kubernetes—you focus on telling Kubernetes what you want (describing the desired state) instead of directly telling it what to do. As your application grows and has more components, managing the cluster using imperative commands becomes impossible. It is a much better idea to use imperative commands for read-only operations, such as `kubectl describe`, `kubectl get`, and `kubectl logs`, and perform all modifications to the clusters desired state using the `kubectl apply` command and Kubernetes object configuration files (also known as manifest files).

There are a couple of recommended practices when using manifest files:

- It's preferable to use YAML manifest files over JSON manifest files. YAML is easier to manage and more commonly used by Kubernetes community.
- Store your manifest files in source control such as Git. Before applying any configuration changes to the cluster, push the changes to the source control first—this will make rollbacks and configuration restoration much easier. Eventually, you should automate this process as part of your CI/CD pipeline.
- Grouping multiple manifest files into a single file is recommended, whenever it makes sense. The official Kubernetes examples repository provides a good demonstration of this approach: `https://github.com/kubernetes/examples/blob/master/guestbook/all-in-one/guestbook-all-in-one.yaml`.
- If you have multiple manifest files for your cluster, you can use `kubectl apply` to recursively apply all manifest files in a given directory.
- Use `kubectl diff` to understand what changes will be applied to the current cluster configuration.
- When deleting Kubernetes objects, use the imperative `kubectl delete` command as it gives predictable results. You can learn more about the declarative deleting of resources in the official documentation but in practice, it is a more risky approach: `https://kubernetes.io/docs/tasks/manage-kubernetes-objects/declarative-config/#how-to-delete-objects`.
- Use labels whenever possible to semantically describe your components: `https://kubernetes.io/docs/concepts/configuration/overview/#using-labels`.

> More best practices regarding manifest files can be found in the official documentation: `https://kubernetes.io/docs/concepts/configuration/overview/`.

Now, let's try demonstrating this approach by deploying an application similar to the one in the last section. This time, we will use Deployment and service objects, which will be defined in separate manifest files—in a real-world scenario, you would group these two manifest files into a single file, but for demonstration purposes, it makes sense to separate them. Follow these steps to deploy the application:

1. Open a PowerShell window.
2. Ensure that your cluster is not running resources from the previous section—you can check that using the `kubectl get all` command and delete them using the `kubectl delete` command.
3. Create a directory for your manifest files, for example, `declarative-demo`:

   ```
   md .\declarative-demo
   cd .\declarative-demo
   ```

4. Create the `windows-example-deployment.yaml` manifest file, which contains the Deployment definition:

   ```yaml
   ---
   apiVersion: apps/v1
   kind: Deployment
   metadata:
     name: windows-example
     labels:
       app: sample
   spec:
     replicas: 1
     selector:
       matchLabels:
         app: windows-example
     template:
       metadata:
         name: windows-example
         labels:
           app: windows-example
       spec:
         nodeSelector:
           "beta.kubernetes.io/os": windows
         containers:
         - name: windows-example
           image: mcr.microsoft.com/dotnet/core/samples:aspnetapp-nanoserver-1809
           ports:
             - containerPort: 80
   ```

5. Create the `windows-example-service.yaml` manifest file, which contains the LoadBalancer Service definition:

```
---
apiVersion: v1
kind: Service
metadata:
  name: windows-example
spec:
  type: LoadBalancer
  ports:
  - protocol: TCP
    port: 8080
    targetPort: 80
  selector:
    app: windows-example
```

6. Apply the manifest files in the current directory using the `kubectl apply` command. Note that if you had a multi-level directory hierarchy, you could use the `-R` flag for recursive processing:

```
PS C:\src\declarative-demo> kubectl apply -f .\
deployment.apps/windows-example created
service/windows-example created
```

7. Use the following command to wait for the service's external IP to be available:

```
PS C:\src\declarative-demo> kubectl get service -w
NAME                 TYPE            CLUSTER-IP      EXTERNAL-IP
PORT(S)              AGE
kubernetes           ClusterIP       10.0.0.1        <none>
443/TCP              44h
windows-example      LoadBalancer    10.0.63.175     51.144.36.7
8080:30568/TCP       3m28s
```

8. Use your web browser to navigate to the external IP and port `8080`.

Now, let's see how you can apply a simple change to your application using the declarative approach—we would like to change the LoadBalancer port to `9090`:

1. Open the `windows-example-service.yaml` manifest file.
2. Modify the `spec.ports[0].port` value to `9090`.
3. Save the manifest file.

4. (Optional but recommended) Verify your changes using the `kubectl diff` command. Remember that you need to have an appropriate *diff* tool installed and defined in the `$env:KUBECTL_EXTERNAL_DIFF` environment variable; you can learn more about this in Chapter 6, *Interacting with Kubernetes Clusters*:

```
kubectl diff -f .\
```

5. Apply the manifest files again:

```
PS C:\src\declarative-demo> kubectl apply -f .\
deployment.apps/windows-example unchanged
service/windows-example configured
```

6. Notice that only `service/windows-example` has been detected as changed in the desired configuration.

7. Now, you can navigate in the web browser to the external IP address and port `9090` to verify the changes.

8. If you want to delete all of the resources that have been created by manifest files in the current directory, you can use the following command:

```
kubectl delete -f .\
```

That's it! As you can see, declarative management may require a bit more of boilerplate configuration but, in the end, managing the applications using this approach is much more predictable and easier to track.

When managing complex applications running in multiple environments, consider using Kustomization files (which can be used with the `kubectl apply` command) or Helm Charts. For example, with Kustomization files, you can organize the configuration files in a convention-friendly directory structure: `https://kubectl.docs.kubernetes.io/pages/app_composition_and_deployment/structure_directories.html`.

In the next section, we will take a quick look at the recommended practices regarding scheduling Pods on Windows nodes.

Scheduling Pods on Windows nodes

To schedule Pods on nodes with specific properties, Kubernetes gives you a few possible options:

- Using `nodeName` in the Pod specification. This is the simplest form of statically scheduling Pods on a given node and is generally not recommended.
- Using `nodeSelector` in the pod specification. This gives you the possibility to schedule your pod only on nodes that have certain label values. We have been already using this approach in the previous section.
- Node affinity and anti-affinity: These concepts expand the `nodeSelector` approach and provide a richer language of defining which nodes are preferred or avoided for your pod. You can read more about the possibilities in the official documentation: `https://kubernetes.io/docs/concepts/configuration/assign-pod-node/#affinity-and-anti-affinity`.
- Node taints and pod tolerations: They provide an opposite functionality to node affinity—you apply a taint to a given node (which describes some kind of limitation) and the pod must have a specific toleration defined to be schedulable on the tainted node.

Scheduling Pods in hybrid Windows/Linux clusters requires at least using `nodeSelector` or a combination of node taints with `nodeSelector`. Every Kubernetes node comes by default with a set of labels, which include the following:

- `kubernetes.io/arch`, which describes the node's processor architecture, for example, `amd64` or `arm`: This is also defined as `beta.kubernetes.io/arch`.
- `kubernetes.io/os`, which has a value of `linux` or `windows`: This is also defined as `beta.kubernetes.io/os`.

You can check the default labels for your Windows node (for example, `7001k8s011`) in your AKS Engine cluster using the following command:

```
PS C:\src> kubectl describe node 7001k8s011
Name:              7001k8s011
Roles:             agent
Labels:            agentpool=windowspool2
                   beta.kubernetes.io/arch=amd64
                   beta.kubernetes.io/instance-type=Standard_D2_v3
                   beta.kubernetes.io/os=windows
                   failure-domain.beta.kubernetes.io/region=westeurope
                   failure-domain.beta.kubernetes.io/zone=0
                   kubernetes.azure.com/cluster=aks-engine-windows-
resource-group
```

```
kubernetes.azure.com/role=agent
kubernetes.io/arch=amd64
kubernetes.io/hostname=7001k8s011
kubernetes.io/os=windows
kubernetes.io/role=agent
node-role.kubernetes.io/agent=
storageprofile=managed
storagetier=Standard_LRS
```

If your pod does not contain `nodeSelector` in the specification, it can be scheduled on both Windows and Linux nodes— this is a problem as Windows containers will not start on Linux nodes and vice versa. The recommended practice is using `nodeSelector` for the predictable scheduling of your Pods for both Windows and Linux containers. For example, in the Deployment definition, the pod template may contain the following:

```
---
apiVersion: apps/v1
kind: Deployment
metadata:
  name: windows-example
spec:
...
  template:
...
    spec:
      nodeSelector:
        "beta.kubernetes.io/os": windows
...
```

Alternatively, you can use, in the latest versions of Kubernetes, the `"kubernetes.io/os":` `windows` selector. For Linux containers, you need to specify `"beta.kubernetes.io/os":` `linux` or `"kubernetes.io/os": linux`.

This approach may cause problems when you are adding Windows nodes to existing large, Linux-only clusters, using Helm Charts or Kubernetes Operators—such workloads may not have the Linux node selector specified out of the box. To solve this issue, you can use taints and tolerations: mark your Windows nodes with a specific `NoSchedule` taints and use matching toleration for your Pods. We will use taint with the `os` key and a value of `Win1809` for this purpose.

To taint Windows nodes, you have two possibilities:

- Taint the node at registration level using the `--register-with-taints='os=Win1809:NoSchedule'` flag for kubelet. Note that this approach is currently not available in AKS Engine as `--register-with-taints` is not user-configurable—you can read more in the documentation: `https://github.com/Azure/aks-engine/blob/master/docs/topics/clusterdefinitions.md#kubeletconfig`.

- Taint the node using kubectl. You can add a taint using the following command: `kubectl taint nodes <nodeName> os=Win1809:NoSchedule` and remove it using `kubectl taint nodes 7001k8s011 os:NoSchedule-`.

Then, your Deployment definition would have to specify the appropriate pod node selector for Windows and taint toleration, which allows scheduling on Windows nodes:

```
---
apiVersion: apps/v1
kind: Deployment
metadata:
  name: windows-example
spec:
...
  template:
...
    spec:
      nodeSelector:
        "beta.kubernetes.io/os": windows
      tolerations:
      - key: "os"
        operator: "Equal"
        value: "Win1809"
        effect: "NoSchedule"
...
```

In this approach, for Linux containers, you do not need to specify any node selector or taint toleration. However, if possible, it is recommended to use the node selector approach without node taints, especially if you are building a new cluster.

In the next section, we will take a look at how you can access your application.

Accessing your application

For accessing your application running in a pod, you have a few possibilities depending on your scenario. In debugging and testing scenarios, you can access your application in the following simple ways:

- Use `kubectl exec` to create an ad hoc, interactive pod. We used this approach in the previous chapters.
- Use `kubectl proxy` to access any service type. This approach works only for HTTP(S) endpoints as it uses proxy functionality provided by Kubernetes API Server.
- Use `kubectl port-forward`. You can use this approach to access individual Pods or Pods running in a Deployment or behind a service.

If you would like to expose the application for end users in production, you can use the following:

- A service object with the LoadBalancer or NodePort type: We have already demonstrated how to use the LoadBalancer Service in the previous section.
- Using an Ingress Controller together with a service of the ClusterIP type: This approach reduces the number of cloud load balancers used (resulting in reduced operational costs) and performs load balancing and routing inside the Kubernetes cluster. Note that this approach uses L7 load balancing so it can be used for exposing HTTP(S) endpoints only.

You can learn in detail about services and Ingress Controllers in `Chapter 5`, *Kubernetes Networking*. Later in this section, we will demonstrate how to use an Ingress Controller for the demo application.

 You can read more about accessing applications running in the cluster in various scenarios in the official documentation: `https://kubernetes.io/docs/tasks/administer-cluster/access-cluster-services/#accessing-services-running-on-the-cluster`.

Let's first demonstrate how to use `kubectl proxy` and `kubectl port-forward`. Perform the following steps:

1. Open a Powershell window.
2. Ensure that the demonstration application from the previous sections is deployed and has a `windows-example` service with port `8080` deployed in the cluster.
3. Run the `kubectl proxy` command:

   ```
   PS C:\src\declarative-demo> kubectl proxy
   Starting to serve on 127.0.0.1:8001
   ```

4. This will expose a simple proxy server on your localhost machine on port `8001` to the remote Kubernetes API Server. You can freely use the API using this endpoint, without additional authentication. Note that using a raw API without a proxy is also possible but then you have to handle the authentication yourself (https://kubernetes.io/docs/tasks/administer-cluster/access-cluster-api/).

5. Your service will be available at http://<proxyEndpoint>/api/v1/namespaces/<namespaceName>/services/[https:]<serviceName>[:portName]/proxy. In our case, navigate to http://127.0.0.1:8001/api/v1/namespaces/default/services/windows-example/proxy/. This approach works for any service type, including just internal ClusterIPs.

6. Terminate the `kubectl proxy` process.

7. Now, execute the following `kubectl port-forward` command:

```
PS C:\src\declarative-demo> kubectl port-forward service/windows-example
5000:8080
Forwarding from 127.0.0.1:5000 -> 80
Forwarding from [::1]:5000 -> 80
```

8. This will forward any network traffic from your localhost `5000` port to `8080` on the `windows-example` service. For example, you can navigate to http://127.0.0.1:5000/ in your web browser. Note that this approach will also work for different protocols than HTTP(S).

9. Terminate the `kubectl port-forward` process.

Now, let's see how to use Ingress Controller to access the demo application. Using Ingress is highly customizable and there are multiple Ingress Controllers available—we will demonstrate the quickest way to get up and running on AKS Engine hybrid cluster using `ingress-nginx` (`https://www.nginx.com/products/nginx/kubernetes-ingress-controller`). Please note that this approach limits the Deployment of Ingress Controllers to Linux nodes only—you will be able to create Ingress objects for services running on Windows nodes but all of the load balancing will be performed on Linux nodes. Follow these steps:

1. Modify the `windows-example-service.yaml` manifest file so that it has `type: ClusterIP`, `port: 80`, and no `targetPort`:

   ```
   apiVersion: v1
   kind: Service
   metadata:
     name: windows-example
   spec:
     type: ClusterIP
     ports:
     - protocol: TCP
       port: 80
     selector:
       app: windows-example
   ```

2. Apply your modifications to the cluster:

   ```
   kubectl apply -f .\
   ```

3. Apply the official generic manifest file for ingress-nginx, which creates a Deployment with one replica running on Linux nodes:

   ```
   kubectl apply -f
   https://raw.githubusercontent.com/kubernetes/ingress-nginx/master/deploy/static/mandatory.yaml
   ```

4. Apply the official cloud-specific manifest file for ingress-nginx. This will create a service of the LoadBalancer type, which will be used for the Ingress Controller:

   ```
   kubectl apply -f
   https://raw.githubusercontent.com/kubernetes/ingress-nginx/master/deploy/static/provider/cloud-generic.yaml
   ```

5. Wait for the Ingress Controller service to receive an external IP address. The external IP address `104.40.133.125` will be used for all services that are configured to run behind this Ingress Controller:

```
PS C:\src\declarative-demo> kubectl get service -n ingress-nginx -w
NAME                TYPE            CLUSTER-IP      EXTERNAL-IP
PORT(S)                         AGE
ingress-nginx   LoadBalancer    10.0.110.35     104.40.133.125
80:32090/TCP,443:32215/TCP      16m
```

6. Create the `windows-example-ingress.yaml` manifest file and define the Ingress object. The `windows-example` service for our application will be registered under the `<ingressLoadBalancerIp>/windows-example` path:

```
apiVersion: networking.k8s.io/v1beta1
kind: Ingress
metadata:
  name: windows-example-ingress
  annotations:
    kubernetes.io/ingress.class: "nginx"
    nginx.ingress.kubernetes.io/rewrite-target: /$2
    nginx.ingress.kubernetes.io/ssl-redirect: "false"
spec:
  rules:
  - http:
      paths:
      - path: /windows-example(/|$)(.*)
        backend:
          serviceName: windows-example
          servicePort: 80
```

7. Apply the changes:

```
kubectl apply -f .\
```

8. Navigate to `http://104.40.133.125/windows-example` to test the Ingress definition.

Of course, you can create multiple Ingress objects with complex rules for different services. A general rule of thumb is that you should use an Ingress Controller to expose your HTTP(S) endpoints whenever possible and use dedicated LoadBalancer services for other protocols.

Now, let's take a look at how you can scale your application!

Scaling the application

In production scenarios, you will definitely need to scale your application—this is where Kubernetes is powerful; you can either manually scale your application or use autoscaling. Let's first take a look at how to perform the manual scaling of your Deployment. You can do it either imperatively or declaratively. To perform scaling by using an imperative command in PowerShell, perform these steps:

1. Execute the `kubectl scale` command, which will scale the `windows-example` Deployment to three replicas:

   ```
   PS C:\src\declarative-demo> kubectl scale deployment/windows-
   example --replicas=3
   deployment.extensions/windows-example scaled
   ```

2. Now watch how the Pods are being added to your Deployment:

   ```
   PS C:\src\declarative-demo> kubectl get pods -w
   NAME READY STATUS RESTARTS AGE
   windows-example-5cb7456474-5ndrm 0/1 ContainerCreating 0 8s
   windows-example-5cb7456474-v7k84 1/1 Running 0 23m
   windows-example-5cb7456474-xqp86 1/1 Running 0 8s
   ```

You can perform a similar operation in a declarative manner, which is generally recommended. Let's scale the application further to four replicas:

1. Edit the `windows-example-deployment.yaml` manifest file and modify `replicas` to 4.

2. Save the manifest file and apply the changes:

   ```
   PS C:\src\declarative-demo> kubectl apply -f .\
   deployment.apps/windows-example configured
   ingress.networking.k8s.io/windows-example-ingress unchanged
   service/windows-example unchanged
   ```

3. Again, use the `kubectl get pods -w` command to observe how the application is scaled up.

The true power of Kubernetes comes with autoscaling. We will cover autoscaling in more detail in Chapter 11, *Configuring Applications to Use Kubernetes Features*, so in this section, we will give only a short overview of how to do it using an imperative command:

1. First, you need to configure the CPU resource limits for the pod template in the Deployment—set this to a small value, for example, 100m. Without CPU resource limits, autoscaling will be not able to apply the scaling policy properly:

```
apiVersion: apps/v1
kind: Deployment
metadata:
  name: windows-example
...
spec:
...
    spec:
...
      containers:
      - name: windows-example
...
        resources:
          limits:
            cpu: 100m
          requests:
            cpu: 100m
```

2. Apply the modifications:

```
kubectl apply -f .\
```

3. Execute the following kubectl autoscale command:

```
kubectl autoscale deployment/windows-example --cpu-percent=15 --min=1 --max=5
```

4. This will create a **Horizontal Pod Autoscaler** (**HPA**) object in the cluster with the default algorithm, a minimum of 1 replica, a maximum of 5 replicas, and configuration based on a target CPU usage of 15% of the limit.

5. Use the following command to check the state of the HPA:

```
kubectl describe hpa windows-example
```

6. You can try to add some CPU load to your Pods by frequently refreshing the application web page. Note that if you are using Ingress, you will hit the cache at the Ingress Controller so the CPU usage may not increase in such a scenario.

7. After some time, you will see that autoscaling kicks in and adds more replicas. When you decrease the load, the Deployment will be scaled down. You can check the timeline using the `kubectl describe` command:

```
PS C:\src\declarative-demo> kubectl describe hpa windows-example
...
  Normal    SuccessfulRescale              11m
horizontal-pod-autoscaler  New size: 3; reason: cpu resource
utilization (percentage of request) above target
  Normal    SuccessfulRescale              4m17s
horizontal-pod-autoscaler  New size: 1; reason: All metrics below
target
```

8. Delete the HPA object to turn off autoscaling using this command:

```
kubectl delete hpa windows-example
```

For managed AKS instances, it is possible to leverage the **node-level** autoscaling feature (`https://docs.microsoft.com/en-us/azure/aks/cluster-autoscaler`), which brings another dimension of scalability for your workloads. Additionally, you can consider using AKS workloads with Azure Container Instances (`https://docs.microsoft.com/en-us/azure/architecture/solution-ideas/articles/scale-using-aks-with-aci`).

Congratulations! You have successfully deployed and autoscaled your first application on an AKS Engine hybrid Kubernetes cluster.

Summary

This chapter has given a brief introduction to how to deploy and manage Windows container applications running on an AKS Engine hybrid cluster. You learned the differences between imperative and declarative management of cluster configuration and when to use each of them. We have used both approaches to deploy a demonstration application—now you know that the recommended declarative approach is easier and less error-prone than using imperative commands. Next, you learned how to predictably schedule Pods on Windows nodes and how to approach adding Windows container workloads to existing Kubernetes clusters. And lastly, we have shown how to access applications running in Kubernetes both for end users and developers and how to scale applications manually and automatically.

In the next chapter, we will utilize all of this new knowledge to deploy a real .NET Framework application to our Kubernetes cluster!

Questions

1. What is the difference between imperative and declarative management for Kubernetes objects?
2. When is using imperative commands recommended?
3. How do you see the changes between local manifest files and the current cluster state?
4. What is the recommended practice to schedule Pods in hybrid clusters?
5. What is the difference between the `kubectl proxy` and `kubectl port-forward` commands?
6. When can you use an Ingress Controller?
7. How do you scale a deployment manually?

You can find answers to these questions in *Assessments* of this book.

Further reading

- For more information about Kubernetes applications management, please refer to the following Packt books:
    - *The Complete Kubernetes Guide* (`https://www.packtpub.com/virtualization-and-cloud/complete-kubernetes-guide`)
    - *Getting Started with Kubernetes -Third Edition* (`https://www.packtpub.com/virtualization-and-cloud/getting-started-kubernetes-third-edition`)
    - *Kubernetes for Developers* (`https://www.packtpub.com/virtualization-and-cloud/kubernetes-developers`)
- Currently, most of the resources regarding hybrid Windows/Linux clusters running on AKS Engine are available online. Please check the official documentation on GitHub for more details:
    - `https://github.com/Azure/aks-engine/blob/master/docs/topics/windows.md`
    - `https://github.com/Azure/aks-engine/blob/master/docs/topics/windows-and-kubernetes.md`

- In general, many of the topics concerning AKS (the managed Kubernetes Azure offering, not AKS Engine itself) are useful, as they touch on how to integrate Kubernetes with the Azure ecosystem. You can find more about AKS itself in the following Packt book:
  - *DevOps with Kubernetes – Second Edition* (`https://www.packtpub.com/virtualization-and-cloud/devops-kubernetes-second-edition`)

10
Deploying Microsoft SQL Server 2019 and a ASP.NET MVC Application

The previous chapters have given you a Swiss Army knife for deploying and operating hybrid Windows/Linux Kubernetes clusters—now, you have all the essential knowledge to deploy a real Windows container application to a Kubernetes cluster. This chapter will focus on demonstrating how you can approach containerizing and deploying a simple voting application written in C# .NET Framework 4.8 and ASP.NET MVC 5, with Microsoft SQL Server 2019 used for the persistence layer. The choice of the technology stack may seem a legacy one (why not use .NET Core?!) but it is intentional—if you are considering using Windows containers in Kubernetes, there is a good chance that you need the classic .NET Framework runtime as you are not ready to migrate to .NET Core.

The topic of migrating existing applications to Kubernetes is broad and will not be fully covered in this book. There are numerous documented best practices for this process, but we will focus on a basic approach, mainly to demonstrate the Deployment instead of focusing on .NET Framework application implementation and migration. The goal of this chapter is to show the following:

- How you can quickly containerize a Windows .NET Framework application
- How to inject environment configuration such as SQL connection strings
- The recommended approach for container logs on Windows
- How to debug the application remotely

More precisely, in this chapter, we will cover the following topics:

- Creating and publishing an ASP.NET MVC application to Docker Hub
- Preparing the **Azure Kubernetes Service Engine (AKS Engine)**
- Deploying a failover Microsoft SQL Server 2019
- Deploying the ASP.NET MVC application
- Accessing the application
- Scaling the application
- Debugging the application

Technical requirements

For this chapter, you will need the following:

- Windows 10 Pro, Enterprise, or Education (version 1903 or later, 64-bit) installed.
- Microsoft Visual Studio 2019 Community (or any other edition) if you want to edit the source code for the application and debug it. **Visual Studio Code (VS Code)** has limited support for the classic .NET Framework.
- An Azure account.
- A Windows/Linux Kubernetes cluster deployed using AKS Engine.

To follow along, you will need your own Azure account in order to create Azure resources for the Kubernetes cluster. If you haven't already created the account for the previous chapters, you can read more about how to obtain a limited free account for personal use here: `https://azure.microsoft.com/en-us/free/`.

Deploying a Kubernetes cluster using AKS Engine has been covered in `Chapter 8`, *Deploying a Hybrid Azure Kubernetes Service Engine Cluster*.

You can download the latest code samples for this book chapter from the official GitHub repository, at `https://github.com/PacktPublishing/Hands-On-Kubernetes-on-Windows/tree/master/Chapter10`.

Creating and publishing an ASP.NET MVC application to Docker Hub

In order to demonstrate the Deployment of a real Windows container application, we will create a Docker image for a voting application that is a small C# .NET Framework 4.8 web application for creating surveys. The application is implemented using the classic ASP.NET MVC 5 stack as it is the most suitable for demonstrating how to approach the containerization of a Windows application. Traditional .NET Framework applications, especially enterprise, heavily rely on Windows-only functionalities, such as **Windows Communication Foundation (WCF)**. In many cases, you may be lucky to easily migrate to .NET Core and use Linux containers for hosting your application, but for some parts of the .NET Framework stack, it may never happen, even in .NET 5.

There are a few assumptions concerning our voting application, as follows:

- There is no dependency on Kubernetes or Windows containers in any way. The application is unaware of being hosted by a container orchestration system.
- **Entity Framework 6.3 (EF 6.3)** (`https://docs.microsoft.com/en-us/ef/ef6/`) with the Code-First approach is used as **object-relational mapping (ORM)**.
- Microsoft SQL Server is used for voting data storage—this is a common stack you see with ASP.NET MVC applications. For local development, we use **Microsoft SQL (MSSQL) Server Express LocalDB** (`https://docs.microsoft.com/en-us/sql/database-engine/configure-windows/sql-server-express-localdb?view=sql-server-ver15`), whereas, for the Kubernetes Deployment, we are going to use MSSQL Server 2019 hosted in Linux containers (`https://docs.microsoft.com/en-us/sql/linux/quickstart-install-connect-docker?view=sql-server-ver15pivots=cs1-bash`).
- Serilog (`https://serilog.net/`) has been chosen as the logging framework.
- Ninject (`https://github.com/ninject/Ninject`) ties everything together as a dependency injector.
- We use simple fat controllers that contain all the business logic and the data access layer (so there are no repositories or other design patterns). This has been chosen specifically to make the application as compact as possible.
- Most of the views and controllers are based on a standard MVC 5 scaffolding for the EF model.
- Usage of view models is limited to places where it is absolutely necessary.

You can find the application source code in the official GitHub repository for the book, at `https://github.com/PacktPublishing/Hands-On-Kubernetes-on-Windows/tree/master/Chapter10/01_voting-application-src`. To open the `VotingApplication.sln` solution file, you need Visual Studio 2019. It is also possible to perform a build by just using the `docker build` command, as explained in the next subsections. At the end of this section, you will have a Docker image for a voting application, ready to be used in Kubernetes. You may follow along with the steps or choose to use a ready-made image from Docker Hub, available at `https://hub.docker.com/repository/docker/packtpubkubernetesonwindows/voting-application`.

Injecting the configuration using environment variables

When developing a container-friendly application, you need to consider how to inject configuration data such as database connection strings. A general rule of thumb is that you should not hardcode any addresses, usernames, passwords, or connection strings into your code. You should be always able to inject such configuration during runtime and, in general, this is also true for non-containerized applications. Kubernetes offers you a wide variety of approaches on how to inject the runtime configuration, as follows:

- Passing arguments to the container commands
- Defining system environment variables for the container
- Mounting ConfigMaps or Secrets as container volumes
- Optionally wrapping everything up using PodPresets

You can read more about all of them in the official documentation (`https://kubernetes.io/docs/tasks/inject-data-application/`). The important takeaway is that all the features integrate with the containerized application using standard **operating system (OS)**-level primitives such as files or environment variables. This means that if you design your application well, you can use it without any changes inside or outside of Kubernetes.

We will demonstrate how to use environment variables to inject an MSSQL Server connection string to our application. This approach is the simplest one but it has a significant limitation—you cannot modify the container's environment variables when the container is running. Once you set the variable, it will have the same value throughout the whole container life cycle. If you need to be able to modify the configuration without restarting the container, you should take a look at ConfigMaps (combined with Secrets), which are described in the next chapter: `Chapter 11`, *Configuring Applications to Use Kubernetes Features*.

Our voting application uses the `VotingApplicationContextFactory` class for creating an EF DbContext for **Model-View-Controller** (**MVC**) controllers. Let's take a look at the `Create()` method of this class (available at `https://github.com/PacktPublishing/Hands-On-Kubernetes-on-Windows/blob/master/Chapter10/01_voting-application-src/Factories/VotingApplicationContextFactory.cs`), as follows:

```
public object Create(IContext context)
{
 var connectionString =
Environment.GetEnvironmentVariable("CONNECTIONSTRING_VotingApplication");
 if (!string.IsNullOrEmpty(connectionString))
 {
 var safeConnectionString = SanitizeConnectionString(connectionString);
 this.log.Info("Using custom connection string provided by environment
variable: {0}", safeConnectionString);
 return new VotingApplicationContext(connectionString);
 }

 this.log.Info("Using default connection string");
 return new VotingApplicationContext();
}
```

The following is a common pattern you can use to inject a configuration into your application, especially in the Linux world, where relying on environment variables is much more common:

1. Check if your chosen environment variable, `CONNECTIONSTRING_VotingApplication`, is defined.
2. If it is, create an EF DbContext using the overridden connection string from the variable.
3. If not, create an EF DbContext using the standard connection string. In this case, it will be retrieved from the `Web.config` application file.

   You can follow this pattern, especially when you are not using custom configuration files. This solution gives you a lot of flexibility and you can use it also when running an application without a container!

 Another approach would be to inject the whole `Web.config` file as a Kubernetes ConfigMap object. We will explore this possibility in the next chapter.

This shows an important principle that you should use when containerizing any application—think about the external interfaces of your application (system) and how it communicates with the outside world. This is the only way you can influence or monitor an application running in a container. Providing and injecting configuration is one of the external interfaces for your application. Similarly, logging defines an output interface for your application—let's see how you can approach this in Windows containers.

Configuring logging for Windows containers log monitor

Kubernetes itself provides simple tools for browsing Pod container logs. Generally, you will have to implement a good cluster-level logging solution—for example, using the Elasticsearch, Logstash, Kibana stack or using Azure Log Analytics (as briefly demonstrated in the previous chapters). The official documentation gives a good overview of possible architectures for logging solutions: `https://kubernetes.io/docs/concepts/cluster-administration/logging/`. In all cases, you will need to expose the application logs from your container to the outside world. From a high-level view, there are three main approaches:

- Use a container **standard output (stdout)** and **standard error (stderr)** entry point and let the container runtime handle the logging. This can be later consumed using a node-level logging agent (for example, Fluentd, Elastic Beats, or Logstash) that forwards the logs to any external logging solution. This works especially well if your containerized applications write everything to the console output out of the box.
- Use an additional sidecar container in your application Pod that gathers the logs from the filesystem, event log, or other sources, and exposes it as stdout or directly to the external logging solution. This approach is useful if your application logs to multiple destinations inside the container.
- Embed log streaming into the application itself. For example, in a C# application, you can use log4net and a dedicated Elasticsearch appender (`https://github.com/ptylenda/log4net.ElasticSearch.Async`) for streaming logs to your Elasticsearch cluster. This approach is the most limited—it creates a tight dependency on an external logging system and may cause an impact on performance that cannot be easily separated from the application workload itself.

For a Windows application, logging to stdout is not common, especially for older applications and when using **Internet Information Services (IIS)** for hosting your web applications. In most cases, using **Event Tracing for Windows (ETW)**, event logs, or custom log files is more common for Windows. For example, our voting application is hosted using IIS. Also, when running in a containerized mode, IIS does not provide a functionality to expose the stdout of an application. You have to rely on event logs or your own log files. On top of that, IIS itself exposes additional application logs in a standard location—c:\inetpub\logs—and streams its own events to ETW.

You can approach the gathering of logs for a voting application in two ways:

- Use an additional sidecar container that runs, for example, Elastic Beats or Winlogbeat (https://www.elastic.co/products/beats/winlogbeat), which gathers all the logs from the application container and exposes it to stdout (https://www.elastic.co/guide/en/beats/filebeat/current/console-output.html) or any other supported output. The logs need to be shared using a volume between the containers inside the Pod.
- Extend the container image with Windows containers log monitor, which has been recently released (https://github.com/microsoft/windows-container-tools). More details regarding the architecture can be found here: https://techcommunity.microsoft.com/t5/Containers/Windows-Containers-Log-Monitor-Opensource-Release/ba-p/973947). This tool uses a different approach than a sidecar container. In the Docker image, instead of directly starting your application, you start LogMonitor.exe with an appropriate JSON configuration file and pass the command line for starting your application as an argument for LogMonitor.exe. In other words, LogMonitor.exe acts as a supervisor for your application process and prints logs to stdout that are gathered from different sources based on the configuration file. There are plans to further extend this solution to be used in the sidecar container pattern.

We are going to use log monitor as it is simple to integrate and easy to configure. The details of the Dockerfile for the application will be shown in the next subsection. Assuming that the command for starting your application (IIS, in this case) is C:\ServiceMonitor.exe w3svc, the general pattern for using Log Monitor is customizing the Dockerfile in the following way:

```
WORKDIR /LogMonitor
COPY LogMonitor.exe LogMonitorConfig.json .
SHELL ["C:\\LogMonitor\\LogMonitor.exe", "powershell.exe"]

ENTRYPOINT C:\ServiceMonitor.exe w3svc
```

The `LogMonitoringConfig.json` file (`https://github.com/PacktPublishing/Hands-On-Kubernetes-on-Windows/blob/master/Chapter10/01_voting-application-src/LogMonitorConfig.json`) for our application has the following JSON configuration:

```json
{
    "LogConfig": {
        "sources": [
            {
                "type": "EventLog",
                "startAtOldestRecord": true,
                "eventFormatMultiLine": false,
                "channels": [
                    {
                        "name": "system",
                        "level": "Error"
                    }
                ]
            },
            {
                "type": "EventLog",
                "startAtOldestRecord": true,
                "eventFormatMultiLine": false,
                "channels": [
                    {
                        "name": "VotingApplication",
                        "level": "Verbose"
                    }
                ]
            },
            {
                "type": "File",
                "directory": "c:\\inetpub\\logs",
                "filter": "*.log",
                "includeSubdirectories": true
            },
            {
                "type": "ETW",
                "providers": [
                    {
                        "providerName": "IIS: WWW Server",
                        "ProviderGuid": "3A2A4E84-4C21-4981-AE10-3FDA0D9B0F83",
                        "level": "Information"
                    },
                    {
                        "providerName": "Microsoft-Windows-IIS-Logging",
                        "ProviderGuid ": "7E8AD27F-B271-4EA2-A783-A47BDE29143B",
                        "level": "Information",
                        "keywords": "0xFF"
```

```
            }
        ]
    }
  ]
}
```

This configuration file subscribes log monitor to the `system` log and
the `VotingApplication` log in the Windows event log, monitors logs in
`C:\inetpub\logs`, and collects ETW data for IIS. The `VotingApplication` log in the
event log contains all the logs produced by Serilog in our application. This is configured in
the `NinjectWebCommon` class (`https://github.com/PacktPublishing/Hands-On-`
`Kubernetes-on-Windows/blob/master/Chapter10/01_voting-application-src/App_`
`Start/NinjectWebCommon.cs`), where we initialize the logger sinks, as follows:

```
private static void RegisterServices(IKernel kernel)
{
    Log.Logger = new LoggerConfiguration()
        .ReadFrom.AppSettings()
        .Enrich.FromLogContext()
        .WriteTo.EventLog(source: "VotingApplication", logName:
"VotingApplication", manageEventSource: false)
        .CreateLogger();

    kernel.Bind<VotingApplicationContext>().ToProvider(typeof(VotingApplication
ContextFactory)).InRequestScope();
    kernel.Bind<IDateTimeProvider>().To<DateTimeProvider>().InRequestScope();
}
```

Note that due to the fact that Windows containers are not running in privileged mode, we
cannot automatically create the log in an event log (`manageEventSource: false`). This
has to be done in the Dockerfile at build time.

With this setup, our voting application will print all our own logs, together with the system
and IIS, to stdout of the container. This means you can easily investigate them using
the `docker logs` command (when running a standalone container) or the `kubectl logs`
command. If you integrate with Azure Log Analytics, your logs will be available for
querying using Kusto.

Creating a Dockerfile

The next step is preparing a Dockerfile for our application. You can check the official documentation on how to approach building .NET Framework applications in a Dockerfile at `https://github.com/microsoft/dotnet-framework-docker/tree/master/samples/dotnetapp`. Our Dockerfile has to cover the following steps:

1. Restore NuGet packages.
2. Build the application, preferably using a publish profile to the local filesystem.
3. Copy tools for applying EF migrations (provided by the EF NuGet package).
4. Create a `VotingApplication` log in the event log.
5. Copy log monitor binaries and configuration.
6. Copy voting application binaries to `C:\inetpub\wwwroot` for IIS hosting.

We need to dwell on the topic of EF migrations a bit more. Applying EF database migrations without application downtime and when having multiple replicas of the application is a complex task. You need to ensure that the migrations can be rolled back and that the database schema is fully compatible with the old and the new application versions. In other words, backward-incompatible changes such as renames have to be handled specially to make them backward-compatible between the individual steps. A skeleton for this process could look as follows—for example, for renaming a column for an entity:

1. Apply database migration that adds a new column with the new name.
2. Roll out a new version of your application that performs writes to both the old and the new column. Reads should be performed using the old column because it always has the proper data.
3. Execute a job that copies data from the old column to the new column.
4. Roll out a new version of your application that reads from the new column.
5. Roll out a new version of your application that writes to the new column only.
6. Apply database migration, which removes the old column.

As you can see, properly handling database migrations for applications running in Kubernetes with no downtime requires strict rules and compatibility/rollback testing—we have brought this topic to your attention, but detailed solutions are out of the scope of this book. There is a good article by Spring that explains the details of how to approach this problem (`https://spring.io/blog/2016/05/31/zero-downtime-deployment-with-a-database`) and another article by Weaveworks dedicated for Kubernetes: `https://www.weave.works/blog/how-to-correctly-handle-db-schemas-during-kubernetes-rollouts`.

For applying migrations, we will use the same Docker image—EF database migrations are applied using application assembly and EF command-line tools, which we will provide in the image. Then, the migrations (and database seeding) will be run using a Kubernetes Job that is suitable for running one-time tasks. In a real-world scenario, this should be scheduled as part of your **Continuous Integration/Continuous Deployment (CI/CD)** process, accompanying the Kubernetes Deployment rollout.

The voting application contains a Dockerfile named `Dockerfile.production` (https://github.com/PacktPublishing/Hands-On-Kubernetes-on-Windows/blob/master/Chapter10/01_voting-application-src/Dockerfile.production) that has layers based on what we have just summarized. Let's analyze it, step by step:

1. The Dockerfile defines a multi-stage build, which means that multiple base images are used throughout the build process. The first stage is the web application build, using a `mcr.microsoft.com/dotnet/framework/sdk` image. This image contains all the .NET Framework build tools that are not required for the runtime. The code for this is illustrated in the following block:

```
FROM mcr.microsoft.com/dotnet/framework/sdk:4.8-windowsservercore-
ltsc2019 AS build
ARG PUBLISH_PROFILE=DockerPublishProfile.pubxml
ARG BUILD_CONFIG=Release

WORKDIR /app

COPY *.sln ./
COPY *.csproj ./
COPY *.config ./
RUN nuget restore

COPY . .
RUN msbuild /p:DeployOnBuild=true
/p:PublishProfile=$env:PUBLISH_PROFILE
/p:Configuration=$env:BUILD_CONFIG
```

The layers are organized in such a way that layer caching during builds is maximized—for example, we run `nuget restore` only if certain solution configuration files change.

2. The build process is performed by a standard `msbuild` command, using a dedicated `DockerPublishProfile.pubxml` publish profile that has the following form:

```
<Project ToolsVersion="4.0"
xmlns="http://schemas.microsoft.com/developer/msbuild/2003">
```

```
<PropertyGroup>
  <WebPublishMethod>FileSystem</WebPublishMethod>
  <PublishProvider>FileSystem</PublishProvider>
<LastUsedBuildConfiguration>Release</LastUsedBuildConfiguration>
  <LastUsedPlatform>Any CPU</LastUsedPlatform>
  <SiteUrlToLaunchAfterPublish />
  <LaunchSiteAfterPublish>True</LaunchSiteAfterPublish>
  <ExcludeApp_Data>False</ExcludeApp_Data>
  <publishUrl>obj\Docker\publish</publishUrl>
  <DeleteExistingFiles>True</DeleteExistingFiles>
</PropertyGroup>
</Project>
```

In principle, it performs a `FileSystem` publish to `obj\Docker\publish`, which is later used for creating the final image.

3. Next, we start the second and final build stage based on the `mcr.microsoft.com/dotnet/framework/aspnet` image dedicated for runtime scenarios, as follows:

```
FROM mcr.microsoft.com/dotnet/framework/aspnet:4.8-
windowsservercore-ltsc2019 AS runtime

WORKDIR /ef6
COPY --from=build
/app/packages/EntityFramework.6.3.0/tools/net45/any/ .
```

In the first step, we perform the copying of EF6 migration command-line tools, which are provided with the EF NuGet package. Here, the key is to copy from the previous stage, using the `--from=build` argument.

4. The next step is creating a dedicated log in an event log for our voting application (this requirement was mentioned in the previous subsection), as follows:

```
RUN powershell.exe -Command New-EventLog -LogName VotingApplication
-Source VotingApplication
```

5. Copy the `LogMonitor` binary and configuration, also overriding the shell command for the container, as follows:

```
WORKDIR /LogMonitor
ADD
https://github.com/microsoft/windows-container-tools/releases/downl
oad/v1.0/LogMonitor.exe .
COPY --from=build /app/LogMonitorConfig.json .
SHELL ["C:\\LogMonitor\\LogMonitor.exe", "powershell.exe"]
```

6. Copy the `build` artifacts from the previous stage to the
   `C:\inetpub\wwwroot` IIS application directory, as follows:

   ```
   WORKDIR /inetpub/wwwroot
   COPY --from=build /app/obj/Docker/publish/. .
   ```

7. And finally, define the default entry point for the image to
   the `ServiceMonitor.exe` starting the IIS service. This is a standard approach
   that you see in the `mcr.microsoft.com/dotnet/framework/aspnet` base
   image. The only difference is that the whole process tree will run under log
   monitor supervision. The code can be seen in the following snippet:

   ```
   ENTRYPOINT C:\ServiceMonitor.exe w3svc
   ```

   That's it! The Dockerfile defines the full build process for the ASP.NET MVC
   application—you could optionally extend it with a testing stage whereby you
   execute appropriate tests. Now, let's build the image and push it to the image
   registry.

Building and pushing the Docker image

The exact details of this process have been covered in `Chapter 3`, *Working with Container
Images*. In short, you can use two approaches here:

1. Performing a manual build of the image on your local machine and pushing it to
   the public Docker Hub. Currently, setting an autobuild for a Windows container
   image is not possible on Docker Hub.
2. If you are interested in having automated builds and GitHub hooks integrated
   into your application, you can use **Azure Container Registry** (**ACR**), as described
   in the chapter mentioned previously.

For the sake of simplicity, we will perform a manual build and push the image to Docker
Hub. In a real-world scenario, you should use at least ACR with GitHub integration as part
of your CI/CD pipeline. Let's perform the build of the Docker image—in the examples, we
will use the `packtpubkubernetesonwindows/voting-application` image repository
name, but if you are following along, you should use your own `<dockerId>/voting-
application` repository. Perform the following steps:

1. Open the PowerShell window and navigate to the main `voting-application`
   source directory.

2. Execute the Docker build using the following command (remember the final dot, which specifies the build context directory):

```
docker build -t packtpubkubernetesonwindows/voting-application -f
.\Dockerfile.production .
```

3. Wait for the build to finish, and tag the image accordingly. This is crucial for Kubernetes Deployments as we can specify a particular version of the image to be rolled out (using the latest version would be ambiguous and is generally not recommended). Using semantic versioning, as described in Chapter 3, *Working with Container Images*, is advised, and this is illustrated in the following code block:

```
docker tag packtpubkubernetesonwindows/voting-application:latest
packtpubkubernetesonwindows/voting-application:1.0.0
docker tag packtpubkubernetesonwindows/voting-application:latest
packtpubkubernetesonwindows/voting-application:1.0
docker tag packtpubkubernetesonwindows/voting-application:latest
packtpubkubernetesonwindows/voting-application:1
```

4. Push all the tags to the image repository, like this:

```
docker push packtpubkubernetesonwindows/voting-application
```

5. Now, you can verify if the tags are properly visible in the Docker Hub page—for example, https://hub.docker.com/repository/docker/ packtpubkubernetesonwindows/voting-application/tags?page=1.

At this point, our Docker image can be used both locally (you need to provide a valid connection string to SQL Server using an environment variable) and in Kubernetes. Let's begin the preparation of AKS Engine cluster Deployment!

Preparing the AKS Engine

If you have followed Chapter 8, *Deploying a Hybrid Azure Kubernetes Service Engine Cluster*, and you have created a hybrid Windows/Linux Kubernetes cluster using AKS Engine, you are ready to go—you can verify in this section if the topology of the cluster is as required. And, if you do not have an AKS Engine cluster deployed yet, we will provide a quick way to deploy it using a PowerShell script provided in the GitHub repository for the book.

Our voting application can be hosted on the smallest possible hybrid Windows/Linux cluster, one Linux master and one Windows node, where the Linux master acts as a regular node. However, to fully demonstrate the principles of Deployment, we will use a cluster that resembles a production one: one Linux master running in **Virtual Machine Scale Sets** (**VMSS**) **High Availability** (**HA**) mode, two Linux nodes, and two Windows nodes. We have used this configuration in the previous chapter for AKS Engine cluster Deployments. In order to quickly deploy an AKS Engine cluster from scratch, you can perform the following steps:

1. Download the following PowerShell script from the book's GitHub repository: `https://github.com/PacktPublishing/Hands-On-Kubernetes-on-Windows/blob/master/Chapter08/01_aks-engine/01_CreateAKSEngineClusterWithWindowsNodes.ps1`.

2. In the PowerShell window, execute the script with the appropriate parameters, as follows:

```
.\01_CreateAKSEngineClusterWithWindowsNodes.ps1 `
    -azureSubscriptionId <subscriptionId> `
    -dnsPrefix <globallyUniqueDnsPrefix> `
    -windowsPassword <windowsNodesPassword>
```

3. This script deploys the cluster to the West Europe location in Azure using the `aks-engine-windows-resource-group` resource group. If there are problems with the AKS Engine Deployment, you can always try specifying a different region—for example, `-azureLocation westus`.

4. When the Deployment finishes, you need to ensure that your default kubeconfig contains the context for the new cluster. You can quickly merge your kubeconfig with one that is generated for the West Europe location by AKS Engine by using the following commands (remember to double-check the contents of the `config_new` file before overwriting your default config file to avoid any loss):

```
$env:KUBECONFIG=".\_output\<globallyUniqueDnsPrefix>\kubeconfig\kubeconfig.westeurope.json;$env:USERPROFILE\.kube\config"
kubectl config view --raw > $env:USERPROFILE\.kube\config_new

Move-Item -Force $env:USERPROFILE\.kube\config_new
$env:USERPROFILE\.kube\config
```

5. In a new PowerShell window, verify that you are able to access the cluster—for example—by running the following command:

```
kubectl get nodes
```

Running an AKS Engine cluster of this size can be costly, so you should always check the estimated cost for **virtual machine** (**VM**) hosting. If you do not need the cluster anymore, you can simply delete it using the `az group delete --name aks-engine-windows-resource-group --yes` command, optionally providing a `--no-wait` parameter.

At this point, you have a cluster ready for running Microsoft SQL Server 2019 and the voting application, so let's proceed!

Deploying a failover Microsoft SQL Server 2019

From MSSQL Server 2017, it is possible to host it in a Linux Docker container. As our application requires MSSQL Server for data persistence, we are going to deploy the latest version—MSSQL Server 2019—to our Kubernetes cluster. Currently, it is possible to deploy MSSQL Server to Kubernetes in two modes, as follows:

1. A single-node instance with failover guaranteed by a Kubernetes Deployment and an Azure Disk persistent volume.
2. A multi-node, HA cluster using a dedicated Kubernetes operator (`https://kubernetes.io/docs/concepts/extend-kubernetes/operator/`).

The second mode was announced for preview as of **Community Technology Preview** (**CTP**) 2.0 version (`https://cloudblogs.microsoft.com/sqlserver/2018/12/10/availability-groups-on-kubernetes-in-sql-server-2019-preview/`) but currently, in the **general availability** (**GA**) version, the Docker images and Kubernetes manifests are not compatible. If you are interested, you can check the official manifest files for this kind of Deployment at `https://github.com/microsoft/sql-server-samples/tree/master/samples/features/high%20availability/Kubernetes/sample-manifest-files`.

For this reason, we are going to deploy SQL Server in the simpler, single-node failover mode. To do this, perform the following steps:

1. Open the PowerShell window.

2. Create a `dev.yaml` manifest file for a new Kubernetes namespace with the following content, and apply it using the `kubectl apply -f .\dev.yaml` command:

```
kind: Namespace
apiVersion: v1
metadata:
  name: dev
  labels:
    name: dev
```

3. Create a `storage-class.yaml` manifest file for a Kubernetes storage class that uses an Azure Disk provisioner, and apply it using the `kubectl apply -f .\storage-class.yaml` command, as follows:

```
kind: StorageClass
apiVersion: storage.k8s.io/v1beta1
metadata:
  name: azure-disk
provisioner: kubernetes.io/azure-disk
parameters:
  storageaccounttype: Standard_LRS
  kind: Managed
```

4. Create a `pvc.yaml` manifest file that defines a `mssql-data` **Persistent Volume Claim (PVC)** for the SQL Server instance. This PVC will be used for mounting data in `/var/opt/mssql` in the container. Apply the manifest using the `kubectl apply -f .\pvc.yaml` command, as follows:

```
kind: PersistentVolumeClaim
apiVersion: v1
metadata:
  namespace: dev
  name: mssql-data
  annotations:
    volume.beta.kubernetes.io/storage-class: azure-disk
spec:
  accessModes:
  - ReadWriteOnce
  resources:
    requests:
      storage: 8Gi
```

5. Define a Kubernetes `mssql` Secret that contains a **System Administrator (SA)** user password for SQL Server, using your own, safe password, as follows:

```
kubectl create secret generic -n dev mssql --from-
literal=SA_PASSWORD="S3cur3P@ssw0rd"
```

6. Create a `sql-server.yaml` manifest file that defines the Kubernetes Deployment for SQL Server, as follows:

```
kind: Deployment
apiVersion: apps/v1
metadata:
  namespace: dev
  name: mssql-deployment
spec:
  replicas: 1
  selector:
    matchLabels:
      app: mssql
  template:
    metadata:
      labels:
        app: mssql
    spec:
      terminationGracePeriodSeconds: 10
      initContainers:
      - name: volume-mount-permissions-fix   # (1)
        image: busybox
        command: ["sh", "-c", "chown -R 10001:0 /var/opt/mssql"]
        volumeMounts:
        - name: mssqldb
          mountPath: /var/opt/mssql
      containers:
      - name: mssql
        image: mcr.microsoft.com/mssql/server:2019-GA-ubuntu-16.04
        ports:
        - containerPort: 1433
        env:
        - name: MSSQL_PID   # (2)
          value: "Developer"
        - name: ACCEPT_EULA
          value: "Y"
        - name: MSSQL_SA_PASSWORD   # (3)
          valueFrom:
            secretKeyRef:
              name: mssql
              key: SA_PASSWORD   # (4)
        volumeMounts:   # (5)
```

```
    - name: mssqldb
      mountPath: /var/opt/mssql
  volumes:
  - name: mssqldb
    persistentVolumeClaim:
      claimName: mssql-data
  nodeSelector:
    "beta.kubernetes.io/os": linux
```

There are a couple of important parts to this manifest file, as follows:

1. First, we need an extra `volume-mount-permissions-fix` init container, which is required for ensuring that directories, after mounting PVC, have proper access permissions for SQL Server—the container will be run before the regular Pod containers are created. This is a good example of how init containers are used.

2. Secondly, we need to accept the **end-user license agreement** (**EULA**) using the `ACCEPT_EULA` environment variable and choose an appropriate SQL Server edition using the `MSSQL_PID` environment variable.

3. We are going to use the Developer edition because our application is hosted for development purposes only. You can read more about usage of these variables in the documentation for the image, at `https://hub.docker.com/_/microsoft-mssql-server`. Additionally, you need to provide a `MSSQL_SA_PASSWORD` environment variable, which contains the SA user password for the instance.

4. For this, we are using the value from the `mssql` Secret that we created earlier.

5. Next, we need to mount the volume provided by the `mssql-data` PVC to the `/var/opt/mssql` path.

6. This will provide a failover similar to SQL Server shared disk failover instances. And lastly, we have to ensure that `nodeSelector` is set to choose only Linux machines.

Now, continue the Deployment using the following steps:

1. Apply the manifest file using the `kubectl apply -f .\sql-server.yaml` command.

2. Create a `sql-server-service.yaml` manifest file to create a Kubernetes service for your SQL Server instance. Depending on your needs, you can use type `ClusterIP`, or, if you expose the SQL Server instance for connections outside from the Kubernetes cluster (for example, for **SQL Server Management Studio (SSMS)**), you can use a `LoadBalancer` type. Apply the manifest file using the `kubectl apply -f .\sql-server-service.yaml` command, as follows:

```
kind: Service
apiVersion: v1
metadata:
  namespace: dev
  name: mssql-deployment
spec:
  selector:
    app: mssql
  ports:
    - protocol: TCP
      port: 1433
      targetPort: 1433
  type: LoadBalancer
```

3. You can observe the Pod creation using the following command:

```
PS C:\src> kubectl get pods -n dev --watch
NAME                                   READY    STATUS    RESTARTS
AGE
mssql-deployment-58bcb8b89d-7f9xz      1/1      Running   0
8m37s
```

At this point, you have an MSSQL Server 2019 instance running in your cluster in the `dev` namespace that is accessible using an `mssql-deployment` **Domain Name System** (**DNS**) name inside of your cluster. Additionally, if you have created a LoadBalancer service, you can verify the instance using SSMS, providing the service's external IP address, user SA, and your chosen password.

We can now proceed to create manifest files for the voting application and deploying the application to the cluster.

Deploying the ASP.NET MVC application

Finally, it is time for the big show! We will now deploy our voting application using a standard Kubernetes Deployment and, in the next section, we will expose it to the external users using the LoadBalancer service. First, we need to briefly summarize what is required for the proper Deployment of our application, as follow:

- A `packtpubkubernetesonwindows/voting-application:1.0.0` Docker image will be used for deploying the application. If you have pushed the image to your own image repository, you need to change the manifest file accordingly. We specify a `1.0.0` tag explicitly as we want to avoid pulling an unexpected container image version. You can read more about the best practices for container images in the documentation at `https://kubernetes.io/docs/concepts/configuration/overview/#container-images`.

- The application requires a `CONNECTIONSTRING_VotingApplication` environment variable to be set if we need a custom connection string. In the case of our Deployment, the connection string should have the following form: `Data Source=mssql-deployment;Initial Catalog=VotingApplication;MultipleActiveResultSets=true;User Id=sa;Password=$(MSSQL_SA_PASSWORD);`, where `$(MSSQL_SA_PASSWORD)` will be retrieved from a Kubernetes Secret.

- Applying the initial database migration is required in order to seed the database data. We will do that using a Kubernetes Job—this approach can be generalized in your CI/CD pipeline. The migration itself is performed using the `ef6.exe database update` command—the image already contains this executable in the `C:/ef6/` directory. Please note that in a production environment, you might want to create a separate Docker image just for migrations that contains all the required tools. In this way, you would keep your application image clean and as small as possible.

- We will not create any dedicated liveness and readiness probes yet as this will be demonstrated in the next chapter: `Chapter 11`, *Configuring Applications to Use Kubernetes Features*.

To deploy the voting application, perform the following steps:

1. Open the PowerShell window.
2. Create a `voting-application.yaml` manifest file for the Kubernetes Deployment with the following contents:

```yaml
apiVersion: apps/v1
kind: Deployment
metadata:
  namespace: dev
  name: voting-application-frontend
  labels:
    app: voting-application
spec:
  replicas: 5  # (1)
  minReadySeconds: 5  # (2)
  strategy:  # (3)
    type: RollingUpdate
    rollingUpdate:
      maxUnavailable: 25%
      maxSurge: 25%
  selector:
    matchLabels:
      app: voting-application
  template:
    metadata:
      name: voting-application-frontend
      labels:
        app: voting-application
    spec:
      nodeSelector:  # (4)
        "beta.kubernetes.io/os": windows
      containers:
      - name: frontend
        image: packtpubkubernetesonwindows/voting-application:1.0.0
# (5)
        env:
        - name: MSSQL_SA_PASSWORD  # (6b)
          valueFrom:
            secretKeyRef:
              name: mssql
              key: SA_PASSWORD  # (6a)
        - name: CONNECTIONSTRING_VotingApplication  # (6c)
          value: "Data Source=mssql-deployment;Initial
Catalog=VotingApplication;MultipleActiveResultSets=true;User
Id=sa;Password=$(MSSQL_SA_PASSWORD);"
        ports:
```

```
        - containerPort: 80
      resources:
        limits:
          cpu: 500m
        requests:
          cpu: 500m
```

Let's explain the most important parts of this manifest file:

1. We define it as a Deployment with 5 initial replicas—we can scale it as we wish, as the frontend application is stateless in our case.
2. In order to have a simple mechanism for preventing the accessing of Pods for which IIS is still initializing, we add `minReadySeconds: 5`. In the next chapter, we will configure a proper readiness and liveness probe.
3. We also explicitly set the Deployment update strategy to `RollingUpdate` with the maximum number of unavailable Pods to `25%`, allowing us to create up to `25%` more Pods than the desired number during rollout (this is controlled by the `maxSurge` parameter).
4. Next, remember to set a proper `nodeSelector` to deploy to Windows nodes only.
5. The image is specified to use a particular tag—if you use your own image, update this accordingly.
6. In order to create the connection string for the database, we have to first retrieve the SA user password from the `mssql` Secret `(6a)` and initialize the `MSSQL_SA_PASSWORD` environment variable `(6b)`, which can be used for creating the actual connection string stored in the `CONNECTIONSTRING_VotingApplication` variable (6c). As demonstrated, you can use existing environment variables to initialize new environment variables: `Data Source=mssql-deployment;Initial Catalog=VotingApplication;MultipleActiveResultSets=true;User Id=sa;Password=$(MSSQL_SA_PASSWORD);`. This is a common pattern when you want to retrieve a value from a Secret and use it for defining another variable.

Now, please continue the Deployment using the following steps:

1. Apply the manifest file using the `kubectl apply -f .\voting-application.yaml` command. Wait for the Pods to start, as follows:

```
PS C:\src> kubectl get pods -n dev
NAME                                          READY    STATUS
RESTARTS    AGE
```

```
mssql-deployment-58bcb8b89d-7f9xz          1/1    Running   0
19h
voting-application-frontend-6876dcc678-kdmcw   1/1    Running   0
19m
voting-application-frontend-6876dcc678-mhdr9   1/1    Running   0
19m
voting-application-frontend-6876dcc678-qsmst   1/1    Running   0
19m
voting-application-frontend-6876dcc678-w5hch   1/1    Running   0
19m
voting-application-frontend-6876dcc678-zqr26   1/1    Running   0
19m
```

The application has been successfully deployed. Before accessing it, we first need to apply the initial database migration—technically, you could access the application without seeding the database as the schema would get initialized automatically, but there would be no data in the tables at all. To perform the database migration, please perform the following steps:

1. Create a `ef6-update-database.yaml` manifest file for the Kubernetes Job with the following content:

```yaml
apiVersion: batch/v1
kind: Job
metadata:
  namespace: dev
  name: voting-application-ef6-update-database3
  labels:
    app: voting-application
spec:
  ttlSecondsAfterFinished: 600   # (1)
  template:
    spec:
      nodeSelector:   # (2)
        "beta.kubernetes.io/os": windows
      containers:
      - name: ef6-update-database
        image: packtpubkubernetesonwindows/voting-application:1.0.0
# (3)
        command: ["c:/ef6/ef6.exe",   # (4)
                  "database", "update",
                  "--verbose",
                  "--assembly",
"/inetpub/wwwroot/bin/VotingApplication.dll",
                  "--connection-string", "Data Source=mssql-
deployment;Initial
Catalog=VotingApplication;MultipleActiveResultSets=true;User
```

```
          Id=sa;Password=$(MSSQL_SA_PASSWORD);",
                    "--connection-provider", "System.Data.SqlClient",
                    "--config", "/inetpub/wwwroot/Web.config"]
        env:
        - name: MSSQL_SA_PASSWORD
          valueFrom:
            secretKeyRef:
              name: mssql
              key: SA_PASSWORD
      restartPolicy: Never
      nodeSelector:
        "beta.kubernetes.io/os": windows
  backoffLimit: 4
```

The key points here are setting a **time-to-live** (TTL) seconds value in order to trigger automatic cleanup of Pods created by the Job (1) and ensuring that the Pods are executed on Windows nodes (2). The last part is setting the container image (3). In our case, we use the same as for the application, as it contains all the migration tools. The (4) command is specific to EF, but in general, you have to provide the path to the .NET assembly that contains the migrations using the --assembly parameter, and a proper connection string, using the --connection-string parameter.

2. Apply the manifest file using the kubectl apply -f .\ef6-update-database.yaml command.

3. Wait for the Job to run to completion, as follows:

```
PS C:\src> kubectl get jobs -n dev
NAME                                       COMPLETIONS   DURATION
AGE
voting-application-ef6-update-database     1/1           50s
103s
```

4. You can check the logs using the standard kubectl logs command, but you have to provide the jobs prefix, as follows:

```
PS C:\src> kubectl logs -n dev jobs/voting-application-ef6-update-
database
Specify the '-Verbose' flag to view the SQL statements being
applied to the target database.
Target database is: 'VotingApplication' (DataSource: mssql-
deployment, Provider: System.Data.SqlClient, Origin: Explicit).
No pending explicit migrations.
Applying automatic migration: 201911201840183_AutomaticMigration.
CREATE TABLE [dbo].[Options] (
...
```

5. Now, if anything went wrong—for example, you cannot access the logs (because the Pod did not even start) or all Job executions completed with a failure—the best way to investigate is describing the Job object and finding the Pods that it has created, as follows:

```
PS C:\src> kubectl describe job -n dev voting-application-ef6-
update-database
. . .
Events:
   Type      Reason           Age      From             Message
   ----      ------           ----     ----             -------
   Normal    SuccessfulCreate 6m23s    job-controller   Created pod:
voting-application-ef6-update-database-chw6s
```

6. Using this information, you can describe any Pods that did not start properly, or you can even directly describe them using the Job name, like this:

```
kubectl describe pod -n dev voting-application-ef6-update-database
```

Our application is ready—we can try accessing it, even if there is no LoadBalancer Service for it yet. To do that, we will use the technique described in the previous chapters, as follows:

1. In the PowerShell window, execute the following command to forward all network traffic from the localhost port 5000 to port 80 on one of the Pods in the voting-application Deployment, as follows:

```
PS C:\src> kubectl port-forward -n dev deployment/voting-
application-frontend 5000:80
Forwarding from 127.0.0.1:5000 -> 80
Forwarding from [::1]:5000 -> 80
```

2. Without closing the PowerShell session, open your web browser and navigate to http://localhost:5000. You should see the following screen:

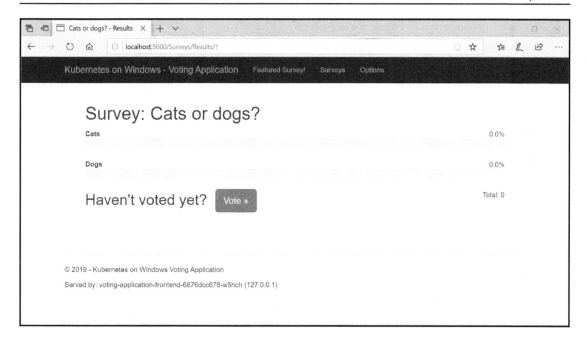

Congratulations! You have successfully deployed the voting application—now, we can proceed to expose the Deployment using a LoadBalancer service.

Accessing the application

In this section, we will expose our voting application to external users by creating a Kubernetes service of the LoadBalancer type. Services have been covered in depth in Chapter 5, *Kubernetes Networking*. At the end of this section, anyone who has the external IP of your new service will be able to access the application.

To create the service, execute the following steps:

1. Open the PowerShell window.
2. Create a `voting-application-service.yaml` manifest file for the Kubernetes service with the following content:

```
apiVersion: v1
kind: Service
metadata:
  namespace: dev
  name: voting-application-frontend
  labels:
```

```
        app: voting-application
spec:
  type: LoadBalancer (1)
  ports:
  - protocol: TCP
    port: 80 (2)
  selector:
    app: voting-application
```

Here, the key points are ensuring that the type of service is `LoadBalancer` (1) and using the proper port for the service (2). In our case, the port on the physical Azure load balancer will be the same as for the application Pods, so we do not need to specify the `targetPort` parameter.

3. Apply the manifest file using the `kubectl apply -f .\voting-application-service.yaml` command.

4. Wait for the external IP to be provided for the new service, as follows:

```
PS C:\src> kubectl get svc -n dev -w
NAME                              TYPE            CLUSTER-IP
EXTERNAL-IP       PORT(S)             AGE
mssql-deployment                  LoadBalancer    10.0.134.237
104.210.54.75     1433:31446/TCP      21h
voting-application-frontend    LoadBalancer    10.0.50.43
104.42.142.217    80:32357/TCP        62s
```

5. In this case, the external IP is `104.42.142.217`. Use your web browser and navigate to `http://104.42.142.217`.

6. You can try refreshing the page multiple times and accessing it from different browsers. You will see in the page footer that you are served by different Pods. If you experience any delays at the beginning, it is caused by IIS starting the app pool in a given Pod when accessed for the first time. The code can be seen in the following snippet:

```
Served by: voting-application-frontend-6876dcc678-zqr26
(10.240.0.44)
```

The application is now accessible to all external users! Now, we will take a look at how you can scale the application.

Scaling the application

In our design, the only component that can scale is the ASP.NET MVC frontend. SQL Server cannot be scaled as it runs in a single node with automatic failover mode. Real scaling of the SQL Server requires the use of **Availability Groups** (**AG**) and a dedicated Kubernetes Operator, as mentioned in the earlier sections.

In the previous chapter, we have shown different declarative and imperative methods on how to scale a Deployment. We will now show the safest, declarative way of scaling the Deployment. Autoscaling will not be covered as it is described in more detail in the next chapter: Chapter 11, *Configuring Applications to Use Kubernetes Features*. To scale the frontend Deployment from 5 replicas to 10, perform the following steps:

1. Open the PowerShell window.
2. Modify your existing `voting-application.yaml` manifest file to change the number of replicas, as follows:

   ```
   apiVersion: apps/v1
   kind: Deployment
   metadata:
     ...
   spec:
     replicas: 10
   ```

3. Apply the manifest file using the `kubectl apply -f .\voting-application.yaml` command.

4. Observe the status of the rollout, as illustrated in the following code block:

   ```
   PS C:\src> kubectl get deployments -n dev -w
   NAME                           READY   UP-TO-DATE   AVAILABLE   AGE
   mssql-deployment               1/1     1            1           21h
   voting-application-frontend    6/10    10           5           125m
   ```

5. You will eventually see that it never reaches 10 ready replicas! What happened? The answer to this is that we have exhausted the CPU reservation limits for our two Windows nodes—each node was scheduled with four Pods, reserving 500m CPU per Pod. If you check the specification of the Standard_D2_v3 Azure VM, you will see that it has two vCPUs, which means that we have reserved all the resources. You can verify this theory by inspecting the Pods that are in Pending status, as follows:

   ```
   PS C:\src> kubectl get pods -n dev
   NAME                                             READY   STATUS
   RESTARTS     AGE
   ```

```
. . .
voting-application-frontend-6876dcc678-9ssc4      0/1      Pending
0               6m1s
. . .
```

6. Describe one of the Pods that is in a `Pending` state, like this:

```
PS C:\src> kubectl describe pod -n dev voting-application-
frontend-6876dcc678-9ssc4
Events:
  Type      Reason            Age         From              Message
  ----      ------            ----        ----              -------
  Warning   FailedScheduling  <unknown>   default-scheduler  0/5
nodes are available: 2 Insufficient cpu, 3 node(s) didn't match
node selector.
```

What can we do in such a case? Consider the following options:

- Scale your Kubernetes cluster up by adding more Windows nodes.
- Do not scale the cluster up; decrease the CPU limits for the Deployment.
- Do not scale the cluster up; do not change CPU limits for the Deployment, but decrease the CPU requests in order to do an overcommit. You can dive deeper into this concept by checking out the official documentation at `https://kubernetes.io/docs/concepts/configuration/manage-compute-resources-container/#how-pods-with-resource-limits-are-run`.

In general, to decide what to do, you have to understand the requirements for your application and how it behaves under low CPU availability. As a demonstration, we will perform an overcommit of CPU resources, as follows:

1. Modify the `voting-application-service.yaml` manifest file.
2. Change the requested CPU value to `250m`, leaving the limits value unchanged. Please note that we also need to modify `maxUnavailable` to allow a larger number of Pods to be unavailable during the rollout. With the previous value of `25%`, we would run into a deadlock situation, as already, 2 of 10 Pods are not available. The code for this is illustrated in the following block:

```
apiVersion: apps/v1
kind: Deployment
. . .
spec:
  strategy:
    . . .
    rollingUpdate:
      maxUnavailable: 50%
```

```
...
template:
  ...
  spec:
    ...
    containers:
    - name: frontend
      ...
      resources:
        limits:
          cpu: 500m
        requests:
          cpu: 250m
```

3. Apply the manifest file using the `kubectl apply -f .\voting-application.yaml` command and observe how the Deployment scales to 10 replicas.

Now that you understand how you can scale our voting application, we can move to the last section in this chapter, which will show how to debug the application.

Debugging the application

Debugging applications is a broad topic and involves a lot of techniques depending on the need—it may involve detailed telemetry, traces, or performance counter analysis. From a developer perspective, there is one technique that is especially important: working with a code debugger. One of the problems with containerized workloads is that they are relatively heavy to debug using standard tools such as Visual Studio—the processes are not running locally and you cannot easily attach the debugger as if it was a local process. In this section we will show the following:

- How to access application logs produced by log monitor
- How to enable Visual Studio remote debugging via `kubectl` port forwarding

Accessing application logs is straightforward as it involves the standard `kubectl logs` command. In production scenarios, you would probably use Azure Log Analytics or Elasticsearch for browsing logs more efficiently. To access voting application logs, execute the following command, which will load logs from all Pods in the Deployment:

```
PS C:\src> kubectl logs -n dev deployment/voting-application-frontend
...
<Source>EventLog</Source><Time>2019-11-20T22:51:17.000Z</Time><LogEntry><Channel>VotingApplication</Channel><Level>Information</Level><EventId>55509</
```

```
EventId><Message>Using custom connection string provided by environment
variable: "data source=mssql-deployment;initial
catalog=VotingApplication;multipleactiveresultsets=true;user
id=sa;password=*****" </Message></LogEntry>
...
```

The current logging settings are quite verbose, but you can see all the log messages logged by Serilog to the Windows event log—for example, the preceding line comes from the `VotingApplicationContextFactory` class (`https://github.com/PacktPublishing/Hands-On-Kubernetes-on-Windows/blob/master/Chapter10/01_voting-application-src/Factories/VotingApplicationContextFactory.cs#L28`).

Now, let's move to the more complicated scenario, which is Visual Studio remote debugging via `kubectl` port forwarding. This use case is not documented yet, but it involves standard techniques known from non-containerized Deployments. We will do the following:

1. Create a dedicated Docker image for debugging that has Visual Studio 2019 remote tools installed (`https://docs.microsoft.com/en-us/visualstudio/debugger/remote-debugging?view=vs-2019`).
2. Push the image to the registry with a special tag.
3. Modify our Deployment so that it uses the new image—for production scenarios, you would rather create a separate Deployment.
4. Copy **program database** (**PDB**) symbol files from the container. We have to perform this step as building an application in the container may result in a slightly different output assembly and symbols.
5. Use `kubectl` port forwarding capabilities to expose the remote debugger to the local development machine.
6. Attach Visual Studio to the `w3wp.exe` process using the forwarded remote debugger.
7. Load any missing debugging symbols.

In our scenario, we are limited to the traditional Visual Studio remote debugger because we are running on the classic .NET Framework. For .NET Core, there are more approaches, which involve both Visual Studio Enterprise and Visual Studio Code. You can read more about Visual Studio Enterprise snapshot debugging for .NET Core running on Linux at `https://github.com/Microsoft/vssnapshotdebugger-docker`, and Visual Studio Code with Azure Dev Spaces at `https://microsoft.github.io/AzureTipsAndTricks/blog/tip228.html`.

Let's start by creating our modified Dockerfile for debugging.

Creating a debug Dockerfile and publishing a debug image

In order to create a debug Dockerfile, we will use our original `Dockerfile.production` file and perform slight modifications. The resulting file is `Dockerfile.debug` (https://github.com/PacktPublishing/Hands-On-Kubernetes-on-Windows/blob/master/Chapter10/01_voting-application-src/Dockerfile.debug). Let's summarize its contents:

1. The build stage in the Dockerfile looks almost the same—the only difference is that we are using a debug configuration for the build. This will ensure that we have proper debug assembly generated, together with PDB symbols, as follows:

```
FROM mcr.microsoft.com/dotnet/framework/sdk:4.8-windowsservercore-
ltsc2019 AS build
ARG PUBLISH_PROFILE=DockerPublishProfileDebug.pubxml
ARG BUILD_CONFIG=Debug

WORKDIR /app

COPY *.sln ./
COPY *.csproj ./
COPY *.config ./
RUN nuget restore

COPY . .
RUN msbuild /p:DeployOnBuild=true
/p:PublishProfile=$env:PUBLISH_PROFILE
/p:Configuration=$env:BUILD_CONFIG
```

2. In the final build stage, we first download and install Visual Studio 2019 remote tools. We are exposing port `4020` as we are going to host the remote debugger using that port, as shown in the following code block:

```
FROM mcr.microsoft.com/dotnet/framework/aspnet:4.8-
windowsservercore-ltsc2019 AS runtime

WORKDIR /temp
RUN powershell.exe -Command Invoke-WebRequest
https://aka.ms/vs/16/release/RemoteTools.amd64ret.enu.exe -OutFile
VS_RemoteTools.exe
RUN powershell.exe -Command ./VS_RemoteTools.exe /install /quiet
EXPOSE 4020
```

3. The rest of the image remains the same except for the `ENTRYPOINT`. We modify it so that the remote debugger process (`msvsmon.exe`) is started in the background. In principle, it is not a recommended practice to start another process in the background in a container, but in our case, we want the quickest way to start the remote debugger together with other services. The syntax of this command is Powershell-specific, and can be seen in the following code block:

```
ENTRYPOINT Start-Process -NoNewWindow 'C:\Program Files\Microsoft
Visual Studio 16.0\Common7\IDE\Remote Debugger\x64\msvsmon.exe' -
ArgumentList
/nostatus,/silent,/noauth,/anyuser,/nosecuritywarn,/port,4020;
C:\ServiceMonitor.exe w3svc
```

With the debug Dockerfile ready, we can create the image and push it to the Docker Hub. Please perform the following steps:

1. We are going to use a convention that debug images will have a `-debug` postfix in the tag—for example, for a production tag 1.0.0, we will use a debug tag `1.0.0-debug`. Another alternative would be creating a new dedicated image repository for debug images. To build the image, execute the following command in the root of the voting application source (use your own image repository name accordingly):

```
docker build -t packtpubkubernetesonwindows/voting-
application:1.0.0-debug -f .\Dockerfile.debug .
```

2. When the build finishes, push the new image to Docker Hub, as follows:

```
docker push packtpubkubernetesonwindows/voting-application:1.0.0-
debug
```

With the image pushed, we are ready to roll out a debug Deployment of our application.

Updating the Kubernetes Deployment

As mentioned earlier, for simplicity, we will reuse the same Kubernetes Deployment and service to enable debugging. We need to make the following modifications to our original `voting-application.yaml` manifest file:

```
apiVersion: apps/v1
kind: Deployment
metadata:
    ...
```

```
spec:
  replicas: 1
  ...
  template:
    ...
    spec:
      ...
      containers:
      - name: frontend
        image: packtpubkubernetesonwindows/voting-application:1.0.0-debug
        imagePullPolicy: Always
```

Modifying the number of replicas to 1 ensures that when debugging, we have only one Pod to which the traffic is redirected. This means that we can easily break on any action performed in the **user interface** (**UI**) using the debugger. On top of that, we have to update the image to our new `packtpubkubernetesonwindows/voting-application:1.0.0-debug` tag and set `imagePullPolicy` to `Always` to make introducing changes easier. For example, if you find a bug and want to quickly redeploy the image and reattach, you build the image with the same tag, push it, and manually delete the currently running Pod in the Deployment. This will recreate the Pod and thanks to the `Always` policy, the image will be pulled again.

Now, apply the manifest file using the `kubectl apply -f .\voting-application.yaml` command. Our setup is ready to attach the Visual Studio debugger.

Attaching the Visual Studio remote debugger

The cherry on top is attaching your Visual Studio 2019 to the IIS app pool process using a remote debugger running inside the container. This process is not fully automated (but could be scripted), and it is possible to further unify PDB symbols between the container image and your local development machine. To attach the debugger, execute the following steps:

1. Open the PowerShell window.
2. Determine the name of your application Pod using the following standard command:

   kubectl get pods -n dev

3. Use the `kubectl cp` command to copy the `VotingApplication.pdb` file to your current directory, as follows:

```
PS C:\src> kubectl cp -n dev voting-application-
frontend-66b95ff674-
mmsbk:/inetpub/wwwroot/bin/VotingApplication.pdb
VotingApplication.pdb
tar: Removing leading '/' from member names
```

4. Alternatively, you can perform this locally using Docker by creating a temporary container and copying the file using the following commands:

```
$id = $(docker create packtpubkubernetesonwindows/voting-
application:1.0.0-debug)
docker cp $id`:/inetpub/wwwroot/bin/VotingApplication.pdb
VotingApplication.pdb
docker rm -v $id
```

5. Use the `kubectl port-forward` command to forward all traffic from your local 5000 port to port 4020 in your Pod—this is where the Visual Studio remote debugger is exposed—as follows:

```
PS C:\src> kubectl port-forward -n dev deployment/voting-
application-frontend 5000:4020
Forwarding from 127.0.0.1:5000 -> 4020
Forwarding from [::1]:5000 -> 4020
```

6. Now, you are ready to attach Visual Studio 2019 to the remote debugger. Open `VotingApplication.sln` in Visual Studio, and navigate to **Debug > Attach to Process...:**, as shown in the following screenshot:

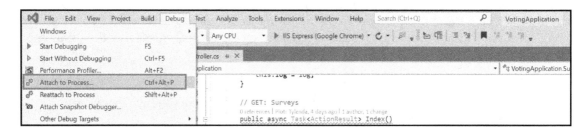

7. In the dialog, set **Connection type** as **Remote (no authentication)**, set **Connection target** to the forwarded port `localhost:5000`, select **Show processes from all users**, and click the **Refresh** button, as shown in the following screenshot:

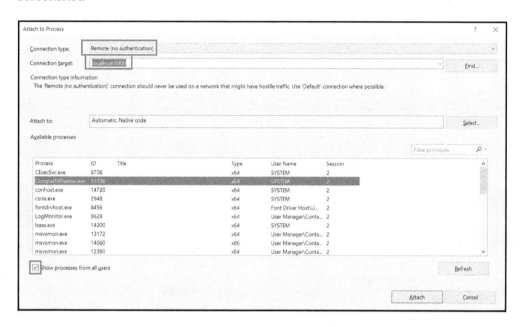

8. You should see the list of all processes running in the container. If, at this point, you have encountered connection problems, you can execute into the container in Kubernetes and check if the `msvsmon.exe` process is still running. If it is not, you can recreate the container or start the process manually using the same command as in the Dockerfile, like this:

```
PS C:\src> kubectl exec -n dev -it voting-application-
frontend-66b95ff674-vn256 powershell
Windows PowerShell
Copyright (C) Microsoft Corporation. All rights reserved.
PS C:\inetpub\wwwroot> Get-Process
...
    218      12     2240       9016     0.06  12360    2 msvsmon
```

9. Now, navigate in the browser to the external IP of the service. We need to ensure that the IIS app pool process (`w3wp.exe`) is started.

10. In the **Attach to Process** dialog, refresh the list of processes, find the `w3wp.exe` process, and click the **Attach** button, as shown in the following screenshot:

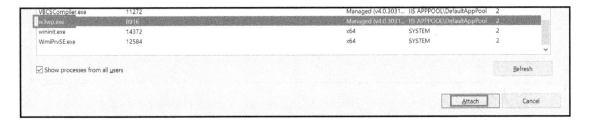

11. The debugger is attached, but it may have missing symbols. You can verify this by placing a breakpoint anywhere in the code, as shown in the following screenshot:

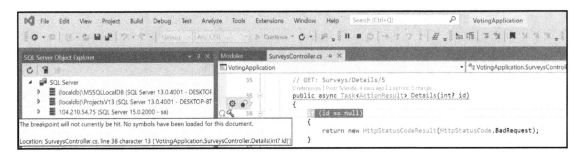

12. If this is the case, to load custom PDB symbols, navigate to **Debug > Windows > Modules**, find the `VotingApplication.dll` assembly, right-click, and choose **Load Symbols**, as shown in the following screenshot:

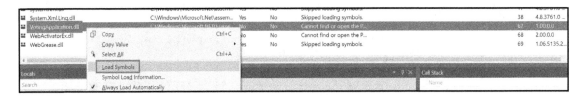

13. Navigate to the directory where you have copied the `VotingApplication.pdb` file. The symbols will be loaded automatically and the breakpoint will become hittable.

14. In the web browser, perform the action that should cause the breakpoint to be hit.

15. Now, depending on your connection speed, Visual Studio may freeze for a bit of time (even a couple of minutes) until the debugger fully attaches. But, after this initial hiccup, the debugging experience should be satisfying, and is shown in the following screenshot:

Congratulations—you have successfully attached a debugger remotely to a process running inside a Kubernetes Pod!

Summary

In this chapter, you have learned how to deploy an ASP.NET MVC application to a Kubernetes cluster, together with a containerized Microsoft SQL Server 2019. We have shown how to approach making an existing .NET Framework application cloud-ready and how to create robust Dockerfiles for such applications. Next, we have prepared an AKS Engine cluster Deployment for our voting application and deployed Microsoft SQL Server 2019 in single-node failover mode, backed by Azure Disk. The application was deployed to the cluster using a Kubernetes Deployment and we have used a Kubernetes Job in order to apply EF database migrations. After that, you have learned a bit more about scaling the Kubernetes Deployments and overcommitting of computing resources. And finally, you had a deep dive into debugging .NET Framework applications running inside Kubernetes Pods using Visual Studio 2019's remote debugger via `kubectl` port forwarding.

The next chapter will focus on more advanced Kubernetes features—we will extend our voting application to fully utilize the power of Kubernetes.

Questions

1. What are the possible ways to inject configuration to an application running in a Kubernetes Pod?
2. What is the purpose of the Windows container log monitor provided by Microsoft?
3. Why is migrating database schema for replicated applications a challenging task?
4. Why are we using a persistent volume backed by Azure Disk for Microsoft SQL Server data?
5. How can you apply EF database migration to an application running in Kubernetes?
6. What is CPU/memory resource overcommitting in Kubernetes?
7. Why do you need `kubectl` port forwarding in order to connect to a Visual Studio remote debugger in a container?

You can find answers to these questions in the *Assessment* of this book.

Further reading

- For more information about Kubernetes applications management, please refer to the following Packt books:
  - *The Complete Kubernetes Guide* (`https://www.packtpub.com/virtualization-and-cloud/complete-kubernetes-guide`).
  - *Getting Started with Kubernetes - Third Edition* (`https://www.packtpub.com/virtualization-and-cloud/getting-started-kubernetes-third-edition`).
  - *Kubernetes for Developers* (`https://www.packtpub.com/virtualization-and-cloud/kubernetes-developers`).
- For alternative approaches to debugging applications running in Kubernetes clusters (for example, Telepresence), you can read the following articles:
  - `https://kubernetes.io/docs/tasks/debug-application-cluster/local-debugging/`.
  - `https://www.telepresence.io/tutorials/kubernetes`.

11
Configuring Applications to Use Kubernetes Features

The last chapter demonstrated how to work with a containerized Windows application in Kubernetes—now, we are going to extend our voting application to use more advanced features which make the orchestration even more robust and automated. Over the years, Kubernetes has been extended with a growing number of features, ranging from fine-grained **Role-Based Access Control** (**RBAC**) or Secrets management to autoscaling using **Horizontal Pod Autoscaler** (**HPA**), the holy grail of container orchestration. Of course, we are not able to cover all of them in the scope of this book, but we are going to include the most useful features that help running containerized Windows applications. Also, please bear in mind that some of the features are not available when you are running an on-premises Kubernetes cluster, for example, cloud-specific StorageClass provisioners—all of the examples we are going to present are assuming that you are running an AKS Engine Kubernetes cluster.

In this chapter, we will cover the following topics:

- Using namespaces to isolate applications
- Health monitoring using liveness and readiness probes
- Specifying resource limits and configuring autoscaling
- Managing application configuration using ConfigMaps and Secrets
- Managing persistent data storage on Windows nodes
- Configuring rolling updates for Deployment
- RBAC

Technical requirements

For this chapter, you will need the following:

- Windows 10 Pro, Enterprise, or Education (version 1903 or later, 64-bit) installed
- Microsoft Visual Studio 2019 Community (or any other edition) if you want to edit the source code for the application and debug it—Visual Studio Code has limited support for the classic .NET Framework
- An Azure account
- Windows/Linux Kubernetes cluster deployed using AKS Engine, ready to deploy the voting application from the previous chapter

To follow along, you will need your own Azure account to create Azure resources for the Kubernetes cluster. If you haven't already created the account for the previous chapters, you can read more about how to obtain a limited free account for personal use at `https://azure.microsoft.com/en-us/free/`.

Deploying a Kubernetes cluster using AKS Engine has been covered in `Chapter 8`, *Deploying a Hybrid Azure Kubernetes Service Engine Cluster*. Voting application Deployment to Kubernetes has been covered in `Chapter 10`, *Deploying Microsoft SQL Server 2019 and ASP.NET MVC Application*.

You can download the latest code samples for this chapter from the official GitHub repository, at `https://github.com/PacktPublishing/Hands-On-Kubernetes-on-Windows/tree/master/Chapter11`.

Using namespaces to isolate applications

In the previous chapter, we already used a namespace (named `dev`) to logically group components of our application into a virtual cluster within an existing physical Kubernetes cluster. The general principle of namespaces is providing resource quotas and a scope for object names—names inside a given namespace must be unique, but they do not have to be unique across different namespaces. By default, Kubernetes provides the following namespaces out of the box:

- `kube-system`: A namespace for objects created by the Kubernetes system, such as `kube-apiserver` or `kube-proxy` Pods.

- `kube-public`: A namespace that can be read by all users, also not authenticated—it will be created in clusters that are bootstrapped by kubeadm and it is generally intended for system use.
- `default`: A namespace for objects with no other namespace.

Depending on your needs and the size of your team, you may be more comfortable with using just object labels (small teams) or separating the objects at namespace level (large team):

- For small teams, where a single developer is capable of understanding the whole system (around 10 microservices) and where the whole development environment can be hosted using local clusters, such as minikube or kubeadm deployment running on VMs, it is possible to stick just to the default namespace for your production services. Alternatively, you may use a dedicated namespace for production workloads and a separate one for the development/staging environment.
- For rapidly growing medium-sized teams, where a single developer is not working in the scope of the whole system, it may be easier to provide dedicated namespaces for each sub-team, especially if it is not possible to create the whole development environment on a local Kubernetes cluster.
- For large teams, where sub-teams operate almost independently, it may be a good idea to have separate production and development namespaces for each team. You may also think about using resource quotas per each namespace and using RBAC.
- For enterprise organizations, where individual teams may not even be aware of other teams, it may be easier to create separate clusters instead of dividing a single cluster using namespaces. This makes resource and billing management easier and provides better boundaries between deployments in case of issues.

When creating a Service object, namespaces influence what is the **Fully-Qualified Domain Name (FQDN)** for the DNS entry of the Service. The FQDNs have a form of `<service-name>.<namespace-name>.svc.cluster.local`—this means that if you use `<service-name>` when calling a Service from a Pod, the call will be scoped to the namespace where this Pod is running. Note that cross-namespace calls to Services are possible but then you need to specify the FQDN.

Let's demonstrate how you can create a namespace for your objects.

Creating namespaces

To create a namespace named `prod`, you can use the following imperative command:

```
kubectl create namespace prod
```

As in the case of other objects, it is generally recommended to use declarative object configuration management and apply manifest files to the Kubernetes cluster. The following `namespace-prod.yaml` manifest file will create the `prod` namespace, additionally specifying the `ResourceQuota` object, which determines the total CPU and memory quota for this namespace:

```
---
kind: Namespace
apiVersion: v1
metadata:
  name: prod
  labels:
    name: prod
---
apiVersion: v1
kind: ResourceQuota
metadata:
  namespace: prod
  name: default-resource-quota
spec:
  hard:
    requests.cpu: 500m
    requests.memory: 1Gi
    limits.cpu: "1"
    limits.memory: 2Gi
```

To apply the manifest file, execute the following command:

```
kubectl apply -f .\namespace-prod.yaml
```

Then, you can use the `kubectl describe` command to check how many resources are used in our namespace:

```
PS C:\src> kubectl describe resourcequota -n prod
Name:              default-resource-quota
Namespace:         prod
Resource           Used  Hard
--------           ----  ----
limits.cpu         0     1
limits.memory      0     2Gi
requests.cpu       0     500m
requests.memory    0     1Gi
```

 Resource quotas in Kubernetes are highly customizable and can be applied to different resources and scoped using sophisticated selectors. You can read more about this in the official documentation at `https://kubernetes.io/docs/concepts/policy/resource-quotas/`.

Now, when you know how to manage namespaces, let's see how you can use them efficiently with `kubectl` commands.

kubectl commands and namespaces

`kubectl` commands, which operate on namespace-scoped objects by convention, use the `--namespace` or `-n` flag to specify the namespace that should be used for the command. If you need to query for objects in all namespaces, you can use the `--all-namespaces` flag instead. For example, to list all Pods in the `prod` namespace, use the following command:

```
kubectl get pods -n prod
```

In the previous chapters, you have used this construct a lot. However, it is good to know that if no namespace is provided for the command, it will use the namespace set as default in the current kubeconfig context. In other words, it does not have to be the default namespace—it all depends on your context settings. We have covered contexts in depth in Chapter 6, *Interacting with Kubernetes Clusters*—for completeness, we will show how to change the namespace used in the current context. To set the `prod` namespace permanently in your current context, use the following command:

```
kubectl config set-context --current --namespace=prod
```

Now, any command that supports specifying namespace will use the `prod` namespace by default.

Deleting namespaces

Similar to other objects, deleting namespaces is recommended to be done imperatively. To delete the `prod` namespace, execute the following command:

```
kubectl delete namespace prod
```

Please note that this command deletes all objects within this namespace, which means it is a highly destructive command and should be used with caution!

In the next section, we will see how you can use probes to configure containers monitoring for liveness and readiness.

Health monitoring using liveness and readiness probes

In Kubernetes, probes are used by kubelet to determine the state of a Pod—you can use them to customize how you check whether a Pod is ready to serve your traffic or a container needs to be restarted. There are three types of probes that you can configure for each container running in a Pod:

- **Readiness probe**: This is used to determine whether a given container is ready to accept traffic. A Pod is considered ready only if all of its containers are ready. Pods that are not ready will be removed from Service Endpoints until they become ready again.
- **Liveness probe**: This is used to detect whether a container needs to be restarted. This can help in situations when a container has been stuck in a deadlock or other issues when the container process is alive but unable to operate properly. Restarting the container may increase the availability of Pods in that case.
- **Startup probe**: This is an additional probe used for determining whether a container has been fully started—readiness and liveness probes are disabled until this probe returns successfully. This is especially useful for containers that have a long startup time due to some initialization. In this way, you can avoid premature kills by the liveness probe.

By default, there are no probes configured on Pod containers. However, Kubernetes will serve traffic only if the Pod containers have been started (in the Docker sense) and restart the containers if they crash (depending on your restart policy of course).

All types of probes can be configured using three types of handler actions:

- Running a command (exec)—if a given command running in the container returns non-zero exit code, the probe is in a failed state.
- Executing an HTTP GET request (httpGet)—the probe is in a successful state only if the container responds to the HTTP GET request with an HTTP code greater than or equal to 200 and less than 400.
- Opening a TCP socket to the container on a specified port (tcpSocket)—the probe is in a successful state if the connection can be established.

> You should additionally consider using the termination grace period for your Pods to properly manage a containerized application life cycle and make your application gracefully exit when a SIGTERM signal is received (https://cloud.google.com/blog/products/gcp/kubernetes-best-practices-terminating-with-grace). Please note that, for Windows Pods, the termination grace period is not supported as of Kubernetes 1.17.

There are a couple of caveats and best practices when working with probes that are true for any large distributed system with many dependent components. We will go through the details when explaining each type of probes—the voting application source code reflecting the examples can be found in the official GitHub repository, at https://github.com/PacktPublishing/Hands-On-Kubernetes-on-Windows/tree/master/Chapter11/02_voting-application-probes-src. First, let's take a look at the most popular probe, the readiness probe.

Readiness probes

Readiness probes are used in Kubernetes to determine whether a Pod container is ready to accept traffic incoming from a Kubernetes Service—Pods that are not ready (a Pod is ready only if all of its containers are considered ready) will be removed from the Service Endpoints list until they become ready again. In other words, it is a signal for notifying that a given Pod can be used for requests incoming to the Service.

There are a couple of established best practices for readiness probes that you should consider:

- Use this probe whenever your containers may not be ready to properly serve traffic as soon as the container is started.
- Ensure that you check the cache warm-up or database migration status during readiness probe evaluation. You may also consider starting the actual process of a warm-up if it hasn't been started yet, but use this approach with caution—a readiness probe will be executed constantly throughout the life cycle of a Pod, which means you shouldn't do any costly operations for every request. Alternatively, you may want to use a startup probe for this purpose, newly-introduced in Kubernetes 1.16.
- For microservice applications that expose HTTP endpoints, consider always configuring the `httpGet` readiness probe. This will ensure that all cases are covered when a container is successfully running but the HTTP server is not fully initialized.
- It is a good idea to use a separate, dedicated HTTP endpoint for readiness checks in your application, for example, a common convention is using `/health`.
- If you are checking the state of dependencies (external database and logging services) in this type of probe, be careful with shared dependencies, such as SQL Server in the voting application. In this case, you should consider using a probe timeout, which is greater than the maximum allowed timeout for the external dependency— otherwise, you may get cascading failures and lower availability instead of occasionally increased latency.

For web applications hosted using **IIS** (short for **Internet Information Services**), a readiness probe makes a lot of sense—the IIS App Pool needs to be fully started and database migrations may not be applied yet. As an example, we will configure a simple readiness probe for our voting application, which will look as follows:

- The ASP.NET MVC application will implement a dedicated controller serving `/health` requests.
- Pending database migrations will be checked. Note that this will indirectly verify the database connection status, which might be not desirable in some cases. Therefore, we will use a probe timeout larger than 30 seconds (the default SQL command timeout).
- Controller actions will return a simple JSON. The HTTP status will be 503 in case of a failed check and 200 in case of success.

To add a readiness probe for the voting application, follow these steps:

1. The implementation of a health check controller action can be found in the `HealthController` class (https://github.com/PacktPublishing/Hands-On-Kubernetes-on-Windows/blob/master/Chapter11/02_voting-application-probes-src/Controllers/HealthController.cs) and looks as follows:

```
public ActionResult CheckHealth()
{
    this.Response.TrySkipIisCustomErrors = true;

    if (!this.db.Database.CompatibleWithModel(throwIfNoMetadata:
true))
    {
        this.Response.StatusCode =
(int)HttpStatusCode.ServiceUnavailable;
        return this.Json(new { status = "Database migrations
pending" }, JsonRequestBehavior.AllowGet);
    }

    return this.Json(new { status = "Ok" },
JsonRequestBehavior.AllowGet);
}
```

2. Additionally, you need to remember to modify routing configuration for your application in the `RouteConfig` class (https://github.com/PacktPublishing/Hands-On-Kubernetes-on-Windows/blob/master/Chapter11/02_voting-application-probes-src/App_Start/RouteConfig.cs), before the default route map:

```
routes.MapRoute(
    name: "Health",
    url: "health",
    defaults: new { controller = "Health", action = "CheckHealth"
});
```

3. As in the previous chapter, build a Docker image of the application, tag it as 1.1.0 version, and push it to Docker Hub. In our demonstration case, we will be using the `packtpubkubernetesonwindows/voting-application:1.1.0` image.

4. Modify the Deployment manifest file, `voting-application.yaml`, to include the following readiness probe configuration for the `frontend` container:

```
apiVersion: apps/v1
kind: Deployment
metadata:
  namespace: dev
```

```
        name: voting-application-frontend
        ...
    spec:
        ...
        template:
            ...
            spec:
                ...
                containers:
                - name: frontend
                    image: packtpubkubernetesonwindows/voting-application:1.1.0
                    ...
                    readinessProbe:
                        httpGet:
                            path: /health
                            port: 80
                        initialDelaySeconds: 30
                        periodSeconds: 10
                        timeoutSeconds: 40
                        successThreshold: 1
                        failureThreshold: 3
                    ...
```

The probe is configured to call the /health endpoint, which will execute the controller action that we have previously implemented. The important parts in the probe configuration are the following:

- initialDelaySeconds is set to 30 seconds to allow IIS for full initialization. It turns out that too early calls to applications running on IIS under ServiceMonitor.exe supervision may result in premature exits of the container (maybe a bug in the ServiceMonitor.exe implementation).
- timeoutSeconds is set to 40 seconds to exceed the SQL Server database timeout, which is set by default to 30 seconds.

5. Now, apply the manifest file using the kubectl apply -f .\voting-application-readiness-probe.yaml command.

6. Inspect the rollout process using the kubectl get pods -n dev and kubectl describe commands as usual. In the Pod events, you can verify whether the Pod had any readiness failures.

7. In the web browser, when you navigate to the application, you should not experience any IIS App Pool startup delays —the web server will be warmed up by readiness checks.

Now, let's take a look at another probe that determines the liveness status of a Pod container.

Liveness probes

The second type of probe is the liveness probe, which can be configured similarly to the readiness probe in the manifest. Liveness probes are used to determine whether a Pod container needs to be restarted. This type of probe may be useful in recovering deadlocks or other types of issues in the container when the process has not exited but is not able to handle any operations.

Similar to readiness probes, there are a couple of guidelines on how and when you should use liveness probes:

- Liveness probes should be used with caution. The wrong configuration of this probe can result in cascading failures in your services and container restart loops. As a quick experiment, you can redeploy the voting application manifest where you replace the readiness probe with a liveness probe, with similar configuration but very short timeouts and delays—you will experience multiple random crashes and poor availability of the application!
- Do not use liveness probes unless you have a good reason for this. A good reason may, for example, be a known issue with a deadlock in your application that has an as yet unknown root cause.
- Execute simple and fast checks that determine the status of the process, not its dependencies. In other words, you do not want to check external dependencies' statuses in the liveness probe—this can lead to cascading failures due to an avalanche of container restarts and overloading a small subset of Service Pods.
- If your process running in the container is able to crash or exit whenever it encounters an unrecoverable error, you probably do not need a liveness probe at all.
- Use conservative settings for `initialDelaySeconds` to avoid any premature container restarts and falling into a restart loop.

Web applications hosted by IIS can be a good candidate for using a liveness probe if you do not know exactly what is going under the hood of the `ServiceMonitor.exe` and `LogMonitor.exe` entry point processes. In theory, they should crash the container whenever there is a problem with IIS or IIS App Pool, but let's assume we need to implement these checks ourselves. We will implement a liveness probe that will check whether IIS App Pool is running using the `exec` handler. To do that, follow these steps:

1. Modify the `voting-application.yaml` manifest file with `Deployment` for our application. Add the following liveness probe configuration for the `frontend` container:

```yaml
apiVersion: apps/v1
kind: Deployment
metadata:
  namespace: dev
  name: voting-application-frontend
  ...
spec:
  ...
  template:
    ...
    spec:
    ...
    containers:
    - name: frontend
    image: packtpubkubernetesonwindows/voting-application:1.1.0
    ...
    livenessProbe:
      exec:
        command:
        - powershell.exe
        - -Command
        - if ((Get-WebAppPoolState DefaultAppPool).Value -ne
"Started") { throw "Default IIS App Pool is NOT started" }
      initialDelaySeconds: 45
      periodSeconds: 10
      timeoutSeconds: 10
      successThreshold: 1
      failureThreshold: 3
    ...
```

The probe is configured so that it executes a PowerShell command, `if ((Get-WebAppPoolState DefaultAppPool).Value -ne "Started") { throw "Default IIS App Pool is NOT started" }`, which checks whether the default IIS App Pool is in a `Started` state. If it is not, an exception will be thrown and the PowerShell process will exit with non-zero exit code causing the probe to go into a failed state.

2. Now, apply the manifest file using the `kubectl apply -f .\voting-application-readiness-probe.yaml` command.

3. Again, inspect the rollout process using the `kubectl get pods -n dev` and `kubectl describe` commands. In the Pod events, you may verify whether the Pods had any liveness failures.

When using the `exec` handler, you should carefully analyze how the chosen command behaves. The `exec` handler has been reported to cause zombie process bloat in some cases.

Finally, let's take a quick look at the last type of probe, the startup probe.

Startup probes

Startup probes have been recently introduced in Kubernetes 1.16 to support cases when a container may require more time for initialization than `initialDelaySeconds + failureThreshold * periodSeconds` set in the readiness probe. In general, you should use the same handler configuration for startup probes that you would for readiness probes but use larger delays. If a container is not ready within `initialDelaySeconds + failureThreshold * periodSeconds` for a readiness probe, then the container will be killed and subject to the Pod's restart policy.

Our voting application does not need a dedicated startup probe, but an example definition in the Deployment manifest file could look like this:

```
apiVersion: apps/v1
kind: Deployment
metadata:
  namespace: dev
  name: voting-application-frontend
  ...
spec:
  ...
  template:
```

```
...
spec:
  ...
  containers:
  - name: frontend
    image: packtpubkubernetesonwindows/voting-application:1.1.0
    ...
    startupProbe:
      httpGet:
        path: /health
        port: 80
      initialDelaySeconds: 30
      periodSeconds: 60
      timeoutSeconds: 40
      successThreshold: 1
      failureThreshold: 5
  ...
```

In the next section, we will focus on assigning resource limits for Pods and how to configure autoscaling for our voting application.

Specifying resource limits and configuring autoscaling

As a container orchestrator, Kubernetes comes out of the box with two important features that help to manage your cluster resources:

- Resource requests and limits for Pod containers
- HPA, which allows automatic scaling of your Deployments or StatefulSets based on CPU resource usage (stable support), memory resource usage (beta support), or custom metrics (also beta support)

Let's first take a look at specifying resource requests and limits.

Resource requests and limits

When you create a Pod, it is possible to specify how much compute resources its containers require—we already performed a short exercise on assigning resources for the voting application in the last chapter. In general, compute resources are CPU and RAM memory—Kubernetes is also able to manage other resources, such as HugePages on Linux or ephemeral storage on the local node.

The Kubernetes resource model provides an additional distinction between two classes of resources: compressible and incompressible. In short, a compressible resource can be easily throttled, without severe consequences. A perfect example of such a resource is the CPU—if you need to throttle CPU usage for a given container, the container will operate normally, just slower. On the other end, we have incompressible resources that cannot be throttled without bad consequences—memory allocation is an example of such a resource.

 There are two great design proposal documents that describe the Kubernetes resource model (`https://github.com/kubernetes/community/blob/master/contributors/design-proposals/scheduling/resources.md`) and resource quality of service (`https://github.com/kubernetes/community/blob/master/contributors/design-proposals/node/resource-qos.md`). We highly recommend reading them to fully understand the vision of Kubernetes resource management and which features are already implemented.

You can specify two values for a Pod container regarding resource allocation:

- `requests`: This specifies the guaranteed amount of a given resource provided by the system. You can also think of this the other way round—this is the amount of a given resource that the Pod container requires from the system to function properly. Pod scheduling is dependent on the `requests` value (not `limits`).
- `limits`: This specifies the maximum amount of a given resource provided by the system. If specified together with `requests`, this value must be greater than or equal to `requests`. Depending on whether the resource is compressible or incompressible, exceeding the limit has different consequences—compressible resources (CPU) will be throttled whereas incompressible resources (memory) can result in container kill.

Using different values of `requests` and `limits` allows for resource overcommit, which is useful for efficiently handling short bursts of resource usage while allowing better resource utilization on average. If you do not specify limits at all, the container can consume as much of the resource on a node as it wants. This can be controlled by namespace resource quotas (introduced earlier in this chapter) and limit ranges—you can read more about these objects in the documentation at `https://kubernetes.io/docs/concepts/policy/limit-range/`.

We covered the details of resource management support on Windows nodes in Kubernetes in Chapter 4, *Kubernetes Concepts and Windows Support*. The important bit is that Windows currently lacks support for an out-of-memory killer (some support for memory limiting may be available with incoming Hyper-V containers features in Kubernetes). This means that exceeding the limits value set for memory for Windows containers will not result in any throttling or container restart. Here, the rule of thumb is to carefully manage scheduling using requests for memory and monitoring for any sudden memory paging.

Before we dive into the configuration details, we need to look at what are the units for measuring CPU resources and memory in Kubernetes. For CPU resources, the base unit is **Kubernetes CPU (KCU)** where 1 is equivalent to, for example, 1 vCPU on Azure, 1 Core on GCP, or 1 hyperthreaded core on a bare-metal machine. Fractional values are allowed: 0.1 can be also specified as 100m (milliCPUs). For memory, the base unit is a byte; you can, of course, specify standard unit prefixes such as M, Mi, G, or Gi.

To demonstrate how to use resource limits and requests, follow these steps:

1. Modify the voting-application.yaml Deployment manifest so that it does not specify any update strategy and has resource allocation set for CPU and memory:

```
apiVersion: apps/v1
kind: Deployment
metadata:
  namespace: dev
  name: voting-application-frontend
  ...
spec:
  replicas: 5
  ...
  # strategy:
  ...
  template:
    ...
    spec:
      ...
      containers:
      - name: frontend
        ...
        resources:
          limits:
            cpu: 1000m
          requests:
            cpu: 1000m
            memory: 256Mi
```

For memory, we follow the current recommendations for Windows nodes—we only specify how much memory we would like to request. For the CPU to simulate resource exhaustion, we specify a large requested value that will consume all of the cluster CPU for Windows nodes. The reason for this is that two nodes with Azure VM type Standard_D2_v3 have two vCPUs each and with five replicas running, we would need five vCPUs in total. The update `strategy` needs to be removed to avoid any deadlocks during the rollout.

2. Apply the manifest file using the `kubectl apply -f .\voting-application.yaml` command.

3. Now, carefully observe the creation of new Pods in your Deployment. You will notice there are Pods that show the `Pending` status:

```
PS C:\src> kubectl get pods -n dev
NAME                                              READY    STATUS
RESTARTS     AGE
voting-application-frontend-54bbbbd655-nzt2n      1/1      Running
0            118s
voting-application-frontend-54bbbbd655-phdhr      0/1      Pending
0            118s
voting-application-frontend-54bbbbd655-qggc2      1/1      Running
0            118s
. . .
```

4. This is expected, as the `voting-application-frontend-54bbbbd655-phdhr` Pod cannot be scheduled to any node because there are no available CPU resources. To check what is the actual reason, describe the Pod and check `Events`:

```
PS C:\src> kubectl describe pod -n dev voting-application-
frontend-54bbbbd655-phdhr
Events:
  Type       Reason         Age          From
Message
  ----       ------         ----         ----                 ------
-
  Warning    FailedScheduling  <unknown>   default-scheduler    0/5
nodes are available: 2 Insufficient cpu, 3 node(s) didn't match
node selector.
```

5. As expected, the Pod cannot be scheduled due to insufficient CPU resources on all nodes that match the node selector. Let's fix the issue by lowering the `requests` and `limits` CPU values for the Pod container—modify the `voting-application.yaml` manifest file so that `requests` is set to `250m` and `limits` is set to `500m` for the CPU.

6. Apply the manifest file using the `kubectl apply -f .\voting-application.yaml` command and observe the successful Deployment.

Now that you know how to allocate and manage resources for your containers, we can demonstrate how to use autoscaling for your application using the HPA.

HPA

The true power of Kubernetes comes with autoscaling implemented by the HPA, which is a dedicated controller backed by the `HorizontalPodAutoscaler` API object. At a high level, the goal of the HPA is to automatically scale the number of replicas in a Deployment or StatefulSet depending on the current CPU utilization or other custom metrics (including multiple metrics at once). The details of the algorithm that determines the target number of replicas based on metric values can be found at `https://kubernetes.io/docs/tasks/run-application/horizontal-Pod-autoscale/#algorithm-details`. HPAs are highly configurable and in this book, we will cover a standard scenario for when we would like to autoscale based on target CPU usage.

Our voting application exposes features that do not require much CPU, which means that it may be hard to trigger autoscaling on demand. To solve this, we will add a dedicated controller action that can simulate a constant CPU load with a given target percentage value. The source code for the `packtpubkubernetesonwindows/voting-application:1.2.0` Docker image for stress simulation can be found at `https://github.com/PacktPublishing/Hands-On-Kubernetes-on-Windows/tree/master/Chapter11/08_voting-application-hpa-src`. If you want to customize the application yourself, open your solution in Visual Studio 2019 and follow these steps:

1. Define the `StressCpuWorker` class (`https://github.com/PacktPublishing/Hands-On-Kubernetes-on-Windows/blob/master/Chapter11/08_voting-application-hpa-src/Services/CpuStressWorker.cs`), which contains the main worker code for simulating CPU stress:

```
private void StartCpuStress()
{
    this.logger.Info($"Environment.ProcessorCount:
{Environment.ProcessorCount}");

    for (int i = 0; i < Environment.ProcessorCount; i++)
    {
        var thread = new Thread(
            () =>
            {
                var watch = new Stopwatch();
```

```
                              watch.Start();

                              while (this.isEnabled)
                              {
                                  if (watch.ElapsedMilliseconds <=
            this.targetCpuLoad)
                                  {
                                      continue;
                                  }

                                  Thread.Sleep(100 - this.targetCpuLoad);

                                  watch.Reset();
                                  watch.Start();
                              }
                        });

                  thread.Start();
            }
        }
```

This code will start several threads, the number of which will be equal to the
currently available processor count in the environment, and each logical
processor will be then stressed for `this.targetCpuLoad` milliseconds by doing
almost empty `while` loops. For the rest of the 100-millisecond "segment", the
thread will be sleeping—this means that, on average, we should have all available
CPUs loaded to `this.targetCpuLoad` percent. Of course, it depends on how
many processors are allotted to the container—this number may vary depending
on your `requests` and `limits` values; you can always check the Pod logs to see
what number of logical processors were available for this Pod. Also, please note
that even if there are two logical processors available to the container, it doesn't
mean that the container will be able to fully utilize them; the load may be
throttled depending on the `limits` value.

2. In the `HomeController` class (`https://github.com/PacktPublishing/Hands-
    On-Kubernetes-on-Windows/blob/master/Chapter11/08_voting-application-
    hpa-src/Controllers/HomeController.cs`), add a new controller action that will
    be available via the `/Home/StressCpu?value={targetPercent}` route. Please
    note that we allow this action to be performed via a GET request (instead of PUT)
    to make the interaction easy when using a web browser. Additionally, inject
    `IStressCpuWorker` into the constructor—the final action implementation will
    be as follows:

    ```
    public ActionResult StressCpu([FromUri] int value)
    {
    ```

```
        this.Response.StatusCode = (int)HttpStatusCode.Accepted;
        var host = Dns.GetHostEntry(string.Empty).HostName;

        if (value < 0)
        {
            this.cpuStressWorker.Disable();
            return this.Json(new { host, status = $"Stressing CPU
    turned off" }, JsonRequestBehavior.AllowGet);
        }

        if (value > 100)
        {
            value = 100;
        }

        this.cpuStressWorker.Enable(value);
        return this.Json(new { host, status = $"Stressing CPU at
    {value}% level" }, JsonRequestBehavior.AllowGet);
    }
```

This implementation will enable CPU stressing if you provide a positive value and for a negative value, stressing will be disabled.

3. Configure dependency injection in the `NinjectWebCommon` class (https:// github.com/PacktPublishing/Hands-On-Kubernetes-on-Windows/blob/master/ Chapter11/08_voting-application-hpa-src/App_Start/NinjectWebCommon. cs). Ensure that the `StressCpuWorker` class is resolved as a singleton:

```
kernel.Bind<ICpuStressWorker>().To<CpuStressWorker>().InSingletonSc
ope();
```

4. Build the Docker image with the tag `1.2.0` and push it to your repository, exactly as we did before.

With the image ready, we can proceed with deploying a new version of the voting application and configure autoscaling. To do that, execute the following steps:

1. Modify the `voting-application.yaml` manifest file and ensure that you use the `1.2.0` tag of the image and that `resources` is specified as follows:

```
resources:
  limits:
    cpu: 500m
  requests:
    cpu: 400m
    memory: 256Mi
```

2. In a PowerShell window, apply the manifest file using the `kubectl apply -f .\voting-application.yaml` command.

3. Wait for the Deployment to finish and observe the CPU usage by Pods using this command:

```
PS C:\src> kubectl top pod -n dev
NAME                                              CPU(cores)
MEMORY(bytes)
mssql-deployment-58bcb8b89d-7f9xz                    339m        903Mi
voting-application-frontend-6b6c9557f8-5wwln         117m        150Mi
voting-application-frontend-6b6c9557f8-f787m         221m        148Mi
voting-application-frontend-6b6c9557f8-rjwmj         144m        164Mi
voting-application-frontend-6b6c9557f8-txwl2         120m        191Mi
voting-application-frontend-6b6c9557f8-vw5r9         160m        151Mi
```

When the IIS App Pool is fully initialized, the CPU usage for each Pod should stabilize around `150m`.

4. Create the `hpa.yaml` manifest file for the HPA:

```
apiVersion: autoscaling/v1
kind: HorizontalPodAutoscaler
metadata:
  namespace: dev
  name: voting-application-frontend
spec:
  minReplicas: 1
  maxReplicas: 8
  targetCPUUtilizationPercentage: 60
  scaleTargetRef:
    apiVersion: apps/v1
    kind: Deployment
    name: voting-application-frontend
```

This HPA will automatically scale the `voting-application-frontend` Deployment to between `1` and `8` replicas, trying to target `60` percent CPU usage. Please note that this target usage is high and in production environments, you should consider using lower, more appropriate values. This manifest file is roughly the same as for the HPA created imperatively using the `kubectl autoscale deployment/voting-application-frontend -n dev --cpu-percent=60 --min=1 --max=8` command.

5. Apply the manifest file using the `kubectl apply -f .\hpa.yaml` command.

6. HPAs are subject to delay for cooldown to avoid thrashing (that is, the replica count fluctuating frequently). The default delay is five minutes. This means that you should expect some delay until the HPA scales the Deployment after you apply it. Monitor the status of the HPA using the `kubectl describe` command:

```
PS C:\src> kubectl describe hpa -n dev voting-application-frontend
...
Metrics:                                                   ( current /
target )
  resource cpu on pods (as a percentage of request): 37% (150m) /
60%
Events:
  Type        Reason                          Age    From
Message
  ----        ------                          ----   ----
-------
...
  Normal      SuccessfulRescale               8m6s   horizontal-Pod-
autoscaler  New size: 4; reason: All metrics below target
  Normal      SuccessfulRescale               3m3s   horizontal-Pod-
autoscaler  New size: 3; reason: All metrics below targetcpu
```

Over time, you will notice that the HPA will tend to scale down to a single replica as there is not enough CPU load.

7. Let's increase the CPU load using our dedicated endpoint. In the web browser, go to the following URL: `http://<serviceExternalIp>/Home/StressCpu?value=90`. This will start stressing the CPU at a target level of 90%—bear in mind that, depending on how the logical processors are allocated for your Pods, the actual usage may be different.

8. You can perform multiple requests to ensure that more Pods in the Deployment start stressing the CPU.

9. After a while, observe what happens in the HPA events:

```
  Normal     SuccessfulRescale               7m44s
horizontal-Pod-autoscaler  New size: 4; reason: cpu resource
utilization (percentage of request) above target
  Normal     SuccessfulRescale               7m29s
horizontal-Pod-autoscaler  New size: 5; reason: cpu resource
utilization (percentage of request) above target
  Normal     SuccessfulRescale               2m25s
horizontal-Pod-autoscaler  New size: 8; reason: cpu resource
utilization (percentage of request) above target
```

The Deployment was automatically scaled up as the CPU resource utilization was above the 60% target! After more Pods are added, the average utilization will decrease because not all Pods are performing CPU stressing.

For AKS and an AKS Engine cluster, it is possible to leverage the cluster autoscaler to automatically adjust the number of nodes in your cluster depending on the resource demands. You can read more in the official Azure documentation (`https://docs.microsoft.com/en-us/azure/aks/cluster-autoscaler`) and in the guide for configuring the cluster autoscaler on Azure (`https://github.com/kubernetes/autoscaler/blob/master/cluster-autoscaler/cloudprovider/azure/README.md`).

Congratulations, you have successfully configured the HPA for the voting application. The next Kubernetes feature that we are going to demonstrate is using ConfigMaps and Secrets for injecting configuration data.

Managing application configuration using ConfigMaps and Secrets

To provide configuration for an application running on Kubernetes, there are a couple of possible approaches, documented in `https://kubernetes.io/docs/tasks/inject-data-application/`:

- Passing arguments to the container commands
- Defining system environment variables for the container
- Mounting ConfigMaps or Secrets as container volumes
- Optionally wrapping everything up using PodPresets

This section will focus on using ConfigMaps and Secrets, which are, in many aspects, similar but have very different purposes.

First, let's take a look at Secrets. In almost every application, you will have to manage sensitive information for accessing dependencies, such as passwords, OAuth tokens, or certificates. Putting such information in a Docker image as hardcoded values is out of the question due to obvious security concerns and very limited flexibility. Similarly, defining a password directly in the Pod manifest file is not recommended—manifest files are intended to be kept in source control and this definitely is not a place for storing such sensitive information. To manage this type of information, Kubernetes offers Secret objects, which can hold technically any type of data consisting of key-value pairs. Optionally, it is possible to encrypt Secrets at rest in `etcd`, which is recommended in production scenarios.

We will now demonstrate how to create a generic (opaque) Secret using `kubectl`. You can also use manifest files for this purpose but how you generate these manifest files depends on your CI/CD pipelines (you do not want to check in these manifest files to your source control!). To create a Secret for a SQL Server password, execute the following steps:

1. Open a PowerShell window.
2. Assuming that you would like to create a Secret named `mssql` in the `dev` namespace, which holds `S3cur3P@ssw0rd` under the `SA_PASSWORD` key, execute the following command:

   ```
   kubectl create secret generic -n dev mssql --from-
   literal=SA_PASSWORD="S3cur3P@ssw0rd"
   ```

3. Now, the Secret can be consumed as a volume mounted in the container (as a file or a directory) or used to define environment variables for a container. In the case of the voting application, it is easier to use the Secret with a SQL Server password as an environment variable. This is achieved in the following way in the Deployment manifest:

   ```
   apiVersion: apps/v1
   kind: Deployment
   metadata:
     namespace: dev
     name: voting-application-frontend
     ...
   spec:
     ...
     template:
       ...
       spec:
         ...
         containers:
         - name: frontend
           image: packtpubkubernetesonwindows/voting-application:1.2.0
           env:
   ```

```
     - name: MSSQL_SA_PASSWORD
       valueFrom:
         secretKeyRef:
           name: mssql
           key: SA_PASSWORD
     - name: CONNECTIONSTRING_VotingApplication
       value: "Data Source=mssql-deployment;Initial
  Catalog=VotingApplication;MultipleActiveResultSets=true;User
  Id=sa;Password=$(MSSQL_SA_PASSWORD);"
```

The key concept here is using `secretKeyRef` to reference a value for the `SA_PASSWORD` key from the `mssql` Secret that we have just created. The value is injected into the `MSSQL_SA_PASSWORD` environment variable (but you can check that it is not possible to see the value when using `kubectl describe`!), which can be accessed by the application running in the container. In our case, we use this variable to define another environment variable named `CONNECTIONSTRING_VotingApplication`. This is a common pattern when you need to create, for example, a connection string that has to include a password but please bear in mind that it may be a less secure solution than using volumes.

There is one significant difference between consuming Secrets as environment variables and as mounted volumes: the Secret data provided via a volume will be updated if the Secret changes. Depending on your needs and implementation details, you may want to choose to mount Secrets as volumes. This, of course, requires your application to be aware of possible changes to the Secrets file, which means it needs to actively monitor the filesystem and refresh any credential providers, connection strings, or certificates, which are often kept in memory. Approaching Secrets as immutable configuration values is the best option (both when mounted as a volume and as environment variables) and makes your application more predictable and less complex. But if your architecture has limitations that prefer as few Pod restarts as possible, then injecting Secrets as a volume and implementing automatic refresh in your application is be the suggested solution.

From a security perspective, injecting Secrets as environment variables is less secure on Linux as, when having root privileges, you can enumerate all environment variables for a process from `/proc/<pid>/environ`. On Windows nodes, the issue is even more complex: you can still access environment variables for processes but volumes cannot currently use the in-memory filesystem. This means that Secrets are then stored directly on the node's disk storage.

To store non-sensitive configuration data for your application, Kubernetes offers ConfigMap objects. This is another concept that you can use to fully decouple Docker images (your build artifacts) from the runtime configuration data. From an API perspective, the concept is similar to Secrets—you can store key-value pairs and inject them either as environment variables for the container or mount them using a volume as a file or a directory. To demonstrate this, we will create a ConfigMap for storing a configuration file, `customErrors.config`, referenced in the `Web.config` file for the ASP.NET MVC application and mount it using a volume.

 As mentioned in `Chapter 4`, *Kubernetes Concepts and Windows Support*, as of Kubernetes 1.17, there is no support for mounting a volume `subPath` as a file on Windows. This means that it is not possible to easily override the whole `Web.config` file for the ASP.NET MVC using ConfigMap.

Please follow these steps:

1. First, we need to perform a small change to the voting application source code (https://github.com/PacktPublishing/Hands-On-Kubernetes-on-Windows/ tree/master/Chapter11/10_voting-application-configmap-src). We will extract the `<customErrors>` node from the `<system.web>` node to a separate file in a subdirectory. In the `Web.config` file, change the `<system.web>` node to this:

   ```
   <system.web>
     <compilation debug="true" targetFramework="4.8" />
     <httpRuntime targetFramework="4.8" />
     <customErrors configSource="config\customErrors.config" />
   </system.web>
   ```

2. Create the `customErrors.config` file in the `config` directory with the following contents. We will override it using a ConfigMap in the next steps:

   ```
   <customErrors mode="On" />
   ```

3. Build a Docker image with the `1.3.0` tag and publish it to Docker Hub, as in the previous examples.

4. Create the `voting-application-customerrors-config.yaml` manifest file for a ConfigMap definition that has the following form and contains the file (https://github.com/PacktPublishing/Hands-On-Kubernetes-on-Windows/ blob/master/Chapter11/10_voting-application-configmap-src/config/ customErrors.config) as data:

   ```
   kind: ConfigMap
   apiVersion: v1
   ```

```
metadata:
  namespace: dev
  name: voting-application-customerrors-config
  labels:
    app: voting-application
data:
  customErrors.config: |
    <customErrors mode="On" />
```

It is possible to create ConfigMaps imperatively using `kubectl`, but we would like to demonstrate the structure of the ConfigMap manifest file. The important part is to keep proper indentation when using a YAML multiline string for bigger config files (|).

5. Apply the manifest file using the `kubectl apply -f .\voting-application-customerrors-config.yaml` command.

6. Modify the `voting-application.yaml` manifest file for Deployment to mount our ConfigMap as a directory in the container (remember to use the new Docker image tag):

```
apiVersion: apps/v1
kind: Deployment
metadata:
  namespace: dev
  name: voting-application-frontend
  ...
spec:
  ...
  template:
    ...
    spec:
      ...
      containers:
      - name: frontend
        image: packtpubkubernetesonwindows/voting-application:1.3.0
        ...
        volumeMounts:
        - name: customerrors-config-volume
          mountPath: C:\inetpub\wwwroot\config\
        ...
      volumes:
      - name: customerrors-config-volume
        configMap:
          name: voting-application-customerrors-config
```

The important part here is to reference the `voting-application-customerrors-config` ConfigMap as a volume (`customerrors-config-volume`) and mount it to `C:\inetpub\wwwroot\config\` in the container. If `subPath` mounts were currently supported on Windows, we could override just a single file instead of the whole directory.

7. Apply the manifest file using the `kubectl apply -f .\voting-application.yaml` command.

8. Now, navigate to the `http://<serviceExternalIp>/Home/StressCpu` address in your browser. This will trigger an exception—we did not provide the required request parameter in the URL. You should see a custom error page that just informs that `An error occurred while processing your request.`

9. Turn off the custom errors page and modify the `voting-application-customerrors-config.yaml` manifest file for ConfigMap so that it contains the node:

```
customErrors.config: |
    <customErrors mode="Off" />
```

10. Apply the manifest file using the `kubectl apply -f .\voting-application-customerrors-config.yaml` command.

> Depending on whether IIS is able to watch for changes in the `C:\inetpub\wwwroot\config\` directory, the IIS App Pool may not be reloaded in the Pod. In such a case, `exec` into the container and execute the `Restart-WebAppPool DefaultAppPool` command.

11. Navigate to `http://<serviceExternalIp>/Home/StressCpu` again. If your IIS App Pool has been reloaded, you will see full exception details instead of the custom error page.

In this way, we have demonstrated how to use Secrets and ConfigMaps in Windows Pods. Now, it is time to familiarize ourselves with managing persistent data storage on Windows nodes.

Managing persistent data storage on Windows nodes

In `Chapter 4`, *Kubernetes Concepts and Windows Support*, we have already covered some storage-related concepts in Kubernetes, such as **PersistentVolumes** (**PV**), **PersistentVolumeClaims** (**PVC**), and **StorageClasses** (**SC**), and how they are supported in Windows workloads. Managing state and storage in containerized applications and using StatefulSets is a broad and complex topic that is not in the scope of this book—the official documentation offers a good introduction, which can be found at `https://kubernetes.io/docs/concepts/storage/`. The key takeaway for PersistentVolume support for Windows Pods is that you can use some of the existing volume plugins but not all. On Windows, there is support for the following:

- In-tree volume plugins:
  azureDisk, azureFile, gcePersistentDisk, awsElasticBlockStore (since 1.16), and vsphereVolume (since 1.16)
- FlexVolume plugins: SMB and iSCSI
- CSI volume plugins (out-of-tree plugins)

This means that, for Windows nodes, in the case of AKS or AKS Engine clusters, you are limited to using the azureDisk and azureFile in-tree volume plugins and technically, you can combine the FlexVolume SMB plugin with Azure Files SMB Share. For on-premises scenarios, you have to rely on the FlexVolume SMB or iSCSI plugins configured to use your own storage or connect to SMB shares exposed as external cloud services. If you are running on vSphere, you can, of course, leverage the vsphereVolume plugin. In general, handling PersistentVolumes for hybrid Windows/Linux clusters running on-premises is still hard.

For on-premises clusters, using Rook (`https://rook.io/`) to orchestrate storage and integrate with Kubernetes is a good solution. Unfortunately, there is no support for Windows yet, even for consuming the volumes.

Our voting application is already using PersistentVolumes for SQL Server running in a Linux Pod—in this case, we have been using StorageClass with the `kubernetes.io/azure-disk` provisioner, which internally uses the azureDisk volume plugin. This scenario concerned Linux Pods—now, we will use PersistentVolumes for Windows Pods. The voting application does not have any particular need for persisting data in frontend containers but as a pure example, we will show how to store a voting log for each Pod.

The source code for this change is available at `https://github.com/PacktPublishing/ Hands-On-Kubernetes-on-Windows/tree/master/Chapter11/12_voting-application- persistentvolume-src`. We will not go into implementation details but the change is simple:

- Add a new `VoteLogManager` class (`https://github.com/PacktPublishing/ Hands-On-Kubernetes-on-Windows/blob/master/Chapter11/12_voting- application-persistentvolume-src/Services/VoteLogManager.cs`), which manages the `C:\data\voting.log` file—you can add new votes to the log and read the log contents. This log file will be persisted using Kubernetes PersistentVolume.
- For each vote that is added in the `SurveyController` class (`https://github. com/PacktPublishing/Hands-On-Kubernetes-on-Windows/blob/master/ Chapter11/12_voting-application-persistentvolume-src/Controllers/ SurveysController.cs`), inform `VoteLogManager`.
- In the `HomeController` class (`https://github.com/PacktPublishing/Hands- On-Kubernetes-on-Windows/blob/master/Chapter11/12_voting-application- persistentvolume-src/Controllers/HomeController.cs`), add a new controller action, `VotingLog`, which returns the contents of the voting log. Then, you can access the voting log for the currently serving replica using `http://<serviceExternalIp>/Home/VotingLog`.

To deploy the application, perform the following steps:

1. Build a Docker image with the tag `1.4.0` for the voting application and push it to Docker Hub as in previous examples.
2. We need to convert our Deployment into a StatefulSet. Therefore, you first need to delete the Deployment from the cluster:

   ```
   kubectl delete deployment -n dev voting-application-frontend
   ```

3. Create the `StorageClass` manifest, `sc.yaml`, with the following contents. We will use the `kubernetes.io/azure-disk` provisioner to use the azureDisk Volume plugin:

```
kind: StorageClass
apiVersion: storage.k8s.io/v1beta1
metadata:
  name: azure-disk
provisioner: kubernetes.io/azure-disk
parameters:
  storageaccounttype: Standard_LRS
  kind: Managed
```

4. Apply the manifest file using the `kubectl apply -f sc.yaml` command.
5. Convert the Deployment into a StatefulSet and use the `1.4.0` version of the Docker image. The full manifest file can be found at `https://github.com/PacktPublishing/Hands-On-Kubernetes-on-Windows/blob/master/Chapter11/13_persistentvolume/voting-application.yaml`. We highlight the changes that are needed compared to the previous `voting-application.yaml` manifest file as follows:

```
apiVersion: apps/v1
kind: StatefulSet
...
spec:
  replicas: 5
  serviceName: voting-application-frontend  # (1)
  ...
  template:
    ...
    spec:
      ...
      initContainers:  # (2)
      - name: volume-mount-permissions-fix
        image: packtpubkubernetesonwindows/voting-application:1.4.0
        command: ["powershell.exe", "-Command", "iisreset.exe
/START; icacls.exe c:\\data /grant '\"IIS
AppPool\\DefaultAppPool\":RW'"]
        volumeMounts:
        - mountPath: C:/data
          name: voting-log-volume
      containers:
      - name: frontend
        image: packtpubkubernetesonwindows/voting-application:1.4.0
        ...
        volumeMounts:  # (3)
        - mountPath: C:/data
          name: voting-log-volume
  volumeClaimTemplates:  # (4)
  - metadata:
      name: voting-log-volume
```

```
labels:
    app: voting-application
spec:
  accessModes:
    - ReadWriteOnce
  resources:
    requests:
        storage: 100Mi
  storageClassName: azure-disk
```

StatefulSet requires providing a Service name that is responsible for this StatefulSet (1). On top of that, we define `volumeClaimTemplates` (4), which will be used for creating a dedicated PersistentVolumeClaim for each Pod replica in this StatefulSet. We reference this PVC for mounting the volume as the `C:/data` directory in the container (3), where `voting.log` will be persisted. Additionally, we also need to give proper read/write permissions to the `C:/data` directory to the IIS App Pool user—otherwise, the web application will not be able to access our PersistentVolume. This is achieved using `icasls.exe` executed in an `init` container (2). Note that you need to first start IIS (`iisreset.exe /START`) to have the IIS App Pool user properly created before assigning the permission!

6. Apply the manifest file using the `kubectl apply -f .\voting-application.yaml` command.

7. When the StatefulSet is ready, navigate to the application in the web browser and vote a few times.

8. Open `http://<serviceExternalIp>/Home/VotingLog` in a web browser and, depending on which Pod replica you have reached, you will see different results:

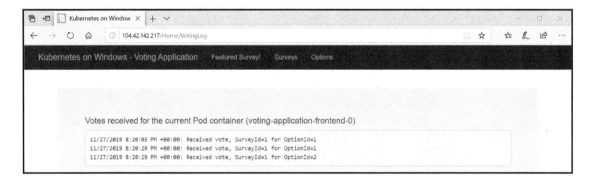

Good, so now we know that writing to the directory in a container works as expected. But let's prove that this directory is indeed backed by a PersistentVolume mount. To do that, perform the following steps:

1. Scale down `statefulset` to 0 replicas. This will remove all of the Pods for the StatefulSet:

   ```
   kubectl scale statefulset/voting-application-frontend -n dev --
   replicas=0
   ```

2. Wait until all Pods are terminated, and observe using the `kubectl get pods -n dev` command.

3. Scale up `statefulset`, for example, to 5 replicas:

   ```
   kubectl scale statefulset/voting-application-frontend -n dev --
   replicas=5
   ```

4. Wait for the Pods to create and become ready. It may take a few minutes due to our readiness probes.

5. Navigate to `http://<serviceExternalIp>/Home/VotingLog` in your web browser. You should see exactly the same voting log for each Pod replica as before. This shows that all Pods have the same PersistentVolumes mounted as previously.

Congratulations! You have successfully mounted azureDisk PersistentVolumes in a Windows Pod for the voting application. Next, we will take a look at how you can configure rolling updates for your application.

Configuring rolling updates for Deployments

In production scenarios, you will definitely need a deployment strategy that provides zero downtime updates for your application. As a container orchestrator, Kubernetes comes with different building blocks that can be used for implementing blue-green Deployments, canary Deployments, or rolling Deployments. A Kubernetes Deployment object has full support for performing a rolling update Deployment—in this type of Deployment, the new version of the application is rolled out by gradually swapping old replicas with new replicas, all of which are behind the same Service. This means that, during the rollout, the end user will reach either the old or new version of the application.

To ensure real zero downtime updates of your Deployments in Kubernetes, you need to configure proper probes, especially readiness. In this way, the user will be redirected to a replica only if this replica can properly respond to the request.

Let's see how you can implement rolling deployment for the voting application. In fact, we have already been using this approach in the previous examples and now we will explain the configuration in more detail. Follow these steps:

1. Delete the StatefulSet, which we created in the previous section, using the `kubectl delete statefulset -n dev voting-application-frontend` command.

2. Let's revert back to the `voting-application.yaml` Deployment manifest file that we used for the HPA demonstration. You can find the file in the GitHub repository at `https://github.com/PacktPublishing/Hands-On-Kubernetes-on-Windows/blob/master/Chapter11/14_rollingupdate/voting-application.yaml`.

3. The rolling update deployment is configured in the following way:

    ```
    apiVersion: apps/v1
    kind: Deployment
    metadata:
      namespace: dev
      name: voting-application-frontend
      ...
    spec:
      replicas: 5
      minReadySeconds: 5
      strategy:
        type: RollingUpdate
        rollingUpdate:
          maxUnavailable: 1
          maxSurge: 1
      ...
        spec:
          ...
          containers:
          - name: frontend
            image: packtpubkubernetesonwindows/voting-application:1.2.0
            ...
    ```

The key part for defining rolling update deployment for your Deployment object is strategy. To configure the rolling update, you need to use type with the RollingUpdate value (which is also the default value). The alternative is using recreate, which will simply kill all Pods before creating new Pods—generally, you do not want to use this strategy type in production unless it is combined with more complex patterns such as blue-green deployments. For the RollingUpdate type, you can define maxUnavailable, which says how many Pods can be in a non-ready state during the update. Similarly, maxSurge defines the maximum number of Pods that can be created over the desired number of Pods during the deployment. You can specify these values as a number or percentage—by default, they are both set to 25%. To better understand what these numbers mean in practice, let's analyze our example. With the desired number of replicas being 5, when you trigger the Deployment rollout, the following sequence of events may happen:

- A new Pod is created. Now, we have six Pods in total, so we have reached the limit set by maxSurge.
- maxUnavailable is set to 1, and we have five Pods ready, so one old Pod can be terminated. We have five Pods in total, with four ready.
- A new Pod is created. We again have six Pods in total but four ready. The rollout has to wait until more Pods become ready.
- One of the new Pods becomes ready. We have six Pods in total, five ready, which means that one old Pod can be terminated and then a new Pod is created.
- This process gradually continues until all five new Pods become ready.

4. Let's see how it works in practice. First, apply the manifest file using the kubectl apply -f .\voting-application.yaml command—this will create the initial version of the application.
5. Rollouts for existing Deployments can be done imperatively by live-editing the object or using the kubectl rollout command. In general, it is better to use the declarative approach: change the manifest file and apply it again. Change the container image tag to packtpubkubernetesonwindows/voting-application:1.4.0 in the manifest file and apply using the kubectl apply -f .\voting-application.yaml command.

6. Quickly after that, start observing `rollout status` using the following command:

```
PS C:\src> kubectl rollout status -n dev deployment/voting-
application-frontend
Waiting for deployment "voting-application-frontend" rollout to
finish: 2 out of 5 new replicas have been updated...
Waiting for deployment "voting-application-frontend" rollout to
finish: 3 out of 5 new replicas have been updated...
Waiting for deployment "voting-application-frontend" rollout to
finish: 4 out of 5 new replicas have been updated...
Waiting for deployment "voting-application-frontend" rollout to
finish: 1 old replicas are pending termination...
Waiting for deployment "voting-application-frontend" rollout to
finish: 4 of 5 updated replicas are available...
deployment "voting-application-frontend" successfully rolled out
```

7. During the rollout, you can use commands such as `kubectl rollout undo -n dev deployment/voting-application-frontend` or `kubectl rollout pause -n dev deployment/voting-application-frontend` to control the Deployment rollout. However, you can still achieve the same just by modifying the manifest file and applying it again—this even includes pausing.

8. You can try accessing the application during the rollout. We have properly configured the readiness probes so you will not experience any unexpected responses from the application!

 StatefulSets also have a customizable strategy for rollouts. Due to state persistence, the strategy is a bit different from Deployments. You can read more in the official documentation, at `https://kubernetes.io/docs/concepts/workloads/controllers/statefulset/#update-strategies`.

Now, let's focus on another important topic in Kubernetes: **Role-Based Access Control (RBAC)**.

Role-Based Access Control

Kubernetes comes with a built-in RBAC mechanism that allows you to configure fine-grained sets of permissions and assign them to users, groups, and service accounts (subjects). In this way, as a cluster administrator, you can control how cluster users (internal and external) interact with the API Server, which API resources they can access, and which actions (verbs) they can perform.

Authentication in Kubernetes is highly configurable and extensible; you can read more in the official documentation, at `https://kubernetes.io/ docs/reference/access-authn-authz/authentication/`. In AKS Engine clusters, it is possible to easily integrate with **Azure Active Directory (AAD)**; you can find more details at `https://github.com/Azure/aks-engine/blob/master/docs/topics/aad.md`.

Using RBAC involves two groups of API resources:

- `Role` and `ClusterRole`: They define a set of permissions. Each rule in `Role` says which verb(s) are allowed for which API resource(s). The only difference between `Role` and `ClusterRole` is that `Role` is namespace-scoped whereas `ClusterRole` is not.
- `RoleBinding` and `ClusterRoleBinding`: They associate users or a set of users with a given role. Similarly, `RoleBinding` is namespace-scoped, `ClusterRoleBinding` is cluster-wide. `ClusterRoleBinding` works with `ClusterRole`, and `RoleBinding` works with either `ClusterRole` or `Role`.

Kubernetes uses a permissive RBAC model—there are no deny rules; everything is denied by default, and you have to define allow rules. Using RBAC is well documented and all of the features have been presented in the official documentation, available at `https:// kubernetes.io/docs/reference/access-authn-authz/rbac/`. There are two key points you should consider for your RBAC strategy:

- Use the principle of least privilege. Your applications should have access to their own resources only (it is recommended that you run each application using a dedicated service account that has access to Secrets or ConfigMaps for the very application). Users should have restricted access depending on their role in the project (for example, a QA engineer may be fine with just read-only access to the cluster).
- Assign `RoleBinding` to groups instead of individual users. This will make your permission management much easier. Note that this requires integrating with external authentication providers to function best.

Let's demonstrate how to use `Role` and `RoleBinding` for the voting application to restrict access to the Deployment to a minimum set of ConfigMaps and Secrets that are needed. We will do that for the ASP.NET MVC application, and using a similar approach for SQL Server can be an additional exercise. For this, we will use the voting application Docker image, `packtpubkubernetesonwindows/voting-application:1.3.0`, which we used for demonstrating ConfigMaps. This Deployment requires both ConfigMaps and Secrets at runtime. Please follow these steps to configure RBAC:

1. Create the `serviceaccount.yaml` manifest file for the dedicated ServiceAccount, named `voting-application`:

   ```
   apiVersion: v1
   kind: ServiceAccount
   metadata:
     name: voting-application
     namespace: dev
   ```

2. Apply the manifest file using the `kubectl apply -f .\serviceaccount.yaml` command.

3. Create the `role.yaml` manifest file for `Role` for reading Secrets and ConfigMaps for the application:

   ```
   apiVersion: rbac.authorization.k8s.io/v1
   kind: Role
   metadata:
     namespace: dev
     name: voting-application-data-reader
   rules:
   - apiGroups: [""]
     resources: ["configmaps"]
     resourceNames: ["voting-application-customerrors-config"]
     verbs: ["get"]
   - apiGroups: [""]
     resources: ["secret"]
     resourceNames: ["mssql"]
     verbs: ["get"]
   ```

4. Use the `kubectl auth reconcile -f .\role.yaml` command to apply `Role`. Using `kubectl auth reconcile` is recommended over `kubectl apply`.

5. Create the `rolebinding.yaml` manifest file for `RoleBinding`, which associates our ServiceAccount with the preceding role:

```
apiVersion: rbac.authorization.k8s.io/v1
kind: RoleBinding
metadata:
  namespace: dev
  name: voting-application-data-reader
subjects:
- kind: ServiceAccount
  name: voting-application
roleRef:
  kind: Role
  name: voting-application-data-reader
  apiGroup: rbac.authorization.k8s.io
```

6. Use the `kubectl auth reconcile -f .\rolebinding.yaml` command to apply `RoleBinding`.

7. Check whether RBAC allows access to the ConfigMap for the ServiceAccount. You can use the `kubectl auth can-i get configmap/voting-application-customerrors-config -n dev --as system:serviceaccount:dev:voting-application` command or visualize all accessible API resources using the `kubectl auth can-i --list -n dev --as system:serviceaccount:dev:voting-application` command.

8. Modify the `voting-application.yaml` manifest file so that the Deployment uses the `voting-application` ServiceAccount:

```
apiVersion: apps/v1
kind: Deployment
metadata:
  namespace: dev
  name: voting-application-frontend
  ...
spec:
  ...
  template:
    ...
    spec:
      serviceAccountName: voting-application
      ...
```

9. Apply the Deployment manifest file using the `kubectl apply -f .\voting-application.yaml` command.

You can perform a similar operation for users in your cluster, for example, by defining Roles that allow read-only access to all API resources.

Congratulations! You have successfully set up RBAC for the voting application.

Summary

In this chapter, we demonstrated several commonly used, advanced features of Kubernetes. First, you learned what the purpose of namespaces in Kubernetes is and how to manage them. Then, we introduced readiness, liveness, and startup probes, which are used for monitoring the life cycle of Pod containers—and we provided you with a set of recommended practices when working with probes and how to avoid common pitfalls. The next step was learning how to specify Pod resource requests and limits and how to combine this with autoscaling using the HPA. To inject configuration data (including sensitive passwords) into our application, we used ConfigMaps and Secrets. On top of that, we have demonstrated how to use PersistentVolumes (backed by the azureDisk Volume plugin) in StatefulSets running on Windows nodes. And lastly, you learned how to approach rolling updates for Deployment objects and what the purpose of RBAC in Kubernetes is.

The next chapter will focus on development workflows with Kubernetes and how you can cooperate with other developers when creating Kubernetes applications.

Questions

1. When should you consider using Kubernetes namespaces?
2. What is the difference between readiness and liveness probes?
3. What are the risks of using a liveness probe with inappropriate configuration?
4. What is the difference between resource `requests` and `limits` values for Pod containers?
5. What is the purpose of delay for cooldown in the HPA?
6. What is the difference between ConfigMaps and Secrets?
7. What is `volumeClaimTemplates` in StatefulSet spec?
8. Why should you ensure the proper configuration of readiness probes when using rolling updates for Deployments?
9. What are the most important rules of thumb when using RBAC in Kubernetes?

You can find answers to these questions in the *Assessment* of this book.

Further reading

- For more information about Kubernetes features and how to manage applications, please refer to the following Packt books:
    - *The Complete Kubernetes Guide* by Jonathan Baier, Gigi Sayfan, Et al (`https://www.packtpub.com/virtualization-and-cloud/complete-kubernetes-guide`).
    - *Getting Started with Kubernetes - Third Edition* by Jonathan Baier, Jesse White (`https://www.packtpub.com/virtualization-and-cloud/getting-started-kubernetes-third-edition`).
    - *Kubernetes for Developers* by Joseph Heck (`https://www.packtpub.com/virtualization-and-cloud/kubernetes-developers`).

12
Development Workflow with Kubernetes

Let's face it—Kubernetes application development is not simple. In the previous chapters, we have been mainly focusing on the cluster provisioning and operations side of Kubernetes, which has its own complexities. As a software developer working with Kubernetes on Windows, you will have quite different challenges. In fact, you may need to switch your design approach to cloud-first, cloud-native, Kubernetes-first, or another modern approach. You have seen that Kubernetes is good at handling Windows applications that were never meant to be hosted in a container at design time, but to fully use the power of Kubernetes, you have to reverse this dependency and start thinking about Kubernetes as the center of the design and your development environment.

In this chapter, we will demonstrate a few popular tools that you can use in your development workflow on Windows, starting with basic integrations for Visual Studio 2019 and Visual Studio Code, and ending with advanced snapshot debugging using Azure Application Insights. You will also learn how to use Helm (version 3) for creating redistributable packages for your Kubernetes application. And as a cherry on top, we will introduce Azure Dev Spaces, which greatly simplifies Kubernetes development for the whole team.

This chapter will focus on the following topics:

- Using developer tooling with Kubernetes
- Packaging applications using Helm
- Debugging containerized applications using Azure Application Insights
- Using the Kubernetes dashboard
- Working on microservices in a team using Azure Dev Spaces

Technical requirements

For this chapter you will need the following:

- Windows 10 Pro, Enterprise, or Education (version 1903 or later; 64-bit) installed.
- Microsoft Visual Studio 2019 Community (or any other edition) if you want to edit the source code for the application and debug it. Please note that, for the Snapshot Debugger feature, you need the Enterprise edition.
- Microsoft Visual Studio Code, if you want to manage Kubernetes clusters using a graphical interface.
- The Chocolatey package manager for Windows (`https://chocolatey.org/`).
- An Azure account.
- A Windows/Linux Kubernetes cluster deployed using the **Azure Kubernetes Service** (**AKS**) engine, ready to deploy the Voting application from the previous chapters.

Using the Chocolatey package manager is not mandatory, but it makes the installation process and application version management much easier. The installation process is documented at `https://chocolatey.org/install`.

To follow along, you will need your own Azure account in order to create Azure resources for the Kubernetes cluster. If you haven't already created the account for the previous chapters, you can read more about how to obtain a limited free account for personal use at `https://azure.microsoft.com/en-us/free/`.

Deploying a Kubernetes cluster using the AKS engine has been covered in `Chapter 8`, *Deploying a Hybrid Azure Kubernetes Service Engine Cluster*. The deployment of the Voting application to Kubernetes has been covered in `Chapter 10`, *Deploying Microsoft SQL Server 2019 and ASP.NET MVC Application*.

You can download the latest code samples for this book chapter from the official *GitHub* repository at `https://github.com/PacktPublishing/Hands-On-Kubernetes-on-Windows/tree/master/Chapter12`.

Using developer tooling with Kubernetes

In your everyday development of .NET applications on Windows, you will most likely use Visual Studio 2019 or Visual Studio Code. In this section, we will show you how to install additional extensions for Kubernetes that allow you to bootstrap applications for container orchestrators.

Support for managing Windows containers in Kubernetes is currently very limited in Visual Studio 2019 and Visual Studio Code. You will not be able to use most of the features, such as integration with Azure Dev Spaces, although this is likely to change in the future. In the case of .NET Core, you can develop on Windows and rely on Linux Docker images.

First, let's take a look at how you can enable Kubernetes support for Visual Studio 2019.

Visual Studio 2019

The latest version of Visual Studio comes with a predefined Azure development workload that you can easily install from the Visual Studio Installer application directly. You do not need to install any additional extensions in order to have Kubernetes support in Visual Studio.

 If you have used Visual Studio Tools for Kubernetes (now deprecated) in the previous editions of Visual Studio, then you can expect a similar functionality in the Azure development workload in the latest version of Visual Studio.

To install an Azure development workload, please go through the following steps:

1. In the start menu for Windows, search for the **Visual Studio Installer** application.
2. Select your version of Visual Studio, click **More**, and select **Modify**.
3. Select **Azure development** and accept the changes by clicking **Modify**:

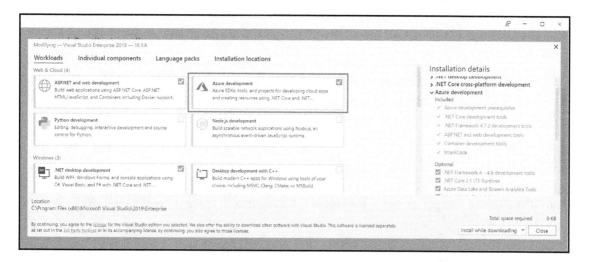

4. Wait for the installation to finish and launch Visual Studio.

Now, you can create new projects for the type container application for Kubernetes, which uses the following:

- *ASP.NET* Core
- Helm charts for packaging
- Azure Dev Spaces for fast iterative development on AKS

It is also possible to add Kubernetes/Helm support for an existing ASP.NET Core:

1. Right-click on the project in **Solution Explorer**.
2. Navigate to **Add** | **Container Orchestrator Support**
3. Choose **Kubernetes/Helm**.

Unfortunately, Visual Studio 2019 currently has limited features for managing Kubernetes clusters. Alternatively, you can use Visual Studio Code for this task.

Visual Studio Code

For Visual Studio Code you can use two *official* extensions from Microsoft:

- **Kubernetes (**`ms-kubernetes-tools.vscode-kubernetes-tools`**)**: Enables you to explore Kubernetes clusters in the tree view, manage Kubernetes objects, and provide IntelliSense for editing manifest files and Helm charts.
- **Azure Dev Spaces (**`azuredevspaces.azds`**)**: Enables Azure Dev Spaces integration, similar to what you have in Visual Studio 2019.

To install these two extensions, open Visual Studio Code and go through the following steps:

1. Open the **Extensions** panel (*Ctrl* + *Shift* + *X*).
2. Search for **Kubernetes** in **Marketplace**.
3. Click **Install**.
4. Repeat the same for Azure Dev Spaces.

In the right menu, you can now use the Kubernetes panel, which automatically loads your kubeconfig. This extension is especially great for working with workspaces containing manifest files, as you get autocompletion, YAML syntax highlighting, and validation.

You can manage your cluster from the tree view or by using commands (*Ctrl + Shift + P*)—this can be used instead of executing `kubectl` commands in PowerShell. For example, you can follow logs for your container:

Visual Studio Code is currently the most useful and advanced tool you can use in Windows for working with Kubernetes and Helm. In the next section, we will show how you can use Helm for packaging applications.

Packaging applications using Helm

Applications need packaging for easy redistribution and dependency management. In Windows, you can use Chocolatey, in Ubuntu you can use **APT** (short for Advanced Package Tool), and for Kubernetes you can use Helm as a package manager (`https://v3.helm.sh/`). There are a couple of alternatives, such as Kustomize (which comes with native support in `kubectl`) and Kapitan, but, in general, Helm is currently regarded as the industry standard, with the largest official repository of Helm charts (`https://github.com/helm/charts`).

The main use cases for Helm are as follows:

- Deploying popular software to your Kubernetes cluster. Packages are distributed as Helm charts.
- Sharing your own applications as Helm charts. This can include packaging a product for consumption by the end users or using Helm as an internal package and dependency manager for microservices in your system.
- Ensuring that the applications receive proper upgrades, including dependency management.
- Configuring software deployments for your needs. Helm charts are basically generic **Yet Another Markup Language** (**YAML**) parametrized templates for Kubernetes manifests. Helm uses Go templates (`https://godoc.org/text/template`) for parametrization. If you are familiar with Go then you will be at home; if not, then you will find it pretty similar to other templating systems, such as Mustache.

 Please note that the architecture of Helm has drastically changed with the recent release of version 3.0.0.

Previously, Helm required a dedicated service deployed on Kubernetes called Tiller, which was responsible for actual communication with Kubernetes API. This has caused various problems, including security and RBAC (short for Role-Based Access Control) issues. As of Helm 3.0.0, Tiller is no longer needed and chart management is done by the client. You can read more about the differences between older Helm versions in the official FAQ at `https://helm.sh/docs/faq/#changes-since-helm-2`.

Helm is distributed as a client (library) with a CLI similar to kubectl. All operations in Helm can be performed using the client now. Let's install Helm on your Windows machine.

Installing Helm

It is recommended that you install Helm on a Windows machine using Chocolatey. To install Helm, go through the following steps:

1. Open the PowerShell window as an administrator.
2. Execute the following installation command:

```
choco install kubernetes-helm
```

3. When the installation is finished, verify that you are running version `3.0.0` or higher:

```
PS C:\src> helm version
version.BuildInfo{Version:"v3.0.0",
GitCommit:"e29ce2a54e96cd02ccfce88bee4f58bb6e2a28b6",
GitTreeState:"clean", GoVersion:"go1.13.4"}
```

4. Check whether you have any repositories that have been added using the `helm repo list` command. If you don't (as in version 3.0.0), add the official `stable` repository and update:

```
helm repo add stable
https://kubernetes-charts.storage.googleapis.com
helm repo update
```

5. Now, try searching for some Helm charts—for example, let's check whether there is a chart for Microsoft SQL Server:

```
PS C:\src> helm search hub mssql
URL                                       CHART VERSION    APP
VERSION        DESCRIPTION
https://hub.helm.sh/charts/stable/mssql-linux    0.10.1
14.0.3023.8       SQL Server 2017 Linux Helm Chart
```

Helm Hub (`https://hub.helm.sh/`) offers a user-friendly interface for browsing the official Helm repository (`https://github.com/helm/charts`).

We have found a stable chart for SQL Server running in Linux containers. It is based on version 2017, but we can still use it for our Voting application.

Deploying Microsoft SQL Server using Helm

Let's now walk through how to deploy Microsoft SQL Server to our AKS Engine cluster. The structure of each chart is similar:

- In the `root` directory, you can find a detailed readme with a description of how to install the chart and what the possible parameters are (`https://github.com/helm/charts/tree/master/stable/mssql-linux`).
- The `Chart.yaml` file contains chart metadata, including dependency information.

- The `templates` directory contains all Go templates for Kubernetes manifests.
- The `values.yaml` file defines the default values for the chart that can be overridden using CLI parameters or by providing a YAML file.

The process of installing a Helm chart is straightforward: define the right values for your needs (and possibly analyze the templates to understand what is happening) and run the `helm install` command. Looking at the chart for SQL Server, we need to specify the following `values.yaml` file:

```yaml
acceptEula:
  value: "y"

edition:
  value: Developer

sapassword: "S3cur3P@ssw0rd"

service:
  type: LoadBalancer

persistence:
  enabled: true
  storageClass: azure-disk

nodeSelector:
  "kubernetes.io/os": linux
```

To deploy SQL Server using Helm, go through the following steps:

1. Open the PowerShell window.
2. Save the preceding file as `values.yaml` in your current directory.
3. Create prerequisites. We need the `dev-helm` namespace and the `azure-disk` StorageClass. Create the following `prereq.yaml` manifest file:

```yaml
---
kind: Namespace
apiVersion: v1
metadata:
  name: dev-helm
  labels:
    name: dev-helm
---
kind: StorageClass
apiVersion: storage.k8s.io/v1beta1
metadata:
  name: azure-disk
```

```
provisioner: kubernetes.io/azure-disk
parameters:
  storageaccounttype: Standard_LRS
  kind: Managed
```

4. Apply the manifest file using the `kubectl apply -f .\prereq.yaml` command.

5. Execute a dry run of the Helm chart installation. You will be able to see which Kubernetes manifest files would be applied:

```
helm install demo-mssql stable/mssql-linux `
    --namespace dev-helm `
    --values .\values.yaml `
    --debug `
    --dry-run
```

This command will perform a dry run of the installation of `stable/mssql-linux` as a `demo-mssql` Helm release in the `dev-helm` namespace.

6. If you are happy with the result, perform the installation:

```
helm install demo-mssql stable/mssql-linux `
    --namespace dev-helm `
    --values .\values.yaml
```

7. Observe the deployment of SQL Server using the following command:

```
kubectl get all --all-namespaces -l release=demo-mssql
```

8. You can also check the status using the Helm CLI:

```
helm status -n dev-helm demo-mssql
```

9. Use a SQL Server Management Studio or SQL Tools container to verify that SQL Server is running properly. You can use an external IP address for the service—we have exposed a LoadBalancer service.

 Commands for managing Helm releases are namespace-scoped in a similar manner to kubectl.

As you can see, using Helm is very efficient for quickly bootstrapping complex applications in your cluster. Now, let's prepare a Helm chart for our Voting application. We will use an SQL Server chart as a dependency.

Creating a Helm chart for our Voting application

In order to package our Voting application as a Helm chart, we will use the manifest files from the previous chapter that we used for the Horizontal Pod Autoscaler demonstration. You can find the base manifest files in the GitHub repository for the book at `https://github.com/PacktPublishing/Hands-On-Kubernetes-on-Windows/tree/master/Chapter12/02_voting-application-base`.

To prepare the Helm chart, we need to go through the following steps:

1. Gather all the required Kubernetes manifest files and determine which parts should be parameterized. We will use these for creating Helm template files and the `default values` file.
2. Define all of the dependencies for our application and define the proper parameter values for them. We will inject these parameters into the `default values` file for our parent chart.
3. Transform the Entity Framework database migrations into post-installation and post-upgrade Helm hooks.

The majority of the work here is transforming the raw Kubernetes manifest files into Helm templates. We will show only the relevant parts of this process in the next few steps. For the best coding experience, use Visual Studio Code for editing the Helm charts. You can find the final Helm chart for our Voting application in the Github repository at `https://github.com/PacktPublishing/Hands-On-Kubernetes-on-Windows/tree/master/Chapter12/03_voting-application-helm`.

Please go through the following steps to create your Helm chart:

1. First, let's uninstall the SQL Server Helm release from the cluster. We will install this chart automatically as a dependency in the Voting application parent chart:

   ```
   helm uninstall -n dev-helm demo-mssql
   ```

2. Run the following command to create a Helm chart scaffolding:

   ```
   helm create voting-application
   ```

   This will create a directory named `voting-application` that contains the basic structure and templates for your Helm chart. We will reuse most of them.

3. Navigate to the chart directory using `cd .\voting-application\` and modify the chart metadata in the `Chart.yaml` file:

```
apiVersion: v2
name: voting-application
description: Voting Application (Windows Containers) Helm chart
type: application
version: 0.1.0
appVersion: 1.4.0
dependencies:
  - name: mssql-linux
    version: 0.10.1
    repository: https://kubernetes-charts.storage.googleapis.com
sources:
  -
  https://github.com/hands-on-kubernetes-on-windows/voting-applicatio
  n
```

The most important bits of the code here deal with defining the proper dependencies and setting the proper `apiVersion`, which will be used as a Docker image tag in the templates. Add `mssql-linux` with the latest chart version (`0.10.1`) from the official stable repository at `https://kubernetes-charts.storage.googleapis.com`.

4. Navigate to the `templates` directory using the `cd .\templates\` command. We will use reuse `_helpers.tpl` (which contains template helper functions), `service.yaml`, `serviceaccount.yaml`, and `ingress.yaml` in the original form. These manifest templates will produce exactly what we need without any changes.

5. The next step is to define a manifest template for our Deployment named `deployment.yaml`; you should inspect the original `deployment.yaml` file in the chart scaffolding, as you can use the majority of it in our template. The final version of this template can be found at `https://github.com/PacktPublishing/Hands-On-Kubernetes-on-Windows/blob/master/Chapter12/03_voting-application-helm/templates/deployment.yaml`. As an example, let's explain how you can parametrize the Docker image tag and inject the SQL Server password:

```
apiVersion: apps/v1
kind: Deployment
metadata:
  name: {{ include "voting-application.fullname" . }}
  labels:
    {{- include "voting-application.labels" . | nindent 4 }}
```

```
spec:
  ...
  template:
    ...
    spec:
      ...
      containers:
        - name: {{ .Chart.Name }}-frontend
          ...
          image: "{{ .Values.image.repository }}:{{
.Chart.AppVersion }}"
          imagePullPolicy: {{ .Values.image.pullPolicy }}
          env:
          - name: MSSQL_SA_PASSWORD
            valueFrom:
              secretKeyRef:
                name: {{ .Release.Name }}-mssql-linux-secret
                key: sapassword
          - name: CONNECTIONSTRING_VotingApplication
            value: "Data Source={{ .Release.Name }}-mssql-
linux;Initial
Catalog=VotingApplication;MultipleActiveResultSets=true;User
Id=sa;Password=$(MSSQL_SA_PASSWORD);"
```

Let's analyze it step by step. The `{{ include "voting-application.fullname" . }}` phrase shows you how to include a template defined in `_helpers.tpl` and use it as the Deployment name. If there is some more advanced templating logic, you should always use this file for defining reusable templates.

The Docker image for the pod container is defined as `"{{ .Values.image.repository }}:{{ .Chart.AppVersion }}"`; you use `.Values` for referencing variables defined in the `values.yaml` file and `.Chart` for referencing chart metadata. And finally, we have used `{{ .Release.Name }}-mssql-linux-secret` in order to reference the secret created by the dependent SQL Server chart.

You need to know the internals of the dependent chart to know what value should be used (https://github.com/helm/charts/blob/master/stable/mssql-linux/templates/secret.yaml).

Unfortunately, Helm does not have an easy referencing process for such values from dependent charts, so you have to either hardcode the name by following the conventions used by Helm (which we did) or define a dedicated template in `_helpers.tpl` (which is a more clean approach, but also more complex).

6. To define RBAC roles and RoleBindings, we create two additional template files, `rolebinding.yaml` and `role.yaml`. You can find the contents in `https://github.com/PacktPublishing/Hands-On-Kubernetes-on-Windows/tree/master/Chapter12/03_voting-application-helm/templates`. Defining RBAC manifests for the application can be made conditional; you can see this practice in the official Helm charts.

7. The last manifest that we need to define is a Helm hook (`https://helm.sh/docs/topics/charts_hooks/`) for running Entity Framework database migrations (`https://github.com/PacktPublishing/Hands-On-Kubernetes-on-Windows/blob/master/Chapter12/03_voting-application-helm/templates/post-install-job.yaml`). A hook is just like any other manifest template, but it has additional annotations that ensure that the manifest is applied at a certain point in the lifecycle of a chart release. Additionally, if the hook is a Kubernetes job, Helm can wait to finish the job and provide cleanup. We want this hook to be a job, the same kind that we have already used for EF migrations, and we want it to be executed after the release is installed or upgraded. Let's see how we can define the annotations for our job in the `post-install-job.yaml` file:

```
apiVersion: batch/v1
kind: Job
metadata:
  name: {{ .Release.Name }}-ef6-database-migrate
  ...
  annotations:
    "helm.sh/hook": post-install,post-upgrade
    "helm.sh/hook-weight": "-5"
    "helm.sh/hook-delete-policy": hook-succeeded
spec:
  backoffLimit: 10
```

The key annotation that turns a manifest template into a hook is `"helm.sh/hook"`. We use `post-install` and `post-upgrade` values to ensure that the hook is executed after installation and after the upgrade of the Helm release. The `"helm.sh/hook-weight"` phrase is used for determining the order of hooks, which in our case doesn't matter, as we have only one hook.

The `"helm.sh/hook-delete-policy"` phrase defines the cases in which the job instances should be automatically deleted. We would like to delete them only on a successful hook execution; otherwise, we want to leave the resources so that we can debug the problem.

Please note that we specify the job `backoffLimit` as `10`; we need this in case of a long SQL Server pod creation, which, in this case, can take even a few minutes; if we don't do this, the hook will fail too quickly.

8. The last step is providing default template values in the `values.yaml` file in the root directory of the chart (`https://github.com/PacktPublishing/Hands-On-Kubernetes-on-Windows/blob/master/Chapter12/03_voting-application-helm/values.yaml`). Let's take a look at some important bits in the file:

```
...
image:
  repository: packtpubkubernetesonwindows/voting-application
  pullPolicy: IfNotPresent
...
nodeSelector:
  "kubernetes.io/os": windows
...
mssql-linux:
  acceptEula:
    value: "y"
  edition:
    value: Developer
  sapassword: "S3cur3P@ssw0rd"
  service:
    type: LoadBalancer
  persistence:
    enabled: true
    storageClass: azure-disk
  nodeSelector:
    "kubernetes.io/os": linux
```

You can organize the values; however, they are already conveniently arranged. For example, everything regarding the Docker image is grouped into the image node, and then you can reference the image repository name in the chart as `{{ .Values.image.repository }}`. A very important thing to remember is to provide a proper `nodeSelector`, which ensures that the pods are scheduled for Windows nodes only. Lastly, you define the values for a dependent chart using its name.

Here, we have used `mssql-linux` because this is the chart that we reference in the `Chart.yaml` file. You can read more about managing dependencies and defining the values in the documentation at https://helm.sh/docs/topics/charts/#chart-dependencies.

 Many aspects of Helm are based on conventions. You can find more about the best practices for implementing charts in the documentation at https://helm.sh/docs/topics/chart_best_practices/. Use the `helm lint` command to check whether there are any issues with your chart.

The chart for our Voting application is ready. Now, we will install this chart to our Kubernetes cluster in the `dev-helm` namespace:

1. Open the PowerShell window in the `root` directory of the chart.

2. Ensure that all the dependent charts are fetched from the repository:

    ```
    helm dependency update
    ```

3. Perform a `dry run` of the Helm chart installation to check the manifest files:

    ```
    helm install voting-application . `
        --namespace dev-helm `
        --debug `
        --dry-run
    ```

    This command will print all the resolved manifest files that will be applied to the installation of the chart in the current directory, `.`, with the default values.

4. Now, install the chart. We need to provide an extended timeout for the installation as our Entity Framework database migration job may need a few minutes to succeed. This depends on how quickly SQL Server is initialized and ready to connect. Use the following command:

    ```
    helm install voting-application . `
        --namespace dev-helm `
        --debug `
        --timeout 900s
    ```

5. The installation will take a bit of time; you can observe the progress of the Deployment for individual Kubernetes objects in a separate PowerShell window:

```
kubectl get all -n dev-helm
```

6. When the installation ends, use `kubectl get -n dev-helm svc -w voting-application` to get the external IP address of the LoadBalancer service for our Voting application. Navigate to the address in a web browser and enjoy!

In a production environment, you should use a Helm chart repository to manage your charts. You can learn more about setting up a repository at `https://v3.helm.sh/docs/topics/chart_repository/`. Additionally, to manage releases for Helm charts *declaratively*, similar to `kubectl apply`, you may consider using `Helmfile` (`https://github.com/roboll/helmfile`).

In the next section, you will learn how to easily add Azure Application Insights to your ASP.NET MVC application running in a Windows container. We will also show you how to perform an upgrade of the Helm release that we have just installed.

Debugging a containerized application using Azure Application Insights

Azure Application Insights is a part of Azure Monitor, which provides **application performance management** (**APM**) capabilities for your applications. It is a large platform, with a rich **UI** (short for **user interface**) in the Azure portal, which provides the following features (among others):

- Request monitoring and tracing, including distributed tracing between multiple microservices
- Exception monitoring and snapshot debugging
- Collecting performance counters for the host machines
- Smart anomaly detection and alerting
- Easy log collection and analytics

The most interesting feature for us is snapshot debugging, which can help diagnose issues in production Deployments where running with an attached remote debugger is not advised. For this, you will need Visual Studio 2019 Enterprise edition if you would like to analyze the snapshots using Visual Studio. Alternatively, you can perform analysis in the Azure portal itself, which has a lightweight web-based debugger available.

Alternatively, you can use zero-instrumentation application monitoring for Kubernetes applications running on Azure using out-of-band instrumentation provided by the Istio service mesh, as explained at `https://docs.microsoft.com/en-us/azure/azure-monitor/app/kubernetes`.

To enable Azure Application Insights together with snapshot debugging, we need to go through the following steps:

1. Enable Azure Application Insights in the Visual Studio project.
2. Install the `Microsoft.ApplicationInsights.SnapshotCollector` NuGet package.
3. Configure snapshot debugging and modify the Serilog configuration to use the sink for sending logs to `System.Diagnostics.Trace`.
4. Add a demonstration exception.
5. Build a new Docker image and push it to Docker Hub.
6. Upgrade the Helm release.

After this, we will be able to analyze trace maps, application logs, and exceptions directly in the Azure portal. Please note that this log collection solution is different from what we demonstrated in `Chapter 8`, *Deploying a Hybrid Azure Kubernetes Service Engine Cluster*, where we used Azure Log Analytics for AKS Engine. They use the same Azure services, but, in the new solution, we will get application logs only—you will not see Kubernetes or container runtime logs in Azure Log Analytics views.

Enabling Azure Application Insights

Please go through the following steps to enable Azure Application Insights in our Voting application. Alternatively, you can use the ready source code available in the Github repository at `https://github.com/PacktPublishing/Hands-On-Kubernetes-on-Windows/ tree/master/Chapter12/04_voting-application-azure-application-insights-src`. If you choose to do so, you need to provide your own Azure Application Insights key in the later steps during the Helm release upgrade:

1. Open the `VotingApplication` solution in Visual Studio 2019.
2. In **Solution Explorer**, right-click on the `VotingApplication` project, choose **Add** and select **Application Insights Telemetry...**:

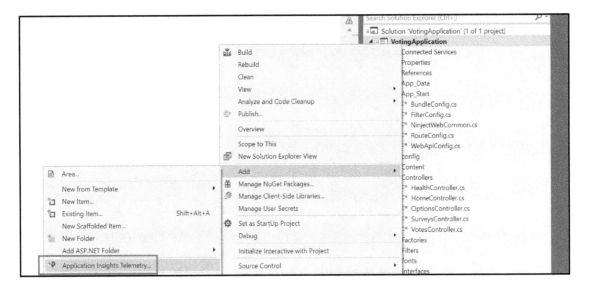

3. Click **Get Started**.
4. Sign in to Azure and provide a new **Resource Group** and **Resource** name (or use the default ones).

5. Click **Register**. The operation will take a few minutes. Once this time has passed, a new Azure Application Insights instance will be created in your Azure subscription, and the appropriate NuGet packages will be added to the Visual Studio project.

6. Update the resource for CodeLens and enable it to collect traces from `System.Diagnostics`:

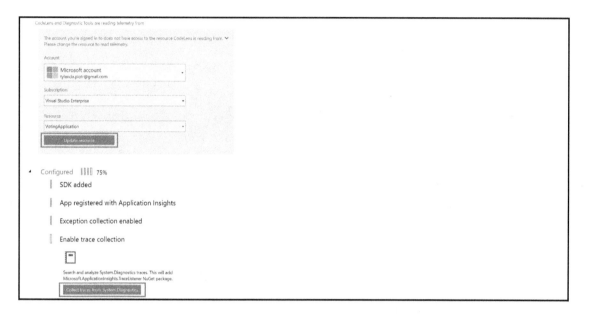

7. We do not want to have the instrumentation key hardcoded into the Docker image. Application Insights supports the ability to inject the key `APPINSIGHTS_INSTRUMENTATIONKEY` environment variable. Navigate to the `ApplicationInsights.config` file in the solution, find the following XML node, write down the key for further usage, and remove the XML node:

```
<InstrumentationKey>4e810bf1-58c4-4af7-
a67d-36fcdcf24a2f</InstrumentationKey>
```

8. Search for all occurrences of your instrumentation key in the solution. You will find one more in `_Layout.cshtml`; replace it with the following value:

```
instrumentationKey:
'@Microsoft.ApplicationInsights.Extensibility.TelemetryConfiguratio
n.Active.InstrumentationKey'
```

9. Right-click the `VotingApplication` project in the Solution Explorer and select **Manage Nuget Packages....** Install the following NuGet package in `Microsoft.ApplicationInsights.SnapshotCollectorandSerilog.Sinks.Trace`.

10. Configure the snapshot debugger. In the `ApplicationInsights.config` file, ensure that, in the root node `ApplicationInsights`, you have the following XML node:

```
<TelemetryProcessors>
 <Add
Type="Microsoft.ApplicationInsights.SnapshotCollector.SnapshotColle
ctorTelemetryProcessor,
Microsoft.ApplicationInsights.SnapshotCollector">
 <IsEnabled>true</IsEnabled>
 <IsEnabledInDeveloperMode>false</IsEnabledInDeveloperMode>
 <ThresholdForSnapshotting>1</ThresholdForSnapshotting>
 <MaximumSnapshotsRequired>3</MaximumSnapshotsRequired>
 <MaximumCollectionPlanSize>50</MaximumCollectionPlanSize>
 <ReconnectInterval>00:15:00</ReconnectInterval>
 <ProblemCounterResetInterval>1.00:00:00</ProblemCounterResetInterva
l>
 <SnapshotsPerTenMinutesLimit>3</SnapshotsPerTenMinutesLimit>
 <SnapshotsPerDayLimit>30</SnapshotsPerDayLimit>
 <SnapshotInLowPriorityThread>true</SnapshotInLowPriorityThread>
 <ProvideAnonymousTelemetry>false</ProvideAnonymousTelemetry>
 <FailedRequestLimit>3</FailedRequestLimit>
 </Add>
</TelemetryProcessors>
```

11. Register the Serilog sink in the `NinjectWebCommon.cs` file in the `RegisterServices` method. Your logger configuration should look like the following:

```
Log.Logger = new LoggerConfiguration()
                .ReadFrom.AppSettings()
                .Enrich.FromLogContext()
                .WriteTo.EventLog(source: "VotingApplication",
logName: "VotingApplication", manageEventSource: false)
                .WriteTo.Trace()
                .CreateLogger();
```

12. In the `HomeController.cs` file, add a new controller action, `TestException`, which we will use for testing the snapshot debugging. It should just throw an unhandled exception:

```
public ActionResult TestException()
{
    throw new InvalidOperationException("This action always throws
an exception!");
}
```

At this point, our Voting application is fully configured to use Azure Application Insights. We can now upgrade the Helm release using the following steps:

1. Build a new Docker image with a `1.5.0` tag, just like we did in the previous chapters, and push it to the Docker Hub. In our case, it will be called `packtpubkubernetesonwindows/voting-application:1.5.0`.

2. Navigate to the directory with the Helm chart for the application.

3. In the `Chart.yaml` file, use `1.5.0` (the same as the Docker image tag) as the `appVersion`. As suggested by our best practices, change the version of the chart—for example, use `0.2.0`.

4. In the `values.yaml` file, add your instrumentation key and increase `replicaCount` to 5:

```
azureApplicationInsightsKey: 4e810bf1-58c4-4af7-a67d-36fcdcf24a2f
replicaCount: 5
```

5. Now we need to inject the instrumentation key to the pod template into `Deployment` for our Voting application. Modify `templates\deployment.yaml` so that `azureApplicationInsightsKey` is injected into the `APPINSIGHTS_INSTRUMENTATIONKEY` environment variable:

```
apiVersion: apps/v1
kind: Deployment
metadata:
  name: {{ include "voting-application.fullname" . }}
  ...
spec:
  ...
  template:
    ...
    spec:
      ...
      containers:
        - name: {{ .Chart.Name }}-frontend
          ...
```

```
env:
- name: APPINSIGHTS_INSTRUMENTATIONKEY
  value: {{ .Values.azureApplicationInsightsKey }}
...
```

6. Perform a `dry run` for the upgrade of the Helm release using the new version of our chart. You should see the instrumentation key being properly resolved in the output manifests:

```
helm upgrade voting-application . `
    --namespace dev-helm `
    --debug `
    --dry-run
```

7. Run the `upgrade`:

```
helm upgrade voting-application . `
  --namespace dev-helm `
  --debug `
  --timeout 900s
```

8. Wait for all replicas to be upgraded to the new version.

Now, your application should be running and sending all of the telemetry to Azure Application Insights. You can navigate to Application Insights from Azure Portal (`https://portal.azure.com/`) or open it directly from Visual Studio by right-clicking `Application Insights` under **Connected Services** and selecting **Open Application Insights Portal**:

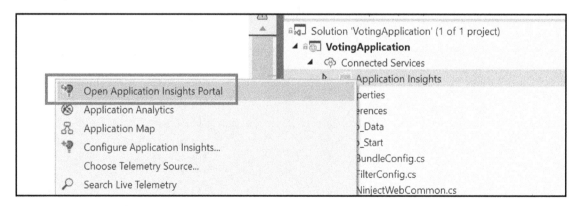

You can explore multiple features that are available out of the box with the current configuration—for example, visualizing the telemetry data as an application map that shows the dependencies between the different components in your application and what their current status is:

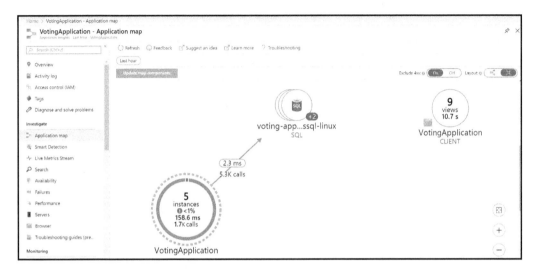

If you are interested in the overall performance of end-user requests, you can check out the dedicated dashboard based on the ASP.NET MVC telemetry:

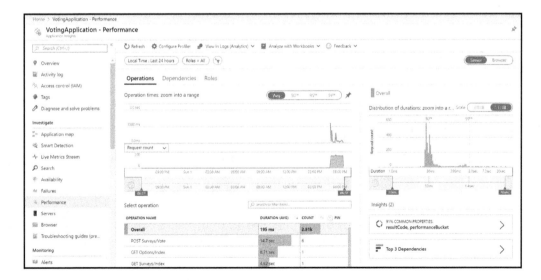

And, of course, you can inspect application **logs**, which are delivered by the Serilog sink. The most important feature in this view is the possibility of running complex queries using the Kusto language (`https://docs.microsoft.com/en-us/azure/kusto/query/`), which is designed for analyzing log data:

You can learn more about the Azure Application Insights features in the official documentation at `https://docs.microsoft.com/en-us/azure/azure-monitor/app/app-insights-overview`.

Now, let's see how you can use the snapshot debugger in order to debug your containerized application, even when you do not have access to a remote debugger.

Snapshot debugger

The Azure Application Insights service offers the snapshot debugger, which is a feature for monitoring exception telemetry from your application, including production scenarios. Whenever there is an unhandled exception (top-throwing), the snapshot debugger collects managed memory dumps that can be analyzed directly in Azure Portal or, for more advanced scenarios, Visual Studio 2019 Enterprise edition. Visual Studio will have this feature installed by default if you selected the ASP.NET workload in the installer.

Snapshot debugging can be configured for regular .NET applications that are not using ASP.NET MVC. You can find out more in the documentation at `https://docs.microsoft.com/en-us/azure/azure-monitor/app/snapshot-debugger-vm#configure-snapshot-collection-for-other-net-applications`.

In the previous paragraphs, we already enabled snapshot debugging in our application by installing the `Microsoft.ApplicationInsights.SnapshotCollector` NuGet package and providing additional configurations. Now, we can test this feature in our Voting application:

1. In your web browser, navigate to the test endpoint that always throws an exception: `http://<serviceExternalIp>/Home/TestException`. Trigger this endpoint twice; by default, we have to hit the same exception more than once to trigger snapshot collection.

2. You will see the default error page for our Voting application. At the same time, the snapshot has already been collected, without any noticeable performance impact for the end user.

3. Navigate to the Application Insights for our Voting application in Azure Portal (`https://portal.azure.com/`).

4. Open the **Failures** pane and select the **Operations** button when viewing the **Operations** tab or select the **Exceptions** button when viewing the **Exceptions** tab:

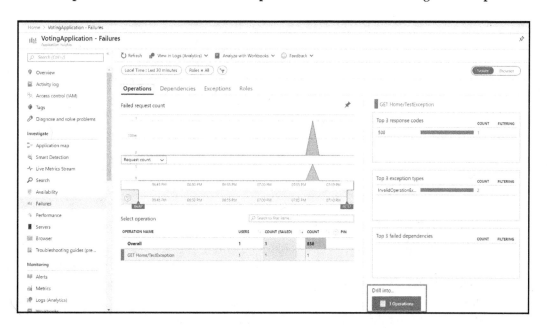

5. From the right, select a **Sample operation** pane and open one of the exception occurrences.

6. At the beginning, you will not see any snapshots on the timeline; you have to first add the Application Insights Snapshot Debugger Role. To do that, click **(Don't see snapshot? Troubleshoot)**:

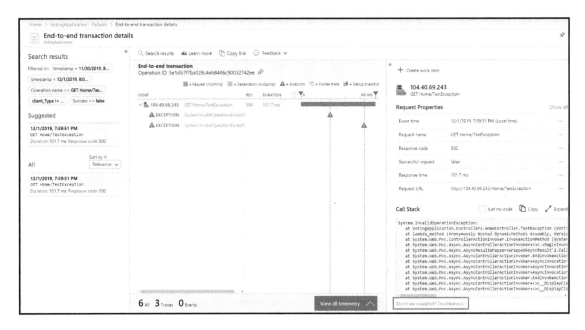

7. Click **Add Application Insights Snapshot Debugger Role**:

8. After that, a basic health check will be executed. Please bear in mind that it takes a few minutes until the snapshots are uploaded, so, if you experience any health check failures, retry in a few minutes.

9. Now, back in the **End-to-end transaction** details view, you will see small icons representing the debug snapshots. Click one of them:

10. The **Debug Snapshot** view offers you lightweight debugger capabilities, including code decompilation. To analyze the snapshot in Visual Studio 2019 Enterprise, click the **Download Snapshot** button:

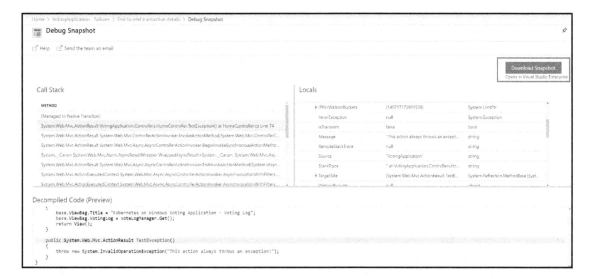

11. When the file downloads, open it in Visual Studio by double-clicking it.

12. In Visual Studio, click **Debug with Managed Only** or **Debug Managed Memory**, depending on your needs. The second option is really useful when you are analyzing memory leaks and other memory-related issues.

13. You may need to select your source code location in order to see the source code view (https://docs.microsoft.com/en-us/visualstudio/debugger/specify-symbol-dot-pdb-and-source-files-in-the-visual-studio-debugger?view=vs-2019).

14. Now, you can use all of the debugging tools that you have always used—for example, you can analyze the Parallel Stacks view:

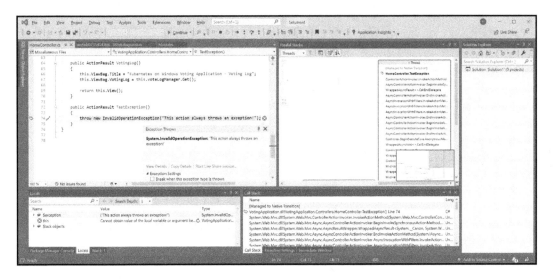

 If you run into any other problems while using the snapshot debugger, check the official troubleshooting guide at `https://docs.microsoft.com/en-us/azure/azure-monitor/app/snapshot-debugger-troubleshoot`.

The snapshot debugger has even more features, which make it possible to set live snap points so that you can create snapshots without waiting for an exception. Unfortunately, right now, this feature is only available for Azure App Service workloads or managed AKS clusters running applications in Linux containers. You can find more in the documentation at `https://docs.microsoft.com/en-us/visualstudio/debugger/debug-live-azure-applications?view=vs-2019`.

In the next section, we will take a look at Kubernetes Dashboard.

Using Kubernetes Dashboard

Kubernetes Dashboard (`https://github.com/kubernetes/dashboard`) is the default, web-based user interface for deploying, managing, and troubleshooting applications running on Kubernetes. Generally, it is recommended that you use declarative kubectl management of the cluster instead of using Dashboard, but it is still a useful tool for having cluster overview, analyzing logs, and quickly executing into pod containers.

To use Dashboard, you have to first install it. You have the following options to do this:

- Deploy using the official manifest by running `kubectl apply -f https://raw.githubusercontent.com/kubernetes/dashboard/v2.0.0-beta6/aio/deploy/recommended.yaml`. You can double-check the latest version in the documentation at `https://kubernetes.io/docs/tasks/access-application-cluster/web-ui-dashboard/`.
- Install the Helm chart using the `helm install kubernetes-dashboard stable/kubernetes-dashboard` command.
- In AKS Engine, use the `kubernetes-dashboard` add-on, which is enabled by default in the cluster ApiModel.

It is important to know that there are strict compatibility rules for the Kubernetes API and Kubernetes Dashboard. You can check the matrix in the official releases page at `https://github.com/kubernetes/dashboard/releases`. Currently, AKS Engine is deployed with version `1.10.1` of Dashboard, which is not compatible with the latest versions of the Kubernetes API. This means that we will deploy Dashboard using the official manifest. The AKS Engine cluster is by default an RBAC-enabled cluster, so we need to configure RBAC in order to use Dashboard as a cluster administrator.

Deploying Kubernetes Dashboard

To deploy and configure RBAC, go through the following steps:

1. Open the PowerShell window.
2. Deploy Kubernetes Dashboard using the official manifest:

```
kubectl apply -f
https://raw.githubusercontent.com/kubernetes/dashboard/v2.0.0-beta6
/aio/deploy/recommended.yaml
```

3. Create the `serviceaccount.yaml` manifest file for `admin-user`:

```
apiVersion: v1
kind: ServiceAccount
metadata:
  name: admin-user
  namespace: kubernetes-dashboard
```

4. Apply the manifest file using the `kubectl apply -f serviceaccount.yaml` command.

5. Create the `clusterrolebinding.yaml` manifest file to give this user a `cluster-admin` role:

```
apiVersion: rbac.authorization.k8s.io/v1
kind: ClusterRoleBinding
metadata:
  name: admin-user
roleRef:
  apiGroup: rbac.authorization.k8s.io
  kind: ClusterRole
  name: cluster-admin
subjects:
- kind: ServiceAccount
  name: admin-user
  namespace: kubernetes-dashboard
```

6. Apply the manifest file using the `kubectl apply -f clusterrolebinding.yaml` command.

7. To get the bearer token for this user, use the following snippet in PowerShell and copy the value after `token::`

```
kubectl -n kubernetes-dashboard describe secrets ((kubectl -n
kubernetes-dashboard get secrets | Select-String "admin-user-
token") -Split "\s+")[0]
```

When granting the `cluster-admin` role to the ServiceAccount that will be used to access the dashboard, you need to understand any security implications. Anyone who has the token for the `admin-user` ServiceAccount will be able to perform any actions in your cluster. In production scenarios, consider creating roles that expose only the necessary functionalities.

Now, you are ready to access Dashboard. To do this, please go through the following steps:

1. In the PowerShell window, start a proxy for connecting to the API using the `kubectl proxy` command. The dashboard is not exposed as an external service, which means we have to use the proxy.

2. Open the web browser and navigate to `http://localhost:8001/api/v1/namespaces/kubernetes-dashboard/services/https:kubernetes-dashboard:/proxy/`.

3. Authenticate using the token option and provide the bearer token that we have retrieved in the previous steps.

4. You will be redirected to the overview of your cluster:

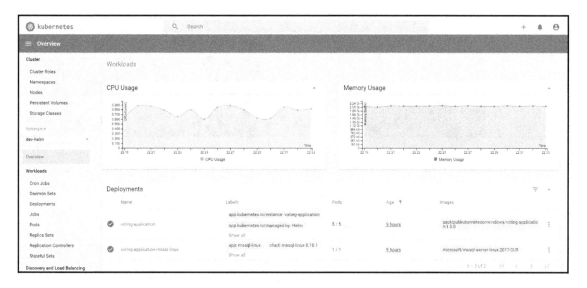

The Kubernetes Dashboard has multiple features that cover many functionalities provided by `kubectl`. In the next sections, we will explore how to access the container logs and execute into pod containers, as they are useful in debugging scenarios.

Accessing pod container logs

Kubernetes Dashboard gives you an easy interface for accessing pod container logs quickly. To access logs for one of the pods for our Voting application, go through the following steps:

1. In the menu, navigate to **Workloads** | **Pods**.
2. Find one of the pods for our Voting application. On the right side, click the three-dot button and select **Logs**.

3. You will be redirected to the logs view where you can inspect the logs in real time, just as if you used the `kubectl logs` command:

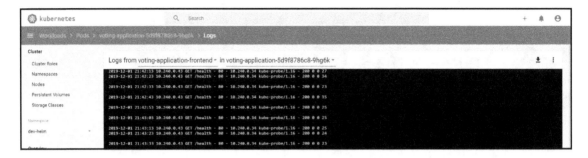

Next, let's see how to `exec` into a pod container.

Executing commands in a pod container

In a similar fashion as for accessing logs, you can exec into a Pod container in order to run ad-hoc commands. This approach can be useful when debugging issues or quickly introducing configuration changes in development clusters. Perform the following steps:

1. In the menu, navigate to **Workloads | Pods**.
2. Find one of the pods for our Voting application. On the right side, click the three-dot button and select `exec`.
3. The PowerShell terminal will open after a few seconds. You can run any arbitrary PowerShell commands and modify the container state:

Congratulations! You have successfully deployed Kubernetes Dashboard and you are now equipped with yet another useful debugging tool. In the next section, you will learn how you can improve your development environment for Kubernetes using Azure Dev Spaces.

Working on microservices in a team using Azure Dev Spaces

Azure Dev Spaces (https://docs.microsoft.com/en-us/azure/dev-spaces/), also known as **AZDS** (short for **Azure Dev Spaces**), is one of the latest offerings from Microsoft for an enhanced Kubernetes development experience. This service provides a rapid and iterative development experience for teams using AKS clusters. Please note that currently, only managed AKS clusters are supported, which means that you cannot use AKS Engine for this service. What is more, the current version does not support the development of Windows container applications; it is possible to interact with existing Windows pods, but they will not be managed by AZDS (https://docs.microsoft.com/en-us/azure/dev-spaces/how-to/run-dev-spaces-windows-containers). From this point of view, AZDS is not useful for Windows container application development, but, as it is likely to receive this support soon, we are going to give you an overview of this offering.

The main features of AZDS are as follows:

- You can minimize the local development environment setup. You can debug and test all components of your distributed application directly in AKS, without replacing or mocking up dependencies (dev/prod parity).
- You can organize the Kubernetes cluster into shared and private Dev Spaces.
- It can run independent updates of microservices without affecting the rest of the AKS cluster and other developers. You can develop your own version of a service, test it in isolation, and, when you are ready to share it with other team members, update the instance so that it is visible to everyone.
- It fully integrates with Visual Studio Code and Visual Studio 2019, including their remote debugging features. It can also be managed from the Azure CLI.
- It can connect your local machine to a Kubernetes cluster and test or debug local applications (with or without containers) with all the dependencies (https://docs.microsoft.com/en-us/azure/dev-spaces/how-to/connect). This feature is similar to telepresence.
- It provides a faster development loop using incremental code compilation directly in the container whenever code changes are detected.

To create an AKS cluster, you can use the Powershell script that we provided in Chapter 4, *Kubernetes Concepts and Windows Support* (https://github.com/PacktPublishing/Hands-On-Kubernetes-on-Windows/blob/master/Chapter04/05_CreateAKSWithWindowsNodes.ps1).

The script can also create a cluster with a two-node Linux pool only. Go through the following steps to create an AKS cluster with AZDS enabled:

1. Download the script and execute it with the appropriate parameters. You need to select an Azure location that supports AZDS (`https://docs.microsoft.com/en-us/azure/dev-spaces/about#supported-regions-and-configurations`) and select the Kubernetes version that is available in the location (use the `az aks get-versions --location <azureLocation>` command). In this example, we will create an AKS cluster instance named `devspaces-demo` in the `westeurope` location and Kubernetes version `1.15.4`. Be sure to select a cluster name that does not contain reserved words or trademarks, or later you will not be able to enable AZDS:

```
.\05_CreateAKSWithWindowsNodes.ps1 `
    -windowsPassword "S3cur3P@ssw0rd" `
    -azureLocation "westeurope" `
    -kubernetesVersion "1.15.4"
    -aksClusterName "devspaces-demo"
    -skipAddingWindowsNodePool $true
```

2. The cluster Deployment can take about 15 minutes. When it is completed, a new context for `kubectl` named `aks-windows-cluster` will be added and set as the default.

3. Enable AZDS for the cluster using the following command:

```
az aks use-dev-spaces `
    --resource-group "aks-windows-resource-group" `
    --name "devspaces-demo"
```

4. The AZDS CLI will be installed. Use the `default` namespace as the Dev Space when prompted.

Now that the AKS cluster has AZDS enabled, we can demonstrate how easy it is to create a new ASP.NET Core 3.0 Kubernetes application in Visual Studio 2019 and debug it directly in the cluster. Go through the following steps to create the application:

1. Open Visual Studio 2019 and select **Create a new project**.
2. Find the **Container Application for Kubernetes** template and click **Next**.
3. Choose the project name and location and click **Next**.
4. Select the **Web Application (Model–View–Controller)** type and click **Create**.

5. We need to introduce small changes to the default configuration. In the `charts\azds-demo\values.yaml` file, ensure that `ingress` is enabled using the following code:

```
ingress:
    enabled: true
```

6. By default, Kestrel listens on port `5000`. We need to change the port to `80` in order to be compatible with Dockerfile and Kubernetes Service. In the `Program.cs` file, ensure that the application startup looks as follows:

```
public static IHostBuilder CreateHostBuilder(string[] args) =>
        Host.CreateDefaultBuilder(args)
            .ConfigureWebHostDefaults(webBuilder =>
            {
                webBuilder
                    .UseUrls("http://0.0.0.0:80")
                    .UseStartup<Startup>();
            });
```

Projects that have AZDS support enabled have the `azds.yaml` file, which defines the Dev Spaces configuration, Dockerfile, and `charts` directory with the Helm chart, ready to be deployed to the cluster by AZDS. Now, let's deploy the application to the `default` Dev Space in our AKS cluster:

1. From the launch settings for your project, select **Azure Dev Spaces**:

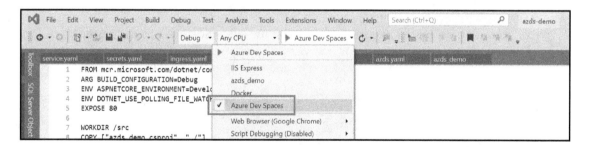

2. Select **devspaces demo AKS cluster** and **default space**, and mark it as **Publicly accessible**, and continue by clicking **OK**.
3. AZDS will build the Dockerfile, install the Helm chart, and attach the debugger. In the web browser, the **Ingress** public endpoint will be automatically opened—for example, `http://default.azds-demo.2dpkt6cj7f.weu.azds.io/`.

4. In the `HomeController.cs` file, add the breakpoint in the index controller action. Refresh the web page in the browser. You will see that the breakpoint is caught exactly as if the application was debugged in a local environment!

5. Stop debugging and introduce a change in the `Index.cshtml` file. For example, change the main header to the following:

```
<h1 class="display-4">Welcome - Modified</h1>
```

6. Launch the application again, using the Azure Dev Spaces configuration. In the **Output** window, you will see that the application is quickly rebuilt, and, after a while, the web browser with the modified main page opens again:

 For more AZDS scenarios in team development, please check the official documentation at `https://docs.microsoft.com/en-us/azure/dev-spaces/team-development-netcore-visualstudio`.

And all of this has happened directly on the AKS cluster. As you can see, development iterations are much faster than they are in a normal dev-loop when building a Docker image, pushing it, and rolling out a new Deployment.

 To delete the AKS cluster, use the `az group delete --name aks-windows-resource-group --yes` command.

Congratulations! You have successfully set up Azure Dev Spaces for your AKS cluster.

Summary

This chapter has focused on how you, as a developer, can improve your development experience with Kubernetes clusters. First, we learned how to configure essential development extensions for Visual Studio Code and Visual Studio 2019. Next, you learned how to use Helm for packaging Kubernetes applications, first by using an official Helm chart for Microsoft SQL Server and later by creating a dedicated chart for our Voting application.

Next, we learned how to integrate Azure Application Insights into your application and how you can leverage advanced features such as the snapshot debugger in order to debug problems in production scenarios for Windows pods. Using our new Docker image with Application Insights instrumentation, we learned how to perform a Helm release upgrade. We introduced Kubernetes Dashboard, which is the most commonly used web UI for Kubernetes. Lastly, you learned what the Azure Dev Spaces service is and how you can use it to increase the development iteration speed when working with AKS clusters.

In the next chapter, we will focus on the important topic of security, especially in the context of Windows containers.

Questions

1. What is Helm and why should you use it?
2. What is the biggest difference between Helm versions two and three?
3. How can you implement automatic Entity Framework database migrations in a Helm chart?
4. How do you perform a rollout of a new version of your application that is installed as a Helm chart?
5. What is the snapshot debugger and how can you use it in production scenarios?
6. Why is it not recommended that you use Kubernetes Dashboard to modify resources in the cluster?
7. What are the advantages of using Azure Dev Spaces?

You can find answers to these questions in the *Assessments* section of this book.

Further reading

- For more information about Kubernetes features and how to manage applications, please refer to the following PacktPub books:
    - *The Complete Kubernetes Guide* (https://www.packtpub.com/ virtualization-and-cloud/complete-kubernetes-guide)
    - *Getting Started with Kubernetes - Third Edition* (https://www. packtpub.com/virtualization-and-cloud/getting-started- kubernetes-third-edition)
    - *Kubernetes for Developers* (https://www.packtpub.com/ virtualization-and-cloud/kubernetes-developers)
- If you are interested in learning more about Azure Application Insights, please refer to the following PacktPub books:
    - *Hands-On Azure for Developers* (https://www.packtpub.com/ virtualization-and-cloud/hands-azure-developers)
    - *Azure for Architects - Second Edition* (https://www.packtpub.com/ virtualization-and-cloud/azure-architects-second-edition)
- For more information regarding Helm, you can check out the following PacktPub book:
    - *Mastering Kubernetes - Second Edition* (https://www.packtpub.com/ application-development/mastering-kubernetes-second- edition)

13
Securing Kubernetes Clusters and Applications

The topic of security deserves special attention—Kubernetes is a huge and complex system where security is not obvious and potential **attack vectors** are not immediately visible. Thinking about security in Kubernetes is even more important if you consider the powerful operations that this system can perform and how deeply it integrates with the operating system internals. Just to shed some light on how things may go south if you overlook configuration details, take a look at an article on how Tesla got cryptojacked because of a *public, unauthenticated* endpoint for Kubernetes Dashboard (`https://blog.heptio.com/on-securing-the-kubernetes-dashboard-16b09b1b7aca`).

In this chapter, we are going to provide you with the general best practices for securing Kubernetes clusters, including the Windows workloads perspective. Windows nodes have some limitations—for example, mounting secrets in clear text directly from the node storage only (not memory)—but they also are more secure than Linux nodes in different ways.

This chapter will cover the following topics:

- Securing Kubernetes clusters
- Securing the container runtime on Windows
- Deploying secure applications using network policies
- Kubernetes secrets on Windows machines

Technical requirements

For this chapter you will need the following:

- Windows 10 Pro, Enterprise, or Education (version 1903 or later, 64-bit) installed
- Azure account
- Windows/Linux Kubernetes cluster deployed using AKS Engine

To follow along, you will need your own Azure account in order to create Azure resources for the Kubernetes cluster. If you haven't already created the account in the previous chapters, you can read more about how to obtain a limited free account for personal use at `https://azure.microsoft.com/en-us/free/`.

Deploying a Kubernetes cluster using AKS Engine has been covered in `Chapter 8`, *Deploying a Hybrid Azure Kubernetes Service Engine Cluster*.

You can download the latest code samples for this book chapter from the official GitHub repository at `https://github.com/PacktPublishing/Hands-On-Kubernetes-on-Windows/tree/master/Chapter13`.

Securing Kubernetes clusters

In this section, we will give some general guidance on how to secure Kubernetes clusters. Additionally, we are going to explore the topic of API user authentication in AKS Engine clusters using **Azure Active Directory** (**AAD**) integration. The list of best practices provided in this chapter is not exhaustive, so please always review the latest official documentation to ensure that you follow the recommendations.

Now, let's go through the list of general recommendations in the following subsections.

Using built-in RBAC for authorization

We have covered the **role-based access control** (**RBAC**) provided by Kubernetes for API authorization in `Chapter 11`, *Configuring Applications to Use Kubernetes Features*. This mechanism allows you to configure fine-grained sets of permissions and assign them to users, groups, and service accounts. In this way, as a cluster administrator, you can control how cluster users (internal and external) interact with the API server, which API resources they can access, and which actions they can perform. At the same time, you should use namespaces to create the first boundary between resources. This also makes applying RBAC policies easier.

For RBAC, use the principle of least privilege and prefer assigning RoleBindings to groups instead of individual users to reduce management overhead. If you use an external authentication provider, you can easily integrate with groups provided by the provider. When bootstrapping the cluster, it is recommended that you use the Node and RBAC authorizers together (use the `--authorization-mode=Node,RBAC` parameter for the API server), in combination with the **NodeRestriction** admission plugin. This is the default way that AKS Engine initializes your cluster.

Using an external authentication provider

All API calls must be authenticated. This is true for both external (normal) users as well as members of the internal Kubernetes infrastructure—for example, kubelet. In the case of the infrastructure, such users generally use ServiceAccounts with tokens or X509 client certificates, which are created when bootstrapping the cluster. Kubernetes itself does not provide the means for managing normal external users who access the cluster; this should be delegated to an external authentication provider that can integrate with Kubernetes—for example, via an authenticating proxy.

You should choose an authentication mechanism that fits your organization and follows the common access patterns for the users. For example, if you are running AKS Engine, it is likely that you are already using Azure Active Directory to manage users and roles in your Azure subscription. On top of that, you should consider using groups to make RBAC policy management easier and more integrated with AAD.

 Apart from AAD, authenticating proxies and authentication webhooks give you the possibility to integrate with different protocols, such as LDAP, SAML, or Kerberos.

At the end of this section, we will demonstrate how to enable AAD integration for your AKS Engine cluster.

Bootstrapping the cluster using kubeadm

If you are deploying the cluster manually, use **kubeadm**, which can bootstrap the cluster securely. It can generate a **self-signed CA** to set up identities for all components in the cluster, generate **tokens** for joining new nodes (TLS bootstrapping), and offer **certificate management** capabilities (`https://kubernetes.io/docs/tasks/administer-cluster/kubeadm/kubeadm-certs/`). Initializing a **secure** Kubernetes cluster is the top design priority for kubeadm (`https://github.com/kubernetes/kubeadm/blob/master/docs/design/design_v1.10.md`).

Disabling public API access

For production scenarios, using proper user authentication with RBAC authorization for the Kubernetes API may not be enough (from a security perspective) if the API is publicly accessible. To reduce the attack vector for your Kubernetes API, consider *disabling* public API access, as well as not exposing any Kubernetes nodes directly to the internet. This will, of course, require you to use a **VPN** or a **jumpbox host** to access the API, but it is definitely more secure.

AKS Engine can configure this for you by a simple change to the cluster apimodel. You can read more about disabling public API access in the official documentation at `https://github.com/Azure/aks-engine/blob/master/docs/topics/features.md#private-cluster`. Alternatively, you may consider hardening the **NAT inbound rules** for master VMs, restricting the range of IPs that are allowed to connect to the machine via HTTPS and SSH.

Disabling the public Dashboard

Similar to the Kubernetes API, you should disable the publicly accessible Kubernetes Dashboard. In common installations, the Dashboard may be exposed as a LoadBalancer service; in the worst case, this will be on a ServiceAccount with a `cluster-admin` role. The recommended practice is to never expose Kubernetes Dashboard using a LoadBalancer service, and to always use `kubectl proxy` to access the page.

Additionally, the ServiceAccount for Kubernetes Dashboard should have the **least privileges** that are enough for your use cases. You will most likely never use Kubernetes Dashboard for creating or editing deployments in production, so why would you need write access for such sensitive API resources?

Running containers in nonprivileged mode

In Kubernetes, it is possible to specify whether a pod is privileged or not. Privileged pods may have containers that are running in privileged mode—this essentially means that the container has access to all devices on the host, which is similar to what processes running with root (or administrative) privileges on the host would have.

It is a good practice to ensure that your pod containers are running in nonprivileged mode in the operating system; this follows the principle of least privilege. Additionally, you should consider using the PodSecurityPolicy admission controller to enforce a set of rules that a pod must fulfill to be scheduled. An example restrictive policy can be found at `https://raw.githubusercontent.com/kubernetes/website/master/content/en/examples/policy/restricted-psp.yaml`.

 Please note that in the case of Windows containers, running privileged containers is not supported. Additionally, for Windows workloads, consider using **Group-Managed Service Accounts** (**gMSAs**, `https://kubernetes.io/docs/tasks/configure-pod-container/configure-gmsa/`).

Encrypting data at rest

Encrypting data at rest is considered a general good practice (and sometimes a law-enforced requirement) for all systems. In Kubernetes, you need to ensure that **etcd cluster** data is encrypted. This will provide an extra layer of security for your API resources and secrets that would otherwise be kept in etcd in unencrypted form. Encrypting secrets at rest is covered as a separate topic in the official Kubernetes documentation at `https://kubernetes.io/docs/tasks/administer-cluster/encrypt-data/`.

For secrets, you should always use late binding by injecting the secrets to pods as volumes or environment variables. Note that injecting secrets as environment variables is less secure on Linux; when you have root privileges, you can enumerate all environment variables for a process from `/proc/<pid>/environ`. On Windows nodes, the issue is even more complex: you can still access environment variables for processes, but volumes cannot currently use the in-memory filesystem. This means that secrets are then stored directly on the node disk storage. This means that you should consider encrypting your Windows node storage to minimize the exposure of credentials. We will take a look at this issue in the next sections.

Using network policies

Network policies act as a firewall between your pods, allowing you to control network access into and out of your containerized applications. In a Kubernetes cluster, there are no limitations in network communication between pods by default—basically, all-to-all traffic is possible. It is a good practice to use a permissive network policy model that, by default, denies all traffic and allows connections only if a dedicated network policy has been defined.

You can read more about network providers that support network policies that are available on AKS Engine in the official documentation at `https://github.com/Azure/aks-engine/tree/master/examples/networkpolicy`. Please take note that currently Windows pods are not supported by these providers, apart from the Enterprise version of Calico that is provided as a part of the Tigera Essentials subscription service (`https://www.tigera.io/media/pr-calico-for-windows`).

Securing the image supply chain and scan images

In `Chapter 3`, *Working with Container Images*, we described how you can sign and verify your Docker images using **Docker Content Trust (DCT)**. You should definitely consider using this approach for your Docker image pipelines in production. Additionally, consider incorporating open source tools, such as **Anchore** (`https://github.com/anchore/anchore-engine`) and **Clair** (`https://github.com/quay/clair`), which can help you identify common vulnerabilities and exposures (**CVEs**) and mitigate them.

Rotating infrastructure credentials and certificates

In general, the shorter the validity time of a credential or a token, the harder it will be for the attacker to make any use of such a credential. Use this principle to set short lifetimes for certificates and tokens that are used in your cluster and implement **automated rotation** whenever possible. This can become your secret weapon when you detect that you are under attack; if you can effectively rotate certificates, you can simply rotate them on demand and make any intercepted credentials useless.

For AKS and AKS Engine, consider using integration with **Azure Key Vault**, which makes your secret and certificate management and rotation much easier. You can read more in the official documentation at `https://github.com/Azure/kubernetes-keyvault-flexvol`.

Additionally, consider integrating an authentication provider for issuing user tokens with a short expiration time. You can use this approach for providing **just-in-time privileged access management**, which can drastically limit the amount of time that a user has *God-mode* access to the resources.

Enabling audit logging

Audit logs should always be available in production clusters. This will make it possible to set up monitoring and alerting for access anomalies and unexpected API calls. The earlier you detect any forbidden API responses, the greater the chance that you will react in time and prevent the attacker from gaining access to the cluster. You can read more about Kubernetes auditing in the official documentation at `https://kubernetes.io/docs/tasks/debug-application-cluster/audit/`.

Make sure you go through the official Kubernetes guide for securing a cluster when you set up a production cluster. You can find more details at `https://kubernetes.io/docs/tasks/administer-cluster/securing-a-cluster/`.

Now, after we have gone through the most important security best practices for Kubernetes clusters, we will take a look at how to enable **Azure Active Directory** (**AAD**) for client authentication in an AKS Engine cluster.

Integrating AAD with AKS Engine

AKS Engine can be easily integrated with AAD in order to provide Kubernetes API client authentication. Together with AAD **groups**, this approach can be used for creating RoleBindings and ClusterRoleBindings for user groups that are mapped to AAD groups.

Let's see how you can create an AKS Engine cluster with AAD integration and create an AAD group for cluster admins. This approach can be extended to manage multiple AAD groups that can have different bindings in RBAC.

Adding AAD integration to an existing AKS Engine cluster is not supported. Therefore, you need to make this decision at cluster deployment time.

The steps for configuring AAD applications for a server and client, as well as the creation of the admin AAD group, have been provided as a Powershell script at https://github.com/ PacktPublishing/Hands-On-Kubernetes-on-Windows/tree/master/Chapter13/01_ AksEngineCreateAadProfile.ps1 for your convenience. You can use the script or go through the following steps:

1. Open the PowerShell window and define the $dnsPrefix variable with a globally unique DNS prefix, which you will later use for AKS Engine deployment—for example:

    ```
    $dnsPrefix = "handson-aks-engine-win-aad"
    ```

2. Create an AAD server application that will represent the Kubernetes API server and store the appId for further use as a $serverApplicationId variable:

    ```
    $serverApplicationId = az ad app create `
        --display-name "${dnsPrefix}Server" `
        --identifier-uris "https://${dnsPrefix}Server" `
        --query appId -o tsv
    ```

3. Update group membership claims for this application:

    ```
    az ad app update `
        --id $serverApplicationId `
        --set groupMembershipClaims=All
    ```

4. Create a **service principal** that will be used for Azure platform authentication:

    ```
    az ad sp create `
        --id $serverApplicationId
    ```

5. Get the **secret** for the service principal and store it for further use as a $serverApplicationSecret variable:

    ```
    $serverApplicationSecret = az ad sp credential reset `
        --name $serverApplicationId `
        --credential-description "AKSPassword" `
        --query password -o tsv
    ```

6. Now, add permissions for the server application to read directory data and sign in and read the user profiles:

```
az ad app permission add `
    --id $serverApplicationId `
    --api 00000003-0000-0000-c000-000000000000 `
    --api-permissions e1fe6dd8-ba31-4d61-89e7-88639da4683d=Scope
06da0dbc-49e2-44d2-8312-53f166ab848a=Scope 7ab1d382-f21e-4acd-a863-
ba3e13f7da61=Role
```

7. Grant the permissions:

```
az ad app permission grant `
    --id $serverApplicationId `
    --api 00000003-0000-0000-c000-000000000000
az ad app permission admin-consent `
    --id $serverApplicationId
```

8. The next steps will be similar, but will apply to an AAD **client application** that represents kubectl. Create the application and store the appId for further use as a $clientApplicationId variable:

```
$clientApplicationId = az ad app create `
    --display-name "${dnsPrefix}Client" `
    --native-app `
    --reply-urls "https://${dnsPrefix}Client" `
    --query appId -o tsv
```

Depending on your AAD tenant configuration, you may require additional permissions to create the service principal. You can read more in the official documentation at https://docs.microsoft.com/en-us/azure/active-directory/develop/howto-create-service-principal-portal#required-permissions.

9. Create the service principal for the application:

```
az ad sp create `
    --id $clientApplicationId
```

10. Determine the OAuth2 ID for the server application and store it as $oauth2PermissionId:

```
$oauth2PermissionId = az ad app show `
    --id $serverApplicationId `
    --query "oauth2Permissions[0].id" -o tsv
```

11. Use the OAuth2 ID to allow the authentication flow between the client and server application:

```
az ad app permission add `
    --id $clientApplicationId `
    --api $serverApplicationId `
    --api-permissions $oauth2PermissionId=Scope

az ad app permission grant `
    --id $clientApplicationId `
    --api $serverApplicationId
```

12. Create an AAD group named `AksEngineAdmins` for AKS Engine administrators and store its ID as a `$adminGroupId` variable:

```
$adminGroupId = az ad group create `
    --display-name AksEngineAdmins `
    --mail-nickname AksEngineAdmins `
    --query "objectId" -o tsv
```

13. We would like to add the current user to this group. First, let's retrieve the `objectId` for the user and store it as a `$currentUserObjectId` variable:

```
$currentUserObjectId = az ad signed-in-user show `
    --query "objectId" -o tsv
```

14. Add the user to the AKS Engine administrators group:

```
az ad group member add `
    --group AksEngineAdmins `
    --member-id $currentUserObjectId
```

15. Determine the AAD Tenant ID for your current subscription and store it as a `$tenantId` variable:

```
$tenantId = az account show `
    --query "tenantId" -o tsv
```

16. Print the JSON object based on the previous variables that will be used in the AKS Engine apimodel:

```
echo @"
"aadProfile": {
  "serverAppID": "$serverApplicationId",
  "clientAppID": "$clientApplicationId",
  "tenantID": "$tenantId",
  "adminGroupID": "$adminGroupId"
```

```
    }
    "@
```

We have everything we need to deploy AKS Engine with AAD integration. To do this, we will use a PowerShell script in almost exactly the same way that we used it in previous chapters (`https://github.com/PacktPublishing/Hands-On-Kubernetes-on-Windows/blob/master/Chapter13/02_aks-engine-aad/CreateAKSEngineClusterWithWindowsNodes.ps1`), together with the apimodel template (`https://github.com/PacktPublishing/Hands-On-Kubernetes-on-Windows/blob/master/Chapter13/02_aks-engine-aad/kubernetes-windows-template.json`). To perform AKS Engine deployment, go through the following steps:

1. Download both the PowerShell script and the apimodel template.
2. Open the PowerShell window in the location of the files.
3. In the `kubernetes-windows-template.json` file, replace `aadProfile` with your own values from the previous paragraph.
4. Execute the script with appropriate parameters:

```
.\CreateAKSEngineClusterWithWindowsNodes.ps1 `
 -azureSubscriptionId <azureSubscriptionId> `
 -dnsPrefix <dnsPrefix> `
 -windowsPassword 'S3cur3P@ssw0rd' `
 -resourceGroupName "aks-engine-aad-windows-resource-group" `
 -azureLocation "westus"
```

5. After a few minutes, the script will execute the `kubectl get pods` command and you will be prompted to *authenticate* in the web browser:

6. Navigate to the URL, provide the code, and log in. After that, you will be authenticated successfully in the Kubernetes API server and be able to use kubectl.

7. To check the definition of the ClusterRoleBinding, which allows you access, execute the following command:

```
PS C:\src> kubectl describe clusterrolebinding aad-default-admin-
group
Name:           aad-default-admin-group
Labels:         addonmanager.kubernetes.io/mode=EnsureExists
                kubernetes.io/cluster-service=true
Annotations:    <none>
Role:
  Kind:    ClusterRole
  Name:    cluster-admin
Subjects:
  Kind    Name                                         Namespace
  ----    ----                                         ---------
  Group   18d047eb-83f9-4740-96be-59555e88138f
```

Depending on your needs, you can now configure more AAD groups, create roles and provide appropriate RoleBindings for them. In the next section, we will take a look at how you can ensure that the Windows container runtime is running securely.

Securing container runtime in Windows

When it comes to securing container runtime, Windows containers are a bit different than Linux containers. For Windows containers, the operating system uses a `Job` object (not to be confused with Kubernetes `Job` object!) **per container** with a system namespace filter for all processes running in a given container. This provides a logical isolation from the host machine that cannot be disabled. You can read more about the Windows container architecture in `Chapter 1`, *Creating Containers*.

This fact has a consequence: **privileged** containers are not available in Windows, though they are available in Linux. Additionally, with the incoming support for Hyper-V containers in Kubernetes, you will be able to secure the container runtime even more and enforce better isolation.

For Linux containers, you would consider using `securityContext` for a pod in order to run as a **nonprivileged** user (with an ID different from 0):

```
apiVersion: v1
kind: Pod
metadata:
  name: secured-pod
spec:
  securityContext:
    runAsUser: 1000
```

Additionally, you can enforce **PodSecurityPolicies**, which are verified by the admission controller before scheduling a pod. In this way, as an example, you can ensure that no pods in a given namespace are running in privileged mode. You have to use RBAC to properly configure policy access.

 AKS Engine comes by default with the PodSecurityPolicy admission controller enabled and **privileged** and **restricted** policies available.

For Windows containers, the standard `securityContext` will not work as it is meant to be used for Linux containers. Windows containers have a dedicated object inside `securityContext` named `windowsOptions`, which can enable some Windows-specific features that are currently still in the **alpha** state:

- Configuring running pod containers with a different user name (`https://kubernetes.io/docs/tasks/configure-pod-container/configure-runasusername/`).
- Configuring Group-Managed Service Accounts (gMSA) for pod containers (`https://kubernetes.io/docs/tasks/configure-pod-container/configure-gmsa/`). The gMSA is a specific type of Active Directory account that provides automatic password management, simplified service principal name management, and the ability to delegate the management to other administrators on multiple servers. Azure Active Directory comes with support for gMSA (`https://docs.microsoft.com/en-us/azure/active-directory-domain-services/create-gmsa`).

In the next section, you will learn more about network policies and how they can be used to deploy more secure applications on Kubernetes.

Deploying secure applications using network policies

In Kubernetes, you can provide better granularity for your application deployments in terms of network isolation using network policies. Represented by `NetworkPolicy` objects, they define how groups of pods can communicate with each other and network endpoints in general—think of them as a basic firewall for enforcing network segmentation at layer 3 of the OSI model. Of course, they are not a substitution for advanced

The `NetworkPolicy` object uses label selectors in order to identify the pods that they are attached to. Similarly, label selectors and IP CIDRs are used for defining ingress and egress rule targets for these pods. A given network policy is used only if it has a label selector that matches a given pod. If there are no network policies matching a given Pod, it can accept any traffic.

Network policy support

In order to use network policies, you need to use one of the **network providers** (used for installing the pod network, as described in `Chapter 5`, *Kubernetes Networking*) that supports network policies. The most popular are as follows:

- Calico (`https://www.projectcalico.org/`)
- Cilium (`https://cilium.io/`)
- Kube-router (`https://www.kube-router.io/`)
- Romana (`https://romana.io/`)
- Weave Net (`https://www.weave.works/docs/net/latest/overview/`)

Unfortunately, there are *no* network providers that currently support Windows nodes, which means you can only use network policies in Linux clusters. The only network provider that has announced incoming support for Windows nodes and network policies is the enterprise version of Calico, provided as a part of the **Tigera Essentials** subscription service (`https://www.tigera.io/media/pr-calico-for-windows`). You can currently try this offering, including Windows node support, in a private preview version. Please note that if you are using AKS or AKS Engine, you are limited to Calico or Cilium, working together with **Azure** or **kubenet** network CNI plugins.

For more details regarding AKS Engine configuration for network policy support, please refer to the official documentation at `https://github.com/Azure/aks-engine/tree/master/examples/networkpolicy`. Additionally, for managed AKS, you may consider using an **advanced networking** feature that allows you to configure your own VNet, define Azure network security groups, and provide automatic connectivity of your pods to the VNet—you can read more in the official documentation at `https://docs.microsoft.com/en-us/azure/aks/configure-azure-cni`.

Let's see how you could use network policies to enforce pod isolation in your clusters.

Configuring network policy

From a security perspective, network policies are important because, by default, Kubernetes allows **all-to-all** communication in the cluster. Namespaces only provide a simple isolation that still allows pods to communicate with each other by IP address. In larger clusters or in multitenant scenarios, you have to provide better network isolation. Even though Windows nodes do not yet support network policies (but eventually they *will* be supported), we feel that it is important to make you aware of how you can approach network segmentation using native Kubernetes constructs.

If you have an AKS Engine Linux cluster with a Calico network on an Azure CNI plugin, you can follow along and configure the network policies for your pods. Deployment of AKS Engine with such a configuration requires a simple change to the cluster apimodel, namely by adding the following property in `properties.orchestratorProfile`:

```
"kubernetesConfig": {
    "networkPolicy": "calico",
    "networkPlugin": "azure"
}
```

Now, we will create a network policy that *blocks all ingress* traffic to all pods in the `default` namespace. This is the opposite of what you have in the cluster by default—the pods in the namespace will be not able to communicate with each other unless you specifically allow it. After that, we will deploy a simple Nginx web server behind a LoadBalancer service and try to communicate internally from a different pod in the cluster and externally from the Azure load balancer. Then we will create a network policy that will act as a **whitelisting rule** just for TCP port 80 for the web server. Please go through the following steps to create the default deny-all rule and deploy the Nginx web server:

1. Create a `default-deny-all-ingress.yaml` manifest file for the `NetworkPolicy` object that denies all ingress traffic to pods in the `default` namespace:

```
apiVersion: networking.k8s.io/v1
kind: NetworkPolicy
metadata:
  namespace: default
  name: default-deny-all-ingress
spec:
  podSelector: {}
  policyTypes:
  - Ingress
```

This is achieved by using an empty `podSelector`, which will select all pods.

2. Apply the manifest file using the `kubectl apply -f .\default-deny-all-ingress.yaml` command.

3. You can use the following command for any network policy if you want to better understand what its effect is:

```
kubectl describe networkpolicy default-deny-all-ingress
```

4. Create a simple manifest file named `nginx-deployment.yaml` for Nginx deployment:

```
apiVersion: apps/v1
kind: Deployment
metadata:
  namespace: default
  name: nginx-deployment
spec:
  selector:
    matchLabels:
      app: nginx
  replicas: 2
```

```
template:
  metadata:
    labels:
      app: nginx
  spec:
    containers:
    - name: nginx
      image: nginx:1.7.9
      ports:
      - containerPort: 80
```

5. Apply the manifest file using the `kubectl apply -f .\nginx-deployment.yaml` command.

6. Create a `nginx-service.yaml` manifest file for the LoadBalancer service for the deployment:

```
apiVersion: v1
kind: Service
metadata:
  namespace: default
  name: nginx-service
  labels:
    app: nginx
spec:
  type: LoadBalancer
  ports:
  - protocol: TCP
    port: 80
  selector:
    app: nginx
```

7. Apply the manifest file using the `kubectl apply -f .\nginx-service.yaml` command.

Be careful when defining very restrictive egress rules. With deny-all egress rules, you will block access to the Kubernetes DNS service for the pods.

With our Nginx web server deployed and the default rule for denying all ingress traffic to pods in the `default` namespace, we can test the connection to the web server:

1. Wait for the external IP of the service to appear using `kubectl get svc -w` and open the address in a web browser. You will see that the connection hangs and eventually times out, as expected.
2. Let's check this using an ad-hoc pod running in the same namespace. Create a `busybox` pod in the interactive mode, running a Bourne shell:

```
kubectl run --generator=run-pod/v1 busybox-debug -i --tty --
image=busybox --rm --restart=Never -- sh
```

4. In the shell session in the pod, try getting the web page hosted by Nginx. You can use both the service DNS name and the IP of one of the pods. In both cases it will fail:

```
wget http://nginx-service:80
wget http://10.240.0.30:80
```

Now, let's create a network policy that allows ingress traffic to Nginx pods on TCP port `80`. After that, you will be able to communicate from both pods in the cluster, as well as from the Azure load balancer. To configure the policy, go through the following steps:

1. Leave the `busybox` interactive session running and open a new PowerShell window.
2. Create a `default-nginx-allow-ingress.yaml` manifest file that allows ingress traffic on TCP port `80` to all pods with label `app=nginx` from all sources:

```yaml
apiVersion: networking.k8s.io/v1
kind: NetworkPolicy
metadata:
  namespace: default
  name: default-nginx-allow-ingress
spec:
  podSelector:
    matchLabels:
      app: nginx
  ingress:
  - from: []
    ports:
    - protocol: TCP
      port: 80
```

3. Apply the manifest file using the `kubectl apply -f .\default-nginx-allow-ingress.yaml` command.

4. In your web browser, navigate again to the external IP for the service. Now, you should be able to reach the web page without any problems!

5. Similarly, try the same in the `busybox` pod container using `wget`. You will also be able to reach the web page.

6. As an exercise, to prove that port filtering works properly, you can modify the network policy to use a different port or run Nginx on a TCP port different than `80`.

Congratulations! You have successfully used network policies to configure permissive networking rules in your Kubernetes cluster. It is a good practice to start with a *permissive* network policy model where you *deny all ingress* traffic to your pods (sometimes also all egress traffic from the pods) and allow the connections by specific network policies. Please note that, for this, you should organize the network policies in a predictable manner, using naming conventions. This will make the management of your networking rules much easier.

In the next section, we will explore how you should handle Kubernetes secrets on Windows machines.

Kubernetes secrets on Windows machines

In `Chapter 4`, *Kubernetes Concepts and Windows Support*, we mentioned that one of Windows's node support limitations is that Kubernetes secrets that are mounted to pods as volumes are written in *clear-text* on node disk storage (not RAM memory). The reason for this is that Windows currently does not support mounting in-memory filesystems to pod containers. This may pose security risks, and needs additional actions to secure the cluster. At the same time, mounting secrets as environment variables has its own security risks—you can enumerate environment variables for processes if you have access to the system. Until it is possible to mount secrets as volumes from in-memory filesystems, there is no completely secure solution for injecting secrets for Windows containers apart from using third-party providers, such as Azure Key Vault.

 Encryption of secrets *at rest* in a Kubernetes etcd cluster is a different and important topic that is covered in the official documentation at `https://kubernetes.io/docs/tasks/administer-cluster/encrypt-data/`.

Let's perform a small experiment to better understand the issue and any possible implications. You will need your AKS Engine cluster with Windows nodes that we used in the previous chapters. Please go through the following steps:

1. Open the PowerShell window and create a `secret-example.yaml` manifest file that contains the username `admin` and password `Password123` encoded in Base64:

```
apiVersion: v1
kind: Secret
metadata:
  name: secret-example
type: Opaque
data:
  username: YWRtaW4=
  password: UGFzc3dvcmQxMjM=
```

2. Apply the manifest file using the `kubectl apply -f .\secret-example.yaml` command.

3. Create the `windows-example-deployment.yaml` manifest file for the deployment of the sample ASP.NET application running on Windows with a `secret-example` secret mounted in the `C:\SecretExample` directory on the pod:

```
apiVersion: apps/v1
kind: Deployment
metadata:
  name: windows-example
  labels:
    app: sample
spec:
  replicas: 1
  selector:
    matchLabels:
      app: windows-example
  template:
    metadata:
      name: windows-example
      labels:
        app: windows-example
    spec:
      nodeSelector:
        "beta.kubernetes.io/os": windows
      containers:
      - name: windows-example
        image: mcr.microsoft.com/dotnet/core/samples:aspnetapp-
```

```
nanoserver-1809
      ports:
        - containerPort: 80
      volumeMounts:
      - name: secret-example-volume
        mountPath: C:\SecretExample
        readOnly: true
    volumes:
    - name: secret-example-volume
      secret:
        secretName: secret-example
```

4. Apply the manifest file using the `kubectl apply -f .\windows-example-deployment.yaml` command.

5. Determine which Windows node is running the pod using the `kubectl get pods -o wide` command. In our case, it is `2972k8s011`.

6. Follow the instructions from Chapter 8, *Deploying Hybrid Azure Kubernetes Service Engine Cluster* in the subsection *Connecting to virtual machines* in order to create a remote desktop connection to node `2972k8s011`.

7. When a command-line prompt initializes, use the `docker ps` command to identify the ID of the Docker container that runs our application. Next, run the `docker inspect -f {{.Mounts}} <containerID>` command to get the *physical* location of the Docker volume data on the *host's* disk storage:

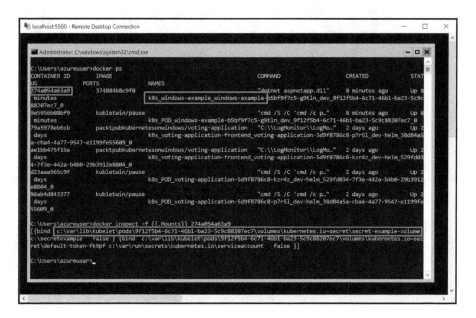

8. Now, simply use this path, check the directory contents, and use the `type` `<filePath>` command to reveal the contents of the file that maps to the `password` key in our secret object:

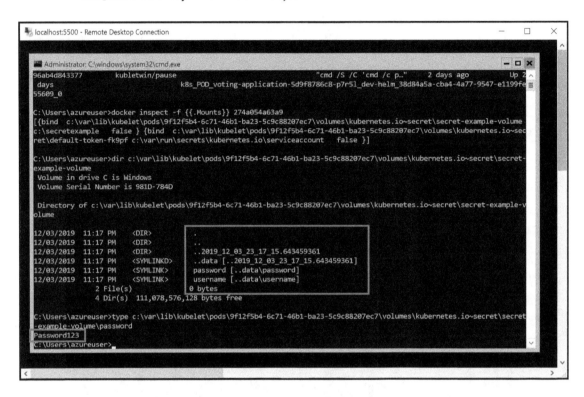

As you can see, we have retrieved the `Password123` value without any problems. On a Linux system that uses an in-memory *tmpfs* filesystem for mounting volumes into secrets, it wouldn't be that easy!

This current design has an obvious security issue: whoever manages to access the node disk storage data can get your secrets (currently used) in *plain-text*. This concerns not only the access to the machine itself (physical or remote) but also the *backups* of your disks that store Docker volumes.

To mitigate this issue, at least to some extent, you should use *disk encryption* for the Windows node disks. In an on-premises scenario, you can consider using BitLocker, which has native support on the Windows server operating system; you can find more details in the official documentation at https://docs.microsoft.com/en-us/windows/security/information-protection/bitlocker/bitlocker-how-to-deploy-on-windows-server.

For Azure deployments, the good news is that Azure VM disks are always *encrypted at rest in Azure data centers*. If your scenario requires you to provide encryption at VM-operating-system level, then this feature is not supported yet for managed AKS (`https://github.com/Azure/AKS/issues/629`), and, in the case of AKS Engine, the node VMs are created by default without encryption (you cannot control them in the cluster apimodel), but you can enable it manually yourself. You can read more about scenarios for Windows VM encryption in the official documentation at `https://docs.microsoft.com/en-us/azure/virtual-machines/windows/disk-encryption-windows`.

To demonstrate how you can encrypt the Windows node disks manually, let's turn on encryption for one of the nodes in our cluster, `2972k8s011`:

1. Open the PowerShell window and create an Azure key vault named `AksEngineEncryptionVault`:

   ```
   az keyvault create `
       --resource-group "aks-engine-windows-resource-group" `
       --name "AksEngineEncryptionVault" `
       --location "westeurope"
   ```

2. Enable the usage of the key vault for disk encryption for Azure VMs:

   ```
   az keyvault update `
       --resource-group "aks-engine-windows-resource-group" `
       --name "AksEngineEncryptionVault" `
       --enabled-for-disk-encryption "true"
   ```

3. Enable encryption of the `2972k8s011` node for `All` disks mounted to the VM:

   ```
   az vm encryption enable `
       --resource-group "aks-engine-windows-resource-group" `
       --name "2972k8s011" `
       --disk-encryption-keyvault "AksEngineEncryptionVault" `
       --volume-type All
   ```

4. When the encryption process is finished, check the current status of the encryption feature:

   ```
   PS C:\src> az vm encryption show `
   >>                 --resource-group "aks-engine-windows-resource-group"
   `
   >>                 --name "2972k8s011"
   {
     "disks": [
       {
         . . .
   ```

```
        "name":
"2972k8s011_OsDisk_1_1986c424c52c46a39192cdc68c9b9cb9",
        "statuses": [
          {
            "code": "EncryptionState/encrypted",
            "displayStatus": "Encryption is enabled on disk",
            "level": "Info",
            "message": null,
            "time": null
          }
        ]
      }
    ]
  }
```

This process would have to be repeated for all Windows nodes in the cluster and repeated whenever you scale your cluster.

Congratulations! You have successfully encrypted a Windows node disk in order to increase Kubernetes secret security.

Summary

This chapter has focused on Kubernetes security in general. We have provided you with 11 recommendations and best practices for securing your Kubernetes cluster, from using RBAC and integrating an external authentication provider, such as Azure Active Directory, to disabling public access for the Kubernetes API and Dashboard and enabling audit logging. We demonstrated how to make your RBAC management and authentication easier on AKS Engine clusters using Azure Active Directory integration. Next, we discussed how to secure container runtime in Kubernetes and the role of network policies (which are not supported on Windows nodes yet).

And lastly, you learned the differences between the injection of Kubernetes secrets on Linux and Windows machines and saw that, with the current design, accessing secrets on Windows machines is easier and can cause security problems. To mitigate this, we showed you how you can encrypt disks for Azure VMs that are used as Windows nodes in your cluster.

In the next chapter, we will focus on how to approach the monitoring of Kubernetes clusters, especially Windows nodes and .NET applications running on Windows nodes.

Questions

1. Why should you use an external authentication provider in Kubernetes, such as AAD?
2. Why is disabling public access to Kubernetes Dashboard important?
3. What is the reason for recommending the encryption of etcd data storage at rest?
4. Can you run privileged containers on Windows machines?
5. What are network policies in Kubernetes and what are the prerequisites to have them enabled?
6. What is the main difference between Linux and Windows nodes when it comes to mounting secrets as volumes?
7. Why is injecting secrets as environment variables considered less safe than using volumes, especially on Linux nodes?

You can find answers to these questions in *Assessments* of this book.

Further reading

- For more information about Kubernetes security, please refer to the following PacktPub books:
  - *The Complete Kubernetes Guide* (https://www.packtpub.com/virtualization-and-cloud/complete-kubernetes-guide).
  - *Getting Started with Kubernetes - Third Edition* (https://www.packtpub.com/virtualization-and-cloud/getting-started-kubernetes-third-edition).
  - *Kubernetes for Developers* (https://www.packtpub.com/virtualization-and-cloud/kubernetes-developers).

14
Monitoring Kubernetes Applications Using Prometheus

Kubernetes as a containers orchestrator is a complex, distributed system that requires monitoring and alerting to function properly at scale. At the same time, you need to monitor your applications running on Kubernetes in the same manner—if you do not have monitoring and alerting in place, you have no idea how your application behaves, whether any failures occur, or whether you should scale up your workload. In fact, the challenges connected with monitoring and alerting are among the most often-reported blockers for the adoption of Kubernetes by enterprises.

Fortunately, over the years, the market has boomed with multiple solutions for log aggregation, telemetry gathering, alerting, and even dedicated **Application Performance Management** (**APM**) systems. We can choose from different Software-as-a-Service (**SaaS**) solutions or open source systems that can be hosted on-premises, all dedicated just for Kubernetes clusters!

But there is the other side of the coin: we are constrained to solutions that can support Windows containers and Windows-based Kubernetes nodes. Production-grade support for Windows in Kubernetes is very recent and there are no turnkey solutions that work just out of the box. Therefore, this chapter aims to provide an overview of the available monitoring solutions for Kubernetes in general and explore how you can implement your own solution that supports Windows nodes.

In this chapter, we will cover the following topics:

- Available monitoring solutions
- Provisioning observable Windows nodes
- Deploying Prometheus using a Helm chart
- Windows Performance Counters
- Monitoring .NET applications using `prometheus-net`
- Configuring dashboards and alerts in Grafana

Technical requirements

For this chapter, you will need the following:

- Windows 10 Pro, Enterprise, or Education (version 1903 or later, 64-bit) installed
- Microsoft Visual Studio 2019 Community (or any other edition) if you want to edit the source code for the application and debug it—Visual Studio Code has limited support for classic .NET Framework
- Helm installed
- An Azure account
- A Windows/Linux Kubernetes cluster deployed using AKS Engine, ready to deploy the voting application from the previous chapter

To follow along, you will need your own Azure account to create Azure resources for the Kubernetes cluster. If you haven't already created the account for the previous chapters, you can read more about how to obtain a limited free account for personal use here: https://azure.microsoft.com/en-us/free/.

Deploying a Kubernetes cluster using AKS Engine has been covered in Chapter 8, *Deploying a Hybrid Azure Kubernetes Service Engine Cluster*. The voting application Deployment to Kubernetes has been covered in Chapter 10, *Deploying Microsoft SQL Server 2019 and ASP.NET MVC Application*.

You can download the latest code samples for this chapter from the official GitHub repository: https://github.com/PacktPublishing/Hands-On-Kubernetes-on-Windows/tree/master/Chapter14.

Available monitoring solutions

The word monitoring is commonly used as an umbrella term that covers the following:

- **Observability**: Providing observability for your components means exposing information about their inner state so that you can access the data easily and do reasoning about the actual state of your components. In other words, if something is observable, you can understand it. A well-known example of a feature that provides observability is logging. Your applications produce logs so that you can examine the flow and the current state of your application. There are three pillars of observability: logging, distributed tracing, and metrics. Distributed tracing provides insight into the flow of a request going through multiple services, for example, using correlation IDs. Metrics can be just numeric information exposed by your application, for example, counters or gauges.
- **Monitoring:** This means collecting observable data for your components and storing it so that it can be analyzed.
- **Analysis and Alerting:** Based on collected monitoring data, you can perform analysis, create rules when a component is considered unhealthy, and configure alerting for your team. More complex scenarios involve, for example, anomaly detection and machine learning.

In Kubernetes, monitoring has even more dimensions than monitoring a single application. Generally, you can divide the monitoring of a Kubernetes cluster into the following separate areas:

- Monitoring hardware and operating system infrastructure of Kubernetes nodes
- Monitoring container runtime
- Monitoring Kubernetes components and resources themselves
- Monitoring containerized applications running in the cluster

And finally, you can look at monitoring systems from the perspective of how the solution is hosted and related to Kubernetes:

- **On-premises monitoring**: Using your own cloud or bare-metal infrastructure, you either provide a separate cluster just for running monitoring tools or use the same cluster as for applications. The second solution is much easier but can be considered only for small Kubernetes clusters. You want to separate application and monitoring workloads; you especially don't want monitoring to negatively influence your application's performance. An example of this approach is deploying your own Prometheus (`https://prometheus.io/`) instance to collect metrics in your Kubernetes cluster, together with a log analytics solution such as the **Elasticsearch, Logstash, Kibana (ELK)** stack (`https://www.elastic.co/what-is/elk-stack`).
- **Internal SaaS monitoring**: If you are running in the cloud, you can use SaaS offerings provided by your cloud service provider, for example, on Azure, you can use Azure Monitor (`https://azure.microsoft.com/en-us/services/monitor/`). Such solutions often easily integrate with other managed services, such as AKS. Additionally, for log monitoring, you can leverage Log Analytics in Azure Monitor (`https://docs.microsoft.com/en-us/azure/azure-monitor/log-query/get-started-portal`).
- **External SaaS monitoring**: In this case, you use a dedicated, generic SaaS offering from an external company that can monitor your cluster running in any cloud or even on-premises. The market of monitoring platforms is big—well-known examples are New Relic (`https://newrelic.com/platform`) and Dynatrace (`https://www.dynatrace.com/technologies/kubernetes-monitoring/`).

Generally, using internal SaaS monitoring is cheaper than external SaaS but you risk more vendor lock-in and increase your dependency on a given cloud service provider. Using on-premises monitoring, which you deploy yourself, is the most flexible and cheapest, but you have to consider the management and operations overhead that comes with an additional large application.

There is still the question of what to monitor. You can learn more about the Four Golden Signals in the following online book from Google: `https://landing.google.com/sre/sre-book/chapters/monitoring-distributed-systems/`. Find out about the **USE** (short for **Utilization Saturation and Errors**) method in the following article: `http://www.brendangregg.com/usemethod.html`.

And now, hybrid Windows/Linux Kubernetes clusters come into the picture. It is important to know that monitoring Windows machines is quite different from monitoring Linux machines—you cannot use the same monitoring agents; they have to be dedicated to a given operating system.

Even in the case of Docker, the way it integrates into the operating system is different from Linux and Windows, which also means that the container runtime monitoring must be done differently. This is the reason why currently there are no turnkey solutions for monitoring Windows nodes in Kubernetes. The closest to providing this is the Container Monitoring solution in Azure Monitor (`https://docs.microsoft.com/en-us/azure/azure-monitor/insights/containers`), which can provide telemetry data for Windows containers but does not integrate with hybrid AKS or AKS Engine yet. You can still, of course, configure it manually on the machines that are part of AKS Engine.

So, what other solution do we have? As a more generic solution, we propose deploying a Prometheus instance that will be able to monitor metrics from Linux workloads by default and can be extended to monitor Windows nodes and containers.

 Distributed tracing and aggregating logs in your cluster are complex monitoring topics on their own. In this book, we will cover metrics monitoring only. If you are interested in logging solutions for Kubernetes, please check the official documentation: `https://kubernetes.io/docs/concepts/cluster-administration/logging/`. For distributed tracing, consider reading about Jaeger: `https://www.jaegertracing.io/`.

Let's take a look at how we can provide metric monitoring for hybrid Kubernetes clusters using Prometheus.

Prometheus and monitoring Windows nodes

Prometheus (`https://prometheus.io/`) is an open source monitoring system for metrics, which uses the PromQL language for exploring time series data. It utilizes the concept of exporters and the HTTP pull model where exporters expose the data on a specified HTTP endpoint and are periodically scraped by the Prometheus server. Alternatively, it can use the HTTP push model, which is generally not recommended but sometimes useful. The format used for exposing metrics is a simple text format where each line represents one value of a metric, which has roughly the following form:

```
http_requests_total{method="post",code="200"} 190
http_requests_total{method="post",code="400"} 5
```

Prometheus stores all data as time series, which are streams of readings for the same metric throughout the time—the exporters expose only the current value of a metric and Prometheus is responsible for storing the history as a time series. In this example, `http_requests_total` is the name of the metric, `method` is a label name, `"post"` is the label value, and `190` is the value of the metric right now. Labels are used for providing dimensions for your time series data, which can then be used for various operations such as filtering and aggregating in PromQL. The general format for a single reading is `<metric name>{<label name>=<label value>, ...}` `<metric_value>`.

You can read more about this format in the official documentation: `https://github.com/` `prometheus/docs/blob/master/content/docs/instrumenting/exposition_formats.md`.

On top of Prometheus, you will commonly use Alertmanager for configuring alerting and Grafana (`https://grafana.com/`) or Kibana (`https://www.elastic.co/products/kibana`) for dashboards and visualizations. The following diagram shows the architecture of Prometheus at a high level and how it monitors Linux workloads running in Kubernetes:

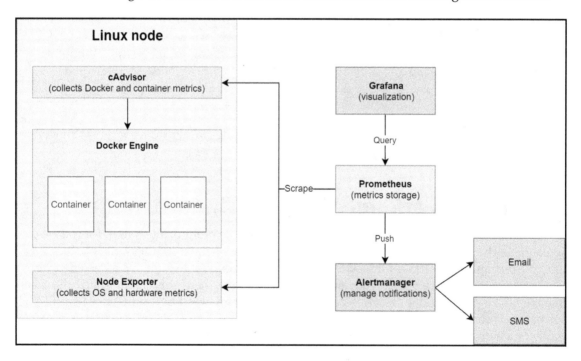

Common Prometheus architecture for monitoring Linux containers on Kubernetes

Apart from standard Prometheus components, there are two key exporters running on each Linux node in the cluster: **cAdvisor**, which exposes container runtime metrics, and **Node Exporter**, which is responsible for exposing the operating system and hardware metrics. For Windows, we can use a similar scheme but we need to use different exporters, as shown in the following diagram:

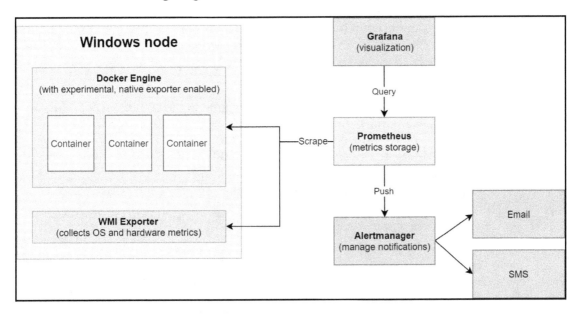

Possible Prometheus architecture for monitoring Windows containers on Kubernetes

In this case, to expose OS and hardware metrics, we use WMI Exporter, which is dedicated to Windows machines. It can also expose some Docker metrics, but we additionally can turn on the experimental feature of exposing metrics with Docker Engine natively, without an additional exporter. You can read more about this Docker feature in the documentation: `https://docs.docker.com/config/thirdparty/prometheus/`.

Generally, on Windows, it is more problematic to deploy exporters as Kubernetes DaemonSets that gather OS metrics. As mentioned in the previous chapters, on Windows, you cannot run privileged containers so you will not have access to container runtime information. This is the main reason why monitoring Windows containers in Kubernetes is a bit harder than Linux containers—we have to configure the exporters outside of the Kubernetes cluster, directly on the host. Now, let's see how you can achieve that in an on-premises scenario and AKS Engine.

Provisioning observable Windows nodes

The HTTP pull model that Prometheus uses perfectly aligns with the separation of concerns between observability and monitoring itself. The component or machine is responsible for exposing appropriate data and metrics—it allows being observed—and Prometheus periodically consumes the available data in the process called scraping. This means that if you have a way of exposing metrics in Prometheus format at some HTTP endpoint, you can use Prometheus for monitoring! It can be hardware telemetry exposed by a system service or even your own metrics accessible by an additional HTTP endpoint in your .NET application.

Now, there is the question of how to gather the metrics data on the Windows operating system and expose it. We are interested in the following:

- Hardware-related metrics, for example, CPU, memory, network, and I/O metrics for the host machine
- Metrics for processes and the host operating system itself and performance counters in general
- Metrics for the container runtime itself
- Metrics for individual containers
- In the case of bare-metal machines, additionally, information about hardware metrics such as CPU temperature and ECC memory correction counts

For Prometheus, the support for exporters on Windows is still expanding but currently, we can already collect most of the preceding metrics. In general, WMI Exporter (`https://github.com/martinlindhe/wmi_exporter`) is the recommended exporter for collecting all hardware-related and OS-related metrics on Windows. For the Docker runtime and containers, we can use an experimental feature of Docker (`https://docs.docker.com/config/thirdparty/prometheus/`) that enables exposing the metrics in Prometheus format. Additionally, WMI Exporter can expose some useful Docker containers metrics when the container collector is enabled in the configuration.

If you are interested in any other Windows Performance Counters, you can use Telegraf (`https://www.influxdata.com/time-series-platform/telegraf/`) to expose them as metrics in Prometheus format. We will do that in the next sections as there are very valid use cases for monitoring Windows Performance Counters on the host as well as inside a container.

Installing WMI Exporter and enabling Metrics Server in Docker

Now, we know a bit of the theory of how to make a Windows machine observable for Prometheus and which components can fulfill our requirements. The installation of WMI Exporter is fairly simple if you use Chocolatey:

```
choco install prometheus-wmi-exporter.install
```

This command will install the exporter with the default configuration and expose the metrics at the endpoint, `http://0.0.0.0:9182`, as described in the documentation for the package: `https://chocolatey.org/packages/prometheus-wmi-exporter.install`. For our use case, we need some specific collectors enabled and this information can be passed to the installer as a parameter. Additionally, we should make the installation unattended and install Chocolatey if it is missing on the machine—our PowerShell script would look like the following:

```
if ((Get-Command "choco" -ErrorAction SilentlyContinue) -eq $null) {
    Invoke-Expression ((new-object
net.webclient).DownloadString('https://chocolatey.org/install.ps1')) | Out-
Null
}

choco install prometheus-wmi-exporter.install -y --force --params
"`"/EnabledCollectors:cpu,cs,container,dns,logical_disk,logon,memory,net,os
,process,service,system,tcp`""
```

To enable Metrics Server, in Docker Engine at `http://0.0.0.0:9323`, we can create another small PowerShell script:

```
Set-Content -Value '{ "metrics-addr" : "0.0.0.0:9323", "experimental" :
true }' -Path C:\ProgramData\docker\config\daemon.json
Restart-Service Docker -Force
```

Now, you have to consider how you are going to perform the installation. For on-premises Deployments, consider the following:

- If you use automation for creating your Kubernetes cluster, for example, Ansible, then you can add additional post-configuration steps.
- If you use bare-metal images or VM images for your machines in the cluster, you can embed the installation steps in the image provisioning process.
- If you manage your machines using Ansible or PowerShell Desired State Configuration, you can also trigger the installation using these tools.

In the case of cloud Deployments, everything depends on whether you are using managed or unmanaged clusters:

- For managed Deployments such as AKS, you are limited to what the service allows; for example, you can use VMSS with Custom Script Extensions.
- For unmanaged Deployments, you can use the same techniques as for on-premises Deployments, for example, providing a custom VM image with preinstalled services, or use solutions specifically for your cloud service provider.

For AKS Engine specifically, you have three options:

- For development and testing purposes, you can use RDP or SSH to connect to the Windows machine and perform the installation manually.
- You can use a custom VM image for Windows nodes (`https://github.com/Azure/aks-engine/blob/master/docs/topics/windows-vhd.md`).
- You can use AKS Engine extensions (`https://github.com/Azure/aks-engine/blob/master/docs/topics/extensions.md`), which are implemented as Custom Script Extensions running as a part of the Deployment.

We are going to demonstrate how you can customize your AKS Engine cluster Deployment using a dedicated extension.

Using extensions for AKS Engine

AKS Engine extensions are a feature that enables additional customization steps as post-provisioning steps in the Deployment. For example, you can execute any PowerShell script that you provide through the extensions repository. The repository can be any HTTP server that follows a convention in directory naming—this also includes raw GitHub repository access endpoints. To learn more about how the extensions work, please refer to the official documentation: `https://github.com/Azure/aks-engine/blob/master/docs/topics/extensions.md`. You can use the `winrm` extension as a good base to understand the implementation details: `https://github.com/Azure/aks-engine/tree/master/extensions/winrm`.

Using extensions is possible during the cluster Deployment only. You cannot enable an extension on a running cluster. Additionally, due to the SQL Server Helm chart requiring four volumes to be mounted on a single node, we need to use a larger VM type for Linux nodes, for example, Standard_D4_v3, which supports up to eight volumes. You can read more about the maximum number of volumes mounted per VM in the documentation: https://docs.microsoft.com/en-us/azure/virtual-machines/windows/sizes-general.

In the GitHub repository for this book, you can find an extension that installs WMI Exporter and enables Docker Metrics Server on Windows: https://github.com/PacktPublishing/Hands-On-Kubernetes-on-Windows/tree/master/Chapter14/03_aks-engine-windows-extensions/extensions/prometheus-exporters. Let's see how the extension is built and how to deploy a new AKS Engine cluster with the extension:

1. The PowerShell script, v1/installExporters.ps1, performs the custom installation logic and has the following contents:

```
Param(
    [Parameter()]
    [string]$PackageParameters =
"/EnabledCollectors:cpu,cs,container,dns,logical_disk,logon,memory,
net,os,process,service,system,tcp"
)

if ((Get-Command "choco" -ErrorAction SilentlyContinue) -eq $null)
{
    Invoke-Expression ((new-object
net.webclient).DownloadString('https://chocolatey.org/install.ps1')
) | Out-Null
}

choco install prometheus-wmi-exporter.install -y --force --params
"`"$PackageParameters`""

Set-Content -Value '{ "metrics-addr" : "0.0.0.0:9323",
"experimental" : true }' -Path
C:\ProgramData\docker\config\daemon.json
Restart-Service Docker -Force
```

It will install WMI Exporter using Chocolatey, enable the Metrics Server for Docker, and restart Docker afterward.

2. The `v1/template.json` JSON file contains an ARM template that triggers the PowerShell script, the key part of which is as follows:

```
"properties": {
    "publisher": "Microsoft.Compute",
    "type": "CustomScriptExtension",
    "typeHandlerVersion": "1.8",
    "autoUpgradeMinorVersion": true,
    "settings": {
      "fileUris": [
        "[concat(parameters('artifactsLocation'),
'extensions/prometheus-exporters/v1/installExporters.ps1')]"
      ]
    },
    "protectedSettings": {
      "commandToExecute": "[concat('powershell.exe -
ExecutionPolicy bypass \"& ./installExporters.ps1 -
PackageParameters ', parameters('extensionParameters'), '\"')]"
    }
}
```

This configures properties for the Custom Script Extension, which will download the installation script and execute it with parameters that you pass in the cluster apimodel.

3. `v1/template-link.json` is a generic file that has placeholders to be replaced by AKS Engine. In this way, your template will be linked to the Deployment.

4. Now, create a GitHub repository and push the extension. Ensure that you follow the directory naming convention, for example, the full path in the repository to `template.json` should be `extensions/prometheus-exporters/v1/template.json`. In the examples, we are going to use the following GitHub repository: https://github.com/ptylenda/aks-engine-windows-extensions.

5. Now, modify your AKS Engine cluster apimodel so that it uses the extension for all Windows nodes (https://github.com/PacktPublishing/Hands-On-Kubernetes-on-Windows/blob/master/Chapter14/04_aks-engine-cluster-with-extensions/kubernetes-windows-template.json) and ensure that you are using `vmSize` for the Linux node pool, which is capable of mounting more than four volumes:

```
{
  "apiVersion": "vlabs",
  "properties":
    ...
    "agentPoolProfiles": [
```

```
{
  "name": "linuxpool1",
  "vmSize": "Standard_D4_v3"
  ...
},
{
  "name": "windowspool2",
  ...
  "extensions": [
      {
          "name": "prometheus-exporters",
          "singleOrAll": "all"
      }
  ]
}
],
...
"extensionProfiles": [
  {
  "name": "prometheus-exporters",
  "version": "v1",
  "rootURL":
"https://raw.githubusercontent.com/ptylenda/aks-engine-windows-exte
nsions/master/",
      "extensionParameters":
"'/EnabledCollectors:cpu,cs,container,dns,logical_disk,logon,memory
,net,os,process,service,system,tcp'"
  }
  ]
  }
}
```

As `rootURL`, you need to provide the HTTP address for raw access to your GitHub repository with the extension. Additionally, we are passing `'/EnabledCollectors:cpu,cs,container,dns,logical_disk,logon,memory,net,os,process,service,system,tcp'` as parameters to the extension, which will be used when executing the PowerShell script.

6. Now, deploy the cluster in the same way as in the previous chapters. You can also use our usual PowerShell script: `https://github.com/PacktPublishing/Hands-On-Kubernetes-on-Windows/blob/master/Chapter14/04_aks-engine-cluster-with-extensions/CreateAKSEngineClusterWithWindowsNodes.ps1`.

7. When the Deployment is finished, use the `kubectl get nodes -o wide` command to determine the private IP of one of your Windows nodes, for example, `10.240.0.65`.

8. SSH to the master node using the `ssh`
   `azureuser@<dnsPrefix>.<azureLocation>.cloudapp.azure.com` comma
   nd and check whether the Windows node exports metrics on ports `9323`
   and `9182`:

```
azureuser@k8s-master-36012248-0:~$ curl
http://10.240.0.65:9323/metrics
# HELP builder_builds_failed_total Number of failed image builds
# TYPE builder_builds_failed_total counter
builder_builds_failed_total{reason="build_canceled"} 0
builder_builds_failed_total{reason="build_target_not_reachable_erro
r"} 0
builder_builds_failed_total{reason="command_not_supported_error"} 0
...
azureuser@k8s-master-36012248-0:~$ curl
http://10.240.0.65:9182/metrics
# HELP go_gc_duration_seconds A summary of the GC invocation
durations.
# TYPE go_gc_duration_seconds summary
go_gc_duration_seconds{quantile="0"} 0
go_gc_duration_seconds{quantile="0.25"} 0
go_gc_duration_seconds{quantile="0.5"} 0
...
```

Congratulations! Now your Windows nodes in AKS Engine cluster are exposing metrics that can be scraped by Prometheus. In the next section, we will install Prometheus in our cluster and configure it to monitor both Linux and Windows nodes.

Deploying Prometheus using a Helm chart

Our cluster infrastructure is now observable—we can deploy Prometheus with appropriate configuration files and start monitoring the cluster. To deploy Prometheus, we have several options:

- Deploy it manually using multiple manifest files.
- Use the `stable/prometheus` Helm chart (`https://github.com/helm/charts/tree/master/stable/prometheus`). This chart provides Prometheus, Alertmanager, Pushgateway, Node Exporter (for Linux nodes), and kube-state-metrics.

- Use the `stable/prometheus-operator` Helm chart (`https://github.com/helm/charts/tree/master/stable/prometheus-operator`) or `kube-prometheus` (`https://github.com/coreos/kube-prometheus`). These solutions aim at providing a way to quickly provision multiple Prometheus clusters in your Kubernetes cluster.

In our case, the best choice is to use the `stable/prometheus` Helm chart as it requires minimum configuration and is not as complex as the generic Prometheus Operator. In production environments, running at a large scale, you should definitely consider using Prometheus Operator so that you can easily deploy multiple Prometheus clusters for different needs.

Installing Helm charts

To deploy Prometheus using Helm chart, perform the following steps:

1. We are going to deploy our monitoring solution in a separate namespace named `monitoring`. Additionally, we need `StorageClass` defined for Prometheus data persistence. Create the `prereq.yaml` manifest file with the following contents:

   ```
   ---
   kind: Namespace
   apiVersion: v1
   metadata:
     name: monitoring
     labels:
       name: monitoring
   ---
   kind: StorageClass
   apiVersion: storage.k8s.io/v1beta1
   metadata:
     name: azure-disk
   provisioner: kubernetes.io/azure-disk
   parameters:
     storageaccounttype: Standard_LRS
     kind: Managed
   ```

2. Apply the manifest file using the `kubectl apply -f .\prereq.yaml` command.

3. Now, we need to define values for the `stable/prometheus` Helm chart (`https://github.com/prometheus/prometheus`). This chart is highly configurable, so check whether you need to override any additional values. Create the `helm-values_prometheus.yaml` file and start editing it with the following contents (`https://github.com/PacktPublishing/Hands-On-Kubernetes-on-Windows/blob/master/Chapter14/05_helm_prometheus/helm-values_prometheus.yaml`):

```
server:
  enabled: true
  global:
    scrape_interval: 50s
    scrape_timeout: 15s
    evaluation_interval: 1m
  service:
    type: LoadBalancer
  nodeSelector:
    "kubernetes.io/os": linux
  persistentVolume:
    storageClass: azure-disk

alertmanager:
  enabled: true
  service:
    type: LoadBalancer
  nodeSelector:
    "kubernetes.io/os": linux
  persistentVolume:
    storageClass: azure-disk

nodeExporter:
  enabled: true
  nodeSelector:
    "kubernetes.io/os": linux

pushgateway:
  enabled: true
  nodeSelector:
    "kubernetes.io/os": linux

kubeStateMetrics:
  enabled: true
  nodeSelector:
    "kubernetes.io/os": linux
```

The most important part is ensuring that the proper `nodeSelector` is set for all components so that the Pods do not get accidentally scheduled on Windows machines. Additionally, we need to provide the name of `storageClass`, which will be used for handling PVCs. Another solution could be setting `azure-disk` as the default `storageClass` in the cluster. In the Helm chart configuration, you can also influence scraping settings, such as how often you would like to execute the scrape jobs. And finally, we are exposing both Prometheus and Alertmanager using the `LoadBalancer` Service—this is, of course, valid only for development and testing purposes in order not to use `kubectl proxy` (which requires additional configuration for Grafana) or use jump boxes.

For production scenarios, consider either limiting access to Prometheus to a private network or expose it behind Ingress, use HTTPS, and provide a safe authentication method. For example, you can integrate Nginx Ingress with Azure Active Directory (`https://kubernetes.github.io/ingress-nginx/examples/auth/oauth-external-auth/`).

Be careful when setting small `scrape_interval` values. Scraping in too short intervals may cause excessive load for your nodes and Pods and result in instability of the system. You should always evaluate how expensive your exporters are in terms of CPU usage and RAM memory.

4. Continue editing the `helm-values_prometheus.yaml` file and provide scraping configuration for Prometheus. We need to ensure that our WMI Exporter and Docker Engine metrics server are scraped by the Prometheus server. You can see the following configuration for the Docker Engine metrics server only; the configuration for WMI Exporter is almost the same apart from the port number:

```
extraScrapeConfigs: |
  - job_name: windows-nodes-docker-metrics-server
    kubernetes_sd_configs:
      - role: node
    scheme: http
    relabel_configs:
    - action: labelmap
      regex: __meta_kubernetes_node_label_(.+)
    - source_labels: [__address__]
      action: replace
      target_label: __address__
      regex: ([^:;]+):(\d+)
      replacement: ${1}:9323
    - source_labels: [kubernetes_io_os]
      action: keep
```

```
        regex: windows
      - source_labels: [__meta_kubernetes_node_name]
        regex: (.+)
        target_label: __metrics_path__
        replacement: /metrics
      - source_labels: [__meta_kubernetes_node_name]
        action: replace
        target_label: node
        regex: (.*)
        replacement: ${1}
    ...
```

Prometheus scrape configurations can get a bit complex; you can check the official documentation for a detailed explanation: `https://prometheus.io/docs/prometheus/latest/configuration/configuration/`. The basic configuration scrapes API resources that are annotated with `prometheus.io/scrape:'true'`, so, for example, if you want your own application Pod to be scraped, you need to use this annotation (together with `prometheus.io/port`). Additionally, you can configure scraping based on API resources directly (`kubernetes_sd_configs`), in this case, `node`. After that, we perform various operations on the labels that were returned by the API for the node: we ensure that the final value of the `__address__` special label contains the required `9323` port, and we define `__metrics_path__` as `/metrics` so in the end, we will be scraping this HTTP endpoint: `http://<nodeAddress>:9323/metrics`.

5. Use the `values` file to install the Helm chart for Prometheus as the `prometheus` release:

```
helm install prometheus stable/prometheus -n monitoring --values
.\helm-values_prometheus.yaml --debug
```

6. While the installation proceeds, you can already define the `helm-values_grafana.yaml` values file for the `stable/grafana` Helm chart, which we are going to use to deploy Grafana for Prometheus:

```
nodeSelector:
  "kubernetes.io/os": linux

service:
  type: LoadBalancer

persistence:
  enabled: true
  storageClassName: azure-disk
  size: 20Gi
```

```
    accessModes:
      - ReadWriteOnce

adminUser: admin
adminPassword: P@ssword

datasources:
  datasources.yaml:
    apiVersion: 1
    datasources:
    - name: Prometheus
      type: prometheus
      url: http://prometheus-server
      access: proxy
      isDefault: true
```

Similarly, we need to ensure that Grafana is scheduled on Linux nodes only. Again, we expose the Service using load balancer—you should consider a different strategy for production Deployments or at least provide proper authentication for this public endpoint. The last important thing is ensuring that our Prometheus instance is added as the default data source in Grafana. Here, you should use the Service name to use discovery via the DNS name.

7. Install the `stable/grafana` Helm chart as the `grafana` release using the following command:

```
helm install grafana stable/grafana -n monitoring --values .\helm-
values_grafana.yaml --debug
```

8. Now, wait for all Pods to be ready and services to receive external IPs:

```
PS C:\src> kubectl get pod,svc -n monitoring
...
NAME                                        TYPE           CLUSTER-IP
EXTERNAL-IP      PORT(S)          AGE
service/grafana                             LoadBalancer   10.0.28.94
104.40.19.54    80:30836/TCP     2h
service/prometheus-alertmanager             LoadBalancer   10.0.0.229
40.78.81.58     80:30073/TCP     2h
service/prometheus-server                   LoadBalancer   10.0.219.93
40.78.42.14     80:32763/TCP     2h
...
```

At this point, you have three web UIs that you can access:

- The Prometheus server (in our example, accessible at `http://40.78.42.14`)
- Alertmanager (`http://40.78.81.58`)
- Grafana (`http://104.40.19.54`)

Verifying the Deployment

Verify whether you can access your external IPs for the Services and perform some basic operations:

1. Open the web UI for your Prometheus server.
2. Navigate to **Status** and choose **Targets**.
3. Scroll down to the `windows-nodes-docker-metrics-server` and `windows-nodes-wmi-exporter targets` scraped by the jobs. They should be green and be executed without errors—if this is not the case, you need to verify your scraping configuration. For debugging purposes, you can introduce changes directly to the appropriate ConfigMap in the cluster:

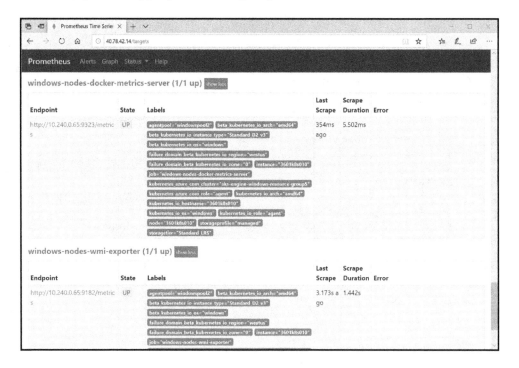

4. Navigate to **Graph** in the menu at the top and switch to the **Graph** tab below the **Execute** button. Run an example query, `rate(wmi_net_bytes_total[60s])`, which plots the average number of bytes received by and sent to Windows nodes per seconds based on the last 60 seconds of the `wmi_net_bytes_total` counter metric:

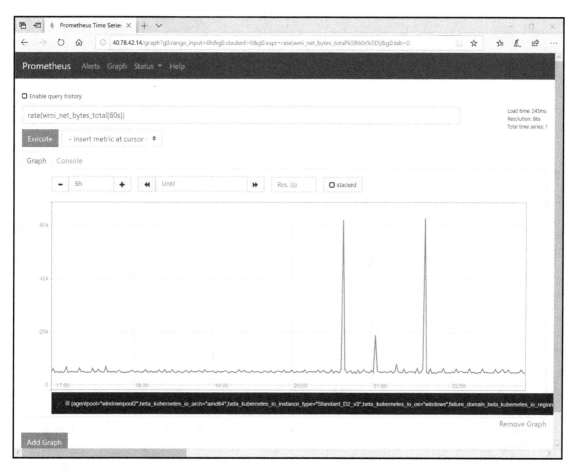

5. Open the Grafana web UI and log in with the credentials that you provided in the Helm chart.
6. Click + in the menu and choose **Dashboard**, then select **Add Query**.

7. Enter an example PromQL query, `wmi_memory_available_bytes / (1024 * 1024 * 1024)`, which will plot the available memory on Windows nodes in GB:

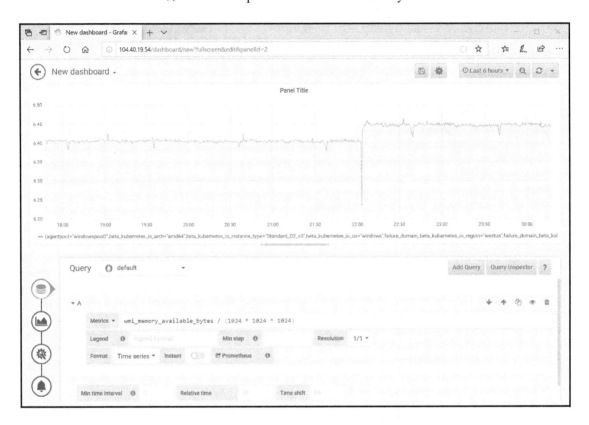

Now, we have a confirmation that our monitoring setup is working correctly! You can explore PromQL in depth in the official documentation: `https://prometheus.io/docs/prometheus/latest/querying/basics/`. It is a broad and powerful language that can implement most of your **Service Level Indicators** (**SLIs**) to monitor your **Service Level Objectives** (**SLOs**).

In the next section, we will explore how you can configure exporting of any Windows Performance Counter using Telegraf.

Windows Performance Counters

Windows provides a feature called Performance Counters, which are used to provide information on how well the operating system, service, application, or driver is performing. Normally, you use **Windows Management Instrumentation** (**WMI**) to get individual metrics values and use more advanced applications such as Perfmon for visualizing the performance data locally. For .NET Framework applications, you can read multiple counters provided directly by the runtime; you can find a list of the counters in the documentation: `https://docs.microsoft.com/en-us/dotnet/framework/debug-trace-profile/performance-counters`. Having access to these metrics, you can easily monitor unusual spikes in the number of exceptions thrown (even without analyzing logs) or analyze garbage collection issues. On top of that, many classic .NET Framework applications expose their own Performance Counters.

For Kubernetes, in addition to the standard Performance Counters collected by WMI Exporter (custom queries are not supported yet: `https://github.com/martinlindhe/wmi_exporter/issues/87`), there are two scenarios that you can consider:

- Collecting Performance Counters for applications running in a container
- Collecting more Performance Counters from the Windows host machine

Both of these can be solved using Telegraf (`https://github.com/influxdata/telegraf`), which is a generic, extensible agent for collecting, processing, aggregating, and writing metrics. One of the input plugins that it supports is `win_perf_counter` (`https://github.com/influxdata/telegraf/tree/master/plugins/inputs/win_perf_counters`), which can collect and transform any Performance Counters available on Windows. At the same time, Telegraf is capable of exposing the collected metrics in the Prometheus format using the `prometheus_client` output plugin (`https://github.com/influxdata/telegraf/tree/master/plugins/outputs/prometheus_client`). The complete solution requires preparing a configuration file, installing Telegraf as a Windows service, and ensuring that Prometheus scrapes the new endpoint.

If you would like to collect more Performance Counters from the host machine, on AKS Engine, you can achieve it using custom extensions, exactly as we did for WMI Exporter and the Docker metrics server. We will demonstrate the first scenario: how you can enrich your Docker image so that your container running on Kubernetes exposes more metrics for Prometheus. Please note that you have to always consider whether it is a valid use case for you—embedding Telegraf in every single container in the cluster comes with increased CPU usage and RAM memory footprint. A general rule of thumb is that you should use this approach only for the key components that may require investigating complex performance problems or as an ad hoc action for debugging purposes.

Extending a Docker image with the Telegraf service

The installation process for Telegraf on Windows is simple: it requires unzipping the file, providing a proper configuration file, and registering Telegraf as a Windows service. To build a new version of Docker image for the voting application, which exposes Performance Counters at port 9273, you can use the source code from the GitHub repository (https://github.com/PacktPublishing/Hands-On-Kubernetes-on-Windows/tree/master/Chapter14/06_voting-application-telegraf) or execute the following steps on the previous version of the source code:

1. In the root directory, create a new file, telegraf.conf, which contains the Telegraf configuration. You can find the contents of this file here: https://github.com/PacktPublishing/Hands-On-Kubernetes-on-Windows/blob/master/Chapter14/06_voting-application-telegraf/telegraf.conf. We are presenting the significant parts only in the following:

```
...
[[outputs.prometheus_client]]
  listen = "0.0.0.0:9273"
  path = "/metrics"
...
[inputs.win_perf_counters]]
  UseWildcardsExpansion = false
  PrintValid = false

  [[inputs.win_perf_counters.object]]
    # Processor usage, alternative to native, reports on a per
core.
    ObjectName = "Processor"
    Instances = ["*"]
    Counters = [
      "% Idle Time",
      "% Interrupt Time",
      "% Privileged Time",
      "% User Time",
      "% Processor Time",
      "% DPC Time",
    ]
    Measurement = "win_cpu"
    # Set to true to include _Total instance when querying for all
(*).
    IncludeTotal=true
...
```

We are using the `prometheus_client` output plugin and
the `win_perf_counters` input plugin, which has a gathering of multiple
Performance Counters configured.

2. Add this file to `votingapplication.csproj` to include it in the build output.
3. Modify the `Dockerfile.production` file so that it includes the part that installs
   Telegraf, right at the beginning of the `runtime` stage:

```
. . .
FROM mcr.microsoft.com/dotnet/framework/aspnet:4.8-
windowsservercore-ltsc2019 AS runtime

WORKDIR /temp
RUN powershell -Command \
    Invoke-WebRequest
https://dl.influxdata.com/telegraf/releases/telegraf-1.12.6_windows
_amd64.zip -OutFile telegraf.zip \
  ; powershell -Command Expand-Archive -Path telegraf.zip -
DestinationPath C:\temp \
  ; Remove-Item -Path telegraf.zip \
  ; mkdir c:\telegraf \
  ; Move-Item -Path c:\temp\telegraf\telegraf.exe -Destination
c:\telegraf

WORKDIR /telegraf
RUN powershell -Command \
    mkdir telegraf.d \
  ; .\telegraf.exe --service install --config
C:\telegraf\telegraf.conf --config-directory C:\telegraf\telegraf.d
COPY telegraf.conf .
RUN powershell -Command \
    Start-Service telegraf
EXPOSE 9273

. . .
```

The preceding commands download the latest release of Telegraf, install it as a
Windows service, and provide the configuration from the previous steps.

4. Build the image with the tag 1.6.0 and push it to Docker Hub as in the previous
   chapters. In our case, it will be `packtpubkubernetesonwindows/voting-application:1.6.0`.

The Telegraf configuration can be modified at container runtime by mounting a custom ConfigMap into the `C:\telegraf\telegraf.d` directory in the container. This is a perfect use case for ConfigMaps.

Now, the Docker image is ready and it can be used in the Helm chart for the voting application.

Deploying an observable version of the voting application

To be able to scrape Performance Counters exposed by Telegraf in the container, we need to update the Helm chart to include the new tag for the Docker image and update the Pod annotations for scraping. You can find the ready Helm chart at: `https://github.com/PacktPublishing/Hands-On-Kubernetes-on-Windows/tree/master/Chapter14/07_voting-application-telegraf-helm` or follow these steps using the previous version:

1. Open a PowerShell window in the root directory of the Helm chart.
2. In the `Chart.yaml` file, increment `appVersion` to be equal with the Docker image tag `1.6.0`. Also, increment the version of the chart itself to `0.3.0`.
3. In the `templates\service.yaml` file, add `annotations` for the Service so that Prometheus can start scrapping all Pods behind the Service at port `9273`:

```
apiVersion: v1
kind: Service
metadata:
  name: {{ include "voting-application.fullname" . }}
  ...
  annotations:
    prometheus.io/scrape: "true"
    prometheus.io/port: "9273"
...
```

4. Update the `templates\deployment.yaml` file so that the voting application frontend Pod exposes port `9273` where Telegraf exports the data at the `/metrics` endpoint:

```
apiVersion: apps/v1
kind: Deployment
...
spec:
  ...
  template:
    ...
    spec:
    ...
      containers:
        - name: {{ .Chart.Name }}-frontend
          ...
          ports:
          ...
            - name: telegraf
              containerPort: 9273
              protocol: TCP
          ...
```

5. Ensure that the `dev-helm` namespace exists. Create the `dev-helm.yaml` manifest file:

```
kind: Namespace
apiVersion: v1
metadata:
  name: dev-helm
  labels:
    name: dev-helm
```

6. Apply the manifest file using the `kubectl apply -f .\dev-helm.yaml` command.

7. The Helm chart is ready to be deployed. Execute the following command in the root directory of the Helm chart for the voting application:

```
helm install voting-application . `
  --namespace dev-helm `
  --debug `
  --timeout 900s
```

Alternatively, if you have already installed a previous version of this chart in your cluster, use the `helm upgrade` command with the same arguments.

8. Wait for the Deployment to finish; you can observe the progress in another PowerShell window using the `kubectl get pods -n dev-helm -w` command.

At this point, the new version of the voting application is deployed to the cluster and Prometheus is already scraping the Pods using the `kubernetes-service-endpoints` scraping job, which is defined in the default configuration. Let's verify whether everything is working correctly:

1. Navigate in the web browser to the external IP for the voting application and create some traffic by using the website for a few minutes.
2. Open the Prometheus server external IP in the web browser, open the **Graph** panel, and change the tab to **Graph**.
3. The Telegraf configuration is set up to output all metrics with the `win_` prefix. Let's query one of these metrics, for example, `win_aspnet_app_Requests_Failed`, which is a counter for the number of failed requests in the ASP.NET application. Use the `rate(win_aspnet_app_Requests_Failed{app_kubernetes_io_name="voting-application"}[5m])` query, which gives the average per-second rate of failed requests in the last five minutes for the voting application for each Pod separately:

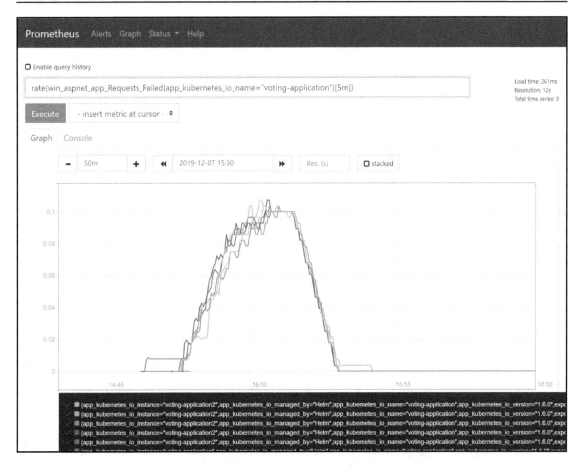

Now, you may be wondering why we see a sudden increase in the number of failed requests at some point—you will most likely see the same situation in your Prometheus. The answer is failed health checks (readiness probes) for a few minutes after deploying the Helm chart. As you probably remember, the SQL Server Helm chart requires up to 10 minutes to fully deploy. This means that, for this interval in time, the readiness probe for the voting application Pods will fail with an HTTP 500 status code.

Calculating `rate` and `irate` requires at least two data points per interval in the time series. This means that you should use the interval value at least two times larger than the scraping interval. Otherwise, you will see missing data in the graph.

You can explore the other Performance Counters that we have exposed for each Pod—this configuration of Telegraf gets a large number of counters, such as the number of exceptions thrown in .NET CLR, the number of locks in .NET CLR (this may be very useful for detecting heavy-locking scenarios!), .NET CLR garbage collection statistics, or IIS performance counters.

In the next section, we will add the last piece of the monitoring puzzle: exposing your own metrics directly from the .NET Framework application using the `prometheus-net` NuGet package.

Monitoring .NET applications using prometheus-net

As part of your monitoring infrastructure, you need to expose custom metrics, directly from your application, which provides additional instrumentation and insights into your business logic. The most popular programming languages have bindings for Prometheus—for C#, one of the libraries that provides integration with Prometheus is `prometheus-net` (`https://github.com/prometheus-net/prometheus-net`). You can use it with the classic .NET Framework and .NET Core as it is targeting .NET Standard 2.0. The features include the following:

- Exporting counters and gauges
- Measuring operation duration and creating a summary or histogram
- Tracking in-progress operations and creating gauges with the number of concurrently executed code blocks
- Exception counting

Additionally, for ASP.NET Core applications, you can use a dedicated middleware package (`https://www.nuget.org/packages/prometheus-net.AspNetCore`) to export ASP.NET metrics. Unfortunately for classic ASP.NET MVC, there is no support for this feature, but it is possible to implement a similar functionality manually.

Installing the NuGet package and adding metrics

The library is provided as a NuGet package (`https://www.nuget.org/packages/prometheus-net`). To enable `prometheus-net` in the voting application, please follow the following steps or alternatively, you can use the ready version of source code available at: `https://github.com/PacktPublishing/Hands-On-Kubernetes-on-Windows/tree/master/Chapter14/08_voting-application-prometheus-net`:

1. Open the voting application solution in Visual Studio 2019.
2. Right-click the **VotingApplication** project and choose **Manage NuGet Packages....**
3. Find the `prometheus-net` package and install it.
4. We need to start an HTTP listener for exporting metrics. In the `Global.asax.cs` file (`https://github.com/PacktPublishing/Hands-On-Kubernetes-on-Windows/blob/master/Chapter14/08_voting-application-prometheus-net/Global.asax.cs`), in the `Application_Start` method at the beginning, add the following lines:

   ```
   var server = new MetricServer(port: 9274);
   server.Start();
   ```

   This will expose the metrics at port `9274` at the `/metrics` endpoint at all network interfaces.

5. Using a custom HTTP listener inside an application running on IIS requires adding a network ACL rule to allow using this port for IIS AppPool user. Therefore, we need to extend the `Dockerfile.production` file to include the following command, for example, after Telegraf installation:

   ```
   RUN "netsh http add urlacl url=http://+:9274/metrics user=\"IIS AppPool\DefaultAppPool\""
   EXPOSE 9274
   ```

Right now, the application is exposing very basic .NET performance counters. We would like to add some custom metrics that will be specific for our voting application. As an example, we are going to add two metrics:

- **Counter**: This is for the number of votes that have been added to the database since the start of the application. We can then use the counter to, for example, calculate the average number of votes added per time interval.
- **Histogram**: This is for the duration to retrieve survey results and summarize them.

To do that, please follow the following steps:

1. In the `SurveyController` class (`https://github.com/PacktPublishing/Hands-On-Kubernetes-on-Windows/blob/master/Chapter14/08_voting-application-prometheus-net/Controllers/SurveysController.cs`), define two metrics, `DbAddedVotesCount` and `GetSurveyResultOperationDuration`, as `static readonly` fields:

    ```
    private static readonly Counter DbAddedVotesCount =
    Metrics.CreateCounter(
        "votingapplication_db_added_votes",
        "Number of votes added to the database.");

    private static readonly Histogram GetSurveyResultOperationDuration
    = Metrics.CreateHistogram(
        "votingapplication_getsurveyresult_duration_seconds",
        "Histogram for duration of GetSurveyResult operation.",
        new HistogramConfiguration { Buckets =
    Histogram.ExponentialBuckets(0.001, 1.5, 20) });
    ```

2. Increment the `DbAddedVotesCount` counter in the `Vote` controller action, just after adding each `Vote` to the database:

    ```
    . . .
        this.voteLogManager.Append(vote);
        this.db.Votes.Add(vote);
        DbAddedVotesCount.Inc();
    }
    . . .
    ```

3. Measure the time of getting survey results to create the histogram. In the `Results` Controller Action, wrap the call to `GetSurveyResult` into the `using` block and use `GetSurveyResultOperationDuration` to measure the time:

    ```
    SurveyResult result;
    using (GetSurveyResultOperationDuration.NewTimer())
    {
        result = this.GetSurveyResult(survey);
    }

    return this.View(result);
    ```

4. After these changes, at the metrics export endpoint, you will see your new metrics:

```
# HELP votingapplication_db_added_votes Number of votes added to
the database.
# TYPE votingapplication_db_added_votes counter
votingapplication_db_added_votes 3
...
# HELP votingapplication_getsurveyresult_duration_seconds Histogram
for duration of GetSurveyResult operation.
# TYPE votingapplication_getsurveyresult_duration_seconds histogram
votingapplication_getsurveyresult_duration_seconds_sum 0.5531466
votingapplication_getsurveyresult_duration_seconds_count 7
votingapplication_getsurveyresult_duration_seconds_bucket{le="0.005
"} 0
votingapplication_getsurveyresult_duration_seconds_bucket{le="0.01"
} 0
...
```

5. Build a new version of Docker image, tag it as `1.7.0`, and push to Docker Hub. We are going to use the `packtpubkubernetesonwindows/voting-application:1.7.0` Docker image in the next section.

As you can see, adding the functionality for exporting your own metrics is quite simple and self-explanatory—you do not need to introduce significant changes to your existing code base!

Now, let's deploy the new version of our application and test the new metrics.

Deploying the new version of the voting application

We have to modify the Helm chart in a similar way as we did in the last section. The Docker image has to be updated and new scraping port registered in annotations for the service—due to Prometheus not supporting multiple ports in a single scraping job (`https://github.com/prometheus/prometheus/issues/3756`), we need to add a second job which will use the new port. You can find the ready Helm chart at: `https://github.com/PacktPublishing/Hands-On-Kubernetes-on-Windows/tree/master/Chapter14/09_voting-application-prometheus-net-helm` or follow these steps using the previous version:

1. Open the PowerShell window in the root directory of the Helm chart.
2. In the `Chart.yaml` file, increment `appVersion` to be equal to the Docker image tag, `1.7.0`. Also, increment the `version` of the chart to `0.4.0`.
3. In the `templates\service.yaml` file, add a new custom annotation, `prometheus.io/secondary-port`, for the Service for port `9274`. We will use this annotation in the new scraping job:

    ```
    apiVersion: v1
    kind: Service
    metadata:
      name: {{ include "voting-application.fullname" . }}
      ...
      annotations:
        ...
        prometheus.io/secondary-port: "9274"
    ...
    ```

4. Update the `templates\deployment.yaml` file so that the voting application frontend Pod exposes port `9274` where the application exposes metrics data at the `/metrics` endpoint:

    ```
    apiVersion: apps/v1
    kind: Deployment
    ...
    spec:
      ...
      template:
        ...
        spec:
        ...
          containers:
            - name: {{ .Chart.Name }}-frontend
              ...
    ```

```
ports:
    ...
    - name: app-metrics
      containerPort: 9274
      protocol: TCP
    ...
```

5. The Helm chart is ready. The Helm release for the voting application can be upgraded—execute the following command in the root directory of the Helm chart for the voting application:

```
helm upgrade voting-application . `
    --namespace dev-helm `
    --debug `
    --timeout 900s
```

6. Wait for the Deployment to finish, you can observe the progress in another PowerShell window using the `kubectl get pods -n dev-helm -w` command.

The last step is adding a Prometheus scrape job that will handle `prometheus.io/secondary-port` annotations. In the future, it should be easier to use multiple ports for scraping, but for now, you have to add multiple jobs for such purposes:

1. In the `helm-values_prometheus.yaml` file (https://github.com/ PacktPublishing/Hands-On-Kubernetes-on-Windows/blob/master/Chapter14/ 10_helm_prometheus-net/helm-values_prometheus.yaml) for the Prometheus Helm chart, add another extra scrape job. This job should have almost exactly the same definition as the default `kubernetes-service-endpoints`, which is present in https://github.com/helm/charts/blob/master/stable/prometheus/ values.yaml but with additional filtering:

```
- job_name: kubernetes-service-endpoints-secondary-ports
  kubernetes_sd_configs:
  - role: endpoints
  relabel_configs:
  - action: keep
    regex: true
    source_labels:
    - __meta_kubernetes_service_annotation_prometheus_io_scrape
  - action: keep
    regex: (\d+)
    source_labels:
    -
__meta_kubernetes_service_annotation_prometheus_io_secondary_port
```

```
...
- action: replace
  regex: ([^:]+)(?::\d+)?;(\d+)
  replacement: $1:$2
  source_labels:
  - __address__
  -
```

__meta_kubernetes_service_annotation_prometheus_io_secondary_port
```
        target_label: __address__
```

The following actions will keep only the targets that have
the `prometheus.io/secondary-port` annotation defined and use it to define
the final `__address__` for scraping.

2. Upgrade the Helm release for Prometheus:

   ```
   helm upgrade prometheus stable/prometheus -n monitoring --values
   .\helm-values_prometheus.yaml --debug
   ```

3. When the upgrade is finished, the only resource that gets updated is the
   ConfigMap, `prometheus-server`. You need to wait a short while before
   Prometheus reloads the configuration.

4. In the Prometheus web UI, navigate to **Status** and **Targets** and verify that
   scraping of the new port works correctly; you should see the `kubernetes-`
   `service-endpoints-secondary-ports` job with a green status:

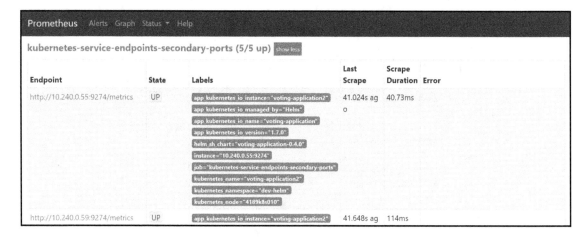

5. Open the voting application web UI and add some votes over a few minutes'
   time.

6. In the Prometheus web UI in the **Graph** tab, run an example query to verify that the solution works. For example, use `sum(votingapplication_db_added_votes)` to get the total number of votes added to the database from all Pods:

Our solution works! In this way, you can export any metrics that you define in your application code and create much more complex queries that can be used for monitoring and analysis purposes.

Now, it's time to configure a dashboard in Grafana and add some alerts.

Configuring dashboards and alerts in Grafana

The web UI of the Prometheus server is very limited and in most cases is used just for performing basic ad hoc queries and checking the configuration. To create more advanced visualizations of the data in Prometheus, you can use Grafana (`https://grafana.com/`), which is an open source analytics and monitoring solution with support for multiple databases. In the previous sections, we have already deployed Grafana using a Helm chart together with Prometheus.

Grafana offers multiple ways to visualize your monitoring data—ranging from simple **line** charts and gauges to complex heatmaps. You can find more information about how to create the visualizations in the official documentation: `https://grafana.com/docs/grafana/latest/`. For our application, we will demonstrate how to configure an example dashboard with the following visualizations:

- A line graph for CPU usage for Windows nodes
- A gauge for the average number of requests per second handled by IIS in the last 5 minutes
- A line graph showing the number of votes added to the database in the last 5 minutes
- A heatmap for visualizing the histogram of the duration of retrieving survey results

Of course, these graphs will not be enough to fully monitor your application but we would like to show the general principle of how to create the dashboards.

Adding visualizations

First, let's create the dashboard and add the first visualization for CPU usage for Windows nodes. Please perform the following steps:

1. Navigate to the Grafana web UI and log in with the credentials provided in the Helm chart release. The default is user `admin` and password `P@ssword`.
2. From the side panel, click the + button and choose **Dashboard**.
3. Click the **Save Dashboard** button and provide `voting application` as the name.
4. Choose **Add Query**.

5. Provide the following query in the first metric: `100 - (avg by (instance) (irate(wmi_cpu_time_total{mode="idle"}[2m])) * 100)`. This query calculates the average CPU usage in the last two minutes using counters for the total CPU idle time.

6. In **Legend**, provide `{{instance}}` to use the node hostname as label.

7. From the left panel, choose **Visualization**. For the Y axis, in **Unit** choose **Misc** and select **percent(0-100)**.

8. From the left panel, choose **General**. Change the **Title** to `Average CPU usage`. Your graph should show the CPU utilization for both Windows nodes:

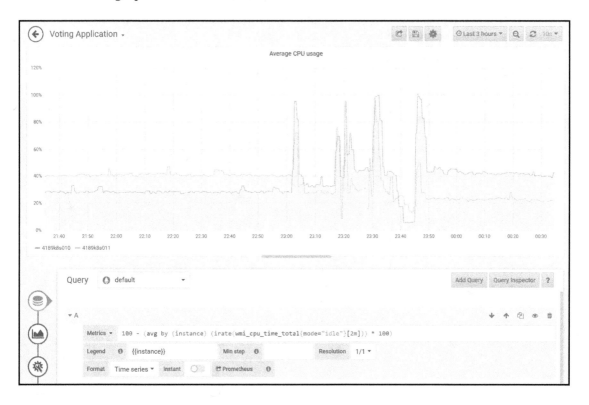

The next step is creating the gauge for the average number of requests per second handled by IIS in the last 5 minutes. Follow the following steps:

1. Return to the dashboard view, click **Add Panel**, and choose **Add Query**.
2. Provide the following query in the first metric: `sum((rate(win_aspnet_app_Requests_Total[5m]))) by (app_kubernetes_io_instance)`. This query calculates the per-second rate of requests in a 5-minute interval per each Pod and summarizes it globally by Kubernetes applications.
3. From the left panel, choose **Visualization**. Choose **Gauge**.
4. In the **Display** area, select **Calc** to be **Last (not null)** and in the **Field** area, change **Unit** to **Throughput > request/sec (reqps)**.
5. From the left panel, choose **General**. Change the **Title** to `IIS average number of requests per second in the last 5m`. Your gauge is showing the current average number of requests per second:

We are going to add the third visualization, which shows a line graph with the number of votes added to the database in the last five minutes. Please follow these steps:

1. Return to the dashboard view, click **Add Panel**, and choose **Add Query**.
2. Provide the following query in the first metric:
   `sum(irate(votingapplication_db_added_votes[5m])) by (app_kubernetes_io_instance) * 300`. This query calculates the rate of increase of the number of votes in a 5-minute interval per Pod and summarizes it globally by Kubernetes application. We need to multiply by 300 (5 minutes) as `irate` calculates the rate per second.
3. Set **Legend format** to `Votes in the last 5 minutes`.
4. From the left panel, choose **General**. Change the **Title** to `Number of votes added to the database in the last 5m`. Now your graph should look like the following:

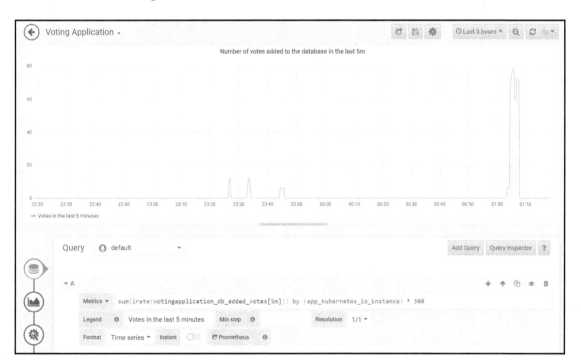

And finally, we are going to add the last visualization, which is a heatmap for visualizing the histogram of the duration of retrieving survey results. Heatmaps are the most effective way of visualizing histogram changes over time and, recently, Grafana was extended with native support for heatmaps for Prometheus histogram metrics. To create the visualization, perform the following steps:

1. Return to the dashboard view, click **Add Panel**, and choose **Add Query**.

2. Provide the following query in the first metric:
   `sum(increase(votingapplication_getsurveyresult_duration_seconds _bucket[2m])) by (le)`. This query will transform our histogram data—we determine the absolute increase rate for each bucket in the last two minutes and summarize each bucket with the `le` label, which is the bucket identifier (`le` is short for **less or equal**—Prometheus histograms are cumulative). In this way, we have buckets that are global per whole application, not individual Pods.

3. Change **Legend format** to `{{le}}` and set **Format** to `Heatmap`.

4. From the left panel, choose **Visualization**. Choose **Heatmap**.

5. In the **Y Axis** area, for **Unit**, choose **Time > seconds (s)** and for **Format** choose **Time series buckets**. Set **Decimals** to `1` to have neat numbers display. Set **Space** to `0` and **Round** to `2`—our heatmap has a relatively large number of buckets, so it will make the display much smoother.

6. In the **Display** area, turn on **Show legend** and **Hide zero**.

7. From the left panel, choose **General**. Change the **Title** to `Heatmap for duration of getting survey results`. Check your heatmap, especially after stressing the main web page in multiple browser tabs with autorefresh! Heatmaps generally look better in the dark theme (which you can change in the **Configuration** menu globally):

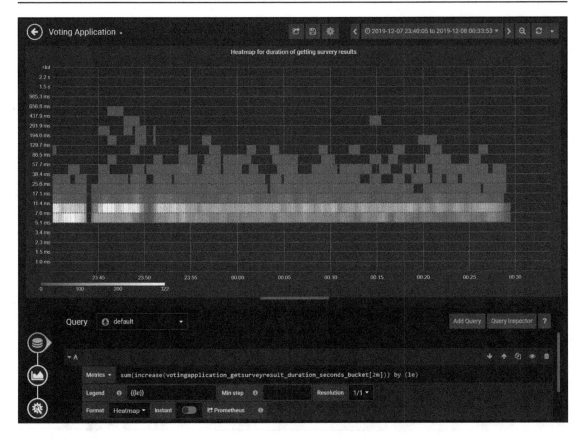

You can clearly see how this operation was performing during stress testing with around 300 requests per minute.

8. And lastly, return to the dashboard view, save all changes, and reorder the visualizations as you wish:

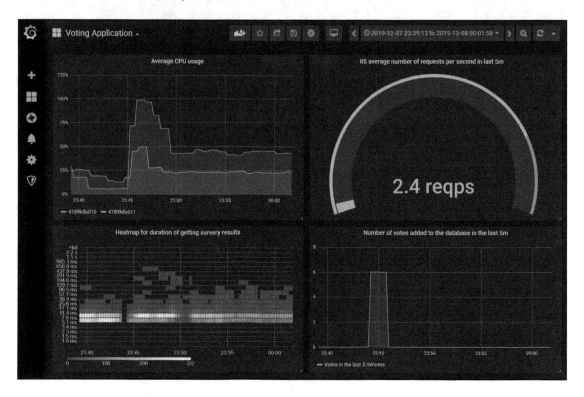

In the next subsection, we will show how to configure email alerting in Grafana.

Configuring alerting

Grafana, apart from creating visualizations and dashboards, is capable of defining alerting rules and sending notifications to multiple channels. You can find a list of supported notification channels in the official documentation: `https://grafana.com/docs/grafana/latest/alerting/notifications/`. The alerts are tied to particular visualizations so you need to have a proper visualization for your use case first. We are going to demonstrate how to create an alert for high CPU usage on a node.

First, we need to configure an email notification channel, so please follow these steps:

1. Grafana requires SMTP configuration to send emails. Obtain these details for your email provider and modify the Grafana Helm chart values file, `helm-values_grafana.yaml`, so that it contains the node:

```
grafana.ini:
  smtp:
    enabled: true
    host: <smtpAddressAndPort>   # For Gmail: smtp.gmail.com:587
    user: <smtpUser>
    password: <smtpPassword>
    skip_verify: true   # Needed for Gmail
    from_address: <emailAddress>
    from_name: <name>
```

 Please note that if you would like to use Gmail, you will need to generate an app password if you have 2FA enabled.

2. Upgrade the Helm release for Grafana:

```
helm upgrade grafana stable/grafana -n monitoring --values .\helm-
values_grafana.yaml --debug
```

3. After the upgrade is finished, navigate to the Grafana web UI. From the left panel, open **Alerting** and select **Notification channels**.
4. Click **New channel**.
5. Fill in the **Name**, select type **Email**, and provide email addresses.
6. Click **Send Test** to test whether your SMTP configuration is correct. If you have any problems, check the logs for the Grafana Pod. After a few minutes, you should receive the test email in your inbox.

When you have confirmed that your notification channel is working correctly, we can continue with creating the alert itself. We would like to receive an alert when average CPU usage on a node is above 80 percent for more than five minutes. Please follow these steps to configure such an alert:

1. Open our dashboard and choose the **Average CPU usage** visualization. From the menu for the visualization, choose **Edit**.
2. From the left panel, open **Alert** and click **Create Alert**.
3. Configure the alert as shown in the following:

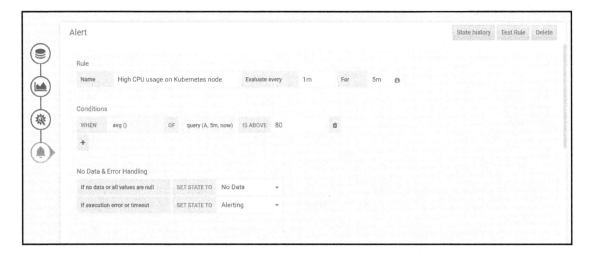

4. Choose your notification channel and optionally customize the notification message.
5. Save the dashboard. You will notice that the dashboard has a heart icon indicating the alert status.

Now, we need to test our rule by creating some load. We can reuse our `StressCpu` action that we created in the previous chapters. Follow these steps to perform the test:

1. In your web browser, navigate to `http://<applicationExternalIp>/Home/StressCpu?value=100` and repeat this action a few times to ensure that a few Pods start to stress the node enough.

2. Check the dashboard. You will notice that the health is still green but the metric is already in the red zone:

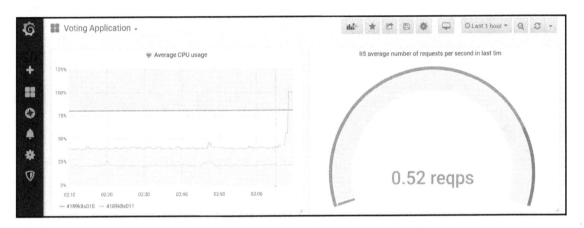

3. Wait for five minutes from the point when the average usage for the last five minutes is above 80 percent. You should receive an email via your notification channel:

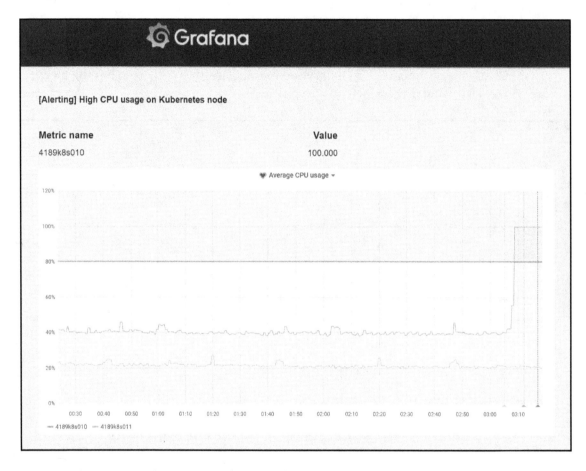

Congratulations! You have successfully configured dashboards for the voting application in Grafana and tested alerting features for our monitoring system.

Summary

In this long chapter, you learned how to set up monitoring of your application running in Windows containers on Kubernetes. First, we took a look at available monitoring solutions and determined which fit our use case with Windows nodes—the best choice currently is using a dedicated instance of Prometheus together with Grafana. Next, you learned how to make Windows nodes observable in terms of hardware, operating system, and container runtime using WMI Exporter and the experimental Docker Engine metrics service. We have shown how you can install and configure these agents on an AKS Engine cluster using extensions.

The next step was the Deployment of Prometheus and Grafana using Helm charts. You needed to ensure that Prometheus scraping jobs are capable of discovering the new metrics endpoints on Windows nodes. After that, we focused on monitoring inside the container and Windows Performance Counters—we exposed several counters using Telegraf and configured scraping of the new endpoint by Prometheus. Additionally, you learned how to use the `prometheus-net` library to export custom metrics to Prometheus directly from your application code. And finally, as the cherry on top, we showed you how to configure a sample dashboard in Grafana for the voting application and how to enable email alerting for high CPU usage on Windows nodes.

The next chapter will focus on disaster recovery and the Kubernetes backup strategy.

Questions

1. Why is observability the key concept in monitoring solutions?
2. What components can you use to monitor Windows nodes using Prometheus?
3. When should you use Prometheus Operator?
4. Why do you need to configure extra scrape jobs in Prometheus for Windows nodes?
5. How can you export any Windows Performance Counters from Windows containers to Prometheus?
6. What is the benefit of using the `prometheus-net` library?
7. How can you configure more than one port for scraping a single Service in Prometheus?
8. What are the benefits of using a heatmap for the visualization of Prometheus histograms?

You can find answers to these questions in the *Assessments* of this book.

Further reading

- For more information about Kubernetes features and monitoring the cluster in general, please refer to the following Packt books:
    - *The Complete Kubernetes Guide* (https://www.packtpub.com/virtualization-and-cloud/complete-kubernetes-guide).
    - *Getting Started with Kubernetes - Third Edition* (https://www.packtpub.com/virtualization-and-cloud/getting-started-kubernetes-third-edition).
    - *Kubernetes for Developers* (https://www.packtpub.com/virtualization-and-cloud/kubernetes-developers).
- You can learn more about Prometheus in the following Packt book:
    - *Hands-On Infrastructure Monitoring with Prometheus* (https://www.packtpub.com/virtualization-and-cloud/hands-infrastructure-monitoring-prometheus).

15
Disaster Recovery

In every production system, **disaster recovery** (**DR**) and **business continuity** (**BC**) are the key concepts that you will have to bear in mind in order to provide the availability of your application workloads. You have to take them into account at an early stage in planning your cluster architecture. The proverb *by failing to prepare, you are preparing to fail* cannot be more true for operating distributed systems, such as Kubernetes. This chapter will focus on DR when running Kubernetes clusters. BC best practices, such as multiregion Deployments and asynchronous replication of persistent volumes, are not included in the scope of the chapter.

Disaster recovery, in general, consists of a set of policies, tools, and procedures to enable the recovery or continuation of vital technology infrastructure and systems following a natural or human-induced disaster. You can read more about the concepts involved in planning for DR in an excellent article from Google at `https://cloud.google.com/solutions/dr-scenarios-planning-guide`. The main difference between DR and BC is that DR focuses on getting the infrastructure up and running following an outage, whereas BC deals with keeping business scenarios running during a major incident. The important thing about DR in Kubernetes is that you can essentially focus on data and state protection for your cluster: you need to have a backup-and-restore strategy for the stateful components. In a Kubernetes cluster, the most important stateful component is the etcd cluster, which is the storage layer for the Kubernetes API server.

In this chapter, we are going to cover the following topics:

- Kubernetes cluster backup strategy
- Backing up the etcd cluster
- Restoring the etcd cluster backup
- Automating backup
- Replacing a failed etcd cluster member

Technical requirements

For this chapter you will need the following:

- Windows 10 Pro, Enterprise, or Education (version 1903 or later, 64-bit) installed
- SSH client installed on your Windows machine
- Azure account
- Multimaster Windows/Linux Kubernetes cluster deployed using AKS Engine or an on-premise cluster (valid for some scenarios)

To follow along, you will need your own Azure account in order to create Azure resources for Kubernetes clusters. If you haven't already created the account for earlier chapters, you can read more about how to obtain a limited free account for personal use at `https://azure.microsoft.com/en-us/free/`.

Deploying a Kubernetes cluster using AKS Engine has been covered in `Chapter 8`, *Deploying Hybrid Azure Kubernetes Service Engine Cluster*.

You can download the latest code samples for this chapter from the official GitHub repository at `https://github.com/PacktPublishing/Hands-On-Kubernetes-on-Windows/tree/master/Chapter15`.

Kubernetes cluster backup strategy

Disaster recovery for Kubernetes essentially involves creating a cluster state backup-and-restore strategy. Let's first take a look at what stateful components are in Kubernetes:

- Etcd cluster (`https://etcd.io/`) that persists the state for Kubernetes API server resources.
- Persistent volumes used by pods.

And surprisingly (or *not*), that is all! For the master node components and pods running on worker nodes, you don't have any nonrecoverable state involved; if you provision a new replacement node, Kubernetes can easily move the workload to the new nodes, providing full business continuity. When your etcd cluster is restored, Kubernetes will take care of reconciling the cluster component's state.

Let's take a look at how to back up and restore persistent volumes. It all depends on how your persistent volumes are provisioned. You can rely on standard filesystem backups stored externally or, in the case of cloud-backed PVs, you can use disk snapshots and manage them as part of the cloud services. There is also an interesting snapshot-and-restore feature (currently in the alpha state) for PVs provisioned using CSI plugins. This will provide better backup-and-restore integration directly at the Kubernetes-cluster level.

 There is a general rule of thumb to keep your cluster workloads as stateless as possible. Think about using external, managed services to store your data (for example, Azure blob storage, Azure Cosmos DB) for which availability and data reliability are guaranteed by SLAs.

For an etcd cluster, the backup-and-recovery strategy depends on two factors: how you store etcd data and what your high-availability topology for Kubernetes masters is. In the case of etcd data storage, the situation is similar to persistent volumes. If you mount the storage using a cloud volume, you can rely on disk snapshots from your cloud service provider (which is the case for AKS Engine), and for self-managed disks, you can employ standard filesystem backup strategies. In all cases, you also have a third option: you can use the snapshot feature of etcd itself. We will later show you how to perform a snapshot-and-restore of etcd using the etcdctl command.

Regarding the high-availability topology for your Kubernetes masters, as mentioned in Chapter 4, *Kubernetes Concepts and Windows Support*, you can run a **stacked** topology or an **external** topology for etcd. In a stacked topology, the etcd member is running as a Kubernetes pod on *every* master node. For the external topology, you run an etcd cluster outside your Kubernetes cluster. It may be fully external, deployed on separate, dedicated hosts, or it may share the same hosts as the master node. The latter is the case for AKS Engine: it runs the external topology, but each master node hosts an etcd member as a native Linux service. For both of these topologies, you can perform backups in the same way; the only difference lies in how you perform the restore. In the stacked topology, which is commonly used for **kubeadm** Deployments, you need to perform a kubeadm init on a new node overriding the local etcd storage. For an external topology, you can simply use the etcdctl command.

 An external topology for an etcd cluster has more components but is generally better at providing business continuity and disaster recovery.

Additionally, if you are running an AKS Engine cluster, you may consider using an Azure Cosmos DB (`https://azure.microsoft.com/en-us/services/cosmos-db/`) instead of a self-managed etcd cluster. Cosmos DB supports exposing an etcd API and can be used as the backing storage for Kubernetes in exactly the same way as a local etcd cluster. In this way, you receive global distribution, high availability, elastic scaling, and data reliability at the levels defined in the SLA. On top of that, you have automatic, online backups with georeplication. You can learn more about this feature and how to configure it in a cluster apimodel in the official documentation at `https://github.com/Azure/aks-engine/tree/master/examples/cosmos-etcd`.

Now, we will take a look at how you can back up your etcd cluster.

Backing up an etcd cluster

The process of backing up an etcd cluster is straightforward, but there are multiple ways that you can approach this task:

- Create a backup or snapshot of the storage disk for etcd. This is especially valid in cloud scenarios where you can easily manage backups outside your Kubernetes cluster.
- Perform a manual snapshot of etcd using the `etcdctl` command. You need to manage the backup files yourself: upload them to external storage, and apply a retention policy.
- Use **Velero** (formerly Heptio Ark (`https://velero.io/`)), which can perform snapshots, manage them in external storage, and restore them if needed. Additionally, it can be used to perform backups of persistent volumes using **Restic** integration (`https://velero.io/docs/master/restic/`).
- Use **etcd-operator** (`https://github.com/coreos/etcd-operator`) to provision etcd clusters on top of Kubernetes. You can easily manage etcd clusters and perform backup–restore operations. Use this approach if you plan to manage multiple Kubernetes clusters in your environment.

We are going to demonstrate the second option, performing manual snapshots of etcd—it is generally good to know what exactly is happening under the hood before switching to advanced automations, such as Velero. For this task, you will need a multimaster Kubernetes cluster; you can create one using AKS Engine. As in the previous chapters, you can use a ready apimodel definition from the Github repository at `https://github.com/PacktPublishing/Hands-On-Kubernetes-on-Windows/blob/master/Chapter15/01_multimaster-aks-engine/kubernetes-windows-template.json` and deploy it using our usual PowerShell script (`https://github.com/PacktPublishing/Hands-On-Kubernetes-on-Windows/blob/master/Chapter15/01_multimaster-aks-engine/CreateAKSEngineClusterWithWindowsNodes.ps1`). This definition will deploy three master nodes together with one Linux worker node and one Windows node.

 Please make sure that you check the estimated costs of hosting a five-node Kubernetes cluster on Azure. The price will depend on the region in which you deploy it.

When your cluster is ready, deploy an application workload—for example, the Voting application from the previous chapters. Then, go through the following steps to create an etcd snapshot:

1. Open the PowerShell window and SSH into one of the master nodes using the following command:

   ```
   ssh azureuser@<dnsPrefix>.<azureLocation>.cloudapp.azure.com
   ```

2. Inspect your Kubernetes cluster configuration. Use the `kubectl cluster-info dump` command to learn more about the etcd setup. You will see that each master node is running its own local instance (but external to the cluster) of etcd, which is passed to the Kubernetes API server as arguments:

   ```
   azureuser@k8s-master-50659983-0:~$ kubectl cluster-info dump
   . . .
                                  "--etcd-servers=https://127.0.0.1:2379",
   . . .
   ```

3. Use the `etcdctl` command to get the topology of the etcd cluster, which has members on the master nodes:

   ```
   azureuser@k8s-master-50659983-0:~$ sudo etcdctl cluster-health
   member b3a6773c0e93604 is healthy: got healthy result from
   https://10.255.255.5:2379
   member 721d9c3882dbe6f7 is healthy: got healthy result from
   https://10.255.255.7:2379
   member 72b3415f69c52b2a is healthy: got healthy result from
   ```

```
https://10.255.255.6:2379
cluster is healthy
```

You can check that these are the private IP addresses of the master nodes in the Azure Portal.

4. Execute the following commands in order to create a snapshot of etcd:

```
sudo mkdir -p /backup
ETCDCTL_API=3 sudo -E etcdctl \
    --endpoints=https://127.0.0.1:2379 \
    --cacert=/etc/kubernetes/certs/ca.crt \
    --cert=/etc/kubernetes/certs/etcdclient.crt \
    --key=/etc/kubernetes/certs/etcdclient.key \
    --debug \
    snapshot save \
    /backup/kubernetes-etcd-snapshot_$(date +"%Y%m%d_%H%M%S").db
```

5. After a short while, the backup should be finished. You can inspect the status of the backup using the following command:

```
azureuser@k8s-master-50659983-0:~$ ETCDCTL_API=3 sudo -E etcdctl --
write-out=table snapshot status /backup/kubernetes-etcd-
snapshot_20191208_182555.db
```

HASH	REVISION	TOTAL KEYS	TOTAL SIZE
b4422ea6	28331	1034	3.2 MB

 Additionally, you should back up the certificates and keys used to access the etcd cluster. In our scenario, it will not be needed because we are going to restore the same master machines. For a general disaster-recovery scenario, you will need them.

With the backup ready, let's see how to upload the file to Azure blob storage. Please note that you *shouldn't* perform these operations directly on production masters, especially when installing Azure CLI *the quick way*. We are demonstrating this in order to later create a Kubernetes **CronJob**, which will run a Docker container to execute these operations. Please go through the following steps for your development cluster:

1. Open a PowerShell window on your local machine and log in to Azure using the `az login` command.

2. Create a service principal that we will use to upload the backup to the Azure blob storage container:

```
PS C:\src> az ad sp create-for-rbac `
    --role="Storage Blob Data Contributor" `
    --
scopes="/subscriptions/<azureSubscriptionId>/resourceGroups/<aksEng
ineResourceGroupName>"

Creating a role assignment under the scope of
"/subscriptions/cc9a8166-829e-401e-
a004-76d1e3733b8e/resourceGroups/aks-engine-windows-resource-group"
...
{
   "appId": "89694083-0110-4821-9510-a74eedf7a27c",
   "displayName": "azure-cli-2019-12-08-19-15-41",
   "name": "http://azure-cli-2019-12-08-19-15-41",
   "password": "67b1f492-caea-463f-ac28-69177f52fecf",
   "tenant": "86be0945-a0f3-44c2-8868-9b6aa96b0b62"
}
```

Copy `appId`, `password`, and `tenant` for further use.

3. Execute the following command to create a dedicated `aksenginebackups` storage account to handle backups. Choose the same Azure location as your AKS Engine cluster:

```
az storage account create `
    --name aksenginebackups `
    --resource-group <aksEngineResourceGroupName> `
    --location <azureLocation> `
    --sku Standard_ZRS `
    --encryption blob
```

4. List the account keys for the new account and copy the value of `key1` for further use:

```
az storage account keys list `
    --account-name $aksenginebackups `
    --resource-group <aksEngineResourceGroupName>
```

5. Continue using the SSH session from the previous paragraph for your development AKS Engine cluster master node. Execute the following command to install the Azure CLI:

```
curl -sL https://aka.ms/InstallAzureCLIDeb | sudo bash
```

6. Log in to Azure using the `appId`, `password`, and `tenant` for your service principal:

```
az login --service-principal \
    -u 1775963c-8414-434d-839c-db5d417c4293 \
    -p 276952a9-fa51-44ef-b6c6-905e322dbaed \
    --tenant 86be0945-a0f3-44c2-8868-9b6aa96b0b62
```

7. Create a new container for backups of our AKS Engine cluster. You can use any name—for example, the DNS prefix for the cluster:

```
az storage container create \
  --account-name aksenginebackups \
  --account-key "<storageAccountKey>" \
  --name <dnsPrefix>
```

8. Create a blob with the backup that we created in the previous paragraph:

```
sudo az storage blob upload \
  --account-name aksenginebackups \
  --account-key "<storageAccountKey>" \
  --container-name <dnsPrefix> \
  --name kubernetes-etcd-snapshot_20191208_182555.db \
  --file /backup/kubernetes-etcd-snapshot_20191208_182555.db
```

9. Remove the backup file from the local disk:

```
sudo rm /backup/kubernetes-etcd-snapshot_20191208_182555.db
```

 For the creation of the service principal and storage account, we have provided a PowerShell script in the GitHub repository at `https://github.com/PacktPublishing/Hands-On-Kubernetes-on-Windows/blob/master/Chapter15/02_CreateBlobContainerForBackups.ps1`.

You have successfully created an etcd snapshot and uploaded it to the Azure blob storage. Now, we will demonstrate how you can restore the backup that we have just created.

Restoring the etcd cluster backup

To demonstrate the restore scenario of etcd for an existing AKS Engine cluster, we first need to modify some Kubernetes objects to later prove that the backup restore has worked. Please note that all the commands shown in this section assume that you are running AKS Engine where an external etcd topology is used with etcd members running on the same machines that host Kubernetes master components. For other clusters, such as an on-premise kubeadm setup, the structure of the directories will be different.

First, let's introduce some changes to the cluster state. For example, if you have our Voting application running, delete the associated `Deployment` object using the following command:

```
kubectl delete deployment -n dev-helm voting-application
```

After a while, all the pods will be terminated—let's assume that this was our **disaster event** that has left the cluster unuseable. We are going to restore the backup named `kubernetes-etcd-snapshot_20191208_182555.db`, which we created earlier and uploaded to Azure blob storage!

 If you have deleted the SQL Server Deployment together with the PVCs, then the restore will not be fully successful. As we mentioned in previous sections, for PVs you need to have a separate backup strategy that is coordinated with etcd backups. Then you can restore both the etcd snapshot and associated PV snapshots.

To perform the restore, you will need to connect to all three Kubernetes nodes at once. This operation can be performed sequentially, but stopping and starting the etcd service on the hosts must be performed simultaneously. Please go through the following steps:

1. Open three PowerShell windows (try to have them all open and visible at the same time to make issuing commands easier). Each window will be used for a separate Kubernetes master.
2. In the Azure Portal, find the private IPs of the master nodes. You can also do this using the Azure CLI. They should follow the convention that master `0` is `10.255.255.5`, master `1` is `10.255.255.6`, and master `2` is `10.255.255.7`.

3. In the first PowerShell window, execute the following command to connect to one of the master nodes (behind the Azure load balancer) and additionally use port forwarding from your local port 5500 to the SSH port for master 0, port 5501 to the SSH port for master 1, and port 5502 to the SSH port for master 2:

```
ssh -L 5500:10.255.255.5:22 `
    -L 5501:10.255.255.6:22 `
    -L 5502:10.255.255.7:22 `
    azureuser@<dnsPrefix>.<azureLocation>.cloudapp.azure.com
```

4. In this way, you can connect to any Kubernetes master you want from your local machine. Check to see which master node you have already connected to and create SSH connections to the *other two* nodes in the remaining PowerShell windows—for example:

```
# Connection to Master 0 already established

# Master 1
ssh azureuser@localhost -p 5501

# Master 2
ssh azureuser@localhost -p 5502
```

5. Now, you have a set of PowerShell windows where you can manage each master node separately. The first step is installing the Azure CLI. Execute the following command *on all masters*:

```
curl -sL https://aka.ms/InstallAzureCLIDeb | sudo bash
```

6. Log in to Azure using the appId, password, and tenant for your service principal, as you did previously. Execute the following command *on all masters*:

```
az login --service-principal \
    -u 1775963c-8414-434d-839c-db5d417c4293 \
    -p 276952a9-fa51-44ef-b6c6-905e322dbaed \
    --tenant 86be0945-a0f3-44c2-8868-9b6aa96b0b62
```

7. Download the `kubernetes-etcd-snapshot_20191208_182555.db` snapshot file. Execute the following command on all master nodes :

```
az storage blob download \
    --account-name aksenginebackups \
    --account-key "<storageAccountKey>" \
    --container-name <dnsPrefix> \
    --name kubernetes-etcd-snapshot_20191208_182555.db \
    --file snapshot.db
```

8. All etcd members must be restored from the same snapshot file. This means that you have to perform a similar operation on all nodes, just with different parameters. On each master, determine the startup parameters for the etcd service (for AKS Engine, it is running as a systemd service). Execute the following command to get the parameters for each master:

```
cat /etc/default/etcd
```

9. You need to capture `--name`, `--initial-cluster`, `--initial-cluster-token`, and `--initial-advertise-peer-urls` for each node. More precisely, `--initial-cluster` and `--initial-cluster-token` will be the same for all masters. We will use these values to initialize a *new* etcd member on each master—for example, for master 0 in our cluster, these parameters are as follows:

```
--name k8s-master-50659983-0
--initial-cluster k8s-
master-50659983-0=https://10.255.255.5:2380,k8s-master-50659983-1=h
ttps://10.255.255.6:2380,k8s-
master-50659983-2=https://10.255.255.7:2380
--initial-cluster-token k8s-etcd-cluster
--initial-advertise-peer-urls https://10.255.255.5:2380
```

10. We can proceed with restoring the data for each etcd cluster member. This restore operation only creates a new data directory. The original data directory that the cluster is currently using is `/var/lib/etcddisk` (which is mounted from a cloud volume). We are going to restore the data to `/var/lib/etcdisk-restored` and later swap the contents. Using the parameters from the previous step, execute this command using matching parameters for each master:

```
# Master 0
ETCDCTL_API=3 sudo -E etcdctl snapshot restore snapshot.db \
   --name k8s-master-50659983-0 \
   --initial-cluster k8s-
master-50659983-0=https://10.255.255.5:2380,k8s-master-50659983-1=h
```

```
ttps://10.255.255.6:2380,k8s-
master-50659983-2=https://10.255.255.7:2380 \
    --initial-cluster-token k8s-etcd-cluster \
    --initial-advertise-peer-urls https://10.255.255.5:2380 \
    --data-dir=/var/lib/etcddisk-restored \
    --debug

# Master 1
ETCDCTL_API=3 sudo -E etcdctl snapshot restore snapshot.db \
    --name k8s-master-50659983-1 \
    --initial-cluster k8s-
master-50659983-0=https://10.255.255.5:2380,k8s-master-50659983-1=h
ttps://10.255.255.6:2380,k8s-
master-50659983-2=https://10.255.255.7:2380 \
    --initial-cluster-token k8s-etcd-cluster \
    --initial-advertise-peer-urls https://10.255.255.6:2380 \
    --data-dir=/var/lib/etcddisk-restored \
    --debug

# Master 2
ETCDCTL_API=3 sudo -E etcdctl snapshot restore snapshot.db \
    --name k8s-master-50659983-2 \
    --initial-cluster k8s-
master-50659983-0=https://10.255.255.5:2380,k8s-master-50659983-1=h
ttps://10.255.255.6:2380,k8s-
master-50659983-2=https://10.255.255.7:2380 \
    --initial-cluster-token k8s-etcd-cluster \
    --initial-advertise-peer-urls https://10.255.255.7:2380 \
    --data-dir=/var/lib/etcddisk-restored \
    --debug
```

11. The snapshot data is ready to be used in a new etcd cluster. But first, we need to gracefully stop the existing Kubernetes master components; otherwise, you will arrive at an inconsistent state after the restore.

12. Kubelet observes the /etc/kubernetes/manifests directory where manifest files for master components are stored. Any change to these manifests is applied by kubelet to the cluster; this is how the Kubernetes master is bootstrapped when there is no Kubernetes API server yet. To stop the master components, including the Kubernetes API server, simply move the manifest files to a different directory and execute the command on all masters:

```
sudo mv /etc/kubernetes/manifests /etc/kubernetes/manifests-stopped
```

After a few seconds, you will see that the Docker containers for master components are being stopped (use the docker ps command to see this).

13. Now, stop the etcd service on all masters:

```
sudo service etcd stop
```

14. Stop the kubelet service on all masters:

```
sudo service kubelet stop
```

15. The final step in preparing the masters for the restore is to remove all other Docker containers that run on the masters, but that are not started using the /etc/kubernetes/manifests directory. Execute the following command on all masters:

```
docker stop $(docker ps -q)
```

16. Perform the actual data directory restore for etcd members. Execute the following commands on all masters.

```
# Backing up old data directory
sudo mkdir /var/lib/etcddisk-old
sudo mv /var/lib/etcddisk/member /var/lib/etcddisk-old/

# Move the contents of the snapshot directory to the target data
directory
sudo mv /var/lib/etcddisk-restored/member /var/lib/etcddisk/
sudo chown etcd -R /var/lib/etcddisk
sudo chgrp etcd -R /var/lib/etcddisk
sudo ls -al /var/lib/etcddisk/member/

# Cleanup
sudo rm -rf /var/lib/etcddisk-restored
```

17. We can now start bootstrapping the cluster with the restored snapshot. The first step is starting the etcd cluster. Execute the following command on all master nodes:

```
sudo service etcd start
```

You can verify the health of your etcd cluster using the sudo -E etcdctl cluster-health command.

18. Move the stopped manifest files back to their original location on all masters. They will be picked up by kubelet once it starts:

```
sudo mv /etc/kubernetes/manifests-stopped /etc/kubernetes/manifests
```

19. Finally, perform the last step: start the kubelet service on all masters:

```
sudo service kubelet start
```

You can quickly verify that the containers for the master components are being started using the `docker ps` command.

20. You can check in a new PowerShell window whether the cluster is already working hard to reconcile the restored state:

```
PS C:\src> kubectl get pods --all-namespaces
NAMESPACE        NAME
READY    STATUS                  RESTARTS    AGE
dev-helm         voting-application-8477c76b67-41krm
0/1      CrashLoopBackOff    6           9h
dev-helm         voting-application-8477c76b67-7tbmw
0/1      CrashLoopBackOff    6           9h
dev-helm         voting-application-8477c76b67-dls6q
0/1      ContainerCreating   7           9h
dev-helm         voting-application-8477c76b67-dvcqz
0/1      ContainerCreating   7           9h
dev-helm         voting-application-8477c76b67-xttml
0/1      CrashLoopBackOff    9           9h
dev-helm         voting-application-mssql-linux-8548b4dd44-hdrpc
0/1      ContainerCreating   0           9h
kube-system      azure-cni-networkmonitor-6dr8c
1/1      Running             1           9h
kube-system      azure-cni-networkmonitor-dhgsv
1/1      Running             0           9h
. . .
```

Our Voting application Deployment is recreating. That is *great news*: the snapshot restore has been *successful*. After a few minutes, all the pods will be ready and you can navigate to the external IP in the web browser and enjoy the application again.

The **Openshift** distribution of Kubernetes implements a native etcd snapshot restore functionality. You can see the details in the scripts in the repository at https://github.com/openshift/machine-config-operator/blob/master/templates/master/00-master/_base/files/usr-local-bin-etcd-snapshot-restore-sh.yaml. The steps there are roughly similar to what we have done in this section.

As you can see, the manual restore scenario is a bit complicated and can be prone to error. In production scenarios, you should use this method when everything else fails; generally, it is better to use automated backup controllers, such as Velero (`https://velero.io/`).

In the next section, you will learn how you can automate the backup procedure on AKS Engine using Kubernetes CronJobs.

Automating backup

In this section, we will demonstrate how to automate the backup procedure for an etcd cluster using Kubernetes CronJob. For this, we will need a Dockerfile that has `etcdctl` and Azure CLI installed for the image in order to create the snapshot and upload it to a selected Azure blob container—exactly as we demonstrated in manual steps. All the configuration and service principal secrets will be injected using environment variables that can be set using Kubernetes secret.

To create the Docker image for the etcd snapshot worker, go through the following steps:

1. Use a Linux machine or switch to the Linux containers in Docker Desktop for Windows.
2. Open a new PowerShell window.
3. Create a new directory for your source code and navigate there.
4. Create a `Dockerfile` file with the following contents:

```
FROM ubuntu:18.04

ARG ETCD_VERSION="v3.3.15"

WORKDIR /temp
RUN apt-get update \
 && apt-get install curl -y \
 && curl -L
https://github.com/coreos/etcd/releases/download/$ETCD_VERSION/etcd
-$ETCD_VERSION-linux-amd64.tar.gz -o etcd-$ETCD_VERSION-linux-
amd64.tar.gz \
 && tar xzvf etcd-$ETCD_VERSION-linux-amd64.tar.gz \
 && rm etcd-$ETCD_VERSION-linux-amd64.tar.gz \
 && cd etcd-$ETCD_VERSION-linux-amd64 \
 && cp etcdctl /usr/local/bin/ \
 && rm -rf etcd-$ETCD_VERSION-linux-amd64

RUN curl -sL https://aka.ms/InstallAzureCLIDeb | bash
```

```
WORKDIR /backup-worker
COPY ./docker-entrypoint.sh .
RUN chmod +x docker-entrypoint.sh

ENTRYPOINT ["/backup-worker/docker-entrypoint.sh"]
```

This Dockerfile is based on the Ubuntu 18.04 Docker image and installs the `etcdctl` command from the official release of etcd. Additionally, we install the Azure CLI and set the `ENTRYPOINT` to a custom shell script that will perform the snapshot operation when the container is started.

5. Now, create a `docker-entrypoint.sh` file with the following contents.

```
#!/bin/bash

snapshot_file="kubernetes-etcd-snapshot_$(date
+"%Y%m%d_%H%M%S").db"

ETCDCTL_API=3 etcdctl \
    --endpoints=$SNAPSHOT_ETCD_ENDPOINTS \
    --cacert=/etc/kubernetes/certs/ca.crt \
    --cert=/etc/kubernetes/certs/etcdclient.crt \
    --key=/etc/kubernetes/certs/etcdclient.key \
    --debug \
    snapshot save \
    $snapshot_file

ETCDCTL_API=3 etcdctl --write-out=table snapshot status
$snapshot_file


az login --service-principal \
    -u $SNAPSHOT_AZURE_PRINCIPAL_APPID \
    -p $SNAPSHOT_AZURE_PRINCIPAL_PASSWORD \
    --tenant $SNAPSHOT_AZURE_PRINCIPAL_TENANT

az storage container create \
    --account-name $SNAPSHOT_AZURE_ACCOUNT_NAME \
    --account-key "$SNAPSHOT_AZURE_ACCOUNT_KEY" \
    --name $SNAPSHOT_AZURE_CONTAINER_NAME

az storage blob upload \
    --account-name $SNAPSHOT_AZURE_ACCOUNT_NAME \
    --account-key "$SNAPSHOT_AZURE_ACCOUNT_KEY" \
    --container-name $SNAPSHOT_AZURE_CONTAINER_NAME \
    --name $snapshot_file \
    --file $snapshot_file
```

```
rm -f $snapshot_file

echo "Backup $snapshot_file uploaded successfully!"
```

The preceding script automates the steps that we have provided in the previous sections. The idea here is that all configurations and credentials that are injected using environment variables, certificates, and keys for accessing an etcd cluster must be mounted as a host volume to the specified location: `/etc/kubernetes/certs/`. For AKS Engine masters, this mapping will be one-to-one.

6. Build the image using a tag containing your Docker ID—we will use `packtpubkubernetesonwindows/aks-engine-etcd-snapshot-azure-blob-job`:

```
docker build -t <dockerId>/aks-engine-etcd-snapshot-azure-blob-job
.
```

7. Tag the image with version `1.0.0` and push the image, along with all of the tags, to Docker Hub:

```
docker tag <dockerId>/aks-engine-etcd-snapshot-azure-blob-
job:latest <dockerId>/aks-engine-etcd-snapshot-azure-blob-job:1.0.0
docker push <dockerId>/aks-engine-etcd-snapshot-azure-blob-job
```

8. You can optionally test your Docker image by running it directly on the AKS Engine master node in a development environment. SSH to the node and execute the following command:

```
docker run \
  -v /etc/kubernetes/certs:/etc/kubernetes/certs \
  -e
SNAPSHOT_ETCD_ENDPOINTS=https://10.255.255.5:2379,https://10.255.25
5.6:2379,https://10.255.255.7:2379 \
  -e SNAPSHOT_AZURE_PRINCIPAL_APPID=1775963c-8414-434d-839c-
db5d417c4293 \
  -e SNAPSHOT_AZURE_PRINCIPAL_PASSWORD=276952a9-fa51-44ef-
b6c6-905e322dbaed \
  -e SNAPSHOT_AZURE_PRINCIPAL_TENANT=86be0945-
a0f3-44c2-8868-9b6aa96b0b62 \
  -e SNAPSHOT_AZURE_ACCOUNT_NAME=aksenginebackups \
  -e SNAPSHOT_AZURE_ACCOUNT_KEY="<storageAccountKey>" \
  -e SNAPSHOT_AZURE_CONTAINER_NAME=<dnsPrefix> \
  packtpubkubernetesonwindows/aks-engine-etcd-snapshot-azure-blob-
job:1.0.0
```

After a short while, the job will end and the snapshot will be uploaded to the container that we created earlier.

With the Docker image ready, we can create a dedicated Kubernetes **CronJob** to run this operation periodically. Please note that we are providing a minimal setup for this job; you should consider using a dedicated service account and set up RBAC in a production environment. Using a Helm chart to efficiently manage this job is also recommended. To create the CronJob, please go through the following steps:

1. Define a *local* file, etcd-snapshot-secrets.txt, that will be used to define the secret object for your CronJob:

```
SNAPSHOT_ETCD_ENDPOINTS=https://10.255.255.5:2379,https://10.255.25
5.6:2379,https://10.255.255.7:2379
SNAPSHOT_AZURE_PRINCIPAL_APPID=1775963c-8414-434d-839c-db5d417c4293
SNAPSHOT_AZURE_PRINCIPAL_PASSWORD=276952a9-fa51-44ef-
b6c6-905e322dbaed
SNAPSHOT_AZURE_PRINCIPAL_TENANT=86be0945-
a0f3-44c2-8868-9b6aa96b0b62
SNAPSHOT_AZURE_ACCOUNT_NAME=aksenginebackups
SNAPSHOT_AZURE_ACCOUNT_KEY="<dnsPrefix>"
SNAPSHOT_AZURE_CONTAINER_NAME=<dnsPrefix>
```

2. Create the etcd-snapshot-azure-blob-job-secrets secret object using the etcd-snapshot-secrets.txt file:

```
kubectl create secret generic `
        -n kube-system `
        etcd-snapshot-azure-blob-job-secrets `
        --from-env-file=etcd-snapshot-secrets.txt
```

3. Now, create the etcd-snapshot-cronjob.yaml manifest file for the CronJob itself:

```
apiVersion: batch/v1beta1
kind: CronJob
metadata:
  name: etcd-snapshot-azure-blob-job
  namespace: kube-system
spec:
  schedule: "0 */6 * * *" # (1)
  successfulJobsHistoryLimit: 2
  failedJobsHistoryLimit: 2
  jobTemplate:
    spec:
      ttlSecondsAfterFinished: 21600
      activeDeadlineSeconds: 600
```

```
template:
  spec:
    tolerations:
    - key: node-role.kubernetes.io/master   # (2)
      operator: Exists
      effect: NoSchedule
    nodeSelector:
      node-role.kubernetes.io/master: ""
    containers:
    - name: snapshot-worker
      image: packtpubkubernetesonwindows/aks-engine-etcd-
snapshot-azure-blob-job:1.0.0   # (3)
      volumeMounts:
      - mountPath: /etc/kubernetes/certs
        name: etcd-certs
      envFrom:
      - secretRef:
          name: etcd-snapshot-azure-blob-job-secrets   # (4)
    volumes:
    - name: etcd-certs
      hostPath:
        path: /etc/kubernetes/certs   # (5)
    restartPolicy: Never
    hostNetwork: true
```

In this manifest file, the most important part is the part that defines an appropriate `schedule` **(1)**. We use a `0 */6 * * *` cron expression that will perform the snapshots *every 6 hours*. For testing purposes, you can set it to `* * * * *` in order to schedule the job *every minute*. Next, we need to ensure that the pod for the CronJob can be scheduled on the master node. We do this by using `tolerations` for taints and a `nodeSelector` **(2)**. The reason for this is that we need access to the etcd certificates and keys, which must be mounted from the master host filesystem. We define the pod to use the `packtpubkubernetesonwindows/aks-engine-etcd-snapshot-azure-blob-job:1.0.0` image that we have just created **(3)**. To populate the environment variables for the container, we use `secretRef` for our secret object, `etcd-snapshot-azure-blob-job-secrets` **(4)**. Lastly, we need to mount the *host* directory, `/etc/kubernetes/certs`, to the pod container so that the worker can access the certificates and keys **(5)**.

4. Apply the manifest file using the `kubectl apply -f .\etcd-snapshot-cronjob.yaml` command.

5. Wait for the first job execution:

```
PS C:\src> kubectl get cronjob -n kube-system -w
NAME                           SCHEDULE       SUSPEND    ACTIVE
LAST SCHEDULE    AGE
etcd-snapshot-azure-blob-job   0 */6 * * *    False      0          2m
16m
```

6. When the job is finished, you can check the logs for the associated pod and also verify in Azure Portal (`https://portal.azure.com/`) that the snapshots are uploaded to your Azure blob container:

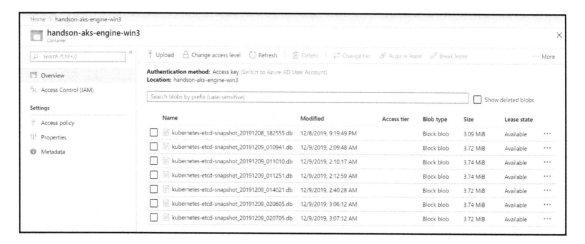

When working with multiple etcd clusters (for multiple Kubernetes Deployments) you can achieve a similar result using the *etcd-operator* (`https://github.com/coreos/etcd-operator`). For a small cluster, such as the one in this demonstration, it doesn't make sense to use such a complex solution.

Congratulations! You have successfully set up an automated CronJob for creating etcd cluster snapshots and automatically uploaded them to the Azure blob container. Now, we are going to demonstrate how you can replace a failed etcd member in order to restore the full operations of the etcd cluster.

Replacing a failed etcd cluster member

As a highly-available database, etcd tolerates minority failures, which means a partial failure where the majority of cluster members are still available and healthy; however, it is a good practice to replace the failed members as soon as possible in order to improve the overall cluster health and minimize the risk of majority failure. It is also highly recommended that you always keep the cluster size greater than two members in production. In order to recover from a minority failure, you need to perform two steps:

1. Remove the failed member from the cluster.
2. Add a new replacement member. If there is more than one failed member, replace them sequentially.

 The etcd documentation provides a list of use cases for runtime configuration changes, as you can see at `https://etcd.io/docs/v3.3.12/op-guide/runtime-configuration/`.

The way that you create a new member depends on what exactly failed. If it is a disk failure or data corruption on the machine that hosts the member, you may consider reusing the same host but with the data directory on a *different* disk. In the case of total host failure, you may need to provision a new machine and use it as a new replacement member. We will demonstrate a case in AKS Engine where we *reuse* the same host and create a member with a different data directory. This is a rather specific use case, but the overall procedure will be the same in all cases.

First, let's simulate the failure of an etcd cluster member. To do that, go through the following steps:

1. Connect to one of the Kubernetes master nodes using SSH:

   ssh azureuser@<dnsPrefix>.<azureLocation>.cloudapp.azure.com

   Let's assume that we connected to master 0 with the private IP 10.255.255.5.

2. Verify the cluster health:

```
azureuser@k8s-master-50659983-0:~$ sudo etcdctl cluster-health
member b3a6773c0e93604 is healthy: got healthy result from
https://10.255.255.5:2379
member 721d9c3882dbe6f7 is healthy: got healthy result from
https://10.255.255.7:2379
member 72b3415f69c52b2a is healthy: got healthy result from
https://10.255.255.6:2379
cluster is healthy
```

3. Stop the etcd service on master 0 using the following command. This will simulate our failure of a member in the cluster:

```
sudo service etcd stop
```

4. Check the cluster health again, but this time provide only the endpoints for master 1 and master 2, which are functioning properly:

```
azureuser@k8s-master-50659983-0:~$ sudo etcdctl --
endpoints=https://10.255.255.6:2379,https://10.255.255.7:2379
cluster-health
failed to check the health of member b3a6773c0e93604 on
https://10.255.255.5:2379: Get https://10.255.255.5:2379/health:
dial tcp 10.255.255.5:2379: connect: connection refused
member b3a6773c0e93604 is unreachable: [https://10.255.255.5:2379]
are all unreachable
member 721d9c3882dbe6f7 is healthy: got healthy result from
https://10.255.255.7:2379
member 72b3415f69c52b2a is healthy: got healthy result from
https://10.255.255.6:2379
cluster is degraded
```

5. Take note of the failed member ID, which in our case is `b3a6773c0e93604`.

Now, let's demonstrate how to replace the failed member. Please go through the following steps:

1. Determine the ID of the failed member. We already have that information from the previous commands, but in general you can use the `sudo etcdctl --endpoints=https://10.255.255.6:2379,https://10.255.255.7:2379 member list` command.

2. SSH into the machine with the failed member.

3. Remove the failed member from the cluster using its ID:

```
azureuser@k8s-master-50659983-0:~$ sudo etcdctl --
endpoints=https://10.255.255.6:2379,https://10.255.255.7:2379
member remove b3a6773c0e93604
Removed member b3a6773c0e93604 from cluster
```

4. Add a new member to the cluster with the name k8s-master-50659983-0-
   replace-0; you can use any name, but in general it is good to follow a
   convention. In our case, the member will have the same IP address as before:

```
azureuser@k8s-master-50659983-0:~$ sudo etcdctl --
endpoints=https://10.255.255.6:2379,https://10.255.255.7:2379
member add k8s-master-50659983-0-replace-0
https://10.255.255.5:2380
Added member named k8s-master-50659983-0-replace-0 with ID
af466a622a247b09 to cluster
```

5. Now, you need to modify the etcd service startup parameters in order to reflect
   the change of the member on this machine. Open /etc/default/etcd as the
   root using a text editor—for example, vim.
6. Modify the --name parameter to k8s-master-50659983-0-replace-0.
7. Modify the --initial-cluster parameter to k8s-
   master-50659983-2=https://10.255.255.7:2380,k8s-master-50659983
   -1=https://10.255.255.6:2380,k8s-master-50659983-0-replace-0=ht
   tps://10.255.255.5:2380.
8. Modify the --initial-cluster-state parameter to existing.
9. Finally, modify the data directory parameter --data-dir to a different one—for
   example, /var/lib/etcddisk-replace-0.
10. Save the file.
11. Create the data directory, ensuring that it is owned by etcd:

```
sudo mkdir /var/lib/etcddisk-replace-0
sudo chown etcd /var/lib/etcddisk-replace-0
sudo chgrp etcd /var/lib/etcddisk-replace-0
```

12. Start the etcd service:

```
sudo service etcd start
```

13. After a while, check the cluster health:

```
azureuser@k8s-master-50659983-0:~$ sudo etcdctl --
endpoints=https://10.255.255.6:2379,https://10.255.255.7:2379
cluster-health
member 1f5a8b7d5b2a5b68 is healthy: got healthy result from
https://10.255.255.5:2379
member 721d9c3882dbe6f7 is healthy: got healthy result from
https://10.255.255.7:2379
member 72b3415f69c52b2a is healthy: got healthy result from
https://10.255.255.6:2379
cluster is healthy
```

Success! The new member is `healthy` and the overall status of the cluster is also `healthy`!

 If you need to use a new machine with a *different* IP address for your etcd replacement member, remember to change the `--etcd-servers` argument for the Kubernetes API server and, if you use a load balancer in front of etcd, don't forget to update the load balancer configuration.

Congratulations! You have successfully performed the replacement of a failed member in an etcd cluster. Even though the new member is hosted on the same virtual machine, it has a new ID (`1f5a8b7d5b2a5b68`) and is treated as a completely new member in the cluster.

Summary

In this chapter, you have learned the key points you should bear in mind when preparing for Kubernetes DR. You have learned about stateful components in the whole Kubernetes cluster and the fact that they require a backup-and-restore strategy using etcd clusters and persistent volumes. Next, you learned how to manually perform a snapshot for your Kubernetes etcd cluster and upload it to an Azure blob container. Then, we used this snapshot to restore a Kubernetes cluster to a previous state and verified that the restore was successful. On top of this, you utilized all your new knowledge in order to create a Docker image for a snapshot worker that created a snapshot of etcd (for AKS Engine) and uploaded it to the Azure blob container. We used this Docker image to create a Kubernetes CronJob for performing backups, which is done every six hours. The last topic that we looked at was how to replace a failed etcd member in AKS Engine. With this knowledge, you should be able to create a reliable disaster-recovery plan for your Kubernetes cluster.

The last chapter of this book will focus on production considerations for running Kubernetes. You can treat this chapter as a set of loosely-coupled recommendations and best practices for different production scenarios.

Questions

1. What is the difference between disaster recovery (DC) and business continuity (BC) and how are they related?
2. Which components do you need to back up in Kubernetes to ensure the possibility of recovering the cluster state?
3. What is an etcd snapshot?
4. What are Velero and etcd-operators and what are their use cases?
5. What are high-level steps for recovering an etcd snapshot?
6. What is a Kubernetes CronJob and how can you use it to automate your backup strategy for etcd clusters?
7. What are high-level steps for replacing a failed etcd cluster member?

You can find answers to these questions in *Assessments* of this book.

Further reading

- For more information about Kubernetes features and disaster recovery in general, please refer to the following Packt books:
    - *The Complete Kubernetes Guide* (https://www.packtpub.com/virtualization-and-cloud/complete-kubernetes-guide).
    - *Getting Started with Kubernetes - Third Edition* (https://www.packtpub.com/virtualization-and-cloud/getting-started-kubernetes-third-edition).
    - *Kubernetes for Developers* (https://www.packtpub.com/virtualization-and-cloud/kubernetes-developers).

- If you are interested in the details about etcd itself and how to handle disaster recovery, you can refer to the official documentation at https://etcd.io/docs/v3.4.0/op-guide/recovery/.
- Additionally, we recommend watching the following excellent webinars from the **Cloud Native Computing Foundation** (**CNCF**) regarding Kubernetes backup strategies using Velero, and operating etcd in production:
    - https://www.cncf.io/webinars/kubernetes-backup-and-migration-strategies-using-project-velero/
    - https://www.cncf.io/webinars/kubernetes-in-production-operating-etcd-with-etcdadm/

16
Production Considerations for Running Kubernetes

You have arrived at the last chapter of this book— well done! In this short chapter, we will provide you with various best practices and recommendations for running Kubernetes in production. There are always two worlds for every software engineering approach or tool—how you use it for development and how you use it in production. For Kubernetes, running in production requires more operations overheads as you want to run your workloads with high availability and reliability, often at a large scale. You have to consider how you are performing upgrades to the cluster itself and how you patch the underlying operating system, ensuring the continuity of your business. If you are running Kubernetes in an isolated network in your enterprise data center, you may need to wire in network proxy configuration in all components of Docker and Kubernetes.

Additionally, it is important to ensure that your clusters are provisioned reproducibly using *infrastructure as code* and *immutable infrastructure* approaches. But this is not everything—you definitely want to manage your cluster workloads declaratively (similar to your infrastructure) and for that, you can employ the GitOps approach. All of the concepts that we describe in this chapter can be applied to Linux-only clusters and hybrid Windows/Linux clusters as well.

This last chapter of this book will cover the following topics:

- Provisioning clusters reproducibly
- Kubeadm limitations
- Upgrading clusters
- OS patching
- Configuring a network proxy for the Docker daemon and Kubernetes

Technical requirements

For this chapter, you will need the following:

- Windows 10 Pro, Enterprise, or Education (version 1903 or later, 64-bit) installed
- An Azure account
- Helm installed
- A Windows/Linux Kubernetes cluster deployed using AKS Engine or an on-premises cluster

To follow along, you will need your own Azure account to create Azure resources for the Kubernetes cluster. If you haven't already created the account for the previous chapters, you can read more about how to obtain a limited free account for personal use here: `https://azure.microsoft.com/en-us/free/`.

Deploying a Kubernetes cluster using AKS Engine has been covered in `Chapter 8`, *Deploying Hybrid Azure Kubernetes Service Engine Cluster*.

You can download the latest code samples for this chapter from the official GitHub repository: `https://github.com/PacktPublishing/Hands-On-Kubernetes-on-Windows/tree/master/Chapter16`.

Provisioning clusters reproducibly

First, let's take a look at how you can approach provisioning your clusters and the underlying infrastructure and how to declaratively manage your application workloads as part of your **Continuous Integration** or **Continuous Deployment (CI/CD)** pipelines. In all cases, setting up any *infrastructure as code* approach is a bit harder and more complex than just using the infrastructure but it pays off greatly in the end game. You gain configuration consistency, simplicity when introducing complex changes, testable/analyzable infrastructure changes, and reproducible environments for any stage of the development workflow.

Infrastructure as code for clusters

Infrastructure as Code (IaC) is, in short, the concept of managing your whole IT infrastructure using declarative configuration files only. What it means is that you aim to havie the state of your infrastructure captured in configuration files and apply changes to the environment using dedicated tools rather than performing physical hardware configuration using scripts or interactive tooling. For Azure, you can use **Azure Resource Manager (ARM)** templates (`https://docs.microsoft.com/en-us/azure/azure-resource-manager/resource-group-authoring-templates`) to describe your infrastructure or use a generic IaC tool such as Terraform (`https://www.terraform.io/`). In fact, you have already used ARM templates indirectly when deploying the AKS Engine cluster—you can think of AKS Engine tools as another layer of abstraction for creating complex ARM templates.

You can take the IaC approach even further: **Immutable Infrastructure (IM)**. In the case of IM, you never modify any configuration on the machines after they are deployed. If you need to perform a fix, you have to build a new machine from a base image with a fix and deprovision the old machines. This may sound extreme but it can be easily achieved both in the virtual machines world as well as bare-metal environments.

Packer (`https://www.packer.io/`) is one of the best tools to help you to introduce this paradigm for virtual and bare-metal machines. But if you think about it carefully, we have already been using IaC and IM in this book a lot but at a different, higher level.

Docker itself is a manifestation of *immutable infrastructure*, where you ship your software as immutable operating system container images, just as if they were VM images.Kubernetes can be seen as a platform for managing your immutable container infrastructure for your application workloads—whenever you create a new Docker image and roll out a new version of a Deployment, you are just creating new containers and throwing away the old ones. If you use a declarative approach to manage your Kubernetes objects (at least using `kubectl apply -f`), you end up with neat *infrastructure as code*.

This long introduction shows us a few things that can be treated as recommendations for provisioning infrastructure for Kubernetes and deploying your clusters, from the lowest to the highest level:

- Always provision your underlying infrastructure for clusters using the *infrastructure as code* or *immutable infrastructure* approach, using the right tools for the job. Terraform or ARM templates suit this task very well in both cases. AKS Engine (`https://github.com/Azure/aks-engine`) is a perfect example of *immutable infrastructure* tooling built on top of ARM templating. If you want to roll out a new version of a VM image for your cluster nodes, you need to create a new node pool with a new image and decommission the old node pool. Avoid using tools that were not originally meant to do that, such as Ansible.

- To create the Kubernetes cluster itself on your infrastructure, use the *infrastructure as code* concept. Tools such as Ansible (`https://www.ansible.com/`), Powershell Desired State Configuration (`https://docs.microsoft.com/en-us/powershell/scripting/dsc/overview/overview?view=powershell-6`), or dedicated kubespray (`https://github.com/kubernetes-sigs/kubespray`) are perfect for this task. AKS Engine excellently combines both infrastructure provisioning and cluster Deployment into one tool. If you need a managed Kubernetes service, then again use Terraform or ARM templates. But do not use them for self-managed clusters to provision software—even if they are capable of doing that, they were not meant to do so in the first place.

- Use Docker and Kubernetes clusters as an *immutable infrastructure* platform for your application workloads. Manage this platform using dedicated, declarative tools such as Kustomize (`https://kustomize.io/`) or Helm (`https://helm.sh/`). Take Helm chart management to an even higher, also declarative, level—use Helmfile (`https://github.com/roboll/helmfile`) or Flux (`https://github.com/fluxcd/flux`). You will not have to worry about running the `helm upgrade` command again! But again, do not use tools that were not meant for this, such as Ansible or Terraform, even though they have modules or providers that are advertised as being capable of managing Kubernetes Objects or Helm Charts. You risk tying to a custom API that does not have all of Kubernetes features and quickly gets outdated.

If you want to manage multiple Kubernetes clusters declaratively, definitely keep an eye on the Kubernetes Cluster API (`https://cluster-api.sigs.k8s.io/introduction.html`), which is currently in alpha state. This Kubernetes project will allow you to create a special Kubernetes management cluster where you can operate on clusters or machines as Kubernetes custom resources.

So, in short, always use the right tool for the job! This is why we will now take a look at Flux and the GitOps approach.

GitOps for application workloads

Flux (`https://github.com/fluxcd/flux`) is a tool that automatically ensures that the state of a Kubernetes cluster matches the configuration (manifests and Helm charts) in Git. This approach complies with GitOps, which is a way of managing Kubernetes clusters and your applications, proposed by Weaveworks (`https://www.weave.works/technologies/gitops/`), where the Git repository is the single source of truth for the declarative infrastructure and your application workloads. This approach fully complies with the *infrastructure as code* paradigm. Moreover, you have a good separation of concerns: the developers introduce the changes to the cluster state or application configuration, which are stored in a Git repository (through a full CI pipeline) and a dedicated GitOps component is responsible for applying the configuration to the Kubernetes cluster. You get this clear boundary and you can always be sure that what is in the repository reflects the actual cluster state.

Let's take a look at how you can use Flux to manage a cluster that runs the Voting Application that we have implemented throughout this book. You will need an AKS Engine cluster for that purpose that has Linux nodes capable of handling more than 4 volume mounts per node—you can use the following cluster ApiModel: `https://github.com/PacktPublishing/Hands-On-Kubernetes-on-Windows/blob/master/Chapter16/01_aks-engine-flux/kubernetes-windows-template.json`.

 Support for Helm 3 in Flux is currently in the development state. You can track progress here: `https://github.com/fluxcd/helm-operator/issues/8`. For this reason, we need to use custom images for Flux components, but by the time you read this, the support may already be in a stable state.

First, let's create our repository with the source of truth for the Kubernetes cluster. Please follow these steps:

1. Create a new GitHub repository. We will be using `https://github.com/hands-on-kubernetes-on-windows/voting-application-flux` for demonstration purposes.

2. In the `charts/voting-application` directory, place the Voting Application Helm chart. You can find the latest one here (with a small workaround for the `post-install` hook and waiting not working correctly in this version of Flux): `https://github.com/PacktPublishing/Hands-On-Kubernetes-on-Windows/tree/master/Chapter16/02_voting-application-flux/charts/voting-application`.

3. In the `namespaces` directory, create the `demo.yaml` file with the namespace definition:

```
apiVersion: v1
kind: Namespace
metadata:
  labels:
    name: demo
  name: demo
```

4. In the `storageclasses` directory, create the `azure-disk.yaml` file with the StorageClass definition:

```
kind: StorageClass
apiVersion: storage.k8s.io/v1beta1
metadata:
  name: azure-disk
provisioner: kubernetes.io/azure-disk
parameters:
  storageaccounttype: Standard_LRS
  kind: Managed
```

5. In the `releases` directory, create the `voting-application.yaml` file with the `HelmRelease` custom resource for our Voting Application. This custom resource is handled by the Flux Helm Operator:

```
apiVersion: helm.fluxcd.io/v1
kind: HelmRelease
metadata:
  name: voting-application
  namespace: demo
  annotations:
    fluxcd.io/automated: "true"
spec:
  releaseName: voting-application
  helmVersion: v3
  timeout: 1200
  wait: false
  rollback:
    enable: false
```

```
chart:
    git: ssh://git@github.com/hands-on-kubernetes-on-
windows/voting-application-flux
    ref: master
    path: charts/voting-application
```

6. Push the changes to your GitHub repository.

> Flux does not follow any directory convention—it is up to you how you
> define the structure. All it does is search for YAML files in the repository.

We have defined our repository with a source of truth. Now, let's deploy Flux to our
cluster, which is capable of handling Helm 3 charts. Execute the following steps (or you can
use the PowerShell script: (https://github.com/PacktPublishing/Hands-On-Kubernetes-
on-Windows/blob/master/Chapter16/03_DeployFlux.ps1):

1. Open a new PowerShell window as Administrator.
2. Install `fluxctl` using Chocolatey:

    choco install fluxctl

3. Create a dedicated `fluxcd` namespace for your Flux components:

    kubectl create namespace fluxcd

4. Add the Flux Helm repository:

    helm repo add fluxcd https://charts.fluxcd.io

5. Install the Flux Helm chart. You need to ensure that all components have
   `nodeSelector` set to run on Linux nodes. Set the `git.url` value to your GitHub
   repository:

    ```
    helm upgrade -i flux fluxcd/flux `
        --namespace fluxcd `
        --set "nodeSelector.`"kubernetes\.io/os`"=linux" `
        --set "memcached.nodeSelector.`"kubernetes\.io/os`"=linux" `
        --set "helmOperator.nodeSelector.`"kubernetes\.io/os`"=linux" `
        `
        --set git.url=git@github.com:hands-on-kubernetes-on-
    windows/voting-application-flux `
        --debug
    ```

6. Apply the official manifest for HelmRelease custom resource definition (here we use the development manifest from the `helm-v3-dev` branch):

```
kubectl apply -f
https://raw.githubusercontent.com/fluxcd/helm-operator/helm-v3-dev/
deploy/flux-helm-release-crd.yaml
```

7. Install the Helm chart for the Flux Helm operator. This is a version of the operator that comes from the development branch with support for Helm 3. Remember to ensure the Linux `nodeSelector`:

```
helm upgrade -i helm-operator fluxcd/helm-operator `
    --namespace fluxcd `
    --set git.ssh.secretName=flux-git-deploy `
    --set configureRepositories.enable=true `
    --set configureRepositories.repositories[0].name=stable `
    --set
configureRepositories.repositories[0].url=https://kubernetes-charts.storage
.googleapis.com `
    --set extraEnvs[0].name=HELM_VERSION `
    --set extraEnvs[0].value=v3 `
    --set image.repository=docker.io/fluxcd/helm-operator-prerelease `
    --set image.tag=helm-v3-dev-ca9c8ba0 `
    --set "nodeSelector.`"kubernetes\.io/os`"=linux"
```

8. Use `fluxctl` to retrieve the public SSH key that has to be added as a deploy key to your GitHub repository:

```
fluxctl identity --k8s-fwd-ns fluxcd
```

9. Copy the key and open your GitHub repository in a web browser.
10. Navigate to **Settings** and **Deploy Keys**.
11. Add your key with write access.
12. Now, you can wait for a short while until the repository is automatically synchronized by Flux or force synchronization using this command:

```
fluxctl sync --k8s-fwd-ns fluxcd
```

13. Observe the creation of components using `kubectl get all -n demo`. You can also use the `kubectl logs` command to follow Helm operator logs, especially in the event of any problems with the process of installing the Helm release:

```
PS C:\src> kubectl get all -n demo
NAME                                                      READY
STATUS     RESTARTS    AGE
```

```
pod/voting-application-5cb4987765-7ht4x                0/1
Running   1              2m
pod/voting-application-5cb4987765-dstml                0/1
Running   1              2m
. . .
```

> In the preceding steps, we used imperative commands, as in the official
> guides from Flux. You can, of course, use declarative manifests and
> YAML files with values for the Helm releases.

As you can see, the whole procedure is completely automatic. You define the state in the
Git repository and Flux automatically takes care of applying the changes to the cluster.
Now, let's test how rolling out a change in the cluster state works. As an example, we will
change the tag for the image that we use in the Voting Application, as if we were rolling out
a new version of the application:

1. In your repository with the cluster state, start editing `charts/voting-application/Chart.yaml`.
2. Change `version` to `0.4.1` to indicate that the chart version itself has changed.
3. Change `appVersion` to a different Voting Application image tag. We can use, for
   example, `1.5.0`, one of the previous versions.
4. Save the changes, commit to the repository, and push to GitHub.
5. Wait for the changes to be synced automatically or force the sync using
   the `fluxctl sync --k8s-fwd-ns fluxcd` command.
6. Execute the `kubectl get pods -n demo` command to see that the resources
   are indeed recreating:

```
PS C:\src> kubectl get pods -n demo
NAME                                              READY    STATUS
RESTARTS    AGE
voting-application-55fb99587d-rjvmq               0/1      Running
0           16s
voting-application-55fb99587d-whrwv               1/1      Running
0           79s
voting-application-55fb99587d-x9j8q               0/1
ContainerCreating   0              79s
voting-application-5cb4987765-g21x8               1/1
Terminating         0              21m
```

7. Describe one of the new pods to verify that it was created with the desired Docker image tag:

```
PS C:\src> kubectl describe pod -n demo voting-
application-55fb99587d-rjvmq
...
Containers:
  voting-application-frontend:
    Container ID:
docker://61e207885bcfc3bde670702e342345127dcf0d6e782609bc68127078fc
007034
      Image: packtpubkubernetesonwindows/voting-application:1.6.0
```

Congratulations! You have successfully set up a GitOps pipeline using Flux. In production, you can easily extend the pipeline by adding CI/CD components integrated with your Git repository, which will perform, for example, the validation of each pull request before it is merged to the cluster state repository. You can learn more about more complex pipelines in the following article: `https://www.weave.works/blog/what-is-gitops-really`.

In the next section, we will take a look at kubeadm limitations for production use cases.

Kubeadm limitations

Kubeadm (`https://github.com/kubernetes/kubeadm`) is a command-line tool for provisioning Kubernetes clusters focused on performing actions necessary to get a minimum viable secure cluster up and running in a user-friendly way—we introduced this tool in `Chapter 4`, *Kubernetes Concepts and Windows Support,* and later used it in `Chapter 7`, *Deploying Hybrid On-Premises Kubernetes Cluster.* This tool is scoped only to a given machine and Kubernetes API communication, so in general, it is intended to be a building block for other automation tools that manage the cluster as a whole. You will find that other complex automation tools such as kubespray are built on top of kubeadm.

Starting with Kubernetes 1.13, kubeadm is considered stable and ready for production use. But even though its current core feature set is in a stable state, you should take into account several limitations that may not make kubeadm the right tool for your production Kubernetes Deployment:

- kubeadm has only initial support for Windows nodes and the API regarding this support is likely to change. This makes production Deployments of hybrid clusters a hard task—the only alternative at this point is manually configuring Kubernetes components on Windows nodes and joining them to an existing Linux cluster. Of course, if you are running on Azure you can use AKS or AKS Engine to run Windows container workloads in production.
- A highly available Kubernetes cluster setup (with stacked and internal etcd topology) is now possible with kubeadm but is still relatively complex. You can read more in the official documentation: `https://kubernetes.io/docs/setup/production-environment/tools/kubeadm/high-availability/`. Additionally, there is no easy way to manage the etcd cluster afterward using kubeadm, which means that solutions such as kubespray give more flexibility. But of course, this comes at the cost of no support for Windows at this point.
- kubeadm cannot be used for joining new nodes to existing clusters that have been bootstrapped without kubeadm.

In general, for hybrid Windows/Linux Kubernetes clusters there is no perfect way for provisioning production-ready clusters if you cannot use AKS or AKS Engine. Using kubeadm is still the only semi-automated way to set up such clusters.

Now, let's take a look at how you can upgrade your Kubernetes cluster to a newer version.

Upgrading clusters

Running a Kubernetes cluster in production will definitely require upgrading the Kubernetes components to newer versions at some point. How you perform the upgrade itself depends on the tools that you use to bootstrap and manage the cluster. But in general, the high-level procedure looks as follows:

1. Upgrade the components running on the primary master node.
2. Upgrade the components running on the additional master nodes.
3. Upgrade the worker nodes.

There is an important rule that you have to follow to ensure safe upgrades: you can only upgrade the cluster by one minor version at once. It means that, for example, a cluster that has version 1.16 can be only upgraded to 1.17—you cannot make a jump straight to 1.18. The reason for this is the version skew policy for Kubernetes master components, which allows running one minor version difference at most only. The expected cadence for releases of minor versions of Kubernetes is three months, which means that you may need to run the upgrade procedure quite often, especially considering that each minor version will be maintained for approximately nine months. You can read about the policies for all components in the official documentation: `https://kubernetes.io/docs/setup/release/version-skew-policy/`.

Depending on how you bootstrapped the cluster, the exact upgrade steps will be different. For example, for kubeadm clusters, the upgrade will be performed in place, on the same machines. But if you use AKS or AKS Engine, the procedure will be compliant with *immutable infrastructure* paradigm: master and worker VMs will be sequentially replaced with VMs running a newer version of Kubernetes components. In more detail, for master nodes, the automated upgrade procedure looks as follows under the hood:

1. `Cordon` (mark the node as unschedulable) one of the master nodes and drain the existing pods.
2. Delete the physical VM. Now, the size of the control plane is `N-1` nodes.
3. Create a new VM with the new version of Kubernetes components.
4. Add the new VM to the cluster and apply any existing labels, annotations, or taints for the node. Now, the size of the data plane is again `N`.

For worker nodes, the procedure is similar and has the following steps:

1. Create a new VM with the new version of Kubernetes components.
2. Add the new VM to the cluster. Now, the size of the data plane is `M+1`.
3. If any pods have already been scheduled to the new node, evict them.
4. Apply any existing labels, annotations, or taints to the new node.
5. `Cordon` the old node and drain the existing pods.
6. Delete the old VM. Now, the size of the data plane is again `M`.

The reason why worker nodes are upgraded by adding an extra node (instead of removing the existing node first) is to ensure that the cluster capacity for data plane workloads does not shrink. This ensures that the upgrade is entirely transparent for the users. You can read more about upgrade procedures for AKS at: `https://docs.microsoft.com/en-us/azure/aks/upgrade-cluster` and for AKS Engine at: `https://github.com/Azure/aks-engine/blob/master/docs/topics/upgrade.md`.

You can use the *immutable infrastructure* approach for upgrades used in AKS and AKS Engine to perform manual upgrades of clusters bootstrapped using different tools, as long as the toolset allows adding new master and worker nodes.

Let's now perform an upgrade of a Kubernetes cluster (with Windows nodes) that has been created using AKS Engine. For this demonstration, we are running a cluster with version 1.16.1, which we have created in the previous sections. You will need the cluster ApiModel, which you used for the initial Deployment. To perform the upgrade, please follow these steps:

1. Open a PowerShell window. Determine what the available Kubernetes versions are that you can use for upgrading your AKS Engine cluster with Windows nodes. Run the following command:

```
PS C:\src> aks-engine get-versions --version 1.16.1 --windows
Version Upgrades
1.16.1 1.17.0-alpha.1, 1.17.0-alpha.2, 1.17.0-alpha.3, 1.17.0-
beta.1
```

2. Let's upgrade the cluster to the latest version, `1.17.0-beta.1`. If you do not have your AKS Engine Service Principal, you have to generate a new one because it is not possible to retrieve the password of an existing one. To do that, use the following command:

```
az ad sp create-for-rbac `
    --role="Contributor" `
    --
scopes="/subscriptions/<azureSubscriptionId>/resourceGroups/<resour
ceGroupName>"
```

Take note of `appId` and `password` to use it during the upgrade command.

3. Execute the following command to perform the upgrade. You have to specify the generated cluster ApiModel:

```
aks-engine upgrade `
            --subscription-id <azureSubscriptionId> `
            --api-model .\_output\<dnsPrefix>\apimodel.json `
            --location <azureLocation> `
            --resource-group <resourceGroupName> `
            --upgrade-version "1.17.0-beta.1" `
            --auth-method client_secret `
            --client-id <appId> `
            --client-secret <password>
```

4. The upgrade can take around 50 minutes (10 minutes per node), depending on the size of your cluster. If you are using a single-node control plane in your cluster, you won't be able to access the Kubernetes API during the upgrade for some time. When the upgrade is finished, run the following command to verify that the nodes are running the desired version of Kubernetes:

```
PS C:\src> kubectl get nodes
NAME                          STATUS   ROLES    AGE     VERSION
1754k8s010                    Ready    agent    17m     v1.17.0-
beta.1
1754k8s012                    Ready    agent    26m     v1.17.0-
beta.1
k8s-linuxpool1-17543130-0     Ready    agent    3m44s   v1.17.0-
beta.1
k8s-linuxpool1-17543130-2     Ready    agent    9m51s   v1.17.0-
beta.1
k8s-master-17543130-0         Ready    master   48m     v1.17.0-
beta.1
```

 In production clusters, especially if you are running a customized cluster with extensions or dedicated VM images, it is recommended to test the upgrade in a separate staging cluster that was created using exactly the same specification.

Congratulations, you have successfully upgraded your AKS Engine cluster to version `1.17.0-beta.1`. In the next section, you will learn how to approach operating system patching in Kubernetes.

OS patching

To ensure the best security of your cluster and the underlying infrastructure, you must ensure that you are running an operating system with the latest patches on your nodes. Fortunately, Kubernetes is flexible when it comes to the maintenance of nodes. The general approach for any maintenance, including applying OS patches that require reboot, is as follows:

1. `Cordon` (mark the node as unschedulable) the node and drain the existing pods.
2. Apply the required updates and reboot the machine.
3. `Uncordon` the node to make it schedulable again.

Alternatively, if you use an *immutable infrastructure* approach, the preceding steps have to be extended by the creation of a new patched machine and the deletion of the old machine. For example, in AKS Engine, this scenario could look as follows, providing that you use Virtual Machine Scale Sets (VMSS) with a custom VM image for your node pools:

1. Build a new version of the VM image.
2. Update the VM image for your VMSS (`https://docs.microsoft.com/en-us/azure/virtual-machine-scale-sets/virtual-machine-scale-sets-upgrade-scale-set#update-the-os-image-for-your-scale-set`), possibly directly in the ARM template.
3. For each VM in the VMSS, sequentially perform the following: `cordon` and drain the node, set the VM image to the latest version for the VMSS instance, and `uncordon` the node.

> If you are interested in creating your own custom VM images for AKS Engine Windows nodes, you can read the following description of the build process, which uses Packer and Azure DevOps: `https://github.com/Azure/aks-engine/blob/master/docs/topics/windows-vhd.md`.

To exercise the manual procedure of maintenance for Windows nodes, please perform the following steps:

1. Let's assume that we would like to patch the `1754k8s010` Windows node.

2. Use the name to get the private IP address of the `1754k8s010` node:

```
PS C:\src> az vm show -g <resourceGroupName> -n 1754k8s010 --show-
details --query 'privateIps'
"10.240.0.35,10.240.0.36,10.240.0.37,10.240.0.38,10.240.0.39,10.240
.0.40,10.240.0.41,10.240.0.42,10.240.0.43,10.240.0.44,10.240.0.45,1
0.240.0.46,10.240.0.47,10.240.0.48,10.240.0.49,10.240.0.50,10.240.0
.51,10.240.0.52,10.240.0.53,10.240.0.54,10.240.0.55,10.240.0.56,10.
240.0.57,10.240.0.58,10.240.0.59,10.240.0.60,10.240.0.61,10.240.0.6
2,10.240.0.63,10.240.0.64,10.240.0.65"
```

3. Use one of the private IPs to create an SSH tunnel from your local `5500` port via the master node to port `3389` (RDP) on the Windows node:

```
ssh -L 5500:10.240.0.35:3389
azureuser@<dnsPrefix>.<azureLocation>.cloudapp.azure.com
```

4. In a different PowerShell window, start the RDP session via the tunnel:

```
mstsc /v:localhost:5500
```

5. Provide your Windows node credentials (as in ApiModel) and connect.
6. Wait for the console to initialize.
7. Now, you are ready to perform the maintenance, but first, we need to drain the node (which also `cordons` the node first). In a new PowerShell window on your local machine, execute this command:

```
PS C:\src> kubectl drain 1754k8s010
node/1754k8s010 cordoned
node/1754k8s010 drained
```

8. When the node is drained, you can start your maintenance procedure. For example, you can use the `sconfig.cmd` utility in the console to apply the updates manually:

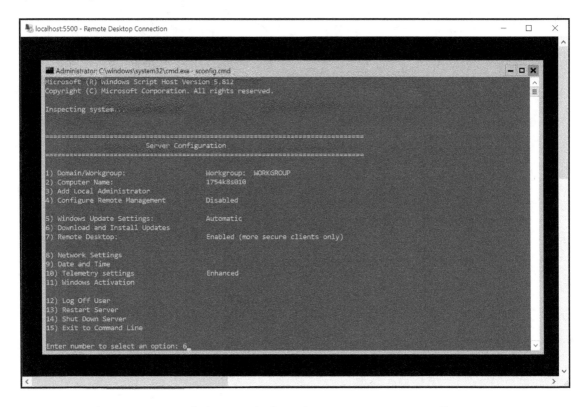

9. Select option 6 and choose which updates you want to install:

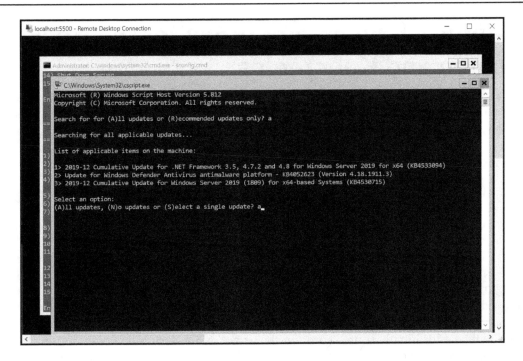

10. Wait for the installation to end and reboot the machine if needed.

11. When the node is fully rebooted, you can `uncordon` the node to make it schedulable again:

```
PS C:\src> kubectl uncordon 1754k8s010
node/1754k8s010 uncordoned
```

Your node will be now fully functional in the cluster again.

 Alternatively, you may consider using Azure Update Management to manage operating system updates and patching in your cluster. You can read more in the official documentation: `https://docs.microsoft.com/en-us/azure/automation/automation-update-management`.

In the last section, we will show which components in Kubernetes require additional configuration if you are running your production cluster behind an HTTP(S) network proxy.

Configuring a network proxy for the Docker daemon and Kubernetes

In enterprise environments, it is a common practice to use HTTP(S) network proxies for connections to external networks and especially the internet. This comes at an additional configuration cost of all components that are running behind a proxy—we are going to give a brief overview of what components in Kubernetes you need to make the proxy aware to use Docker images from external registries and propagate the proxy settings to the containers.

Let's assume that our proxy addresses are as follows:

- `http://proxy.example.com:8080/` for HTTP proxy
- `http://proxy.example.com:9090/` for HTTPS proxy

Configuration for other standard proxies, such as SFTP, can be done similarly. You may also need appropriate no-proxy variables to exclude the Kubernetes nodes and local network, otherwise, you will be not able to communicate between the nodes or the traffic to nodes, will be additionally routed through the proxy! Now, for Linux nodes and masters (assuming a Debian-based distribution, such as Ubuntu), you will need to ensure that the following settings are configured:

1. Define proxy settings for the default environment, `/etc/environment`. This will make tools such as APT honor the proxy settings:

    ```
    HTTP_PROXY=http://proxy.example.com:8080/
    HTTPS_PROXY=http://proxy.example.com:9090/
    http_proxy=http://proxy.example.com:8080/
    https_proxy=http://proxy.example.com:9090/
    ```

2. Proxies are set for the Docker daemon environment. This will ensure that the containers receive the proxy variables as well. You can define the `/etc/systemd/system/docker.service.d/http-proxy.conf` file with the following contents:

    ```
    [Service]
    Environment="HTTP_PROXY=http://proxy.example.com:8080/"
    "HTTPS_PROXY=http://proxy.example.com:9090/"
    ```

3. For building Docker images on machines behind a proxy, consider passing the proxy settings as arguments:

```
docker build --build-arg
http_proxy=http://proxy.example.com:8080/ \
  --build-arg https_proxy=http://proxy.example.com:9090/ \
  -t someimage .
```

For your Windows worker nodes, you can take the following steps:

1. Define global environment variables from PowerShell as an Administrator:

```
[Environment]::SetEnvironmentVariable("HTTP_PROXY",
"http://proxy.example.com:8080/",
[EnvironmentVariableTarget]::Machine)
[Environment]::SetEnvironmentVariable("HTTPS_PROXY",
"http://proxy.example.com:9090/",
[EnvironmentVariableTarget]::Machine)
```

2. Additionally, ensure that any traffic that uses a web browser engine also respects the proxy settings:

```
reg add
"HKCU\Software\Microsoft\Windows\CurrentVersion\Internet
Settings" /v ProxyServer /t REG_SZ /d proxy.example.com:8080 /f
reg add
"HKCU\Software\Microsoft\Windows\CurrentVersion\Internet
Settings" /v ProxyEnable /t REG_DWORD /d 1 /f
```

These configuration steps should let you pull Docker images, bootstrap the cluster, and later make pod containers aware of these settings when connecting to an external network.

Summary

In this chapter, we focused on common operational best practices for Kubernetes clusters running in production. First, we covered the approaches for provisioning infrastructure for Kubernetes and deploying the clusters reproducibly—we introduced the concepts of *infrastructure as code* and *immutable infrastructure* and have showed how they fit into the Kubernetes landscape. Additionally, we provided a recommendation on the best tools for provisioning infrastructure and cluster Deployments. Next, you learned what GitOps is and how to apply this philosophy using Flux and Git repositories. We focused on the operational aspects of upgrades and the patching of both the underlying cluster infrastructure and Kubernetes itself. And lastly, you learned how to ensure that your Kubernetes cluster can run behind HTTP(S) network proxies in enterprise environments.

Congratulations! This has been a long journey into the (almost) *uncharted territory* of Kubernetes on Windows—good luck with your further Kubernetes journey and thanks for reading.

Questions

1. What is the difference between *infrastructure as code* and *immutable infrastructure*?
2. Why is Kubernetes considered to be a platform that uses the *infrastructure as code* approach?
3. What is GitOps?
4. What are the benefits of using Flux in your Kubernetes clusters?
5. What are the steps during the upgrade of a Kubernetes cluster version?
6. What is the procedure for performing maintenance on a Kubernetes node?

You can find answers to these questions in *Assessments* of this book.

Further reading

- For more information about Kubernetes features and running the cluster in production, please refer to the following Packt books:
    - *The Complete Kubernetes Guide* (https://www.packtpub.com/virtualization-and-cloud/complete-kubernetes-guide)
    - *Getting Started with Kubernetes - Third Edition* (https://www.packtpub.com/virtualization-and-cloud/getting-started-kubernetes-third-edition)
- If you are interested in exploring *infrastructure as code* concepts, you can check out the following Packt book:
    - *Infrastructure as Code (IaC) Cookbook* (https://www.packtpub.com/virtualization-and-cloud/infrastructure-code-iac-cookbook)
- The Kubernetes documentation offers some more best practices for running clusters: https://kubernetes.io/docs/setup/best-practices/.

Assessments

Chapter 1: Creating Containers

1. Object Namespaces, Process Table, Job Objects, and Windows Container Isolation Filesystem. Additionally, on top of these low-level functionalities, **Host Compute Service** (**HCS**) and **Host Network Service** (**HNS**) abstract the public interface for running and managing containers.

2. Windows Server containers require the host OS version to match the container base image OS version. Additionally, on Windows, you can use Hyper-V isolation, which enables running containers with a non-matching base image OS version.

3. In Hyper-V isolation, each container is running inside a dedicated, minimal Hyper-V virtual machine. Containers do not share the kernel with host OS; there are no compatibility limitations between the host OS version and the container base OS version. Use Hyper-V isolation if you need to run containers with a non-matching base image OS version and in multi-tenant environments with untrusted code execution scenarios.

4. To enable LCOW support in Docker Desktop (version 18.02 or later), you have to enable the experimental features option in **Docker Settings | Daemon**. Creating an LCOW container requires specifying the `--platform linux` parameter for the `docker run` command.

5. `docker logs <containerId>`

6. For Windows containers that have Powershell installed, you can use the following command: `docker exec -it <containerId> powershell.exe`.

Chapter 2: Managing State in Containers

1. The container layer is the top writeable layer in the filesystem for each Docker container.

2. Bind mounts provide a simple functionality of mounting any file or directory from the container host to a given container. Volumes provide similar functionality but they are fully managed by Docker, so you do not have to worry about physical paths in the container host filesystem.

3. The writeable container layer is coupled with the container host, which means it is not possible to easily move the data to a different host. Layer filesystems provide worse performance than direct access to the host filesystem (for example, using volumes). You cannot share the writeable layer between different containers.

4. Use the SMB Global Mapping feature on Windows host, which is provided to mount SMB shares visible to the containers. Then, you can mount the SMB share in a container as a regular directory from the host machine.

5. No. To persist your storage data for Hyper-V containers, you have to use Docker volumes. If you need to use bind mounts (for example, for SMB Global Mappings), you have to use process isolation.

6. `docker volume prune`

7. Volume drivers in Docker can be used to manage volumes that are hosted on remote machines or in cloud services.

Chapter 3: Working with Container Images

1. A Docker registry is an organized, hierarchical system for storing Docker images, providing scalable distribution of images. Docker Hub is the official, public Docker registry hosted and managed by Docker, Inc.

2. A tag is a versioning label for a single image in a repository.

3. `<dockerId>/<repositoryName>:<tag>`

4. **Azure Container Registry** (**ACR**) is a fully managed private Docker registry provided by the Azure cloud. In the case of ACR, you store the images using your own Azure storage account and you can make the registry fully private, for your own infrastructure needs.

5. `latest` is the default tag used when you pull or build images (if you do not specify an explicit tag). In general, you should not use the `latest` tag apart from in development scenarios. In production, always specify an explicit tag for your Kubernetes manifests or in the Dockerfile instructions.

6. Semver suggests the following scheme of using three numbers, major, minor, and patch, separated with dots: `<major>.<minor>.<patch>`, where each number is incremented as needed.

7. **Docker Content Trust** (**DCT**) provides a means of verifying digital signatures of data being transferred between Docker engine and the Docker registry. This verification allows the publishers to sign their images and the consumer (Docker engine) to verify the signatures to ensure the integrity and source of the images.

Chapter 4: Kubernetes Concepts and Windows Support

1. The control plane (master) consists of a set of components that are responsible for global decisions regarding the cluster, such as the scheduling and deployment of application instances to worker nodes and managing cluster events. The data plane consists of worker nodes that are responsible for running container workloads scheduled by the master.

2. Cluster management is performed using a declarative model, which makes Kubernetes very powerful—you describe the desired state and Kubernetes does all of the heavy lifting to transform the current state of the cluster to the desired state.

3. A Kubernetes Pod consists of one or more containers that share kernel namespaces, IPC, a network stack (so you address them by the same cluster IP and they can communicate via localhost), and storage. In other words, Pods can contain multiple containers that share some resources.

4. A Deployment API object is used for the declarative management of ReplicaSet rollouts and scaling. This is the key API object for ensuring the smooth rollout of a new version of your application.

5. Windows machines can only join the cluster as worker nodes. There is no possibility and no plans for running master components on Windows. The setup of a local Kubernetes development environment for hybrid Linux/Windows clusters is complex and currently no standard solutions, such as Minikube or Docker Desktop for Windows' support such a configuration.

6. Minikube aims at providing a stable environment for local development with Kubernetes. It is available on Windows, Linux, and macOS but can provide Linux clusters only.

7. **AKS** (short for **Azure Kubernetes Service**) is a fully managed Kubernetes cluster offering by Azure. AKS Engine is an official, open source tool for provisioning self-managed Kubernetes cluster on Azure. Internally, AKS uses AKS Engine but they cannot manage clusters created by one another.

Chapter 5: Kubernetes Networking

1. Pods running on a node must be able to communicate with all Pods on all nodes (including the Pod's node) without NAT and explicit port mapping. All Kubernetes components running on a node, for example, kubelet or system daemons/services, must be able to communicate with all Pods on that node.

2. You can use Flannel with host-gw only if there is Layer 2 (L2) connectivity between the nodes in the cluster. In other words, there cannot be any L3 routers between the nodes.

3. A NodePort Service is implemented as a ClusterIP Service with the additional capability of being reachable using any cluster node IP address and a specified port. To achieve that, kube-proxy exposes the same port on each node from the range of 30000–32767 (which is configurable) and sets up forwarding so that any connections to this port will be forwarded to ClusterIP.

4. Reduced cost (you use only one cloud load balancer to serve the incoming traffic) and L7 load balancing capabilities

5. A container runtime uses CNI plugins to connect containers to the network and remove them from the network when needed.

6. An internal vSwitch is not connected to a network adapter on the container host, whereas an external vSwitch is connected and provides connectivity with external networks.

7. Docker network modes (drivers) are a concept coming from Docker that is part of the **Container Network Model** (**CNM**). This specification was proposed by Docker to solve container networking setup and management challenges in a modular, pluginable way. CNI is a CNCF project aiming at providing a simple and clear interface between any container runtime and network implementation. They solve almost the same problem but in different ways. On Windows, the implementation of Docker network modes and CNI plugins is the same—they are lightweight adapters for HNS.

8. On Windows, overlay network mode creates a VXLAN overlay network using VFP at an external Hyper-V vSwitch. Each overlay network has its own IP subnet, determined by a customizable IP prefix.

Chapter 6: Interacting with Kubernetes Clusters

1. kubectl uses the kubeconfig file, which is located in `~\.kube\config`. This YAML configuration file contains all of the parameters required for kubectl to connect to the Kubernetes API for your cluster

2. You can use a `KUBECONFIG` environment variable or the `--kubeconfig` flag for individual commands to force kubectl to use a different kubeconfig.

3. Contexts are used for organizing and coordinating access to multiple Kubernetes clusters.

4. `kubectl create` is an imperative command to create new API resources, whereas `kubectl apply` is a declarative management command for managing API resources.

5. `kubectl patch` updates a resource by merging the current resource state and a patch that contains only the modified properties. A common use case for patching is when you need to enforce a node selector for an existing DaemonSet in hybrid Linux/Windows clusters.

6. `kubectl logs <podName>`

7. `kubectl cp <podName>:<sourceRemotePath> <destinationLocalPath>`

Chapter 7: Deploying a Hybrid On-Premises Kubernetes Cluster

1. Use an internal NAT Hyper-V vSwitch if you plan to use the cluster for local development only. Any external inbound communication (apart from your Hyper-V host machine) will require NAT. Use an external Hyper-V vSwitch if your network has DHCP and DNS servers that you (or the network administrator) can manage. This will be the case in most production deployments.

2. In short, changing operating system configuration, such as disabling swap, installing a Docker container runtime, installing Kubernetes packages, and performing `kubeadm init`.

3. The Service subnet is a virtual subnet (non-routable) used by Pods for accessing services. Routable address translation from virtual IPs is performed by kube-proxy running on nodes. The Pod subnet is a global subnet used by all Pods in the cluster.

4. `kubeadm token create --print-join-command`

5. `kubectl taint nodes --all node-role.kubernetes.io/master-`

6. The Flannel network with a host-gw backend (win-bridge CNI plugin on Windows nodes): A host-gw backend is preferable as it is in a stable feature state, whereas an overlay backend is still in alpha feature state for Windows nodes.

7. In short, download `sig-windows-tools` scripts, which install the Docker and Kubernetes packages; prepare JSON configuration file for the scripts; and execute them.

8. `kubectl logs <podName>`

Chapter 8: Deploying a Hybrid Azure Kubernetes Service Engine Cluster

1. AKS is a fully managed Kubernetes cluster offering by Azure. AKS Engine is an official, open source tool for provisioning self-managed Kubernetes clusters on Azure. Internally, AKS uses AKS Engine, but they cannot manage clusters created by one another.

2. AKS Engine generates an **Azure Resource Manager** (**ARM**) template based on a supplied configuration file (cluster apimodel). Then, you can use this ARM template to deploy a fully functional, self-managed Kubernetes cluster on Azure infrastructure.

3. No. Even if AKS internally uses AKS Engine, it is not possible to use AKS Engine to manage AKS and vice versa.

4. The Azure CLI, Azure Cloud Shell, kubectl, and optionally the SSH client for Windows if you would like to connect to the nodes using SSH.

5. AKS Engine uses the apimodel (or cluster definition) JSON file to generate ARM templates, which can be used for deploying Kubernetes clusters directly to Azure.

6. Use SSH and execute the following command: `ssh azureuser@<dnsPrefix>.<azureLocation>.cloudapp.azure.com`.

7. Assuming that `10.240.0.4` is the private IP of the Windows node, create an SSH connection to the master that forwards the RDP port to the Windows node using the `ssh -L 5500:10.240.0.4:3389 azureuser@<dnsPrefix>.<azureLocation>.cloudapp.azure.com` command. In a new command-line window, start an RDP session using the `mstsc /v:localhost:5500` command.

Chapter 9: Deploying Your First Application

1. The imperative approach consists of executing imperative kubectl commands, such as `kubectl run` or `kubectl expose`. In the declarative approach, you always modify object configurations (manifest files) and create or update them in the cluster using the `kubectl apply` command (alternatively, you can use Kustomization files).

2. The imperative `kubectl delete` command is preferred over declarative deletion as it gives predictable results.

3. `kubectl diff -f <file/directory>`

4. The recommended practice is using `nodeSelector` for the predictable scheduling of your Pods for both Windows and Linux containers.

5. You can use `kubectl proxy` to access any Service API object. `kubectl port-forward` is a more low-level command that you can use for accessing individual Pods or Pods running in a deployment or behind a service.

6. Using an Ingress Controller is possible only if you have nodes that are capable of running Ingress Controller Pods. For example, for ingress-nginx, the deployment of an Ingress Controller is possible for Linux nodes only—you will be able to create Ingress objects for services running on Windows nodes but all of the load balancing will be performed on Linux nodes.

7. `kubectl scale deployment/<deploymentName> --replicas=<targetNumberOfReplicas>`

Chapter 10: Deploying Microsoft SQL Server 2019 and ASP.NET MVC Applications

1. You can choose from the following: passing arguments to the container commands, defining system environment variables for the container, mounting ConfigMaps or Secrets as container volumes, and optionally wrapping everything up using PodPresets.

2. `LogMonitor.exe` acts as a supervisor for your application process and prints logs to standard output, which are gathered from different sources based on the configuration file. There are plans to further extend this solution to be used in the sidecar container pattern.

3. You need to ensure that the migrations can be rolled back and that the database schema is fully compatible with the old and new application versions. In other words, backward-incompatible changes such as renames have to be handled specially to make things backward compatible between the individual steps.

4. This guarantees data persistence when the Pod is terminated and ensures SQL Server failover, even if the new Pod is scheduled on a different node.

5. You need to use the `ef6.exe` command to apply the migrations. This can be executed using the Kubernetes Job object.

6. If you use a `requests` value for resources that is lower than the `limits` value, you can enter the state of resource overcommitting. This makes it possible for Pods to temporarily use more resources than they have requested and enables the more effective bin-packing of Pod workloads.

7. The VS remote debugger is exposed at the `4020` TCP port from your container. To connect to it, without exposing it as a Service object, you need to use kubectl port forwarding.

Chapter 11: Configuring Applications to Use Kubernetes Features

1. The general principle of namespaces is providing resource quotas and a scope for object names. You will organize the namespaces depending on the size of your cluster and your team.

2. The readiness probe is used to determine whether a given container is ready to accept traffic. The liveness probe is used to detect whether a container needs to be restarted.

3. The wrong configuration of this probe can result in cascading failures in your services and container restart loops.

4. `requests` specifies the guaranteed amount of a given resource provided by the system. `limits` specifies the maximum amount of a given resource provided by the system.

5. Avoiding thrashing (replica count fluctuating frequently).

6. ConfigMaps and Secrets can hold technically any type of data consisting of key-value pairs. The purpose of Secrets is keeping sensitive information for accessing dependencies, whereas ConfigMaps should be used for general application configuration purposes.

7. `volumeClaimTemplates` is used for creating a dedicated PersistentVolumeClaim for each Pod replica in this StatefulSet.

8. To ensure real zero-downtime updates of your deployments in Kubernetes, you need to configure proper probes, especially readiness. In this way, the user will be redirected to a replica only if this replica can properly respond to the request.

9. The principle of least privilege: Your applications should have access to their own resources only (it is recommended that you run each application using a dedicated service account that has access to Secrets or ConfigMaps for the very application), and users should have restricted access depending on their role in the project (for example, a QA engineer may be fine with just read-only access to the cluster).

Chapter 12: Development Workflow with Kubernetes

1. Helm is used to create redistributable packages for your Kubernetes application. You can use it to deploy applications provided by others or use it for your own applications as an internal package and dependency manager for microservices in your system.

2. Helm 2 required a dedicated service deployed on Kubernetes named Tiller, which was responsible for actual communication with Kubernetes API. This has caused various problems, including security and RBAC issues. As of Helm 3.0.0, Tiller is no longer needed and chart management is done by the client.

3. Use a Kubernetes Job object as a post-installation hook in Helm.

4. Use a new Docker image in the Helm chart manifest or values file and perform `helm upgrade`.

5. The Snapshot Debugger is a feature of Azure Application Insights that monitors exception telemetry from your application, including production scenarios. Whenever there is an unhandled exception (top-throwing), the Snapshot Debugger collects managed memory dumps, which can be analyzed directly in the Azure portal or, for more advanced scenarios, using Visual Studio 2019 Enterprise edition.

6. You should prefer proper declarative management of Kubernetes.

7. The Azure Dev Spaces service provides a rapid and iterative development experience for teams using AKS clusters.

Chapter 13: Securing Kubernetes Clusters and Applications

1. Kubernetes itself does not provide a means for managing normal external users who access the cluster. This should be delegated to an external authentication provider that can integrate with Kubernetes, for example, via Authenticating Proxy.

2. To reduce the attack vector, the recommended practice is to never expose Kubernetes Dashboard using a LoadBalancer service and always use a kubectl proxy for accessing the page.

3. This will provide an extra layer of security for your API resources and Secrets, which otherwise would be kept in etcd in unencrypted form.

4. No, this feature is supported only in Linux containers.

5. NetworkPolicy objects define how groups of Pods can communicate with each other and network endpoints in general—think of them as a basic firewall for enforcing network segmentation at Layer 3 of the OSI model. To use network policies, you need to use one of the network providers that support network policies.

6. On Windows, Kubernetes Secrets that are mounted to Pods as volumes are written in cleartext on node disk storage (not RAM). The reason for this is that Windows currently does not support mounting an in-memory filesystem to Pod containers. This may pose security risks and entails additional actions to secure the cluster.

7. When you have root privileges, you can enumerate all environment variables for a process from `/proc/<pid>/environ`, including Secrets injected in that way. For Secrets mounted as volumes, it is not possible as you use `tmpfs`.

Chapter 14: Monitoring Kubernetes Applications Using Prometheus

1. Providing observability for your components means exposing information about their inner state so that you can access the data easily and reason about the actual state of your components. In other words, if something is observable, you can understand it.

2. WMI Exporter can be used to monitor a Windows node host OS and hardware. For monitoring the Docker Engine itself, you can use the experimental metrics server exposed by the Engine.

3. In production environments running at a large scale, you can use Prometheus Operator to easily deploy and manage multiple Prometheus clusters for different needs.

4. WMI Exporter and the Docker Engine metrics server are exposing the metrics on dedicated ports on each node. We need two extra scraping jobs that handle them individually.

5. Use the Telegraf service hosted directly in your container.

6. Providing additional instrumentation and insights into business logic for your applications.

7. In your Service Object manifest, define an additional annotation, for example, `prometheus.io/secondary-port`. After that, you have to create a dedicated scraping job, which will consume the new annotation, in a similar way to `prometheus.io/port`.

8. Heatmaps are the most effective way of visualizing histogram changes over time and recently Grafana was extended with native support for heatmaps for Prometheus histogram metrics.

Chapter 15: Disaster Recovery

1. The main difference between DR and BC is that DR focuses on getting the infrastructure up and running following an outage, whereas BC covers keeping the business scenarios running during a major incident.

2. The `etcd` cluster is used by the master and persistent volumes are used by Pods.

3. A snapshot is a backup file provided by the v3 API of etcd.

4. Velero can perform `etcd` snapshots, manage them in external storage, and restore if needed. Additionally, it can be used for performing backups of persistent volumes using Restic integration. Etcd-operator is used for provisioning of multiple `etcd` clusters on top of Kubernetes. You can easily manage the `etcd` clusters and perform backup-restore operations. Use this approach if you plan to manage multiple Kubernetes clusters in your environment.

5. Access all Kubernetes master nodes and, on all machines, perform the same steps in parallel: download the target snapshot file, restore it to a local directory, stop Kubernetes master components, stop the `etcd` service, stop the kubelet service, swap the `etcd` data directory, start the `etcd` service, and finally start the kubelet service.

6. A Kubernetes CronJob gives you the ability to schedule Kubernetes Jobs at a fixed schedule, similar to cron in Linux systems.

7. Remove the failed member from the cluster, add a new replacement member, and if there is more than one failed member, replace the members sequentially.

Chapter 16: Production Considerations for Running Kubernetes

1. In immutable infrastructure, you additionally do not perform any modifications to the configuration of machines once they are provisioned. If you need a configuration change or a hotfix, you need to build a new machine image and provision new machines.

2. Kubernetes can be seen as a platform for managing your immutable container infrastructure for your application workloads—whenever you create a new Docker image and roll out a new version of deployment, you are just creating new containers and throwing away the old ones. If you use a declarative approach for managing your Kubernetes Objects, you end up with neat Infrastructure-as-Code.

3. GitOps is a way of managing the Kubernetes cluster and your applications, proposed by WeaveWorks, where the Git repository is the single source of truth for the declarative infrastructure and your application workloads. This approach fully complies with the Infrastructure-as-Code paradigm.

4. Flux can be used for easily implementing GitOps for your Kubernetes clusters.

5. Upgrade the components running on the primary master node, upgrade the components running on the additional master nodes, and upgrade the worker nodes.

6. Cordon (mark the node as unschedulable) the node and drain the existing Pods, then apply the required updates and reboot the machine, and uncordon the node to make it schedulable again.

Other Books You May Enjoy

If you enjoyed this book, you may be interested in these other books by Packt:

Hands-On Kubernetes on Azure
Shivakumar Gopalakrishnan, Gunther Lenz

ISBN: 978-1-78953-610-2

- Use the Kubernetes dashboard to review clusters and deployed applications
- Find out the benefits and limitations, and how to avoid potential problems while using AKS
- Understand the implementation of Microsoft toolchains such as Visual Studio Code and Git
- Implement simple and advanced AKS solutions
- Ensure automated scalability and high reliability of your applications with Microsoft AKS
- Apply kubectl commands to monitor applications

DevOps with Kubernetes
Hideto Saito, Hui-Chuan Chloe Lee, Et al

ISBN: 978-1-78839-664-6

- Learn fundamental and advanced DevOps skills and tools
- Get a comprehensive understanding for container
- Learn how to move your application to container world
- Learn how to manipulate your application by Kubernetes
- Learn how to work with Kubernetes in popular public cloud
- Improve time to market with Kubernetes and Continuous Delivery
- Learn how to monitor, log, and troubleshoot your application with Kubernetes

Leave a review - let other readers know what you think

Please share your thoughts on this book with others by leaving a review on the site that you bought it from. If you purchased the book from Amazon, please leave us an honest review on this book's Amazon page. This is vital so that other potential readers can see and use your unbiased opinion to make purchasing decisions, we can understand what our customers think about our products, and our authors can see your feedback on the title that they have worked with Packt to create. It will only take a few minutes of your time, but is valuable to other potential customers, our authors, and Packt. Thank you!

Index

www.ingramcontent.com/pod-product-compliance
Lightning Source LLC
LaVergne TN
LVHW081506050326
832903LV00025B/1404